I0093842

Kulturstiftung Sibirien

Jochelson, Bogoras and Shternberg
A Scientific Exploration of Northeastern Siberia
and the Shaping of Soviet Ethnography

Edited by Erich Kasten

Verlag der Kulturstiftung Sibirien
SEC Publications

Bibliografische Informationen der Deutschen Nationalbibliothek:
Die Deutsche Nationalbibliothek verzeichnet diese Publikation in der Deutschen
Nationalbibliografie: detaillierte bibliografische Daten sind im Internet über
<http://dnb.d-nb.de> abrufbar.

Cover photo based on the image *Group outside winter tent of Tundra Yukaghir chief,*
#338343, American Museum of Natural History Library, with a photo composition of
cuttings from portraits in this book.

Design and Production:
Kulturstiftung Sibirien gGmbH, Fürstenberg/Havel

Printing:
Books on Demand GmbH, Norderstedt

Electronic edition: www.siberian-studies.org/publications/jochbogshtern.html

ISBN: 978-3-942883-34-4

CONTENTS

INTRODUCTION

Erich Kasten

The idea for this book arose when new editions of earlier classic monographs in northeastern Siberian ethnography were in preparation[1] for which some of the contributors to this volume had written their forewords. On request of the editor they submitted these texts as reprints for this book. In this way, their essays can now be presented here again in a coherent form, whereas they were previously scattered in the above-mentioned new publications of Jochelson's and Bogoras's monographs. These two men, along with Shternberg, made up the so-called *etnotroika* that shaped early Soviet ethnography. More contributions were solicited in order to do justice to Shternberg's significant role in this process and to Bogoras's later far-reaching scientific and educational programs that he launched in Leningrad upon conclusion of his fieldwork projects in northeastern Siberia. Two of these essays, those by Elena Liarskaya and Anna Sirina & Tat'iana Roon, were published in Russian before, and with their English translation they can now reach an even broader international readership. The chapters by Matthias Winterschladen and Sergei Kan were written for this volume in order to round it out in necessary ways.

The authors of this volume review the fascinating and changeable biographies of Waldemar Jochelson, Waldemar Bogoras and Lev Shternberg, with a focus on how they became involved in ethnography towards the end of the 19th century, while spending many years in remote parts of the country as political exiles. The initial aim of their former revolutionary activities was to better the lives of underprivileged people, which was also reflected in the later ambitious community-oriented research programs that they conceptualized at Leningrad State University, until these pioneering efforts were eventually impeded during Stalin's repressions. Consequently, their invaluable scientific legacy encompasses not only the enormous volumes in which they documented the cultures of the peoples of northeastern Siberia—the Yakut, Yukaghir, Even, Koryak, Chukchi and the Nivkh—at the turn of the 20th century, shortly before their lives and many of their unique cultural features underwent rapid transformations during Soviet times. But Jochelson, Bogoras and Shternberg also shaped significantly the emerging Soviet ethnography and had a strong impact on the next generations of scholars in the Soviet Union who worked in this field.

---

1 http://www.siberian-studies.org/publications/bisp_E.html. Another series covers significant monographs by German-Baltic scientists who travelled through Kamchatka in the 18th and 19th centuries (http://www.siberian-studies.org/publications/bika_E.html).

In his introductory chapter, *The Forgotten Member of the "Etnotroika?,"* Matthias Winterschladen calls our attention to the fact that Jochelson had for many years not received the attention that he deserved, as Bogoras and Shternberg did, though this has changed, notably since *perestroika*.[2]

The next section of articles acknowledges Jochelson's scientific legacy with regard to his monographs on the Yakut, the Yukaghir and the Koryak. But first, Erich Kasten explores in his chapter, *From Political Exile to Outstanding Ethnologist for Northeastern Siberia*, how Jochelson became interested in ethnography towards the end of the 19th century, while spending many years in faraway parts of the country as a political exile. His initial strong revolutionary commitment explains much of his empathetic approach towards indigenous peoples, as well as his fieldwork methods. Some of them pointed the way ahead and became relevant later in more recent ethnographic research. Jochelson incorporated new ideas from American cultural anthropology during his later collaboration with Franz Boas, after which one can notice changes to his earlier fieldwork as well as his ethnographic style and thematic emphasis.

This is shown in even more detail in the following chapter by Erich Kasten and Michael Dürr, *Waldemar Jochelson and the Koryak during the Jesup North Pacific Expedition*. A biographical sketch of his years after the Sibiriakov Expedition reveals the obvious shifts in Jochelson's methods and in the presentation of his results between his first ethnographic fieldwork and the later Jesup North Pacific Expedition, for which he was recruited by Franz Boas and with whom he continued to work at the American Museum of Natural History in New York until his death. By means of selected themes, Jochelson's particular ethnographic interests and outcomes are further discussed, such as his assessments of political economy and his investigations into material culture and the arts as well as shamanic performances and other ritual practices.

In his chapter, *Reading the Ethnographic Past in the Present*, Thomas R. Miller focuses on Jochelson's work on the Yukaghir, based on his two expeditions with them. The author first summarizes the most prominent themes and conclusions that Jochelson drew in his extensive monograph on the Yukaghir and neighboring peoples with whom they closely interacted, such as the "Yukaghirized Tungus." A particular topic is then more thoroughly discussed—shamans and singing diseases. In contrast to Jochelson's later descriptions of similar performances by the Koryak, it becomes obvious that he gained more insight into these sensitive issues of indigenous worldviews and ritual practices with the Yukaghir, most likely due to the fact of his deeper immersion and particular ways of collaboration with local experts there.

---

2   In a forthcoming Russian publication the significant results of Jochelson's early Sibiriakov Expedition will be compiled and thoroughly discussed: Kasten, Erich, and Anna Sirina (eds.) 2019. *Vladimir Iokhel'son i Sibiriakovskaia (Iakutskaia) ekspeditsiia (1894–1897 gg.)* [Waldemar Jochelson and the Sibiriakov (Yakut) Expedition (1894–1897)], Fürstenberg/Havel: Kulturstiftung Sibirien [in preparation].

Tat'iana Argounova-Low emphasizes in her chapter on Waldemar Jochelson's monograph, *The Yakut and Continuing Traditions of Ysyakh*, the particular impact that Jochelson's work still has on present-day ritual practices. The descriptions in the monograph confirm the authenticity of Sakha contemporary celebrations. As already indicated by Winterschladen and Miller, Jochelson's attitude towards local people and his documentation of their cultural heritage was always and is even more today acknowledged by the Sakha community.

In his chapter on Bogoras's "classical monograph," *The Chukchee*, Igor Krupnik first reviews his personal background and the course and results of both of his expeditions—the Sibiriakov and Jesup North Pacific—during which he worked closely with his friend Waldemar Jochelson. Just as for Jochelson, Bogoras's later publication of his exhaustive descriptions of Chukchi culture was strongly promoted and supported by Boas. But Bogoras had already become more active in the Bolshevik Revolution than the other two members of the *etnotroika*, which caused some delays in the completion of his *opus magnum*. Krupnik points out a conflict faced by Bogoras during his work was that he presumably felt persuaded by Boas to present the material according to a different template than he might have had in mind himself. This raises the question, if this was the reason he made his local partners in these publications more "invisible," whereas their contribution was still fully acknowledged by him and Jochelson in their letters from the foregoing Sibiriakov Expedition, as already indicated by Kasten in his chapter above. Krupnik also directs our attention to other "invisible" partners, whose role and valuable contribution during the Jesup North Pacific Expedition remain largely unmentioned by both Bogoras and Jochelson—specifically their wives, Sof'ia Volkova Bogoras and Dina Jochelson-Brodskaia.

Elena Liarskaya's chapter, *Penelope's Cloth: "The Bogoras Project" in the Second Half of the 1920s–1930s*, ties neatly into Bogoras's scientific activities after the Bolshevik Revolution at Leningrad State University. Together with Lev Shternberg he established there the so-called Leningrad ethnographic school that became most influential for the next generations of ethnographers in the Soviet Union. Liarskaya analyses key elements of the "Bogoras project," i.e. its structure and Bogoras's principal aims and efforts to realize his ambitious and complex program. Such combined scientific and community-oriented research involving training and participation of local partners was definitively innovative for that time. According to Liarskaya, the "Bogoras project" that he launched with his colleagues worked well until the mid-1930s—and it's probably lucky that Bogoras himself did not experience Stalin's repressions that started one year after his death in 1937, and which severely affected the continuation of his work.

Anna Sirina and Tat'iana Roon provide us in their chapter on Lev Iakovlevich Shternberg, *At the Outset of Soviet Ethnography*, with much information about this outstanding scientist, who became the other prominent founder of the Leningrad ethnographic school. After the preceding chapter on Bogoras it becomes clearer how they complemented each other in pursuing their tasks. We first learn that Shternberg's personal background was very similar to Jochelson's and Bogoras's, and then about the beginning of his ethnographic work as an exile on Sakhalin, where he developed his fieldwork methods on his own. His research eventually resulted in comprehensive and thorough descriptions of Nivkh culture in particular, corresponding to those by Jochelson and Bogoras on the peoples of northeastern Siberia. The authors follow up with how Shternberg prepared his materials for publication during his work at the Museum of Anthropology and Ethnography beginning in 1901 and later at Leningrad State University. They portray the new generation of ethnographers that he strongly influenced by his teaching while also carrying out more expeditions in the Amur area. At the same time he was involved in acquiring exhibits for the museum as well as compiling linguistic collections. The authors underline the importance of his friendship with Franz Boas and they touch upon Shternberg's relations with Sergei Shirokogoroff, another prominent ethnographer on Tungus peoples in eastern Siberia. They inform us of the complex network that he was able to establish with other scholars in Leningrad. Furthermore, they discuss the impact of his theoretical studies on relevant ethnological themes at that time.

Closely related to this is the closing chapter by Sergei Kan, *Was Lev Shternberg Just Another Classical Evolutionist?,* in which he challenges the still prevalent understanding that Shternberg was a classical evolutionist. However this may be, his ideas obviously coexisted with those of other scholars who clearly represented different views, and Shternberg was open to modifying some of his positions accordingly. The author reveals that—despite Boas's rejection of Shternberg's principal theoretical conclusions —they had much in common with regards to their methods. In one of his lectures Shternberg gives a definition of culture which is much closer to Boas's views than those of Morgan or Tylor. In other lectures and articles he modified evolutionist theories regarding particular developments in religion. And last but not least, the drastic changes during and in the wake of the Russian Civil War made Shternberg rethink some of his earlier evolutionary judgements.

In this volume a particular emphasis was placed on the comprehensive monographs by Jochelson, Bogoras and Shternberg in English language, but one has to also keep in mind their abundant materials that were published before or at the same time in Russian editions. For this, a forthcoming publication (see footnote 2) will compile and discuss such informative documents with regard to Waldemar Jochelson in order to achieve an even more complete and balanced view of the events.

1 THE FORGOTTEN MEMBER OF THE "ETNOTROIKA"? WALDEMAR JOCHELSON IN THE MIRROR OF RESEARCH AND HIS SCIENTIFIC LEGACY

Matthias Winterschladen

As Waldemar Bogoras [Vladimir Germanovich Bogoraz] (1865–1936) in 1934 finally succeeded in publishing at least the first part of his magnum opus *The Chukchee* in Russian translation, which dealt with the social organization of the Chukchi people, once more he proclaimed the contributions of his generation of scientists comprising former *Narodnaia Volia* (The People's Will) revolutionaries, who became researchers into the indigenous peoples of the farthest Northeast of Siberia:

> "The social mission of the epoch of the last zemlevol'tsy and narodovol'tsy, who ended up in the remote exile in the far north-east, consisted of the study of the peoples scattered there, who were primeval, half exterminated and almost completely unknown. In general, this was a collective work. It was done by entire groups of political exiles, who became scholars and researchers."

> ["Sotsial'noe zadanie epokhi dlia poslednikh zemlevol'tsev i narodovol'tsev, popavshikh v dalekuiu ssylku na krainem severo-vostoke, sostoialo v izuchenii narodnostei, razbrosannykh tam, pervobytnykh, poluistreblennykh i pochti sovershenno neizvestnykh. Eta rabota v obshchem byla kollektivnaia. Eiu zanimalis' tselye gruppy politicheskikh ssyl'nykh, stavshikh uchenymi issledovateliami."] (Bogoras 1934:XIII)

Here Bogoras referred in particular to the widespread group of members of the Yakutian Historic-Ethnographic Expedition of 1894 to 1897—later named the Sibiriakov Expedition after its donor Innokentii Mikhailovich Sibiriakov (1860–1901)—to research the indigenous population of Yakutia that was largely drawn from banished public enemies of the Russian Empire. He mentioned namely the linguist and ethnographer Eduard Karlovich Pekarskii (1858–1934) and his "monumental dictionary" (*monumental'nyi slovar'*) of the Yakut language (ibid.).[1] Above all though he named his close friends and loyal companions Lev Iakovlevich Shternberg (1861–1927) and Waldemar Jochelson [Vladimir Il'ich Iokhel'son] (1855–1937), together with whom he formed—as Bogoras himself phrased it—an "etnotroika" (ethno-troika) (ibid.).

---

1 See also Pekarskii (1907–1930; 1958/59). For the work and life of E.K. Pekarskii see Kharitonov (1958) and Okoneshnikov (1982).

Already during the waning decades of imperial Russia these three protagonists together with their revolutionary comrades and scientific colleagues from the Sibiriakov Expedition played an immensely important role in the process of the emergence and differentiation of anthropology as an academic discipline, which at the turn of the 20th century was still undergoing its formation. Their "generation" of anthropologists, ethnographers, linguists, folklorists and archeologists inherited the legacy of the German Baltic scientific elite who once came from the in 1893 Russified University of Dorpat, and—after the Russian sailings around the world—during the remainder of the 19th century practically dominated research into the Siberian subcontinent and the north Pacific. On the one hand they formed the foundation of a new scientific cohort of researchers of the huge region with a strong focus on its indigenous peoples. On the other hand, as the revolutionary activities of many of its representatives had led to their either spending several years in western European countries or at least having good contacts with Russian exile communities in Switzerland, Paris, London or Berlin, this generation was able to take over the role of mediator between the Russian Empire and Western Europe (Dahlmann 2016:46–47; see also Kasten 2013). Within this constellation the *etnotroika* of Jochelson, Bogoras and Shternberg took on a special role. Whereas, contrary to the tradition of Soviet research literature even still in the 1960s (see Gurvich 1963:248, 252–253; Gorokhov 1965:52, 75)[2], their methods and scientific approach were based not only on the practical experiences they had been able to acquire through their initially autodidactic research within the framework of the Sibiriakov Expedition in northern Yakutia (Jochelson and Bogoras) or in the course of the Russian Empire Census of 1897 on Sakhalin, where Shternberg had been banished. Thanks to the participation of Jochelson and Bogoras in the Jesup North Pacific Expedition (1897–1902) under the leadership of the German-American anthropologist Franz Boas (1858–1942) and Shternberg's later integration into Boas's scientific network, all three came under the influence of his philosophy of cultural relativism on the history of mankind. Also, Boas's historical and inductive approach left clear traces on the understanding of science of his three Russian colleagues. Although they integrated Boas's perspective and methodology into their own research concepts, his scientific approach based on a holistic understanding of indigenous peoples and cultures by the study of museum collections, anthropometric data, folklore, language and material culture was received as well by the following generation of Soviet and Russian scientists as a result of the *etnotroika's* transfer of knowledge (see Krupnik 1998:205–208; Winterschladen 2016:78–79; Weber 2016:136-146). Moreover, thanks to Boas's introduction, the three remained for a long time virtually the only Russian scientists who regularly took part in the International Congresses of Americanists (Krupnik 1998:205–206). This close entanglement with the classical Boasian anthro-

---

2 Both authors refer to a thesis from of a paper from Sergei Aleksandrovich Tokarev (Tokarev 1956:11–12). Tokarev published this article including his thesis for the first time in 1948 (see Tokarev 1948:191–192).

pological school and the acceptance in the international research community made possible the expansion of the above-described mediator role onto the two American continents, this even still in early Soviet times. Finally, similar to the way the German Baltic "functional elites" of imperial Russia, who, according to Jan Kusber, "epitomized the socialization results" of the "Europeanization process" initiated by Peter I and who saw their research as a means towards the modernization of the Russian Empire (see Kusber 2009:105)[3]; after the Bolshevik Revolution Bogoras and Shternberg did not just place their scientific know-how into the service of the new rulers, but even became founding members of the *Komsev*, the "Committee for the Assistance to the Peoples of the Northern Borderlands" (or shortly "Committee of the North", Russian: *Komitet sodeistviia malym narodnostiam severnykh okrain*) which was created in 1924 (see Weiser 1989:35–43; Slezkine 1994:150–163), thus putting themselves actively in the service of the Bolshevik modernization project towards the comprehensive reorganization of the traditional society (Winterschladen 2016:80).

While Bogoras and Shternberg are counted self-evidently in Soviet as well as Russian historiography as "outstanding ethnologists and anthropologists of the fatherland" (*vydaiushchiesia otechestvennye etnologi i antropologi*)[4], and while both are celebrated for their roles as theoretical pioneers as well as practical organizers and creators of new scientific institutions, as eminently important representatives of the founding generation of Soviet ethnography, or rather, that "of the fatherland" (*otechestvennaia etnografiia*)—as it is called then in Russian—(see for example Sirina and Roon 2004; Mikhailova 2004; Vakhtin 2016: in particular 125–126); Jochelson's contribution towards the professionalization and differentiation of the science of man, as well as towards the further scientification of its theoretical concepts and research methods has not so far received anything close to the same attention. Even the interest in Jochelson's biography is much less. While the lives and works of both of his friends are not only well investigated but have also repeatedly been the cause of recent new research (Rezvan 2012; Antropologicheskii forum 2016 (29):101–219)[5], there is so far no major work on Jochelson's life and career available. To be sure, in Soviet times—

3　In his article Jan Kusber refers to a central thesis of Ilya Vinkovetsky [Il'ia Vin'kovetskii] (Vinkovetsky 2001:198–201). See also Dahlmann (2016:41–42).

4　This is also the title of an anthology published in 2004 under the editorship of Valerii Aleksandrovich Tishkov and Daniil Davydovich Tumarkin (Tishkov and Tumarkin 2004) which contains two longer biographic articles about L.Ia. Shternberg and W. Bogoras (see Sirina and Roon 2004; Mikhailova 2004).

5　The anthology under the editorship of Efim Anatol'evich Rezvan was published in honor of the 150th birthday of L.Ia. Shternberg by the MAE RAN. In analogy to this book the MAE RAN journal *Antropologicheskii forum* (Anthropological Forum) dedicated an entire issue to the 150th birthday of W. Bogoras which includes new studies around him, for example, even about his wife Sof'ia Konstantinovna Bogoras [Bogoraz] (born Volkova) (see Mikhailova 2016). For Shternberg's biography see also the still fundamental work of Sergei Kan (2009); for Bogoras see Gernet (1999: in particular 63–91) which presents a bibliography of works about his life and scientific creation.

and on the initiative and with the assistance of Bogoras—a short biographical essay by Konstantin Borisovich Shavrov in honor of Jochelson's 80th birthday was published in 1935 in the journal *Sovetskaia Etnografiia* (Soviet Ethnography) (Shavrov 1935:3); but Jochelson was almost forgotten in the following decades, with the only exception of the few works by Il'ia Samuilovich Gurvich (see Gurvich 1963; 1972; Gurvich and Kuzmina 1985).

Fig. 1 Waldemar Jochelson (1900). The photo was taken in San
Francisco before his departure to northeastern Siberia for the
Jesup North Pacific Expedition. Image #129123,
American Museum of Natural History Library.

This changed only after the collapse of the Soviet Union. In the mid-1990s the Vladivostok ethnographer Nikolai Vladimirovich Kocheshkov was one of the first to bring Jochelson back into the consciousness of Russian society with a few smaller essays, for example in the periodical *Zabytye imena* (Forgotten Names) (see Kocheshkov 1994a, b).[6] Then, from the end of the 1990s much more Russian researchers came along to work intensively on Jochelson's scientific legacy. Among them the Yakutsk art historian pair Vladimir Kharlamp'evich Ivanov (1937–2000) and Zinaida Ivanovna Ivanova-Unarova or the Magadan historian Sergei Borisovich Slobodin, as well as ethnologists Nikolai Borisovich Vakhtin from St. Petersburg and Anna Anatol'evna Sirina from Moscow stand out (Ivanov 2000; Ivanov and Ivanova-Unarova 2003; Slobodin 2005; Vakhtin 2004a; 2005; Sirina 2007; Sirina and Shinkovoi 2007). In August 2005 even a conference in honor of Jochelson's 150th birthday took place in Yakutsk from which also appeared an anthology (Gogolev 2008)[7]. Moreover, also in western research circles Jochelson became better known again through the research project *Jesup II* that was initiated by the Smithsonian Institution in Washington, D.C. at the beginning of the 1990s and which for the first time since Boas's days brought American and Russian scientists together onto a common path to research the North Pacific Rim and to reappraise the Jesup Expedition. This research initiative is understood to be a long-term scientific undertaking with the aim of an international investigation into the indigenous population of the north Pacific in the tradition of the Jesup Expedition (Fitzhugh and Krupnik 1993).[8] Nevertheless, Michael Knüppel, who in 2013 presented a first comprehensive bibliography of the works of Jochelson, including those widely scattered unpublished materials of his legacy in Russian, American and Western European archives (Knüppel 2013)[9], laments that the "great pioneer of the Yukaghir studies and founder of the north Pacific archeology" has not yet been awarded the "due attention" which he deserves (ibid.:8). In spite of the recently increased movement in research on Jochelson, even outside Russia (Winterschladen et al. 2016)[10], one cannot completely escape this conclusion. And so, the year 2017 passed without the 80th anniversary of Jochelson's death being memorialized, through a conference at a prominent place or a major publication, either in his Russian homeland or in the USA, where he mostly spent his sunset years from 1922 until his death in 1937 and completed his scientific work, among other things on the North American indigenous people of the Aleuts (Jochelson 1925; 1933).

---

6   The academic supervisor of N.V. Kocheshkov was Sergei Vasil'evich Ivanov (1895–1986) who himself was a student of L.Ia. Shternberg and W. Bogoras (see Reshetov 2003).

7   See here in particular Ivanova-Unarova (2008).

8   This project has already produced a large number of common scientific publications, and not just by American und Russian scholars. See Fitzhugh and Crowell (1988); Fitzhugh and Krupnik (2001); and Kendall and Krupnik (2003).

9   This book also includes a bibliography of scholarly works about W. Jochelson. As already mentioned, a detailed biography of W. Jochelson is still a desideratum, but around 20 biographical articles from encyclopedias can be found in the above-mentioned literature list by Michael Knüppel (2013:126–131).

10   In this volume see in particular the articles Winterschladen (2016), Knüppel (2016), Krumholz and Winterschladen (2016), and Kleinmanns (2016).

Although Jochelson has returned nowadays to the centers of both the Russian and American scientific landscape, the general societal interest in his person remains slight. Furthermore, it seems at first glance paradoxical that the newly awakened interest in his scientific accomplishments is rooted precisely at the peripheral places where Jochelson's career as a researcher of the indigenous peoples of east Siberia and the north Pacific took its course—in Yakutia where Jochelson, the banished political enemy of the state, revolutionized the Yukaghir studies (Knüppel 2016:200–213); in Vladivostok, from where he set out in the service of the AMNH to the Koryaks, the ethnography of whom would become his most important work (Jochelson 1908). For all three of the big research undertakings in which Jochelson had participated (the Sibiriakov, Jesup and finally, from 1908 until 1911, the Riabushinskii expeditions) proceeded under the patronage of central scientific institutions of the Russian Empire or the USA, while anthropology as freshly "emancipated" former auxiliary discipline of geography did not just aim at new knowledge. Already the German Baltic Karl Ernst von Baer (1792–1876), one of the most significant founding figures of the IRGO, on which orders the Sibiriakov and Riabushinskii expeditions were sent, had pleaded that research results—for example of Siberia's indigenous population—be put in the service of the civilization of the non-European territories of imperial Russia (Knight 1998:116–118). In the USA, however, Boas had cleverly understood how to use the great interest of the elites of the young state in the question of the origin of the indigenous peoples of the Americas to convince the president of the AMNH, Morris Ketchum Jesup (1830–1908) of the necessity of financing a big expedition to the North Pacific Rim. This interest of the American elites still had its roots in the 18th century. Thomas Jefferson, the third US President, had already written about the "probability" of the relatedness of the indigenous peoples of the Americas to those of Asia (Jefferson 1801:147–149). Nevertheless, that this focus on the "prehistory" of the USA in the discourse of the late 19th century was closely connected to the idea of "American chosenness", with the *Manifest Destiny* of the American nation to take possession of the entire continent "allotted by Providence" to realize a "godly mission of progress and freedom" (see O'Sullivan 1845:5,7,9)[11]; Boas, the cultural relativist, had no scruples about putting the central idea of legitimization of US expansion into the service of his scientific career. At this point one should reference the important thesis written by German historian Jürgen Osterhammel, who described geography as an "imperial science", as "a sort of accomplice subject of European expansion" (Osterhammel 2009:1164), which can be expanded quite well to include anthropology as accomplice subject of the European civilization mission with respect to "primitive cultures".

Although Jochelson also at least partly placed his abilities as a scientist in the service of the young Soviet state, though far less actively than his friends Bogoras and

---

11   The American publicist John O'Sullivan was the first who in 1845 explicitly used the term *Manifest Destiny*. See O'Sullivan (1845:5). See also O'Sullivan (1839:430); Horsman (1981); and Weinberg (1935).

Shternberg, a look at Vasilii Afanas'evich Robbek's (1937–2010) opening speech at the Yakutsk Conference to honor Jochelson's 150th birthday makes clear why the "rediscovery" of his research work precisely through representatives of Jochelson's once-investigated indigenous peoples poses no paradoxes. Robbek, who himself originated from a nomadic reindeer herder family from Verkhnekolymsk, described Jochelson not only as an "outstanding researcher of the peoples of the north" (*vydaiushchiiisia issledovatel' narodov Severa*), but integrated him into his own agenda of "further development of the Yukaghir studies" (*dal'neishee razvitie iukagirovedeniia*) as well as a new way towards a "revival and preservation of the Yukaghir people" (*vozrozhdenie i sokhranenie iukagirskogo naroda*) (Robbek 2010:1st paragraph; see also Robbek 2008). After the loss of the mostly Soviet-influenced identities of many indigenous peoples, not only in Siberia as a result of the collapse of the USSR, which in its northern peripheries to a much greater degree than in the European part of Russia had led to the decay of economy, infrastructure, culture and social integration (see Rohr 2011:395–399; Heleniak et al.:371–372, 374–379), the interest of precisely such indigenous communities in the scientific legacy of researchers like Jochelson is very large. In the case of Jochelson's works on the Yukaghirs or Koryaks, this concerns especially his comprehensive research results on spiritual culture and world views as well as shamanism and traditional rituals and customs of both of these peoples (see Jochelson 1908:13–382; 1910–1926:135–342). While these components of the indigenous cultures that Jochelson himself experienced were almost extinguished as a result of the radical socio-economic reorganization of the indigenous societies under Stalin from the Soviet modern as "outmoded" (*otzhivshie*) cultural phenomena (Ivanova-Unarova 2015:29), Jochelson's highly detailed portrayals of the immaterial culture of indigenous peoples of the former Soviet Union are used at present as a blueprint for a new spiritual rootedness.

However, the fact that the general consciousness in Russian majority society placed Jochelson in a subordinate position vis-à-vis his two friends, Bogoras and Shternberg, has much to do with his personal attributes—with his in many ways *hybrid identity* as a historical actor in "borderless transnational areas" (see Patel 2004:13–14; Gassert 2010:1–2); but this absolutely also in combination with his often crazy or better to say shifted (German: *ver-rückt*) path through life. Not only Jochelson but also his two friends found themselves first as societal outsiders—on the basis of their Jewish origin and their revolutionary activism in the *Narodnaia Volia*, which in imperial Russia brought them the banishment to eastern Siberia and in Soviet Russia the negative stamp of belonging to the "wrong" wing of the Russian revolution movement, and the defamation of having formed a "surrogate of bourgeois social science" (*surrogat burzhuaznogo obshchestvovedeniia*) (Kan 2006:44; 2007:205)[12]. In contrast to both of his companions and in spite of even having quite a close connection to his Russian homeland, Jochelson spent much more time outside the borders of the Russian Empire or

---

12 This defamation is a citation out of a speech by the Soviet linguist Valerian Borisovich Aptekar' (1899–1937) at the conference of the Moscow and Leningrad ethnologists in Leningrad in 1929.

far from its European centers since his first forced stay in Berlin in the mid-1870s than they did—either as an agent of *Narodnaia Volia* and student at Bern University or as a banished public enemy and expedition participant in the Siberian northeast and North-American northwest or finally as a freelance scientist living often in Western Europe or since 1922 in his last exile in New York. Compared to Bogoras he did not take an active part in the Russian Revolution of 1905/06, but instead in 1908 he left on his third large scientific enterprise (the Riabushinskii Expedition). In the end his increasing age and poor health prevented him from serving in the imperial army in World War I, as Bogoras did, or from participating in the building of the young Soviet state after the fall of the Russian Empire. A university career was denied him after his emigration to the USA at beginning of the 1920s, while his poor health sent him back to Europe to the Côte d'Azur for some years. This hardly straight and often nonlinear life path outside all common patterns of national historical narratives must have had the effect of removing Jochelson from national historiography. It explains clearly why Jochelson—in contrast to Bogoras and Shternberg or even Boas—has not yet been accepted equally into the national pantheon of scientific geniuses of Russia or the USA (see also Ivanova-Unarova 2015).

A further problem of the research on Jochelson, that, though beyond ideological or political scientific matters, is not insignificant, is posed by the situation of the sources or much more the confused scattering of Jochelson's mostly unpublished legacy in Russian, western European and American archives. Major parts of his written legacy are principally in St. Petersburg in the AV IVR RAN, the Archive of the Orientalists, and in New York where records in the archive of the Division of Anthropology and in the Research Library of the AMNH as well as in the NYPL are stored. In the case of the archive materials in the AV IVR RAN the collection consists of Jochelson's direct legacy which at the moment of his death was in his personal possession. These sources were shipped from the New World back to Russia on Jochelson's own wishes after the death of his wife Dina Lazarevna Jochelson-Brodskaia [Iokhel'son-Brodskaia] (1864–1943) in New York (Slobodin 2005:112). They contain extensive material and many manuscripts from almost all of Jochelson's creative phases as well as Dina's field diaries from the Jesup and Riabushinskii expeditions. In the archives of the AMNH the private correspondence of Jochelson and his wife is especially worthy of consideration (see AV IVR RAN: f. 23/631; AMNH DAA: .J634; AMNH RL: D66; NYPL: MssCol 1565).[13] In addition, significant ego documents are to be found in the legacies of other scholars with whom Jochelson maintained active correspondence, foremost among them in the APS in Philadelphia which houses among other things the exchange of letters between Boas and Jochelson (APS: Mss.B.B61.inventory07, b. 48; see also Knüppel 2013:34–39); but also for example in the ASL in Juneau, where the Russian-American historian and ethnographer Michael Z. Vinokouroff's

---

13   For the archive collection in the AV IVR RAN see also Gurvich (1963:248–249); for the archive
     collections in the New York archives see also Knüppel (2013:29–30, 40–43).

(Mikhail Zinov'evich Vinokurov) (1894–1983) written exchange with Jochelson is to be found (ASL: MS 81, b. 4/ PCA 243, b. 4, f. 3, 10; see also Knüppel 2013:31–33; Martin 1986:30–31/ suppl. 22–23). A further major collection is housed in the ANLA in Fairbanks. Its core is formed by original documents of Jochelson's research work on the Aleutian Islands during the Riabushinskii Expedition (see Knüppel 2013:49–58). A special part of Jochelson's legacy are the collections of audio-documents, which are divided mostly among three archives. These are the FA IRLI RAN, the phonogram archive of the Institute for Russian Literature in St. Petersburg (see Burykin 2005:5,9,14; 2008; Burykin et al. 2005), the Archives of Traditional Music (ATM) of Indiana University in Bloomington and the BPA in Berlin (see Knüppel 2013:44–45; Keeling 2001:287–288). Additionally, Russian researchers also found further materials in the state archives of Yakutsk, Khabarovsk and Irkutsk: The Soviet historian Georgii Prokop'evich Basharin (1912–1992) published a number of documents from the Sibiriakov Expedition in the journal *Iakutskii arkhiv* (Yakutsk Archive) in 1972, among them some letters from Jochelson that today lie in the National Archive of the Sakha Republic (Yakutia) (see Basharin 1972; NARS (Ia): f. 12, op. 12, d. 299); while researching in the State Archive of the Khabarovsk Krai, N.B. Vakhtin found manuscripts by Jochelson on the unrealized project of the Encyclopedia of the Far Eastern Krai of the USSR (see Vakhtin 2004b; GAKhK: f. 537, op. 1, d. 17, ll. 191–194/ f. 537, op. 1, d. 69, ll. 2–5); and A.A. Sirina discovered unexpectedly in the State Archive of the Irkutsk Oblast the correspondence of Jochelson and Bogoras with the direction of the VSOIRGO during the Sibiriakov Expedition (see Sirina 2007; Sirina and Shinkovoi 2007; GAIO: f. 293, op. 1, d. 94).

Just the above-explained excessive "distribution" of Jochelson's legacy in 13 archives on three continents, in three different countries, and partly in peripherally located regions such as eastern Siberia or central Alaska makes it clear why even serious and engaged researchers find it difficult to get a comprehensive look at Jochelson's personal life and scientific work; why no one has so far dared to tackle the mammoth task of a scientifically demanding biography of Jochelson. In addition, in view of Jochelson's time in Berlin or Switzerland before and after his banishment, as well as after the Jesup Expedition, urgent research work in German and Swiss archives would be called for. That could be useful because now as then, little is known of these periods of Jochelson's life, as far as his autobiographical accounts go (see Jochelson 1918; 1922; 1923a,b). It is absolutely valid to consider that these texts by Jochelson were written under the impression of the Bolshevik Revolution and the subsequent Russian Civil War (1917–1922), as well as in memory of his former comrades from the *Narodnaia Volia*. Their publication resulted not least from Jochelson's need to emphasize his loyalty to the Russian revolution movement. Further new findings could also be lying dormant in other archives, for example in the Scientific Archive of the MAE RAN, where Jochelson at least worked for a decade between 1912 and 1922 as a curator. There, a look into the "mixed employee collection" (*smeshannyi fond sotrudnikov*)

Matthias Winterschladen

could be fruitful (NA MAE RAN: f. 40). And N.B. Vakhtin indicated that discoveries might also be made in the SPbF ARAN (see Vakhtin 2004a:47–48, fn. 3, 6).

A further technical problem is posed by the fact that Jochelson's works and legacy exist not only in Russian, but also in German and English. Besides, the work with linguistic and folkloristic materials from his three expeditions demands at least rudimentary knowledge of the individual indigenous languages, especially Yukaghir, Koryak, Even, Aleut, Itelmen or Yakut languages. This task would require an international and interdisciplinary research team in order just to deal with the research desiderata around the materials of Jochelson from the Sibiriakov and Riabushinskii expeditions, which have so far hardly been scientifically evaluated or appraised.

The first important steps have already been taken with regard to the formerly hard-to-access early works of Jochelson in German (Jochelson 2017). Furthermore, a publication in Russian on Jochelson first "tentative scientific steps" is currently being prepared (Kasten and Sirina 2018). This edition will present important source texts by Jochelson and early scientific works in Russian as well as the photograph collection arising from the still-young researcher's participation in the Sibiriakov Expedition at the end of the 19th century. The core among these documents being a complete transcript of Jochelson's field diary of the trip right through the Kolymskii Okrug. It remains to be hoped that on the one hand this will expand the interest in this fascinating researcher and scientist, and on the other hand will prompt an intensive exploration of his life and work within a framework of inquiry into Transnational or Global History. For precisely the scientific works of Jochelson or his life and career offer a wide spectrum for detailed, deeper-searching scientific inquiry beyond the "national fixation", in this context also many new findings about the development of anthropology as a science, but also in general about the global history of the late 19th and early 20th centuries outside the national historical narratives.

Abbreviations

AMNH DAA Division of Anthropology Archives of the American Museum of Natural History, New York
AMNH RL   Research Library of the American Museum of Natural History, New York
AMNH   American Museum of Natural History, New York
ANLA   Alaska Native Language Archive, Fairbanks AK
APS   American Philosophical Society, Philadelphia PA
ASL   Alaska State Library, Juneau AK
ATM   Archives of Traditional Music, Bloomington IN
AV IVR RAN Arkhiv vostokovedov Instituta vostochnykh rukopisei Rossiiskoi akademii nauk [Archive of the Orientalists of the Institute of Eastern Manuscripts of the Russian Academy of Sciences], St. Petersburg

BPA   Berliner Phonogrammarchiv (der Abteilung für Musikethnologie des Ethnologischen Museum), Berlin

FA IRLI RAN   Fonogrammarkhiv Instituta russkoi literatury Rossiiskoi akademii nauk [Phonogram Archive of the Institute of Russian Literature of the Russian Academy of Sciences], St. Petersburg

IRGO   Imperatorskoe Russkoe geograficheskoe obshchestvo [Imperial Russian Geographic Society], St. Petersburg

MAE RAN   Muzei antropologii i etnografii Rossiiskoi akademii nauk [Museum of Anthropology and Ethnography of the Russian Academy of Sciences], St. Petersburg/ Petrograd/ Leningrad

NYPL   New York Public Library, New York

SPbF ARAN   Sankt-Peterburgskii filial Arkhiva Rossiiskoi akademii nauk [St. Petersburg Branch of the Archive of the Russian Academy of Sciences], St. Petersburg

VSOIRGO   Vostochno-Sibirskoe Otdelenie Imperatorskogo Russkogo geograficheskogo obshchestva [Eastern Siberian Department of the Imperial Russian Geographic Society], Irkutsk

References

Unpublished Sources

AMNH DAA – American Museum of Natural History. Division of Anthropology Archives, New York: .J634, Jochelson, Waldemar, 1855-1937, 4 Boxes.

AMNH RL – American Museum of Natural History. Research Library, New York: D66, Domherr-Jochelson Collection, 9 Boxes.

APS – American Philosophical Society, Philadelphia PA: Franz Boas Papers, Inventory (I-K), Mss.B.B61.inventory07, Box No. 48.

ASL – Alaska State Library, Juneau AK: Historical Collection, MS 81, Michael Z. Vinokouroff Papers, 1764–1884, Box No. 4.

ASL – Alaska State Library, Juneau AK: Historical Collection, PCA 243, Michael Z. Vinokouroff Photograph Collection, ca. 1880's–1970's, Box No. 4, Folder No. 3 and 10.

AV IVR RAN – Arkhiv vostokovedov Instituta vostochnykh rukopisei Rossiiskoi akademii nauk [Archive of the Orientalists of the Institute of Eastern Manuscripts of the Russian Academy of Sciences], St. Petersburg: fond 23/631, Iokhel'son, Vladimir Il'ich (1856-1937), etnograf, issledovatel' tuzemtsev severnoi Sibiri, uchenyi khranitel' MAE, professor SPb universiteta, chlen-sotrudnik Russkogo Geograficheskogo obshchestva, nachal'nik ekspeditsii N'iu-Iorkskogo muzeia estestvennykh nauk na krainii severo-vostok Sibiri v 1900–1902 gg. [Jochelson, Waldemar (1856–1937), Ethnographer, Researcher of the Indigenous Peoples of Northern Siberia, Scientist and Curator of the St. Petersburg Museum of Anthropology and

Ethnography, Professor of the St. Petersburg University, Member and Colleague of the Russian Geographic Society, Leader of the Expedition of the American Museum of Natural History, New York, to the Far Northeast of Siberia from 1900 to 1902], 2 opisi [2 Inventories].

GAIO – Gosudarstvennyi arkhiv Irkutskoi oblasti [State Archive of the Irkutsk Oblast] Irkutsk: fond 293, Sibiriakovskaia (Iakutskaia) ekspeditsiia [The Sibiriakov (Yakut) Expedition], opis' 1, delo 94.

GAKhK – Gosudarstvennyi arkhiv Khabarovskogo kraia [State Archive of the Khabarovsk Krai], Khabarovsk: fond 537, opis' 1, delo 17, listy 191–194, text: Aleuty i ikh ostrova [The Aleuts and Their Islands].

GAKhK – Gosudarstvennyi arkhiv Khabarovskogo kraia [State Archive of the Khabarovsk Krai], Khabarovsk: fond 537, opis' 1, delo 69, listy 2–5, text: Iukagiry i chuvantsy [The Yukaghirs and the Chuvans].

NA MAE RAN – Nauchnyi arkhiv Muzeia antropologii i etnografii Rossiiskoi akademii nauk [Scientific Archive of the Museum of Anthropology and Ethnography of the Russian Academy of Sciences], St. Petersburg: fond 40, smeshannyi fond sotrudnikov [Inventory of the Research Associates].

NARS (Ia) – Natsional'nyi arkhiv Respubliki Sakha (Iakutiia) [National Archive of the Republic Sakha (Yakutia)], Yakutsk: fond 12, opis' 12, delo 299.

NYPL – New York Public Library, New York: MssCol 1565, Waldemar Jochelson Papers (1855–1937), 10 Boxes.

Encyclopedia

BSE-III – Bol'shaia Sovetskaia Entsiklopediia [The Great Soviet Encyclopedia], 3rd edition, 31 vols., Moscow: Sovetskaia Entsiklopediia.

Printed Sources and Secondary Literature

Antropologicheskii forum 2016. *K 150-letiiu so dnia rozhdeniia V.G. Bogoraza* [To the 150th Anniversary of V.G. Bogoras's Birthday]. In *Antropologicheskii Forum* 29:101–219 (five articles by Dmitrii V. Arziutov, Nikolai B. Vakhtin, Elena A. Mikhailova, and Elena V. Liarskaia).

Basharin, Georgii P. 1972. *Iz istorii organizatsii Sibiriakovskoi ekspeditsii* [From the History of the Sibiriakov Expedition]. In *Iakutskii Arkhiv*, issue 4: 201–229.

Bogoras, Waldemar [Bogoraz Vladimir G.] 1934. Predislovie avtora k russkomu izdaniiu [Foreword by the Author to the Russian Edition]. In *Chukchi. Chast' I: Sotsial'naia organizatsiia* [The Chukchee. Part I.: Social Organization], V.G. Bogoras, XIII–XXX. Leningrad: Izdatel'stvo Instituta narodov severa TsIK SSSR.

Burykin, Aleksei A. 2005. Materialy po iazykam i fol'kloru korennykh malochislennykh narodov Severa, Sibiri i Dal'nego Vostoka v kollektsiiakh Fonogrammarkhiva IRLI (Pushkinskii Dom) RAN [Linguistic and Folkloristic Materials of the Small Indigenous Peoples of the North, Siberia, and the Far East in the Collections of the Phonogram Archive of the Institute of Russian Literature (Pushkinskii House) of the Russian Academy of Sciences], http://lingsib.iea.ras.ru/ru/round_table/papers/burykin1.pdf [17.01.2018], 1–14. In *"Kruglyi stol po problemam iazykov korennykh narodov Sibiri, nakhodiashchikhsia pod ugrozoii ischeznoveniia", Institut etnologii i antropologii RAN, g. Moskva, 27–28 oktiabria 2005 g.,* ["Round Table About the Problems of the Languages of the Indigenous Peoples of Siberia, which are at Risk of Extinction", Institute of Ethnology and Anthropology of the Russian Academy of Sciences, Moscow, October 27–28th, 2005]: http://lingsib.iea.ras.ru/ru/round_table/ [6.04.2018].

— 2008. Fonograficheskie kollektsii V.I. Iokhel'sona iz fondov Fonogrammarkhiva Instituta russkoi literatury (Pushkinskii Dom) RAN [The Phonographic Collections of W. Jochelson in the Inventories of the Phonogram Archive of the Institute of Russian Literature (Pushkinskii House) of the Russian Academy of Sciences]. In *Sever Azii v etnokul'turnykh issledovaniiakh. Materialy mezhdunarodnoi i nauchno-prakticheskoi konferentsii, posviashchennoi 150-letiiu so dnia rozhdeniia V.I. Iokhel'sona (g. Iakutsk, 15-16 avgusta 2005 g.).* [Northern Asia in Ethnic and Cultural Research. Materials of An International Scientific and Practical Conference Dedicated to the 150th Anniversary of W. Jochelson's Birthday]. A.I. Gogolev (ed.), 31–39. Novosibirsk: Nauka.

Burykin, Aleksei A., Girfanova, Al'bina Kh., Kastrov, Aleksandr Iu. et al. (eds.) 2005. *Kollektsii narodov Severa v Fonogrammarkhive Pushkinskogo Doma. Materialy po iazykam i fol'kloru narodov Krainego Severa, Sibiri i Dal'nego Vostoka Rossii, khraniashchiesia v Fonogrammarkhive Instituta russkoi literatury (Pushkinskii Dom) RAN* [The Collections of the Peoples of the North in the Phonogram Archive of the Pushkinskii House. Linguistic and Folkloristic Materials of the Peoples of the Outmost North, Siberia, and the Far East of Russia stored in the Phonogram Archive of the Institute of Russian Literature (Pushkinskii House) of the Russian Academy of Sciences]. St. Petersburg: Filologicheskii institut SPbGU.

Dahlmann, Dittmar 2016. Deutschbaltische Forschungsreisende und Wissenschaftler und die Universität Dorpat in der ersten Hälfte des 19. Jahrhunderts – Ein Überblick. In *Auf den Spuren der modernen Sozial- und Kulturanthropologie. Die Jesup North Pacific Expedition (1897–1902) im Nordosten Sibiriens.* M. Winterschladen, D. Ordubadi, and D. Dahlmann (eds.), 11–49, Fürstenberg/Havel: Kulturstiftung Sibirien.

Fitzhugh, William W., and Aron Crowell (eds.) 1988. *Crossroads of Continents. Cultures of Siberia and Alaska*, Washington, D.C.: Smithsonian Institution Press.

Fitzhugh, William W., and Igor Krupnik 1993. Jesup II Research Initiative. In *Arctic Studies Center Newsletter* 2: 5–9.

Gassert, Philipp 2010. Transnationale Geschichte, Version 1.0. In *Docupedia-Zeitgeschichte*: 1–13. http://docupedia.de/images/0/08/Transnationale_Geschichte_Version_1.0_Philipp_Gassert.pdf) [13.01.2018].

Gernet, Katharina 1999. *Vladimir Germanovič Bogoraz (1865–1936). Eine Bibliographie.* München: Osteuropa-Institut München.

Gogolev, Anatolii I. (ed.) 2008. *Sever Azii v etnokul'turnykh issledovaniiakh. Materialy mezhdunarodnoi i nauchno-prakticheskoi konferentsii, posviashchennoi 150-letiiu so dnia rozhdeniia V.I. Iokhel'sona (g. Iakutsk, 15–16 avgusta 2005 g.)* [Northern Asia in Ethnic and Cultural Research. Materials of An International Scientific and Practical Conference Dedicated to the 150th Anniversary of W. Jochelson's Birthday]. Novosibirsk: Nauka.

Gorokhov, Kirill I. 1965. Issledovaniia i materialy uchastnikov Iakutskoi (Sibiriakovskoi) ekspeditsii VSORGO v 1894–1896 gg. v oblasti etnografii Iakutov [Research and Materials of the Participants of the Yakut (Sibiriakov) Expedition of the VSORGO in 1894–1896 in the Field of the Yakut Ethnography]. In *Iz istorii Iakutii XVII–XIX vekov. (Sbornik statei)* [The History of Yakutia from the 17th to the 19th Century. (Collection of Essays)]. K.I. Gorokhov, V.V. Nikolaeva, and F.G. Safronov (eds.): 52–75, Yakutsk: Iakutknigoizdat.

Gurvich, Il'ia S. 1963. Polevye dnevniki V.I. Iokhel'sona i D.L. Iokhel'son-Brodskoi [The Field Journals of W. Jochelson and D.L. Jochelson-Brodskaia]. In *Ocherki istorii russkoi etnografii, fol'kloristiki i antropologii. Trudy instituta etnografii* 2: 248–258.

– 1972. Iokhel'son, Vladimir Il'ich. In *BSE III* 10: 390.

Gurvich, Il'ia S., and Liudmila P. Kuzmina 1985. W.G. Bogoras et W.I. Jochelson. Deux éminents représentants de l'ethnographie Russe. In *Inter-Nord* 17: 145–151.

Heleniak, Thimothy, Tobias Holzlehner, Elena V. Khlinovskaia 2001. Der große Exodus. Demographische Trends an Russlands nördlicher Peripherie. In *Osteuropa* 61(2–3): 371–386.

Horsman, Reginald 1981. *Race and Manifest Destiny. The Origins of American Racial Anglo-Saxonism.* Cambridge MA: Harvard University Press.

Ivanov, Vladimir Kh. 2000. Vladimir Iokhel'son i Dina Iokhel'son-Brodskaia. Issledovateli etnicheskoi kul'tury narodov Severo-Vostoka Sibiri [Waldemar Jochelson and Dina Jochelson-Brodskaia. Investigators of the Ethnic Culture of the Peoples of Northeastern Siberia]. In *Tsirkumpolarnaia kul'tura. Pamiatniki kul'tury narodov Arktiki i Severa. Materialy nauchno-prakticheskoi konferentsii* [Circumpolar Culture. Monuments of the Culture of the Arctic and Northern Peoples. Materials of a Scientific and Practical Conference], L.I. Vinokurova and V.Kh. Ivanov (eds.), 119–128.Yakutsk: Severoved.

Ivanov, Vladimir Kh., and Zinaida I. Ivanova-Unarova 2003. The Revitalization of the Traditional Culture of Northeast Siberian Peoples. The Role of the Jesup Expedition. In *Constructing Cultures Then and Now. Celebrating Franz Boas and the Jesup North Pacific Expedition.* L. Kendall and I. Krupnik (eds.), 336–347, Washington,

D.C.: Arctic Studies Center, National Museum of Natural History, Smithsonian Institution.

Ivanova-Unarova, Zinaida I. 2008. Vladimir Iokhel'son i ego vklad v izuchenie Severo-Vostoka Azii i Severnoi Ameriki. (K 150-letiiu so dnia rozhdeniia) [Waldemar Jochelson and his Contribution to the Studies of Northeastern Asia and North America. (To the 150th Anniversary of His Birthday)]. In *Sever Azii v etnokul'turnykh issledovaniiakh. Materialy mezhdunarodnoi i nauchno-prakticheskoi konferentsii, posviashchennoi 150-letiiu so dnia rozhdeniia V.I. Iokhel'sona (g. Yakutsk, 15–16 avgusta 2005 g.)* [Northern Asia in Ethnic and Cultural Research. Materials of An International Scientific and Practical Conference Dedicated to the 150th Anniversary of W. Jochelson's Birthday]. A.I. Gogolev (ed.), 20–30. Novosibirsk: Nauka.

— 2015. Iokhel'son, Vladimir Il'ich. In *Arctic Megapedia*: http://arctic-megapedia.ru/wiki/Йохельсон,_Владимир_Ильич [13.01.2018].

Jefferson, Thomas 1801. *Notes on the State of Virginia.* 3rd edition. Newark: Pennington & Gould.

Jochelson, Waldemar [Iokhel'son, Vladimir I.] 1908. The Koryak. *The Jesup North Pacific Expedition* 6, Memoirs of the American Museum of Natural History 10, Pt. 1–2. New York. New edition 2016, edited by E. Kasten and M. Dürr. Fürstenberg/Havel: Kulturstiftung Sibirien.

— 1910-1926. The Yukaghir and Yukaghirized Tungus. *The Jesup North Pacific Expedition* 9, Memoirs of the American Museum of Natural History 13; Pt. 1, 1910; Pt. 2, 1924; Pt. 3, 1926. New York. New edition 2018, edited by E. Kasten and M. Dürr. Fürstenberg/Havel: Kulturstiftung Sibirien.

— 1918. Dalekoe proshloe. Iz vospominanii starago narodovol'tsa [Distant Past. From the Memories of an Old Narodovolets]. In *Byloe* 13: 53–75.

— 1922. *Pervye dni Narodnoi voli* [First Days of the *Narodnaia Volia*]. St. Petersburg: Gosudarstvennaia Tipografiia.

— 1923a. Iz perepiski s P.L. Lavrovym [Petr Lavrovich Lavrov, 1823–1900]. [From the Correspondence with P.L. Lavrov]. In *Byloe* 23: 147–155.

— 1923b. Kalendar' Narodnoi voli. Iz vospominanii [Yearbook of the Narodnaia Volia. From the Memories]. In *Muzei Revoliutsii* 1: 44–51.

— 1925. *Archaeological Investigations in the Aleutian Islands.* Washington, D.C.: Carnegie Institution of Washington.

— 1933. *History, Ethnology and Anthropology of the Aleut.* Washington, D.C.: Carnegie Institution of Washington.

— 2017. *Aus dem Fernen Osten Russlands. Deutschsprachige Schriften (1881–1908).* E. Kasten (ed.). Fürstenberg/Havel: Kulturstiftung Sibirien.

Kan, Sergei 2006. "My Old Friend in a Dead-End of Skepticism and Empiricism". Boas, Bogoras, and the Politics of Soviet Anthropology of the Late 1920s – Early 1930s. In *Histories of Anthropology Annual* 2: 32–68.

— 2007. "Moi drug v tupike empirizma i skepsisa". Vladimir Bogoraz, Franz Boas i politicheskii kontekst sovetskoi etnologii v kontse 1920-kh – nachale 1930-kh gg. ["My Friend in a Dead-end of Skepticism and Empiricism". Waldemar Bogoras, Franz Boas, and the Political Context of Soviet Anthropology of the Late 1920s– Early 1930s]. In *Antropologicheskii Forum* 7: 191–230.

— 2009. *Lev Shternberg. Anthropologist, Russian Socialist, Jewish Activist.* Lincoln NE, London: University of Nebraska Press.

Karmaat, Joachim 2016. In Theorie und Praxis. Der Boas'sche Kulturrelativismus bei Iochel'son und Bogoraz. In *Auf den Spuren der modernen Sozial- und Kulturanthropologie. Die Jesup North Pacific Expedition (1897–1902) im Nordosten Sibiriens.* M. Winterschladen, D. Ordubadi. and D. Dahlmann (eds.), 263–290. Fürstenberg/Havel: Kulturstiftung Sibirien.

Kasten, Erich 2013 (ed.). *Reisen an den Rand des Russischen Reiches. Die wissenschaftliche Erschließung der nordpazifischen Küstengebiete im 18. und 19. Jahrhundert.* Fürstenberg/Havel: Kulturstiftung Sibirien.

Kasten, Erich, and Anna Sirina (eds.) 2019. *Vladimir Iokhel'son i Sibiriakovskaia (Iakutskaia) ekspeditsiia (1894–1897 gg.)* [Waldemar Jochelson and the Sibiriakov (Yakut) Expedition (1894–1897)], Fürstenberg/Havel: Kulturstiftung Sibirien [in preparation].

Keeling, Richard 2001. Voices from Siberia. Ethnomusicology of the Jesup Expedition. In *Gateways: Exploring the Legacy of the Jesup North Pacific Expedition, 1897–1902.* I. Krupnik and W.W. Fitzhugh (eds.), 279–296. Washington, D.C.: Arctic Studies Center, National Museum of Natural History, Smithsonian Institution.

Kendall, Laurel, and Igor Krupnik (eds.) 2003. *Constructing Cultures Then and Now. Celebrating Franz Boas and the Jesup North Pacific Expedition*, Washington, D.C.: Arctic Studies Center, National Museum of Natural History, Smithsonian Institution.

Kharitonov, Luka N. 1958. *Eduard Karlovich Pekarskii. K 100-letiiu so dnia rozhdeniia* [Eduard Karlovich Pekarskii. To the 100th Anniversary of His Birthday], Yakutsk: Iakutskskoe knizhnoe izdatel'stvo.

Kleinmanns, Marit 2016. Salvage Ethnography in Ostsibirien. Die Sammlungen indigener Mythen und Sagen durch Vladimir Bogoraz und Vladimir Iochel'son im Rahmen der Jesup North Pacific Expedition. In *Auf den Spuren der modernen Sozial- und Kulturanthropologie. Die Jesup North Pacific Expedition (1897–1902) im Nordosten Sibiriens.* M. Winterschladen, D. Ordubadi, and D. Dahlmann (eds.), 291–331, Fürstenberg/Havel: Kulturstiftung Sibirien.

Knight, Nathaniel 1998. Empire and Nationality. Ethnography in the Russian Geographical Society, 1845–1855. In *Imperial Russia. New Histories for the Empire.* J. Burbank and D. L. Ransel (eds.), 108–141. Bloomington: Indiana University Press.

Knüppel, Michael 2013. *Paraphernalia zu einer Biographie des Sibiristen, Anthropologen und Archäologen Vladimir Il'ič Iochel'son (1855–1937).* Wiesbaden: Harrassowitz Verlag.

— 2016. Vladimir Il'ič Iochel'son und die Bedeutung der Jesup North Pacific Expedition für die jukagirischen Studien. In *Auf den Spuren der modernen Sozial- und Kulturanthropologie. Die Jesup North Pacific Expedition (1897–1902) im Nordosten Sibiriens.* M. Winterschladen, D. Ordubadi, and D. Dahlmann (eds.), 195–214, Fürstenberg/Havel: Kulturstiftung Sibirien.

Kocheshkov, Nikolai B. 1994a. Rossiiskii etnograf. (Vladimir Il'ich Iokhel'son) [A Russian Ethnographer. (Waldemar Jochelson)]. In *Zabytye imena. Stat'i i ocherki* 1: 92–101.

— 1994b. Zabytoe imia. Zhizn' i trudy V. Iokhel'sona [A Forgotten Name. Life and Efforts of W. Jochelson]. In *Rossiia and ATR* 2: 44–51.

Krumholz, Yvonne, and Matthias Winterschladen 2016. Zwei Schriften – zwei auseinander divergierende Darstellungen? Oder: warum Vladimir Iochel'son für die Jesup North Pacific Expedition zwei unterschiedliche Werke verfasste. Eine Untersuchung am Beispiel seiner Schamanismusdarstellung. In *Auf den Spuren der modernen Sozial- und Kulturanthropologie. Die Jesup North Pacific Expedition (1897-1902) im Nordosten Sibiriens.* M. Winterschladen, D. Ordubadi, and D. Dahlmann (eds.), 215–262, Fürstenberg/Havel: Kulturstiftung Sibirien.

Krupnik, Igor 1998. Jesup Genealogy. Intellectual Partnership and Russian-American Cooperation in Arctic/ North Pacific Anthropology. Part I: From the Jesup Expedition to the Cold War, 1897–1948. In *Arctic Anthropology* 35(2): 199–226.

Krupnik, Igor, and William W. Fitzhugh (eds.) 2001. *Gateways: Exploring the Legacy of the Jesup North Pacific Expedition, 1897–1902*, Washington, D.C.: Arctic Studies Center, National Museum of Natural History, Smithsonian Institution.

Kusber, Jan 2009. Imperiale Wissenschaften und Expansion. Das Beispiel Fedor Petrovič Litke. In *Russland, der Ferne Osten und die „Deutschen".* H. Duchhardt (ed.), 103–117. Göttingen: Vandenhoeck & Ruprecht.

Martin, Louise 1986. *Michail Z. Vinokouroff. A Profile and Inventory of His Papers (MS 81) and Photographs (PCA 243) in the Alaska Historical Library*, with a supplement (pages 1–26), Juneau: Alaska Department of Education, Division of State Libraries.

Mikhailova, Elena A. 2004. Vladimir Germanovich Bogoraz. Uchenyi, pisatel', obshchestvennyi deiatel' [Waldemar Bogoras. Scientist, Writer, Social Activist]. In *Vydaiushchiesia otechestvennye etnologi i antropologi XX veka* [Outstanding Russian Ethnologists and Anthropologists of the 20th Century]. V.A. Tishkov and D.D. Tumarkin (eds.), 95–136, Moscow: Nauka.

— 2016. Sof'ia Konstantinovna Bogoraz (1870–1921): Shtrikhi k potretu Vladimira Germanovicha Bogoraza [Sof'ia Konstantinovna Bogoras (1870-1921): Accents to the Portrait of Waldemar Bogoras]. In *Antropologicheskii Forum* 29: 109–124.

O'Sullivan, John 1839. The Great Nation of Futurity. In *The United States Magazine and Democratic Review* 6(23): 426–430.

— 1845. Annexation. In *The United States Magazine and Democratic Review* 17(85): 5–10.

Okoneshnikov, Egor I. 1982. *E.K. Pekarskii kak leksikograf* [E.K. Pekarskii as a Lexicographer]. Novosibirsk: Nauka.

Osterhammel, Jürgen 2009. *Die Verwandlung der Welt. Eine Geschichte des 19. Jahrhunderts.* München: C.H. Beck.

Patel, Kiran Klaus 2004. *Nach der Nationalfixiertheit. Perspektiven einer transnationalen Geschichte.* Berlin: Humboldt-Universität.

Pekarskii, Eduard K. 1907–1930. *Slovar' iakutskogo iazyka* [Dictionary of the Yakut Language], 13 vols. St. Petersburg / Petrograd / Leningrad. 2nd edition 1958/59, Leningrad: Akademiia nauk SSSR.

Reshetov, Aleksandr M. 2003. Vsia zhizn' v poiske. S.V. Ivanov [The Whole Life in Search. S.V. Ivanov]. In *Znamenitye universanty. Ocherki o pitomtsakh Sankt-Peterburgskogo universiteta* [Famous Graduate Students. Sketches about Wards of the St. Petersburg University]. Published in 3 volumes, 2002–2005. N.Ia. Olesich (ed.), vol. 2: 401–421. St. Petersburg: Izdatel'stvo Sankt-Peterburgskogo Universiteta.

Rezvan, Efim A. (ed.) 2012. *Lev Shternberg – grazhdanin, uchenyi, pedagog. K 150-letiiu so dnia rozhdeniia* [Lev Shternberg – Citizen, Scientist, Pedagogue. To the 150th Anniversary of His Birthday]. St. Petersburg: Kunstkamera.

Robbek, Vasilii A. 2008. Nauchnoe nasledie V.I. Iokhel'sona i iukagirovedenie v Respublike Sakha (Iakutiia) [The Scientific Heritage of W. Jochelson and the Yukaghir Studies in the Sakha Republic (Yakutia)]. In *Sever Azii v etnokul'turnykh issledovaniiakh. Materialy mezhdunarodnoĭ i nauchno-prakticheskoĭ konferentsii, posviashchennoi 150-letiiu so dnia rozhdeniia V.I. Iokhel'sona (g. Iakutsk, 15–16 avgusta 2005 g.)* [Northern Asia in Ethnic and Cultural Research. Materials of An International Scientific and Practical Conference Dedicated to the 150th Anniversary of W. Jochelson's Birthday]. A.I. Gogolev (ed.), 9–19. Novosibirsk: Izdatel'stvo Nauka.

— 2010. Nauchnoe nasledie V.I. Iokhel'sona i iukagirovedenie v Respublike Sakha (Iakutiia) [The Scientific Heritage of W. Jochelson and the Yukaghir Studies in the Sakha Republic (Yakutia)]. In *Voprosy istorii i kul'tury severnykh stran i territorii 4.* http://www.hcpncr.com/journ1210/journ1210robbek3.html [13.01.2018].

Rohr, Johannes 2001. Anpassung und Selbstbehauptung. Die indigenen Völker in Russlands Hohem Norden. In *Osteuropa* 61(2–3): 387–415.

Shavrov, Konstantin B. 1935. V.I. Iokhel'son. In *Sovetskaia Etnografiia* 2: 3–15.

Sirina, Anna A. 2007. "Skoro budet dva goda, kak my zanimaemsiia ekspeditsionnymi rabotami…. Neizvestnye pis'ma V.I. Iokhel'sona i V.G. Bogoraza iz Sibiriakovskoi (Iakutskoi) ekspeditsii ["Soon it will be Two Years, Since We have Started Working on the Expedition…". Unknown Letters of W. Jochelson and W. Bogoras from the Sibiriakov (Yakut) Expedition]. In *Ilin* 5: 90–97.

Sirina, Anna A., and Tat'iana P. Roon 2004. Lev Iakovlevich Shternberg. U istokov sovetskoi etnografii [Lev Iakovlevich Shternberg. At the Origins of the Soviet Ethnography]. In *Vydaiushchiesia otechestvennye etnologi i antropologi XX veka* [Outstanding Russian Ethnologists and Anthropologists of the 20th Century]. V.A.

Tishkov and D.D. Tumarkin (eds.), 49–94, Moscow: Nauka.

Sirina, Anna A., and Anatolii I. Shinkovoi 2007. Neizvestnoe nasledie Sibiriakovskoi (Iakutskoi) ekspeditsii (1894–1896 gg.). Pis'ma V.I. Iokhel'sona v VSOIRGO [The Unknown Heritage of the Sibiriakov (Yakut) Expedition. Letters of V.I. Jochelson to the VSOIRGO]. In *Rasy i Narody* 33: 331–368.

Slezkine, Yuri 1994. *Arctic Mirrors. Russia and the Small Peoples of the North*. Ithaca NY, London: Cornell University Press.

Slobodin, Sergei B. 2005. Vydaiushchiisia issledovatel' severnykh narodov. (K 150-letiiu so dnia rozhdeniia V.I. Iokhel'sona [An Outstanding Investigator of the Northern Peoples. To the 150th Anniversary of V.I. Jochelson's Birthday]. In *Etnograficheskoe Obozrenie* 2: 96–115.

Tishkov, Valerii A., and Tumarkin, Daniil D. (eds.) 2004. *Vydaiushchiesia otechestven-nye etnologi i antropologi XX veka* [Outstanding Russian Ethnologists and Anthro-pologists of the 20th Century]. Moscow: Nauka.

Tokarev, Sergei A. 1948. Vklad russkich uchenykh v mirovuiu etnograficheskuiu nauku [The Contribution of Russian Scientists to the World's Ethnography]. In *Sovetskaia Etnografiia* 2: 184–207.

— 1956. Vklad russkikh uchenykh v mirovuiu etnograficheskuiu nauku [The Contri-bution of Russian Scientists to the World's Ethnography]. In *Ocherki istorii russkoi etnografii, fol'kloristiki i antropologii. Trudy instituta etnografii*, vol. 30(1): 5–29.

Vakhtin, Nikolai B. 2004a. "Nauka i zhizn'". Sud'ba Vladimira Iokhel'sona (po mate-rialam ego perepisi 1897–1934 gg.) ["Science and Life". The Destiny of Waldemar Jochelson (based on His Correspondences between 1897–1934)]. In *Biulleten'. Antropologiia, men'shinstva, mul'tikul'turalizm* 5: 35–49.

— 2004b. Za uspekh beznadezhnogo dela. (Istoriia nevykhoda Entsiklopedii Dal'ne-Vostochnogo kraia) [To the Success of a Hopeless Project. (The History of the Encyclopedia of the Far-Eastern Krai]. In *Geopanorama russkoi kul'tury. Provin-tsiia i eë lokal'nye teksty* [Geopanorama of the Russian Culture. The Province and its Local Texts]. L.O. Zaionts (ed.), 43–60. Moscow: Iazyki slavianskoi kul'tury.

— 2005. Tikhookeanskaia ekspeditsiia Dzhesupa i eë russkie uchastniki [The Jesup North Pacific Expedition and its Russian Participants]. In *Antropologicheskii Forum* 2: 241–274.

— 2016. "Proekt Bogoraza". Bor'ba za ogon' [The "Bogoras Project". The Battle for Fire]. In *Antropologicheskii Forum* 29: 125–141.

Vinkovetsky, Ilya 2001 [Vin'kovetskii, Il'ia]. Circumnavigations, Empire, Modernity, Race. The Impact of Round-the-World Voyages on Russia's Imperial Conscious-ness. In *Ab Imperio* 1-2: 191–210.

Weber, Johannes 2016. Vladimir G. Bogoraz und Lev Ja. Šternberg. Protagonisten des Kulturtransfers der Ideen Franz Boas'? Die Entwicklung der Kulturanthropologie in Russland im ersten Drittel des 20. Jahrhunderts. In *Auf den Spuren der modernen Sozial- und Kulturanthropologie. Die Jesup North Pacific Expedition (1897–1902) im*

Nordosten Sibiriens. M. Winterschladen, D. Ordubadi, and D. Dahlmann (eds.), 119–149. Fürstenberg/Havel: Kulturstiftung Sibirien.

Weinberg, Albert K. 1935. *Manifest Destiny. A Study of Nationalist Expansionism in American History*, Baltimore: The John Hopkins Press.

Weiser, Adelheid 1989. *Die Völker Nordsibiriens unter sowjetischer Herrschaft von 1917 bis 1936*. Hohenschäftlarn bei München: Renner.

Winterschladen, Matthias 2016. Zwischen Revolution und Wissenschaft. Iochel'son, Bogoraz und die Verflechtung von Wissenschaft und Politik – ein biographischer Zugang. In *Auf den Spuren der modernen Sozial- und Kulturanthropologie. Die Jesup North Pacific Expedition (1897–1902) im Nordosten Sibiriens*. M. Winterschladen, D. Ordubadi, and D. Dahlmann (eds.), 77–118, Fürstenberg/Havel: Kulturstiftung Sibirien.

Winterschladen, Matthias, Diana Ordubadi, and Dittmar Dahlmann (eds.) 2016. *Auf den Spuren der modernen Sozial- und Kulturanthropologie. Die Jesup North Pacific Expedition (1897–1902) im Nordosten Sibiriens*. Fürstenberg/Havel: Kulturstiftung Sibirien.

2 FROM POLITICAL EXILE TO OUTSTANDING ETHNOLOGIST FOR NORTHEASTERN SIBERIA: JOCHELSON AS SELF-TAUGHT FIELDWORKER DURING HIS FIRST SIBIRIAKOV EXPEDITION 1894-1897.

Erich Kasten

The scientific exploration of the peoples and cultures of northeastern Siberia entered a new phase towards the end of the 19th century with Waldemar Jochelson. During the preceding 150 years, traveling scholars—mostly natural scientists of German or German-Baltic origin—had dedicated themselves to these tasks on behalf of the Russian authorities (Kasten 2013).[1] Jochelson, however, had a different background. First and foremost, his socio-critical convictions and his early career as a political activist distinguished him from most mainstream scientists of that time. Clearly, this had a considerable impact on his first encounters and acquaintances and his later research collaborations with indigenous people in these remote areas. Throughout his fieldwork he elaborated new methods of his own that, in some cases, gave direction to the emerging new discipline of Ethnology.

Due to intense experiences in extreme situations Jochelson's life took distinct turns: from an activist against social injustice to a political exile in Siberia, where he became interested in the indigenous peoples among whom he had to live. Then, many years later, he concluded his academic career in New York with his monumental opus in the form of significant monographs on the cultures of several peoples of northeastern Siberia. Throughout this time, he was substantially involved in the early shaping of Soviet ethnography.

Jochelson participated prominently in three major ethnographic expeditions in northeastern Siberia: the Sibiriakov Expedition (1894–1897), the Jesup North Pacific Expedition (1897–1902) and the Riabushinskii Expedition (1908–1911). The Jesup North Pacific Expedition under the direction of Franz Boas has attracted considerable recent international attention (Krupnik and Fitzhugh 2001). In these and following discourses Boas's potential influence on Jochelson's later field research and the elaboration of his published works was a substantive issue though probably at times somewhat overestimated (Kasten and Dürr 2016:27ff.). However, this view may be more qualified and rated differently if one considers Jochelson's earlier writings that have so far been less well known, as they were

---

1   See also the new editions of earlier monographs from the 19th century in the series *Bibliotheca Kamtschatica* at the Foundation for Siberian Cultures: http://www.siberian-studies.org/publications/bika_E.html

difficult to access. He wrote these articles immediately after his first fieldwork during the Sibiriakov Expedition, where main features of his unique and often innovative research approach were already visible. This study will therefore focus on Jochelson's earlier works that were initially published not only in Russian but also in German language. As Jochelson's life and complete works have already been extensively presented and discussed elsewhere,[2] only a brief biographical outline will be given here. In the following, the period of his early ethnographic work during the Sibiriakov Expedition will be investigated and analyzed more closely with regard to his primal attitudes and approaches from which he gradually developed his distinct methodology.

Biographical outline

Waldemar Jochelson [Vladimir Il'ich Iokhel'son] was born in Wilna (Vilnius) in 1855, where he grew up in a Jewish-orthodox family. Due to his revolutionary activities (see next paragraph), he was arrested in 1885 and first served a prison sentence at the Peter and Paul Fortress in St. Petersburg. Thereafter he was condemned to ten years in exile in northeastern Siberia.

During his years in exile he became acquainted with Waldemar Bogoras, who was sent there for the same political reasons. Both were obviously looking for intellectual challenges, and they discovered their common interest in ethnography. This also dovetailed with their unbroken revolutionary calling "to go into the people", and a long-lasting friendship evolved. Thus, Jochelson and Bogoras gratefully accepted the invitation, sanctioned by the authorities, to participate in the Sibiriakov Expedition, whose purpose it was to conduct ethnographic-historical research in this region. The experiences ensuing from this work clearly gave rise to some noticeable turns or shifting ambitions in Jochelson's later life, in that an academic career became a possibility, and his former political activities faded into the background.

After his return to St. Petersburg in 1898, Jochelson went first to Switzerland to finish his studies there. But shortly afterwards a new opportunity arose which tied in with his ethnographic interests and gave him the prospect of expanding them. For Franz Boas had invited him—at the recommendation of Friedrich Wilhelm Radloff, the director of the Museum of Anthropology and Ethnography in St. Petersburg—to participate in the Jesup North Pacific Expedition. During the years 1900 to 1902 of the expedition, Jochelson and his wife Dina Brodskaia worked with the Koryak on the northern coast of the Okhotsk Sea and on the Taigonos Peninsula. On the way back he sojourned for some time with the Yukaghir near Verkhnekolymsk, who he knew from earlier, lengthy visits.

---

2   See Winterschladen 2016; Knüppel 2013; Brandišauskas 2009; Vakhtin 2001. The first two paragraphs will summarize and draw mostly on these earlier works.

After the expedition, Jochelson secured with Boas's support a temporary appoint-
ment at the American Museum of Natural History in New York, where he began to
work up most of his research materials. The Jochelson couple also stayed for some
time in Zurich, London and Berlin, where Waldemar Jochelson took part in various
international congresses. Subsequently, he worked for a short time at the Museum
of Anthropology and Ethnology in St. Petersburg. Eventually, in 1908, Jochelson was
appointed director of the ethnological branch of another wide-ranging expedition.
During the years 1908 to 1911 of this expedition, named after Russian entrepreneur
and sponsor of the expedition Fedor Pavlovich Riabushinskii and organized by the
Imperial Russian Geographical society, Jochelson investigated together with his wife
and other collaborators the archaeology, culture, and language of the Aleut and the
Itelmen on Kamchatka. At the same time, other members of the expedition devoted
themselves independently to research in natural science.

After their return to St. Petersburg, the Jochelsons again found themselves in a precarious professional and economic situation (see this volume, 66f.) and the decided in
1922 to move and settle in New York once and for all. There again, Boas helped them
to establish themselves by means of minor appointments at the American Museum of
Natural History. Before his death in 1937, Jochelson managed to publish most of his
research materials, though some of them came out only after his death. All of them
still rank among the most significant ethnographies of this region.

Socio-critical ideas and revolutionary activities

The rabbinic seminary that Jochelson attended in Vilnius was not just an educational
institution for Jewish clergymen. It was there that in his youth Jochelson came into
contact with the socio-critical and revolutionary thinking that fascinated him. After
initial attempts by the government to close this facility, resistance to the Russian
authorities arose there. From these student circles emerged—with recourse to the
writings of philosophers und publicists such as Nikolai Chernyshevskii, Petr Lavrov
and Aleksandr Gertsen—the *Narodnik* ("Friend of the People") movement, a forerunner of later organizations such as *Zemlia i Volia* ("Land and Freedom") and *Narodnaia Volia* ("The Will of the People") that Jochelson joined. Members of the rabbinic
seminary also offered "continued political education" to the public at large and dis-
seminated socio-critical circulars of their own.

After attracting the attention of the secret police in 1875, Jochelson managed to
escape arrest and went to Berlin, where he worked as a lathe operator in an engineer-
ing factory. Before then he had acquired shoemaking skills—as part of his endeavor
to see things from the laborers' perspective. At the same time he attended open lectures and other events by social democratic organizations to upgrade his education
in philosophy and political economy. On those occasions he met with distinguished

social democrats such as Eduard Bernstein and Karl Johann Kautsky. Already at that time, Jochelson was publishing his first articles in Berlin on the situation in Russia for *Vorwärts* and *The Social Democrat,* journals of the social democratic party, as well as for a Russian language journal released in London.

In 1876, Jochelson traveled illegally to Russia, where for some years he pursued political agitation in the Ukraine. Later, revolutionary missions took him back and forth between Moscow and St. Petersburg. He helped with the manufacture of fake passports and other documents, and organized the transport of illegal writings abroad. In the meantime, Jochelson again traveled to Kiev to learn more about agriculture and to study land surveying. Acting on his maxim "to go into the people" he attempted to better understand even this group of people—the peasants who had to suffer in particular under the rule of the Czar—while staying with them most of the time for agitation purposes. Aside from all this, there is the rumor that Jochelson also worked in a dynamite factory to acquire—the same as other activists—knowledge of the manufacture of explosives. As dynamite was later found in the apartment that the revolutionary organization had provided him, he would have been within the neighborhood of the terrorists who were responsible for the assassinations of the Head of the Secret Police N.V. Menzentsov (1878) and Czar Alexander II (1881). However, direct involvement by Jochelson in these events could never be proven, as he left the country again in 1880.

Jochelson then sojourned in Switzerland, where he taught children of wealthy Russian families at a school on Lake Geneva while at the same time studying social sciences at the University of Bern.[3] Aside from that he assisted in editorial work for various Russian propaganda newsletters. At that time, Jochelson also authored articles for the journal *Der Sozialdemokrat* (The Social Democrat), in which he reported on the trials in Russia of the organizers of the successful assassination of Alexander II on March 1, 1881. As Jochelson was in some cases well known to the defendants, he was able to write thoroughly and authentically about their history (Jochelson 1881; see also Jochelson 2017:35–38). His clearly expressed sympathy for the convicted revolutionaries probably led to his being arrested once more at the Russian border when he tried to enter the country again in 1885. The authorities were obviously informed beforehand and found illegal writings with him. He managed to escape through the window of the guardhouse, but was captured again only a short time later and brought to St. Petersburg.

He spent the first two years of his prison term at the Peter and Paul Fortress in St. Petersburg. Then he was condemned to ten years in exile and sent to remote places

---

3   In the short curriculum vitae that he compiled in the USA, Jochelson mentioned that he had studied philosophy, which corresponded at that time to the human sciences with its broad curriculum in German-speaking countries. With regard to his teachers at the University of Bern, who could have had an impact on Jochelson's later academic interests, see Krumholz and Winterschladen (2016:230ff.).

in northeastern Siberia, where he again met with many former fellow campaigners of the revolutionary movement. Jochelson went first to Olekminsk via Tobolsk. After the local police found something suspicious in his correspondence he was sent to even more outlying locations. As Bogoras reported, Jochelson had mentioned in the particular letter that the exiles should pay particular attention to the indigenous people of these northern territories. It is said that the mocking government officials consequently had sent Jochelson to the Kolyma region; not to Srednekolymsk, where exiles had already established a small community of their own, but to even more remote places, where living conditions were much more difficult (Shavrov 1935:7).

With the help of the local population Jochelson acquired skills in fishing and hunting to survive in the wilderness. But in spite of surveillance by the authorities, the exiles traveled freely to nearby trade fairs. During this time—1894 and 1895—Jochelson was able to publish notes of his impressions (Jochelson 1894; 1895). In these works he discussed at length the question of agriculture in Yakutia, while trying to show new prospects for its possible further development in even such regions of the far north. In appreciation, he received the silver medal from the Imperial Russian Geographic Society in 1895 (Slobodin 2005:97).

The fact that Jochelson had already gained firsthand knowledge of the Yakut, Even, and probably also the Yukaghir languages, underlines his interest in and desire to empathize with the difficult living conditions of the indigenous people, whose everyday life practices and worldviews he sought to better understand by means of their own narratives. Thus, Jochelson could hardly have been better qualified for the upcoming opportunity to participate in the Sibiriakov Expedition, which turned out to be a particularly lucky happenstance, not only for him but also for science.

The Sibiriakov Expedition

The East Siberian Branch of the Imperial Russian Geographical Society in Irkutsk had organized the Yakut Historical Ethnographical Expedition for the years 1894–1897,[4] during which Jochelson had to conduct fieldwork in the area along the Kolyma River. The expedition was later named after its sponsor, Innokentii M. Sibiriakov, a businessman and philanthropist from Irkutsk whose family had made their fortune in gold mines.[5] Among other things, Sibiriakov was interested in the impact of gold

---

4   Often, 1894–1896 is given as the time period for the expedition, whereas Jochelson had— according to his field diary (cf. Gurvich 1963:249–251)—conducted his fieldwork from 1895– 1897. Jochelson set off for the first of his altogether eight journeys on December 15, 1894 from Yakutsk. The last trip he made from January 15 to July 15, 1897 (Jochelson 1898b:10f.). One reason for the diverging dates could be that Jochelson and Bogoras carried out some census work directly after the expedition in the region while also making use of that time for further ethnographical investigations.

5   I.M. Sibiriakov was apparently not involved with these affairs, but as a member of the family

mining on the indigenous people. As a result, the expedition had practical development aims as well as scientific ones (Sirina 2007:91). Thus, the expedition followed the
tradition of former ethnographic research in northeastern Siberia, by such scientists
as the agronomist Johann Karl Ehrenfried Kegel (1841–1847) and the geologist and
mining engineer Karl von Ditmar (1851–1855) on Kamchatka (Gülden 2011; Ditmar
2011a,b; Kasten 2013).

According to Dahlmann (2016:44), the composition of the 26-person research
team alone marked the beginning of a new era in the scientific exploration of northeastern Siberia. The participants were no longer recruited from the "classical imperial
military and scientific elites of Russia" (ibid.), but the team was formed by civil servants and intellectuals from the Yakut region, among them—with special permit of
the government—mostly political exiles and "enemies of the state". Besides Jochelson
and Bogoras, these were well-known ethnographers such as Eduard K. Pekarskii, Ivan
I. Mainov, Sergei V. Iastremskii and Nikolai A. Vitashevskii. One of the two directors
of the expedition, Dmitrii A. Klements, had served his term as an exile in the east
Siberian town of Minusinsk. Klements and Jochelson had already gotten to know each
other in Vilnius in 1875, whereupon they worked together for some years in the revolutionary movement. Jochelson wrote later that Klements had at that time "influenced
the direction of my revolutionary activities, and 20 years later he recruited me as a
participant for the Yakut expedition. By doing so he opened up the possibility of a
scientific career to me" (Jochelson 1922:45).

These "enemies of the state" were now needed as an "intellectual resource" (Dahlmann 2016: 45), which—as a result of increasing scientific isolation—had been thin-
ning out after the decay of the "transnational phase" of ethnographic research
(Schweitzer 2013) that was characterized by collaborative international research.
Furthermore, the Sibiriakov Expedition was a research initiative that originated in
Irkutsk, the new and growing intellectual center of Siberia in the second half of the
19th century. The expedition was conceived of there by the East Siberian Branch of the
Imperial Russian Geographical Society, and was also regionally financed and orga-
nized. For this expedition one had to draw upon the existing intellectual potential of
that region to which belonged above all well-educated political exiles.

Through the control of Andrei I. Popov, loyal imperial public servant, later
vice-governor of the Yakut district and second director of the expedition, the authorities came to the understanding that they could risk this unusual association. At least,
there was no known interference by the government, whereas later, during the Jesup
North Pacific expedition, obstruction by the secret police was reported, which Jochelson attributed to his former political background, among other things (Jochelson
1903; see also Jochelson 2017:153–158).

---

he held shares in the enterprise and dedicated himself more to charitable activities.

Fig. 1 Political exiles, 1900. Jochelson (to the right), presumably at Olekminsk [EK].
Image #11092, American Museum of Natural History Library.

For a long time, Jochelson's fragmentary publications on the results of the Sibiria-kov Expedition in the form of articles for various journals received little notice, as outside Russia special attention was directed mostly to Jochelson's later monographs that were published as a result of the Jesup North Pacific Expedition (Jochelson 1908a; 1910–1926; 1933). In the Soviet Union, the journal *Sovetskaia Etnografiia* published an article for his 80th birthday in 1935, in which Shavrov (1925: 7–8) wrote about the organization and the course of the Sibiriakov Expedition. He emphasized that one of its main outcomes was that Jochelson had discovered "the communistic sharing of the kill and other rare characteristic traits of primitiveness" among the Yukaghir.

First comprehensive studies of Jochelson's Sibiriakov Expedition were authored by Gorokhov (1958; 1965), and were based on local archival materials. Gurvich (1963) directed our attention to Jochelson's field diaries in Russian archives and presented some of them in more detail.[6] For Jochelson's 150th birthday, Slobodin (2005) honored his academic merits in a substantial article in *Etnograficheskoe obozrenie*. An important discovery of his correspondence—that for a long time was believed to be lost —was made by Anna Sirina during her work at the State Archive of the Irkutsk District (*gosudarstvennyi arkhiv Irkutskoi oblasti*) in 2005–2006. This entails 18 letters by Jochelson and Bogoras (11 of them by Jochelson) that they sent from their expedition to the administration of the East Siberian Branch of the Imperial Rus-

---

6   These diaries will be published in the forthcoming volume by Kasten and Sirina (2019).

sian Geographical Society in Irkutsk, and which were published by Sirina (2007) and Sirina and Shinkovoi (2007).[7] Most of the unique photographs that Jochelson had taken during the expedition are now stored in the archives of the Regional Irkutsk museum of local history (see Manushkina 2019), at the Museum of Anthropology and Ethnology in St. Petersburg, and at the American Museum of Natural History in New York—where some of these photos were mistakenly attributed to the later Jesup North Pacific expedition.

For a comparative evaluation of Jochelson's earlier articles and later monographs, the above-mentioned diaries and letters shed much light on the way Jochelson, like Bogoras, first developed his fieldwork methods, more or less autodidactically, and eventually brought them to great mastery. From these sources it also becomes apparent how—in comparison to later expeditions—the successful realization of such field-work methods was dependent on the particular local conditions, which obviously turned out to be very beneficial for Jochelson in his work with the Yukaghir.

In his preliminary research report Jochelson emphasizes that he has taken two different kinds of notes during his trips. First, he noted comments regarding the given research questions. Second, under the rubric "travel notes" (*Putevye zametki*), his diaries contained besides travel routes spontaneous impressions and sentiments, or "what appeared simply interesting to him" (Jochelson 1898b:25). And especially the latter notes contain insightful information, not only about the country and the people, but above all also about Jochelson's personal perceptions and sentiments, and how he interacted with indigenous people.

First, Jochelson's main interest was directed towards the Yakut of the Kolymski district (Argounova-Low, *this volume*). Only during later trips, which took him to the Yasachnaia River via Verkhnekolymsk, did he become more intensely involved with the daily practices, languages and folklore of the Yukaghir (Miller, *this volume*). In his diary he notes that the Yukaghir—like the Evenk (Tungus) and Even (Lamut)[8] —follow similar ritualized rules during the sharing of the kill *nimat* (cf. Sirina 2012: 316–335), as also in social interaction between the sexes (Jochelson 2017:53–55; cf. Gurvich 1963:251).

The diary also reveals that Jochelson devoted much of his time to the study of the Yukaghir language by recording texts with their translations, as well as individual Yukaghir words. During his stay with the Tundra Yukaghir, Jochelson was also interested in their relations with the Chukchi, and which impact their reindeer herding had on the decline of reindeer hunting among the Yukaghir. Some of the Yukaghir

---

7   See also their comprehensive publication in Kasten and Sirina (2019).
8   Jochelson's use of the ethnonyms Tungus and Lamut is sometimes confusing, as both belong to the same tungusic language family. By "Tungus" Jochelson usually meant Evenk and by "Lamut" Even. But according to Anna Sirina (personal communication), he didn't always use these terms consistently, especially if these ethnonyms were used by others, for example by K.P. Patkanov.

subsequently switched to reindeer herding as well—which he does not mention in his official reports (Gurvich 1963:251). Jochelson describes in his diaries the course of the devastating pox epidemics from which the local people suffered, and questions why certain areas were spared. Furthermore, he notes how he and Bogoras developed methods to study the cultures and languages of various groups of people. However, the extent to which this turned out to be useful during the later Jesup North Pacific Expedition, as mentioned by Gurvich (1963:253), is questionable (see p. 69, *this volume*). A central point for Jochelson was the knowledge of indigenous languages:

> "Above all it became apparent that without a knowledge of the languages any ethnographic work is inconceivable, to which not only superficial observations of the daily routines belong." (Jochelson, in Gurvich 1963:252)

The organizational difficulties under which the expedition suffered are described by Sirina (2007:92). Obviously, the number of participants, named "excursionists" (ekskursanty), was too high. As these were in most cases political exiles, their status did not always clarify, if or to what places they had a permit to travel. With the early withdrawal of the important initiator and patron Sibiriakov, who retired in 1896 to the monastery Athos where he died in 1901, interest in the expedition soon faded. Apparently, strong leadership was missing, one which should have been committed to the further and well-structured elaboration of the results. No means were foreseen for publications, with the result that these came out only later—and if at all—in a dispersed way. Little attention was given by the leadership of the expedition to the whereabouts of important research materials, such as the valuable photographs, which are therefore today scattered over many different collections and not archived in any coherent form.

In particular the letters by Jochelson and Bogoras to the East Siberian Branch of the Imperial Russian Geographical Society in Irkutsk reveal obvious shortcomings in communication between the administration and the members of the expedition, which affected their work in the field considerably. In each letter there are complaints that money and needed equipment had not yet arrived, and that therefore certain trips could not be taken, while these had to be undertaken within the strict time constraints of the seasons. In one case, Jochelson had to procure a loan in the community to proceed with his trip (in Sirina 2007:95). It's also informative that Jochelson repeatedly—and often in vain—ordered special literature to further his study of ethnographic methods while he was already in the field (in Sirina and Shinkovoi 2007: 343f.). What obviously irritated Jochelson most was that many of the letters remained unanswered. Again and again he pointed out the uncertainties of mail delivery, reaching Srednekolymsk from Yakutsk only three times a year. Climate and weather conditions exacerbated this uncertainty (Jochelson 2017:44–45, 91ff., 115ff.). From the letters we can also learn a lot about his travel logistics and his routes at certain times of the

Fig. 2 Post boat, Lena River, 1897. Image #11006, American Museum of Natural History Library.

Fig. 3 Jochelson [presumably at Srednekolymsk, EK].
Image #11016, American Museum of Natural History Library.

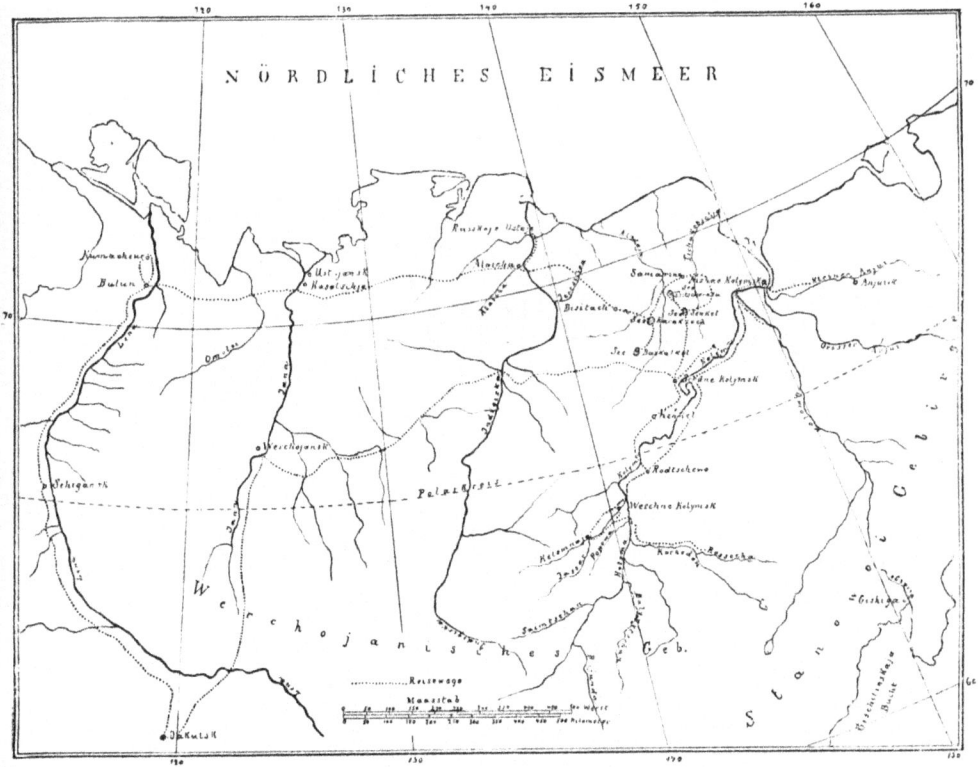

Fig. 4 x x x x x x x Yukaghir settlements.
•••••••• Areas, where still Yukaghir is spoken. Between Alasei and Chukochia a tundra
vernacular is spoken. (Jochelson 1899a: 7)

year, and how Jochelson and Bogoras divided up their work with regard to various
ethnic groups (in Sirina and Shinkovoi 2007:341).

Jochelson gives more details about how his activities proceeded, in particular in his
letters from 1896–1897 (in Sirina 2007). For example, on January 20, 1896, Jochelson
went to Verkhnekolymsk (ibid.:92f.), where he collected some economic data on two
Yakut settlements. At the same time, he also became interested in shamanism, and
recorded the full text of a shamanic ritual. In the beginning of February he returned
to Srednekolymsk. Together with his companion Aleksei Dolganov, who came from
Verkhnekolymsk, he set off a few days later for the middle upper reaches of the Omolon River, where Yukaghir lived. From there he traveled further by himself to the Aniui
outpost (*krepost'*) to meet Bogoras. Both visited the seasonal trade fair (*iarmarka*)
there. After that, Jochelson undertook a short trip up the Aniui River to investigate
some burial sites. Finally, he returned to Yukaghir settlements along the Omolon River.

In another letter dated July 25, 1896, Jochelson again mentions his keen interest in the exploration of the burial sites, after he had found a skeleton with special funeral clothing (in Sirina 2007:94f.). From April 18 until June 15, 1896, he stayed at the confluence of the Omolon and Kolyma rivers, where he devoted himself "almost exclusively to linguistic work" (ibid.)—in fact concurrently with speakers of Yukaghir and Evenk (Tungus) languages living in the area. From there he reports:

"My knowledge of the Yukaghir language has improved so much […] that I hope to soon be capable of drafting a grammar. But I will not hurry with that, i.e. for this I need further theoretical preparation. My Yukaghir word list is growing so much that I have already stopped counting the words. Furthermore, I can now generate all word forms from each template. My assumptions with regard to the language of the Kolymski Tungus [Evenk] have proved to be completely true—they speak a Yukaghir dialect. […] In general, the composition of the language is completely Yukaghir, but it differs from Yukaghir in a considerable number of Tungusic words and the consonant change. […] Tungus [Evenk] live in the Tundra, but along the Yasachnaia River the Lamut [Even] have switched to the Yukaghir language, while at the same time the Yukaghir tribe has declined. Further research, one should hope, will provide more data that will confirm this situation." (ibid.)

Thereafter Jochelson traveled further up the Omolon River to document more gravesites. While writing this letter, he had already stayed three weeks in Srednekolymsk, where he was awaiting urgently requested money for further travel to Verkhnekolymsk. Yukaghir from the Korkodon area were waiting for him, with whom he wanted to travel upstream.

Eventually he enclosed several photographs with the letter, two of gravesites, one view over the settlement and a fourth image that shows "his teacher, the Tungus and Yukaghir from Verkhoiansk, Dolganov. Dolganov was also one of the boatmen with whom Jochelson traveled to the Korkodon, and he wrote that he would have wished to take him along later to Yakutsk. There he could have been of much use to him as an interpreter, as besides his Yukaghir mother tongue Dolganov had also mastered the Yakut and Lamut [Even] languages, as well as some Russian. Jochelson also thought that he could have regularly practiced Yukaghir language with him. Dolganov was prepared to join him, but that would have cost Jochelson 200 more rubles. Therefore it had "under the given circumstances to remain a dream" (ibid.:95).

In his letter of October 25, 1897 to the East Siberian Branch of the Imperial Russian Geographical Society, Jochelson requested accounts of earlier travels that he needed for comparative studies (ibid.:96). In the same letter he also introduced Aleksei Dolganov as his most valuable collaborator, together with Vasilii Shalugin, with whom he was underway along the Yasachnaia River, as well as Ivan Spiridonov and Fedos'ia Sontseva from the Korkodon River area. He appealed to the administration to confer an award through the general governor to the first two of them for their special merits, and to make specified presents to the latter in the name of the Imperial Russian Geographical Society. In another letter dated November 11, 1897, Jochelson lists in detail other assistants from the Cossack population (ibid.:96).

Fig. 5 Jochelson's Yukaghir collaborators.
Image #22188, American Museum of Natural History Library.

As soon as the expedition had come to an end, Jochelson published first results in the form of some articles for Russian journals (Jochelson 1898a,c,d) and a preliminary research report (Jochelson 1898b). In the latter he describes in detail his travel routes (Jochelson 1898b:10). He eventually also drafted a plan for how he meant to proceed with the elaboration of the collected materials and their publication (Jochelson 1898b:43). He also addresses some first important insights to the effect that for the—according to his estimate—700 Yukaghir "within about 50 years it could be too late to restore their language, religion and social system (Jochelson 1898b:19), but he was obviously wrong about that. Jochelson also provided important clues in this report to the decrease in multilingualism of the indigenous people—from an often-encountered capability of four languages (Yukaghir, Yakut, Even and Chukchi) from east to west, to usually only two languages (Even and Yakut) beyond the Indigirka River, while west of the Yana River, only Yakut was spoken (Jochelson 1898b:32). Also remarkable are Jochelson's assessments of the cultural dynamics and overlays between different ethnic groups, which were at the center of his investigations. In one case, for the Yukaghir and Even, this led "to a compromise between both influences" (Jochelson 1898b:36).

Shortly afterwards, in 1899, Jochelson used German versions of his first publications for lectures in Switzerland. These lectures were published there in the reports of meetings of prestigious scientific societies (Jochelson 1900a,b). Jochelson had already published parts of one lecture (Jochelson 1900a) in *Mutter Erde* ("Mother Earth") (Jochelson 1899a), one of those popular scientific journals that were in vogue among the general educated public at that time. There he also released other, less scientific-ethnographic reports that described more empathetically the everyday life of the local people, and which provide valuable insights into how they dealt with each other (Jochelson 1899b–e; also in 2017:91–137). One of these articles had been published previously in a similar popular scientific Russian journal, *Niva* (Jochelson 1898c).

Only many years later were Jochelson's research results from this time released in a complete publication, his monograph *The Yukaghir and Yukaghirized Tungus* (Jochelson 1910–1926). He wrote this comprehensive work later in New York after another period of research in that area during the Jesup North Pacific Expedition, though it contains for the most part results from the Sibiriakov Expedition. In this monograph Jochelson eventually takes up themes in which he was obviously particularly interested during the Sibiriakov Expedition, for example gravesites and funeral customs that were often mentioned in his letters (see p. 45, *this volume*), but which he did not follow up on in his early articles in the aforementioned journals. However, before the Jesup North Pacific Expedition, his second research trip, Jochelson was able to publish a text collection in St. Petersburg that contains about 150 stories and song lyrics, which he had recorded in Russian and Yukaghir languages during the Sibiriakov Expedition (Jochelson 1900c). His Yukaghir word list had more than 9,000 entries that revealed to him, as he wrote, basic insights into the grammatical composition of this language. Whereas the Yukaghir were considered among scientists at that time to have already become extinct, Jochelson discovered that the Yukaghir language was split into two different dialects, the Kolyma und the Tundra Yukaghir (Jochelson 1905). Furthermore, Jochelson ascertained already in 1899 a "relationship between the peoples of northeast Asia and tribes on the northwest coast of North America" (Jochelson 1900a; see also 2017:47)—which, Franz Boas also made independently at the same time as the basic paradigm for the Jesup North Pacific Expedition.

Jochelson's results from the Sibiriakov Expedition in relation to his later works

Particularly revealing is a more in-depth study, most notably of his early publications from the years 1898 and 1899 in comparison with his later works that originated many years later in connection with the Jesup North Pacific Expedition, and obviously under some influence by Franz Boas in New York. This underlines an oft-suggested assumption (Vakhtin 2004:36) that there probably was a distinct turn in Jochelson's life towards an expected career as a scientist, which had already become apparent during his earlier stay in Switzerland, i.e. shortly after his return from the Sibiriakov Expedition. The reason for this can only be guessed at. There were certainly ample reasons for his disappointment with the later course of the revolutionary movement, but these he experienced during his later stays in St. Petersburg in the early 1920s. Another reason could have been his acquaintance and marriage to Dina Brodskaia, who he got to know in Switzerland shortly after his expedition, and keeping up with her academic profile could have been another incentive for him. However, after a closer look, foremost into his letters and diaries, one gets the impression that he had already shifted his interests towards science at an earlier stage in the light of his desire to study autodidactically the languages and knowledge systems of these peoples, which obviously fascinated him tremendously and which he wanted to explore more deeply with scientific methods. The question to what extent Jochelson had already come into contact with ethnography during his university studies, must remain unresolved. Arguing against this possibility could be the fact that he first obtained (or ordered) specialized ethnological literature during his fieldwork. On the other hand, he might have already received important incitements in this direction during his studies in Bern, where he attended classes with professors who taught geography with a clear connection to Russia (see footnote 3). Reinforced by his immediate experiences in the field, Jochelson's scientific interests obviously moved into the foreground, but without him giving up his earlier socio-critical attitudes and outlooks.

Thus, one sees in his earlier writings Jochelson's clearly expressed empathy for the local people, which helped him to see their often precarious living situation from their own perspective. He was evidently following here his former revolutionary approach, to improve the wellbeing of deprived and suppressed people. Furthermore, he could not conceal his emotional involvement, as he had himself lived under most difficult conditions among the indigenous people. He had experienced firsthand the ever-present dangers of their travels, when he, for example, got separated from the caravan for some time while he was en route on his sledge in hazardous weather conditions (Jochelson 1899c; see also 2017:101). His account of how he had to deal with his fellow travelers while all of them were starving (Jochelson 1900a; see also 2017:72ff.) opened his eyes to similar situations that were reported to him, for example, when a person who was starving to death refused to allow the last remaining reindeer of a friend should to be slaughtered for him (Jochelson 1899c; see also 2017:112). Jochelson describes with striking sensitivity how indigenous people treated community members who were suffering from pox and were doomed to die, and how they organized special caring facilities outside the settlement for these lepers—while they of course also had to protect themselves. In the face of his affection for and attachment to the indigenous people, however, Jochelson also describes in very measured words certain traits that divide humans in extreme situations, such as selfishness and the greed of a helper at the funeral of a wealthy person who had died of pox. Afterwards he secretly took the festive funeral clothing of the deceased—and the thief later fell ill himself from the same disease after wearing the coat (Jochelson 1899d; see also 2017:123f.).

Fig. 6 Yakut with leprosy expelled from village.
Image #1953, American Museum of Natural History Library.

He openly criticized the "crooked tradesmen"—also a frequent motif in Russian literature in the late 19th century—with whom indigenous people were confronted. Thus Jochelson accused the government of not caring about these people, but instead "brought so much alcohol into the Kolymsk region that half of the income of this poor district went to vodka" (Jochelson 1898a:274).

It is remarkable that these deeply sympathetic descriptions are mostly missing in his later extensive monographs on the Koryaks and Yukaghirs. However, it is unlikely that Jochelson's attitude could have fundamentally changed in the meantime. It is more likely that he would—during his later close collaboration with Boas—have adapted his writings to a "scientific" style, which he might have perceived more useful to academic recognition and his career in his chosen new professional environment. Reports containing the author's emotions were, at that time, certainly not compatible with such aims.

It is also disconcerting that he no longer acknowledges the contributions of local collaborators in his later monographs (see Kasten and Dürr 2016:18), whereas he still expressed this clearly, most notably in his letters during the Sibiriakov Expedition (see p. 46f., *this volume*). The same thought occurred to Igor Krupnik (2017:32) with regard to Waldemar Bogoras's work *The Chukchee* that was published—like Jochelson's *The*

Koryak, after the Jesup North Pacific Expedition. In the case of Bogoras, Krupnik explains it as follows:

"As Bogoras returned from his JNPE [Jesup North Pacific Expedition] field-work loaded with data and ideas, he was persuaded to accept a Boasian template of 'basic ethnography' for his writings for the JNPE series" (Krupnik 2017: 30). ... [He] "was pressured to present his data under an academic template not quite to his personal liking" (2017:31).

That the last sentence might also apply to Jochelson can hardly be assessed. On the other hand, during the Sibiriakov Expedition Jochelson already anticipates a lot of what Boas later made essential to his method:

"Therefore it appeared to be very important to me to document the ethnographic material by means of its unbiased representation in the narratives [Mitteilungen] of the indigenous people in their own words und in the original language, as only in this way does one become aware of the original meaning" (Boas 1910:7).

In his diaries and letters (see above) Jochelson underlines in 1894 how important it is for the understanding of indigenous cultures to record their narratives in their own languages, as he had done for his own text collection.

Beyond this, Jochelson studied the origin of indigenous communication systems from pictographic scripts that could have been guided by close monitoring of natural phenomena, in particular animal tracks (Jochelson 1900a; see also 2017:85ff.). In his detailed descriptions of hunting behavior Jochelson captures elementary human-animal relations that are characteristic of the given (and other indigenous) peoples:

"There is a mysterious tie between hunter and animal. If the hunter did not love the animal, he could not kill it. What a strange kind of love to offer oneself for consumption! But the guardian spirit of the animal, *Pädshul,* who treats the hunter with indulgence, who kills the animal for consumption, is upset if people kill animals pointlessly" (Jochelson 1900a; 2017:55).

With regard to fishing, Jochelson makes the not irrelevant observation that one lets pass the first school of fish ascending from the sea in order "not to frighten the fish", and only after that does the fishing begin (Jochelson 1900a; see also 2017:60). This behavior—even if reasoned here in a different way—reflects traditional ecological behavior and knowledge to let pass sufficient fish for spawning and for other settlements at the upper reaches of the river.[9] All this reveals Jochelson's intimate understanding of indigenous knowledge systems that an outsider can only grasp during long periods of participatory observation.

---

9   Similar ecologically motivated behavior in fishing was also observed by Georg Wilhelm Steller in the mid-18th century with the Itelmen on Kamchatka (Kasten 2012:70).

Also in other cases the particular quality of Jochelson's early writings becomes apparent. He describes in detail trade disputes in which he became involved (Jochelson 1900a; see also 2017:74–75), and notes characteristic behaviors and traits of different ethnic groups. While these may be valid, Jochelson avoids talking them up to ethnic stereotypes, as often happens. With remarkable intensity he captures—as also on other occasions—interethnic relations that underlie exchange networks of the five different ethnic groups in that area (Yukaghir, Even, Evenk, Yakut and Russians) that are obviously indispensable for survival under the given conditions.

It is striking, however, that such detailed descriptions and explanations are missing in Jochelson's later writings on the Koryak and Itelmen. The reasons may be different to the above-mentioned case, where certain emotional statements were not appropriate to his later scientific template. For in contrast to Jochelson's many years of travel within a relatively confined area during the Sibiriakov Expedition (and already before that), the Jesup North Pacific Expedition suffered from a number of shortcomings. One of them was the extreme time pressure as a consequence of Boas's demand to follow up a multitude of research questions for wide-ranging cultural comparisons. The latter caused in particular Bogoras's far-flung travel activities that made it impossible for him to stay in any one place long enough to conduct serious stationary or participatory observation. Therefore his Boas-style ethnographic method evokes more the impression of a hectic "collecting trip" in accordance with "salvage anthropology", the prevalent paradigm of that time.

Regarding Jochelson's research with the Koryak during his later Jesup North Pacific Expedition, it stands out by contrast to his earlier work with the Yukaghir, how difficult it obviously was for him to build up similar trusting relations with Koryak people, while these are clearly reflected in his earlier writings. In his later monograph on the Koryak he himself expresses his frustration after he felt cheated by a shaman, who he had commissioned for a performance, while certain important seasonal ritual practices such as the Kilvei feast remained concealed from him (Kasten and Dürr 2016:25). The anthropological measuring of indigenous people that was part of the prescribed research program sometimes provoked severe resistance.[10] This could often only be broken by some—also known from Boas—"tricks of the trade", by which the indigenous people were promised that the Czar would have fine clothing custom-made and sent to them as a gift (Kasten and Dürr 2016:20).

In general, one gets the impression that the Koryak viewed the taking of body measurements—perceived by them as a senseless transgression of their intimate sphere—as occurring under the orders of government authorities that Jochelson had to execute. That must have created even more distance between them, as Jochelson was already sometimes addressed this way (ibid.). His relations with the Yukaghir

---

10 Cf. the commentary by Dina Jochelson-Brodskaia who was mainly in charge of this task during the expedition: "Then not even pleas or gifts could persuade the stubborn and wild Koryak women to take off their clothes for the purpose of measuring" (1906:1).

during the Sibiriakov Expedition differed significantly from this. Among other things, Jochelson's earlier status as an exile probably played a part, when—in the eyes of the indigenous people—he suffered from the despotism of the authorities, just as they did.[11]

In contrast to his later difficulties with getting body measurements, it is revealing how sensitively Jochelson tried to explain to the indigenous people during the Sibiriakov Expedition the procedure of taking pictures that was completely unknown to them—in order to make it understandable to them. In their view, each person had a "shadow", and they imagined this to be captured in the photograph. However, what was then irritating for them was the fact that Jochelson could take a photo of a person who had just died, as—in their understanding—the shadow had left the body already (Jochelson 1899e; see also 2017:133).

Another handicap during Jochelson's research with the Koryak could have been that he didn't have sufficient time to concern himself with the Koryak language, and that he obviously was not always satisfied with the proficiency of his interpreter. First and foremost one can see the difference that it made that Jochelson was accompanied during his work with the Yukaghir by a team of local experts whose members were knowledgeable of specific regional conditions. For that he could draw on a wide pool of well-suited and knowledgeable local collaborators, with some of whom he was already familiar from his earlier stay in the area as an exile and with whom he had maintained long-standing mutually trusting relationships.

The obvious lack of adequate local experts during his later expeditions might have caused irritation and frustration for Jochelson, as is reflected in his emotionless descriptions of the Koryak. Even more striking is this in his ethnography of the Itelmen (Kamchadal) during the Riabushinskii Expedition in the years 1910–1911 (Koester and Kasten 2019). Here one can even assume some sluggishness or resignation,[12] when for example it seems that Jochelson in his remarks is almost more interested in his „Kamchadal" dog than in indigenous people themselves. From the beginning of this expedition there was a stronger interest by Jochelson in the archaeology, language and culture of the Aleut (Jochelson 1908b; see also 2017:150). With regard to the inclusion of Kamchatka into the research program, he was likely responding to the wish of the donor F.P. Riabushinskii. Hence Jochelson's ethnography on the Itelmen did not bring forward particularly illuminating new insights—which could be the reason he postponed again and again the publication of the results, and finally

---

11 In the most remote settlements of the Kolyma area, where Jochelson was not known from before, he was received, however, with deep respect and submissiveness, as was common with Russian authorities.

12 A reason for this could also have been that towards the end the expedition was facing financial problems, after the concealment of money in Petropavlovsk after the death of the sponsor F.P. Riabushinskii, who initiually wanted to participate in the expedition himself (pers. communication M. Winterschladen)

for so long that he never did complete this work during his lifetime. Besides his short-comings in mastering the Itelmen language, another fact might have contributed to Jochelson's disappointment—the strong Russian influence under which Itelmen culture had apparently already been for a long time.[13] This had already made ethnological research with these people less attractive.[14] But the question arises—did this have its origin in the new scientific *Zeitgeist* that was also shaped by the Boas school? In the beginning— before and during the Sibiriakov Expedition—Jochelson had worked unbiased and with great interest even with old Russian settlers (Jochelson 1899a; also in 2017:50f.) as he wanted in particular to learn more about the specific linguistic-cultural dynamics between all ethnic groups of this area (Jochelson 1900b,c).

In light of the publications on the results of the three expeditions in which Jochelson took part, clear differences can be seen in the kind and quality of his ethnography. Any judgments—from various perspectives—should be left aside here. However, there are indications as to how such significant variations might be explained. In any case, we did not only learn more about Jochelson's successful methods during his early ethnographic fieldwork that pointed the way forward to this new discipline, but also about the conditions under which these could be applied with good results.

In his manifold publications on the Yukaghir, it appears that Jochelson intentionally highlighted different themes and chose different genres in presenting them, as these publications were first directed to a heterogeneous readership. For example, in his articles on social movements in Russia that were published in German journals he aimed to appeal to revolutionary circles in western Europe, with the German social democracy as its driving force at that time. His first scientific reports were published in Russia in order to immediately inform the East Siberian Branch of the Imperial Russian Geographical Society and other participants of the Sibiriakov Expedition, as well as other scientists in Russia of his research results from this expedition. Shortly afterwards, he had used German translations of these articles for lectures at prominent scientific societies in other countries with the aim of recommending himself for a possible academic career in western Europe. That he had already published these articles a year earlier in popular scientific journals such as *Mutter Erde* could be explained by a possible shortage of money, as even Boas had to finance his first field trips this way (Kasten 1992:11). Beyond that, these journals provided Jochelson with the opportunity to become better known within a wider well-educated public.

Jochelson's later publications, in which he—as in his monograph *The Yukaghir and the Yukaghirized Tungus*—again drew on materials from his earlier Sibiriakov Expedition, were directed again at another audience that he then had in mind in his quest

---

13 Already during his planning Jochelson added "that much could still be done there in spite of the Russification of the Kamchadal" (Jochelson 1908b; 2017:147).

14 See Bergman (1928:175ff.), who evidently was relieved to stay again with his "wild people" (the Even) in the interior of the peninsula, after his side trip to the Itelmen on the west coast. These people "had already been mixed with the Russians."

for a future professional career—namely international colleagues from the new discipline of cultural anthropology that had authoritatively been shaped by Franz Boas in America.

References

Bergman, Sten 1928. *Auf Schi und Hundeschlitten durch Kamtschatka*. Stuttgart: Strecker und Schröder.

Boas, Franz 1910. *Die Resultate der Jesup-Expedition*. Verhandlungen des XVI. internationalen Amerikanisten-Kongresses, 1908. Erste Hälfte: 3–18. Wien und Leipzig: Hartleben.

Brandišauskas, Donatas 2009. Waldemar Jochelson – A Prominent Ethnographer of North-Eastern Siberia. *Acta Orientala Vilnensia* 10(1–2): 165–179.

Dahlmann, Dittmar 2016. Deutschbaltische Forschungsreisende und Wissenschaftler und die Universität Dorpat in der ersten Hälfte des 19. Jahrhunderts – Ein Überblick. In *Auf den Spuren der modernen Sozial- und Kulturanthropologie. Die Jesup North Pacific Expedition (1897–1902) im Nordosten Sibiriens*. M. Winterschladen, D. Ordubadi, and D. Dahlmann (eds.), 11–49. Fürstenberg/Havel: Kulturstiftung Sibirien.

Ditmar, Karl von 2011a [1890]. *Reisen und Aufenthalt in Kamtschatka in den Jahren 1851–1855*. Erster Teil: Historischer Bericht nach den Tagebüchern. St. Petersburg. Neuausgabe: Michael Dürr (Hg.). Fürstenberg/Havel: Kulturstiftung Sibirien.

— 2011b [1900]. *Reisen und Aufenthalt in Kamtschatka in den Jahren 1851–1855*. Zweiter Teil: Allgemeines über Kamtschatka. St. Petersburg. Neuausgabe: Michael Dürr (Hg.). Fürstenberg/Havel: Kulturstiftung Sibirien.

Gorokhov, K.I. 1958. *Deiatel'nost' Iakutskoi ekspeditsii 1884–1886 gg.* [The Work of the Yakut Expedition 1884–1886]. Trudy Iakutskogo filiala AN SSSR: 37–65. Yakutsk.

— 1965. Issledovateli i materialy uchastnikov Iakutskoi (Sibiriakov) ekspeditsii VSORGO v 1994–1996 gg. v oblasti etnografii iakutov [Researchers and materials of the participants in the Yakut (Sibiriakov) Expedition]. *Istoriia Iakutii XVII–XIX vv.*: 52–75. Yakutsk.

Gülden, Werner Friedrich (Hg.) 2011. *Johann Karl Ehrenfried Kegel: Forschungsreise nach Kamtschatka. Reisen und Erlebnisse des Johann Karl Ehrenfried Kegel von 1841 bis 1847*. Fürstenberg/Havel: Kulturstiftung Sibirien.

Gurvich, I.S. 1963. *Polevye dnevniki V.I. Iokhel'sona i D.L. Iokhel'son-Brodskoi* [The Field Diaries of V.I. Jochelson and D.L. Jochelson-Brodskaia]. Ocherki istorii russkoi etnografii, fol'kloristiki i antropologii. Vyp. II: 248–258.

Jochelson, Waldemar [Iokhel'son, Vladimir I.] 1881. Aus Russland. *Der Sozialdemokrat*, Nr. 17, vom 24.04.1881.

— 1894. Olekminskie skoptsy. Istoriko-bytovoi ocherk. [The Skoptsy of Olekminsk:

A Historical and Lifestyle Account]. *Zhivaia Starina*, Otd. 1, Vyp. II: 191–203, Otd. 2, Vyp. 3: 301–324.

— 1895. Zametki o naselenii Iakutskoi oblasti v istoriko-etnograficheskom otnoshenii" [Notes on the Population of the Yakut Oblast' in Historic and Geographic respects]. *Zhivaia Starina*, Vyp. II: 1–37.

— 1898a. Obrazy materialov po izucheniiu iukagirskogo iazyka i fol'klora sobrannykh v iakutskoi ekspeditsii [Materials on the Study of the Yukaghir Language and Folklore, Collected During the Yakut Expedition]. *Izvestiia Imperatorskogo Akademiia Nauk*, Ser. 5, Bd. IX (2): 151–177.

— 1898b. Predvaritel'nyi otchet ob issledovaniiakh inorodtsev Kolymskogo i Verkhnoianskogo okrugov [Preliminary Report on the Research of the Indigenous People of the Kolymsk and Verkhoiansk Districts]. *Izvestiia VSOIROGO* XXIX (1): 9–52. (Summary in German: 48–52, see also Jochelson 2017: 39–41).

— 1898c. V polarnomu kraiu putevye nabroski [Travel Notes From the Polar Region]. *Niva* 29 (19): 394–396.

— 1898d. Po rekam Iasachnoi i Korkodonu. Drevnii i sovremennyi iukargiskii byt i pis'mena. [On the Rivers Yasachna and Korkodon. Earlier and Present Yukaghir Customs and Writings]. *Izvestiia VSOIROGO* XXXIV (3): 255–290. St. Peterbug.

— 1899a. Die Jukagiren im äussersten Nordosten Asiens. In *Mutter Erde – Technik, Reisen und nützliche Naturbetrachtung in Haus und Familie*. Bd. 1: 261–266, 453–456, 467–470, 481–484; Bd. 2: 207–210, 228–229, 245–247. Berlin und Stuttgart: Spemann. (see also Jochelson 2017: 43–78)

— 1899b. In Polargegenden: I. Das Eisen-Mädchen (Timir-Kyß). In *Mutter Erde – Technik, Reisen und nützliche Naturbetrachtung in Haus und Familie*. Bd. 1: 285–288. Berlin und Stuttgart: Spemann. (see also Jochelson 2017: 91–97)

— 1899c. In Polargegenden: II. Ein „Tanner" in der Tundra. In *Mutter Erde – Technik, Reisen und nützliche Naturbetrachtung in Haus und Familie*, Bd. 1: 303–308, 325–328. Berlin und Stuttgart: Spemann. (see also Jochelson 2017: 99–114)

— 1899d. In Polargegenden: III. Die Blattern im äussersten Norden. In *Mutter Erde – Technik, Reisen und nützliche Naturbetrachtung in Haus und Familie*, Bd. 1: 364–366, 385–388. Berlin und Stuttgart: Spemann. (see also Jochelson 2017: 115–125)

— 1899e. In Polargegenden: IV. Die Aussätzigen im äussersten Nordosten. In *Mutter Erde – Technik, Reisen und nützliche Naturbetrachtung in Haus und Familie*. Bd. 2: 471–473, 487–490. Berlin und Stuttgart: Spemann. (see also Jochelson 2017: 127–137)

— 1900a. Die Jukagiren im äussersten Nordosten Asiens. *Sitzungsberichte der Geographischen Gesellschaft in Bern* XVII: 1–48. (see also Jochelson 2017: 43–78)

— 1900b. Über die Sprache und Schrift der Jukagiren. *Sitzungsberichte der Geographischen Gesellschaft in Bern* XVII: 49–63. (see also Jochelson 2017: 79–89)

— 1900c. *Materialy po izucheniiu iukagirskago iazyka i fol'klora, sobrannye v Kolymskom okruge* [Materials on the Study of the Yukagir Language and Folklore Collected in the Kolyma District]. St. Peterburg.

— 1903. Dvulikii Ianus [Two-faced Janus]. *Osvoboždenie* 15: 255–256. (German translation in Jochelson 2017: 153–158)

— 1905. *Essays on the Grammar of the Yukaghir Language*. Academy of Sciences. Annals March 1905, Bd. XVI, Teil II: 97–152. New York.

— 1908a. The Koryak. *The Jesup North Pacific Expedition* 6, *Memoirs of the American Museum of Natural History* 10, Pt. 1–2. New York. New edition 2016, edited by E. Kasten and M. Dürr. Fürstenberg/Havel: Kulturstiftung Sibirien.

— 1908b. Die Riabouschinsky-Expedition nach Kamtschatka. *Globus* 94: 224–225. (see also Jochelson 2017: 147–151)

— 1910–1926. The Yukaghir and Yukaghirized Tungus. *The Jesup North Pacific Expedition* 9, *Memoirs of the American Museum of Natural History* 13; Pt. 1, 1910; Pt. 2, 1924; Pt. 3, 1926. New York. New edition 2018, edited by E. Kasten and M. Dürr. Fürstenberg/Havel: Kulturstiftung Sibirien.

— 1922. *Pervye dni Narodnoi Voli* [The First Days of the People's Will]. Petrograd.

— 1933. The Yakut. In *Anthropological Papers of the American Museum of Natural History*, 37–221. New York: American Museum of Natural History. New edition 2018, edited by M. Dürr and E. Kasten. Fürstenberg/Havel: Kulturstiftung Sibirien.

— 2017. *Aus dem fernen Osten Russlands. Deutschsprachige Schriften (1881–1908)*. E. Kasten (ed.). Fürstenberg/Havel: Kulturstiftung Sibirien.

Jochelson-Brodsky, Dina 1906. *Zur Topographie des weiblichen Körpers nordostsibirischer Völker*. Inaugural-Dissertation. Medizinische Fakultät der Universität Zürich.

Kasten, Erich 1992. Franz Boas. Ein engagierter Wissenschaftler in der Auseinandersetzung mit seiner Zeit. In *Franz Boas. Ethnologe, Anthropologe, Sprachwissenschaftler*. M. Dürr, E. Kasten, and E. Renner (eds.), 7–38. Berlin: Staatsbibliothek zu Berlin / Wiesbaden: Reichert.

— 2012. Koryak Salmon Fishery: Remembrances of the Past, Perspectives for the Future. In *Keystone Nations: Indigenous Peoples and Salmon Across the North Pacific*. B.J. Colombi and J.F. Brooks (eds.), 65–88. Santa Fe: SAR Press.

Kasten, Erich (ed.) 2013. *Reisen an den Rand des Russischen Reiches: Die wissenschaftliche Erschließung der nordpazifischen Küstengebiete im 18. und 19. Jahrhundert*. Fürstenberg/Havel: Kulturstiftung Sibirien.

Kasten, Erich, and Michael Dürr 2016. Jochelson and the Jesup North Pacific Expedition. A New Approach in the Ethnography for the Russian Far East. In *Waldemar Jochelson: The Koryak*. E. Kasten and M. Dürr (eds.), 9–34. Fürstenberg/Havel: Kulturstiftung Sibirien.

Kasten, Erich, and Anna Sirina (eds.) 2019. *Vladimir Iokhel'son i Sibiriakovskaia (Iakutskaia) ekspeditsiia (1894–1897 gg.)* [Waldemar Jochelson and the Sibiriakov (Yakut) Expedition (1894–1897)], Fürstenberg/Havel: Kulturstiftung Sibirien (in preparation).

Knüppel, Michael 2013. *Paraphernalia zu einer Bibliographie des Sibiristen, Anthropologen und Archäologen Vladimir Il'ič Iochel'son (1855–1937)*. Wiesbaden: Harrassowitz.

Koester, David, and Erich Kasten (eds.) 2019. *Jochelson's Anthropological Investigations in Kamchatka: Results of the Riabushinskii Expedition*. Fürstenberg/Havel: Kulturstiftung Sibirien (in preparation).

Krumholz, Yvonne, and Matthias Winterschladen 2016. Zwei Schriften – zwei divergierende Darstellungen. Oder: warum Vladimir Iochel'son für die Jesup North Pacific Expedition zwei unterschiedliche Werke verfasste. Eine Untersuchung am Beispiel der Schamanismusforschung. In *Auf den Spuren der modernen Sozial- und Kulturanthropologie. Die Jesup North Pacific Expedition (1897–1902) im Nordosten Sibiriens*. M. Winterschladen, D. Ordubadi and D. Dahlmann (eds.), 215–262. Fürstenberg/Havel: Kulturstiftung Sibirien.

Krupnik, Igor 2017. Waldemar Bogoras and The Chukchee: A Maestro and a Classical Ethnography. In *Waldemar Bogoras: The Chukchee*, 2017 [1904–1909]. New edition 2017, M. Dürr and E.Kasten (eds.), 9–45. Fürstenberg/Havel: Kulturstiftung Sibirien.

Krupnik, Igor, and William W. Fitzhugh (eds.) 2001. *Gateways. Exploring the Legacy of the Jesup North Pacific Expedition, 1897–1902*. Washington, D.C.: Arctic Studies Center, National Museum of Natural History, Smithsonian Institution.

Manushkina, E.G. 2019. Materialy Iakutskoi (Sibiriakov) ekspeditsii v fondakh Irkutskogo oblastnogo kraevedcheskogo muzeia [Materials of the Yakut (Sibiriakov) Expedition in the Archives of the Regional Irkutsk Museum of Local History]. In *Vladimir Iokhel'son i Sibiriakovskaia (Iakutskaia) ekspeditsiia (1894–1897 gg.)*, E. Kasten and A. Sirina (eds.), 2019. Fürstenberg/Havel: Kulturstiftung Sibirien (in preparation).

Schweitzer, Peter 2013. Naturforscher, Weltreisende und nationale Forschungstraditionen: Bemerkungen zur ethnologischen Erforschung Sibiriens im 18. und 19. Jahrhundert. In *Reisen an den Rand des Russischen Reiches: Die wissenschaftliche Erschließung der nordpazifischen Küstengebiete im 18. und 19. Jahrhundert*. E. Kasten (ed.), 11–28. Fürstenberg/Havel: Kulturstiftung Sibirien.

Shavrov, K.B. 1935. V.I. Iokhel'son. *Sovetskaia Etnografiia* (2): 3–15.

Sirina, A.A. 2007. "Skoro budet dva goda, kak my zanimaemsa ekspeditsionnymi rabotami ...". Neizvestnye pis'ma V.I. Iokhel'sona i V.G. Bogoraza iz Sibiriakov (Iakutskoi) ekspeditsii [Soon It Will Be Two Years That We Occupy Ourselves With the Expedition Work ...Unknown Letters by W. Jochelson and W. Bogoras From the Sibiriakov (Yakut) Expedition]. *Ilin. Istoriko-geograficheskoi, kul'turologicheskii zhurnal* (5): 91–96.

— 2012. *Evenki i Eveny v sovremennom mire. Samosoznanie, prirodopol'zovanie, mirovozzrenie* [Evenk and Even in the Present World. Self-confidence, Nature Use and Worldview]. Moskva: Izdatel'skaia firma "Vostochnaia literatura".

Sirina, A. A, and Shinkovoi A. I. 2007. Neizvestnoe nasledie Sibiriakovskoi (Iakutskoi) ekspeditsii (1894–1896): pis'ma V. I. Iokhel'sona vo VSOIRGO. [Unknown Remains of the Sibiriakov (Yakut) Expedition 1894–1896: Letters by Waldemar Jochelson to the Eastern Siberian Department of the Imperial Russian Geographic Society, Irkutsk]. *Rasy i narody. Ezhegodnik* 33: 331–368.

Slobodin, S. B. 2005. Vydaiushchiisia issledovatel' severnykh narodov (k 150 letiiu so dnia rozhdeniia V. I. Iokhel'sona) [A Prominent Researcher of the Northern Peoples (to the 150th anniversary of V.I. Jochelson)]. *Etnograficheskoe Obozrenie* 5: 96–115.

Vakhtin, Nikolai 2001. Franz Boas and the Shaping of the Jesup Expedition Siberian Research, 1895–1900. In *Gateways. Exploring the Legacy of the Jesup North Pacific Expedition, 1897–1902*. I. Krupnik and W.W. Fitzhugh (eds.), 71–89. Washington, DC: Arctic Studies Center, National Museum of Natural History, Smithsonian Institution.

— 2004. "Nauka i zhizn'". Sud'ba Vladimira Iokhel'sona (po materialam ego perepisi 1897–1934 gg.) ["Science and Life". The Destiny of Waldemar Jochelson (based on His Correspondences Between 1897–1934)]. In *Biulleten'. Antropologiia, men'shinstva, mul'tikul'turalizm* 5: 35–49.

Winterschladen, Matthias 2016. Zwischen Revolution und Wissenschaft. Vladimir Iochel'son, Vladimir Bogoraz und die Verflechtung von Wissenschaft und Politik – Ein biographischer Zugang. In *Auf den Spuren der modernen Sozial- und Kulturanthropologie. Die Jesup North Pacific Expedition (1897–1902) im Nordosten Sibiriens*. M. Winterschladen, D. Ordubadi and D. Dahlmann (eds.), 77–118. Fürstenberg/Havel: Kulturstiftung Sibirien.

3 WALDEMAR JOCHELSON AND THE KORYAK DURING THE JESUP NORTH PACIFIC EXPEDITION: SHIFTING FIELDWORK APPROACHES AND NEW ACADEMIC AMBITIONS[1]

Erich Kasten and Michael Dürr

Jochelson's involvement in the expedition and his later reviewing of the results

During his participation in the Sibiriakov Expedition (1894–1897) Waldemar Jochelson had gained broad knowledge of the cultures of the Yakut, Evenk, Even, and the Yukaghir. At the same time, he had already developed—as a self-taught scientist—a remarkable fieldwork methodology of his own (see Kasten, *this volume*). But most important, his work with the indigenous peoples in these remote areas had kindled his keen interest in ethnology. After his release from exile in northeastern Siberia and before returning to St. Petersburg in 1898, he went back to Switzerland to finish his studies there, where he also prepared the outcomes of his ethnographic research for various audiences (Jochelson 2017). But eventually, due to fortunate circumstances, the opportunity arose for Jochelson to build upon his former studies and follow his new academic ambitions.

Around the same time, in 1897, Franz Boas made a proposal to Morris K. Jesup, the president of the American Museum of Natural History in New York. Boas envisaged an ambitious program to examine the mutual cultural influences between northeastern Asia and northwestern America. He supposed that these could be traced by studying the contemporary peoples of the North Pacific rim.

While Franz Boas was setting up a research team to study the Asian sector of the region, he faced difficulties with his candidates. The Austrian Erwin Ritter von Zach unexpectedly withdrew his initial commitment. Boas had little trust in the young German Berthold Laufer, who was expected to take part in the Amur expedition. In the end, Boas turned for advice to Friedrich Wilhelm Radloff, the director of the Museum of Anthropology and Ethnography in St. Petersburg. Standing in opposition to other trends in Russian ethnography, Radloff was interested in promoting the same kinds of research that Boas favored (Kan 2004:30). He was immediately able to recommend Jochelson and Bogoras. Already in the autumn of 1898, Boas met Jochelson for the first time in Berlin. In the correspondence that ensued, Boas drafted the

---

1 This chapter is a slightly abridged version of the foreword to the new edition of Jochelson's *The Koryak* (Jochelson 1908 [2016]).

research plan and defined the conditions of the resulting contract.[2] Jochelson was appointed to be the leader of the Siberian team. He was slated to work primarily with the Koryak, where he was expected to collect a number of artifacts and a body of anthropometrical data, take photographs and make sound recordings employing the new technology of wax cylinders. A special focus was to be on the study of Koryak languages and mythologies, as well as on the acquisition of ethnographic artifacts for the collection of the American Museum of Natural History.

For Boas it was crucial that, in advance of the project, Jochelson should come to New York and receive clear, detailed instructions in person. The upcoming fieldwork was expected to take about one and a half years. Following the fieldwork, Jochelson was expected to spend a similar length of time in New York to work up the material there. It turned out that, for several reasons, the start of the expedition had to be delayed by an additional year. Jochelson was eager, first, to complete his dissertation in Bern. Moreover, both he and Bogoras were still working on the publication of results from the Sibiriakov Expedition.[3] There were also protracted negotiations with Boas over questions of payment. And both men had suggestions of their own to make about the best routes to take and other details of the expedition. Eventually, Jochelson succeeded in convincing Boas to expand his research to include the Yukaghir. Likewise, Bogoras wanted to include additional research among the coastal Chukchi and the Siberian Yup'ik, where he had not worked before.

In March 1900, Jochelson and Bogoras arrived in New York and signed the contract with Jesup. Besides the zoologist Norman G. Buxton and his assistant Aleksandr Akselrod, it was agreed that Jochelson could bring his wife, Dina Jochelson-Brodskaia, along on the expedition. She had studied medicine in Zürich and was now appointed to be in charge of the photography and the collection of anthropometrical data. Bogoras's wife Sofiia was also permitted to join her husband on the expedition.[4] Detailed instructions about particular themes and locations for the research were noted by Boas in a written letter. According to the contract, the overall aim of the expedition was to conduct an "ethnological and biological survey of northwestern Asia."

Buxton's zoological results were later published at the American Museum of Natural History by J. A. Allen (1902, 1905; Allen and Buxton 1903). This was despite the fact that these descriptions do not contain information about traditional uses of key wildlife resources. Most of the conversation that Jochelson had with Buxton about the collected zoological specimens was apparently limited to Jochelson's concurrence that certain mammals also existed in the Kolyma area, where Buxton did not carry out investigations. Among his achievements, Jochelson is credited with having collected some important mammal specimens. In fact, a mouse that he collected was named

---

2 For further details, see Vakhtin (2001:80ff.).
3 Apart from some articles, both the Yukaghir and Chukchee text collections appeared in Russian (Iokhel'son 1900, Bogoraz 1900).
4 For more on the team members, see Winterschladen (2016:87).

after him—*Evotomys jochelsoni, sp. nov.* (Kolyma red-backed mouse; Allen and Buxton 1903:148). The most informative part of the Buxton papers, for our purposes, is his diary. It provides a clearer picture of the course and conditions of their journey, even though the two men traveled apart from each other most of the time (Allen and Buxton 1903:104–119).

Fig. 1 Waldemar Jochelson, N.G. Buxton, and Waldemar Bogoras in
San Francisco before their departure for Siberia, spring 1900.
Image #338343, American Museum of Natural History Library.

Before Jochelson and Bogoras finally arrived in Vladivostok on May 16, 1900, Boas had asked Radloff to inform the Imperial Academy of Sciences of their plans and to request the assistance and cooperation of the Russian government (Vakhtin 2001:86). This was granted to Jochelson and Bogoras in a formal letter. Although, as has often been the case in Russia, orders were sent simultaneously to the local authorities calling for surveillance of their work. Jochelson later published an anonymous article in Stuttgart (1903) describing the situation and even quoting from the secret letters

(Jochelson 2017:153–158). He speculates that the obstructions caused by these secret orders could easily have prevented the success of the expedition, "If the travelers had not known the district well and had not had broad knowledge as well as personal relationships with the native people, the expedition would have remained without results." […] "It must be questioned what these secret orders meant? Did the ministry fear the propagation of separatist ideas among the Chukchi? Where is the logical connection between the 'earlier anti-government activity' of the travelers, for which they had already been punished, and their later involvement in the commissioned scientific work? If it is correct that there was seen to be such a connection, why did the ministry not respond to the applications by the Academy of Science and the Geographical Society by saying that it was not required to assist these travelers with their scientific work?" (ibid.:157–158)

On July 24, 1900, Jochelson and his wife Dina Jochelson-Brodskaia left Vladivostok together with Buxton and Akselrod. Heading north, they arrived on August 16 at the village Kushka, near the mouth of the river Gizhiga, only to find the place uninhabited. A measles epidemic had decimated the population the previous winter, and survivors had withdrawn to the interior (Allen 1903:108). The Jochelsons decided to move on to Koryak settlements located along the Penzhina and Gizhiga bays, where they worked during the following winter. They were joined there in December 1900 by Bogoras, who then traveled until April 1901 among the eastern branch of the Koryak.

Fig. 2 The Jochelsons travel with Reindeer Koryak, 1901.
Image #4155, American Museum of Natural History Library.

Fig. 3 Dina Jochelson-Brodskaia in front of a native sod-covered hut, summer 1900. Image #337626, American Museum of Natural History Library.

Fig. 4 Jochelson and his team rafting down the Korkodon River, fall 1901. Image #4194, American Museum of Natural History Library.

Bogoras also visited the Itelmen to collect texts in both languages[5] as well as some ethnographic objects from the eastern Koryak.

From their base camp, Jochelson and his wife undertook field trips to the interior of the Gizhiga district and to the Reindeer Koryak on the peninsula of Taigonos. It was no doubt a wise decision to concentrate on this area, rather than traveling under uncertain weather conditions to more distant places in northern Kamchatka or along the Pacific coast. This allowed Jochelson to focus on his thorough case study of the local whale festival in the village of Kuel. He was forced to miss similar festivals at the other locations farther to the east. But the lengthy travel time would have precluded this, as they were held almost simultaneously. In summer 1901, the Jochelsons set off for Verkhnekolymsk to conduct further studies on the Yukaghir. They stayed there until the beginning of March 1902, eventually returning to New York in November 1902.

As an appointed assistant of the American Museum of Natural History, Jochelson began to work up the collected material. His hope for secure employment did not materialize, however, due to a conflict between Boas and Jesup over the financing of publications resulting from the expedition. In early 1904, therefore, Jochelson decided to return to Europe without having finished his work on the collected materials. Nevertheless, the friendship that Boas had already established with Jochelson (and Bogoras) endured. In the coming years, Boas was able to arrange for their participation at various congresses of Americanists. Jochelson and his wife spent time living in Zürich, London and Berlin. He was offered a position as junior curator at the Museum of Anthropology and Ethnology in St. Petersburg. He considered it inadequate but ultimately accepted and moved there in 1907.

In the meantime, Jochelson continued to prepare his publication on the Koryak, which eventually appeared in 1908 under the imprint of the American Museum of Natural History (Jochelson 1908). He had assumed that this would enhance his reputation, leading to further scientific work in Russia. This proved to be correct. While planning for another expedition to the North Pacific, he received an offer to participate as the head of the ethnological section in the Kamchatka Expedition of the Russian Geographical Society. This venture, also named for its sponsor, Fedor Riabushinskii, spanned the years from 1908 until 1911. Jochelson was sent to the North Pacific to conduct fieldwork in Kamchatka. He was able to bring the Commander Islands and the people of the Aleutian Islands into the program as well (see Kasten, 53f., *this volume*).

Upon his subsequent return to St. Petersburg, Jochelson once again found himself in uncertain circumstances. While struggling to complete his publication on the Yukaghir, which he still owed Boas, he was also eager to work on his new materials from the recent Riabushinskii Expedition. His situation became even worse after the October Revolution of 1917. Bogoras and Lev Shternberg (1861–1927) obtained pro-

---

5   Bogoras (2019)

fessorships in the Faculty of Ethnography at the newly founded Institute of Geography in Petrograd (see Sirina and Roon; Kan, *this volume*), but Jochelson did not find steady employment there, which could have provided him a comfortable living. In his unsuccessful applications to other similar institutions, he pointed out that his concern was to preserve the languages and the peoples of the Yukaghir, Aleut and Itelmen, as these were threatened by assimilation. Alluding to the rhetoric of the Bolsheviks, he added that these peoples had been disadvantaged during tsarists times and needed the support of the new socialist state (Winterschladen 2016:100). After the Kronstadt uprising of 1921, however, the political climate began again to change, bringing with it further repressions. Meanwhile, like many others, Jochelson faced increasing poverty. He decided to leave Russia again and return to the United States. Together with his wife Dina, he moved to New York in 1922.

Even in the US, however, it was difficult for them to become established as scientists with stable incomes. Mainly through the support of Boas and commissioned work projects that he had arranged for them, they were able to eke out a subsistence living. In spite of the difficulties, Jochelson was able to publish most of the materials that he had collected during his earlier expeditions (Jochelson 1925; 1926; 1933a,b) as well as a monograph written under contract for the American Museum of Natural History titled *Peoples of Asiatic Russia* (1928). However, he never managed to complete the publication of his materials on the language and culture of the Itelmen and on the language of the Aleut, both of which were from the Riabushinskii Expedition.

Jochelson died on November 2, 1937, leaving this work to posterity. The Itelmen (Kamchadal) texts that he had collected were eventually edited by Dean Stoddard Worth (1961),[6] and the Aleut texts by Knut Bergsland (1990). His manuscript on the ethnography of the Itelmen living on the west coast of Kamchatka will be published for the first time as a chapter of an edited volume (Koester and Kasten 2019).

Motivations

At the outset one might wonder what could have motivated Jochelson to return of his own free will to such faraway and uneasy places, where he had been exiled for many years? He had complained repeatedly about the harsh living conditions while traveling in rough circumstances and while staying in local communities (Jochelson 1899a, vol. 2:228–229). But over the years, he had certainly also experienced the hospitality of the people, which he may well have come to appreciate (Jochelson 1908:425 [447 in the 2016 edition]). But while he obviously enjoyed close relations with Yakut and Yukaghir communities, Jochelson's accounts, with regard to his Koryak collaborators, do not indicate that he was eager to establish long-lasting ties to the local peoples

---

6   New edition converted into contemporary Itelmen orthography with partial reconstruction of the phonemics: Khaloimova, Dürr and Kasten (2014).

with whom he worked. Instead one gets the impression that the collected data was now meant for his new immediate scientific purposes, and that he didn't intend to visit the particular region again. Consequently, he also did not think about proper ways or specific later publication formats to return the documented materials to the local community—which has become a big concern in present-day co-productions in ethnography.[7]

Jochelson's—the same as Bogoras's—motivation was most likely in part morally founded in their aim not to let these peoples "fall into oblivion" (Winterschladen 2016:89). And yet, their approach of "salvage anthropology" by no means aimed at sustaining the endangered languages and cultures. Thus Michael Krauss is "struck, even shocked, that as revolutionaries, discoverers of cultural relativism, they [Boas, Jochelson, and Bogoras] wrote so little in their JNPE contributions to protest or even express regret about the then very active colonial suppression of the languages and cultures" (2003:215).

For Bogoras, the humanitarian imperative and concern for native peoples apparently did not yet involve their re-education toward socialist values and ways of thinking. That only appears as part of his missions and commitments in the 1920s and later (see Liarskaia, *this volume*). It seems that he simply wanted to support their aspirations to a better life, which had been blocked so far by the tsarist regime (Winterschladen 2016:82). At first, Jochelson obviously shared this attitude. Probably after meeting Boas, however, his priorities shifted. The prospects of a scientific career became increasingly realistic and attractive to him. Through participation in this prestigious expedition, he apparently realized, he would get the opportunity to enhance his reputation and collect abundant data for later publishing projects.

Fieldwork and research methods

To what extent are Jochelson's motivation and primary research aim reflected in his fieldwork methods, and in the way he met and interacted with local people? Unfortunately, his publication on the Koryak tells us very little about these questions. In accordance with Boas's instructions, this monograph was written in an academic descriptive style. As a result, the text is almost devoid of personal or emotional comments about his relations with local collaborators or informants. At several points, Jochelson briefly mentions "his" Cossack, a man who seems to have assisted him and his wife mainly with sledge transportation. He occasionally also refers to their interpreter, Nicholas Vilkhin, a "Russianized Koryak" from the settlement of Gizhiginsk. Jochelson characterizes him as being "in equal command of the local Russian dialect

---

7   See, for example, Krupnik and Bogoslovskaia (2017); Lavrillier and Gabyshev (2017); Baztan et al. 2017 and the corresponding program of the Foundation for Siberian Cultures (http://www.siberian-studies.org/publications/lc_E.html).

and the Koryak language, [...] although I had to labor hard before I had him trained for the work" (Jochelson 1908:15 [56]). Only in one instance does Jochelson describe in somewhat greater detail the way in which they worked together: "Very few of the women were able to dictate to me two tales in succession. Usually, after having told one tale, they would ask to be relieved, for they were tired. In taking my notes, I was obliged to stop frequently, for I could see that my interpreter was tired, and unable to follow my questions with proper attention" (ibid.:426 [448]). This quote is also reveal-ing in other ways. It provides a rare case of deeper insight into Jochelson's fieldwork and recording techniques, which may be considered questionable according to our present standards (Kasten 2016b:16–18).

Another critical aspect is that the texts most likely were not dictated in the Koryak language. Jochelson does not explain whether the various tales and explanations were told to him and Vilkhin in Koryak or in Russian. This issue cannot be resolved, because the texts are only known through their published English translations (Jochelson 1908:125–340 [167–357]) and no original fieldnotes seem to exist.[8] Moreover, Jochel-son relied entirely on the linguistic expertise of Bogoras,[9] as "he has revised and cor-rected the transcriptions of all Koryak names, words, incantations, and other Koryak phrases, contained in this book" (ibid.:15 [56]). Bogoras explains this division of labor in his edition of Koryak Texts: "I undertook the study of their language, because my practical knowledge and previous studies of the Chukchee language put me in a posi-tion to acquire with ease a knowledge of the Koryak, which is closely related to the Chukchee" (Bogoras 1917:1). Bogoras also mentions the role of Vilkhin in the process of data collection (ibid.:4). Although this division of labor permitted the collection of quite reliable linguistic data from the Koryak, despite their single brief field trip, one may wonder whether Bogoras's understanding of Koryak was to a certain degree Chukchi-biased: "The rules of pronunciation, which are strict and consistent in the Chukchee language, are quite lax in all the Koryak dialects" (ibid.:4). The English translations of the Koryak texts, later edited in Bogoras (1917), and of the hitherto unpublished Itelmen (Kamchadal) texts, recorded by Bogoras, were published first in Jochelson (1908) and amount to more than 25 % of the text's entire corpus (Jochelson 1908:284–297, 309–340 [309–321, 331–357]).

Beyond this method of acquiring dictated texts, Jochelson employed for the first time in that region the revolutionary new technique of phonograph or wax cylin-der recordings.[10] With some amusement, he describes the reaction of the speakers or

---

8   cf. the lists of the unpublished materials in Jakobson et al. (1957) and Knüppel (2013).
9   Nevertheless, Jochelson was a linguist in his own right, as his work on the Yukaghir language (Jochelson 1905;1926) as well as on Aleut and on Itelmen, demonstrates.
10 Bogoras notes that two of the songs he published in his Koryak Texts were transcribed from the phonographic recordings of Jochelson (Bogoras 1917:103). Most of Jochelson's wax cylin-ders are now in the holdings of the Archive of Traditional Music in Bloomington, and a few are in the Phonogram Archive of the Ethnological Museum in Berlin (Knüppel 2013:44–48).

singers toward this unknown device, which was mostly used for recording shaman's incantations or healing songs: "Our phonograph made the most striking impression wherever we went. Often a hundred persons would crowd into the house where we put up our phonograph, and gather around it in a ring" (Jochelson 1908:426f. [448]). And "after eating two fungi, he [a Reindeer Koryak] began to sing in a loud voice, gesticulating with his hands. I had to support him, lest he fall on the machine; and when the cylinder came to an end, I had to tear him away from the horn, where he remained bending over it for a long time, keeping up his songs" (ibid.:583 [609]).

The expedition's visual ethnographic documentation was also altered and enhanced by the newly introduced technology of photography. For earlier accounts, and well into the 19th century, we still have to rely on hand-sketched or painted illustrations. Some of these images were created by artists who never actually saw the particular scenery or subject in person, which inevitably led to distortions (ibid.:13ff. [54f.]). Others, however, such as the watercolors of Friedrich Heinrich von Kittlitz (2011) from his journey through Kamchatka in 1828, looked almost as natural and precise as later photographs. During the expedition, Dina Jochelson-Brodskaia was responsible for the photographs, which were primarily taken for the purpose of documenting "physical types" (Miller and Mathé 1997:19). As a result, many of the pictures are portraits of individuals. There are also, however, many scenes of daily and ceremonial life as well as views of the landscape. The documentary accuracy or pre-

Fig. 5 They often set up two tents in the field. One served as living and writings quarters, the other as portable studio and darkroom.
Image #4148, American Museum of Natural History Library.

cision of the plates and figures in the edited volume should not be overrated, though. Some of the original photographs were modified prior to publication with the aim of enhancing their value as interpretative reconstructions: "Plate xxix, Fig. 1, represents two Koryak in armor, with bent bows. The plate is the reproduction of a photograph taken by me, except that the artist, Mr. Rudolf Cronau, sketched in under my direction the missing wing of the armor" (Jochelson 1908:563 [588]).

When taking the anthropometric measurements, which was mostly done by Dina Jochelson-Brodskaia, the couple encountered difficulties and frequent resistance among those to be investigated in this way. They feared "that they would die if they allowed themselves to be measured" (ibid.:49 [86]). With the help of a Koryak elder, Jochelson employed a trick-of-the-trade, much like some that are well-known from Boas's methods on similar occasions (Cole 1985:107). "He [the elder] assured the Koryak, half in jest and half in earnest, that their heads and bodies were being measured in order to get caps, boots, and coats which the Czar was to send them the next year. However, he himself refused for a long while to allow me to take his measurements" (Jochelson 1908:409 [426]). Unfortunately, Jochelson did not inquire further as to whether these kinds of body measurements were felt to be an intrusion into a person's privacy. It is possible that the resistance was in response to a recent campaign against foreigners. There may have been fear that such unknown practices would cause an epidemic, as had happened a few years earlier, following the visit of another researcher, N.V. Slunin. In any case, the inhabitants of the Taigonos peninsula subsequently referred to Jochelson as "face-measuring chief." Those of Paren were obviously more impressed by his abilities in recording texts, so they called him "tales chief."

There is another aspect of Jochelson's nearly ethnohistorical approach that characterizes the later sections of his work (ibid.:761–811 [787–837]), namely the consultation of archival materials from the 18th and early 19th centuries housed in the Government Archives of the Gizhiga district. This was to supplement his information from earlier published sources. Besides contributing to a better understanding of the demographic and economic situation in past times, these materials enabled Jochelson to demonstrate the Russian influence on Koryak pictographic memoranda and commercial notes: "Later on I found in the archives of the natives on the Kolyma River receipts of Russian officials of the eighteenth and the beginning of the nineteenth centuries. The receipts testified as to the payment of tribute in furs by the native chiefs, and the number of fur skins or rubles received as tax was indicated by Russian letters and also by means of the system used by Qačilqut, evidently for the benefit of the illiterate natives" (ibid.:727 [754]).

Jochelson (and Bogoras) also made use of another pioneering new genre of ethnographic documentary. Obviously following Boas's instructions and based on his own experiences during his earliest fieldwork on Baffin Island in 1883 (Müller-Wille 2014:111–117) Jochelson encouraged native people to make drawings on their own (Jochelson 1908:723ff. [750ff.]), even though he had earlier already collected

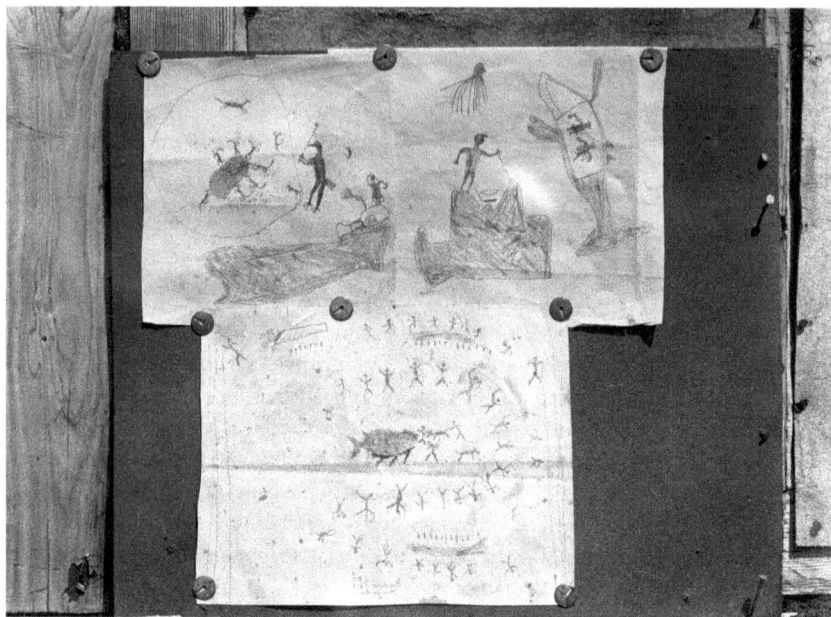

Fig. 6 Drawings by Koryak illustrating mythological themes, 1901.
Image #1585, American Museum of Natural History Library.

illustrations from them (1899c). This corresponds with an overall intention and aim to let them document, without censorship, scenes and perceptions as seen from their own viewpoints (see below). Thus Jochelson points out that "the collections of draw-ings were made on paper with pencil [...] who drew at my request, and without any instruction or explanation on my part" (Jochelson 1908:724 [751]). The same method is often employed in contemporary ethnographic research. Sometimes this has the additional purpose of showing and emphasizing community participation in the design of text collections and learning tools (Kasten 1998; 2015a).

Jochelson and Bogoras collected hundreds of traditional tales from the Russian Far East and compared them with those compiled in North America by Boas and oth-ers (Jochelson 1904; 1906; 1908; Bogoras 1902; 1910; 1917; 1928). This was an important objective and accomplishment of the Jesup Expedition and one that closely followed the practices of Boas himself. He had published similar work on the peoples of the Pacific Northwest coast, the goal being to reconstruct migrations and cultural con-tacts from borrowings and adaptations of mythological elements (Boas 1895:329–363; Dürr 1992:392–394). Jochelson summarized the results of this comparative study: "In concluding my review of the Koryak folk-lore, I deem it necessary to state, that I regard the identity of the Koryak folk-lore with that of North America as established" (Jochelson 1908:362 [380]).

Jochelson also referred to texts as a source for reconstructing earlier stages of the cultures under consideration, e.g.: "One tale [...] points to their former possession of subterranean dwellings" (ibid.:465 [487]). At another point he speculated about an earlier stage when Koryak used driving-dogs while referring to mythology: "From this myth it may be concluded that the creator of the Koryak world is conceived of as having driving-dogs" (ibid.:502, note [526f.]). And in his discussion of reindeer-breeding he stated: "The myths give no tangible data as to the origin of reindeer-breeding" (ibid.:474 [499]). This approach is related to Boasian methods. Boas himself, however (Boas 1916; 1935), mainly abstained from speculations about the past. He usually restricted himself to seeking either reflections of, or contradictions to, cultural practices that had been documented elsewhere. It may be worth noting in this context that Jochelson not only assumed that myths can be seen as preserving older cultural practices. He also tended to speculate on earlier cultural stages, based on the assumption that certain artifacts, such as funeral costumes, materialize these older stages: "Women's funeral costumes have no caps—a fact, which shows that in former times the Koryak women did not wear caps" (Jochelson 1908:597 [624]).

Selected themes

Regarding the treatment of specific ethnographic themes, Jochelson's conclusions are usually based on far-reaching and thorough comparative discussions of the existing academic literature at that time. A good example is the origins of reindeer breeding (Jochelson 1908:469–501 [493–526]). He strives to combine these results with his own observations and assessments. In making recommendations on possible developments for a more sustainable Koryak economy, Jochelson diverges noticeably from Boas's defined project aims and adopts applied approaches that were characteristic of mid-19th century German-Baltic ethnographic research in Kamchatka.[11] Thus he questions "if it would become possible for the latter [the Russians] to raise the civilization of the natives?" (ibid.:805 [831]). Toward this end, Jochelson believes in the success of practical school education that pays particular attention to enhancing the efficiency of traditional branches of the native economy, so "that their further development could be left in their own hands" ibid.:806 [832]). Here Jochelson is a forerunner of later developments in native self-government that have been realized at least in some parts of North America. His concern is underscored by his harsh critique of the colonial policy of the Russian Empire, which "maintains its remote northeastern colonies solely for the glory of possessing a territory" (ibid.:804 [830]), or for "a petty national pride, but [...] paid for by the government through a costly administration of unprofitable colonies" (ibid.:802 [828]). At the same time, Jochelson gives a blunt account of the

---

11   Kasten (2013b). See in particular the research program of Kegel (2011) and Ditmar (2011).

brutal excesses in the way this policy was put into practice. Today, this is celebrated by state authorities in Kamchatka as the annexation (*prisoedinenie*) of these far eastern provinces to Russia.

On the other hand, Jochelson obviously endorsed the testimony of an elder herdsman who believed in "the source of power in the Russian government, and not in the customs of his people" (ibid.:769 [794]). When discussing potential prospects for further economic development, he concludes that the "primitive state of the material life of the Koryak, left almost intact by outside influence, determines the primitive state of their mental culture" (ibid.:405 [423]). This view differs clearly from what we have learned, for example, from the much earlier Georg Wilhelm Steller. A reason for this might be that Jochelson already looked at native cultures more from the perspective of current anthropological science. Steller, in contrast, gained his thorough insights and deep respect for traditional environmental knowledge through his role as a thoughtful participant observer. It was an approach that he employed to a considerable extent already in the mid-18th century (Kasten 2013a:249–251; 2019)—and which could even be noticed with Jochelson's earlier work during the Sibiriakov Expedition (see Kasten, *this volume*). Unlike Steller, Jochelson seems—in particular during the Jesup North Pacific Expedition—to have been less interested in documenting actual work processes regarding traditional resource use or when constructing tools. From the perspective of the collector of ethnographic specimens—which was one of his main assignments— he viewed and described items primarily according to their material makeup and practical functions. Because he tended to disregard more comprehensive ideas and motivations that underlie such work processes, Jochelson often failed to conceive the important emotional and social meanings that these activities entail (Kasten 2016b). Such a more encompassing viewpoint also receives short shrift whenever Jochelson is describing and analyzing objects of native art. In contrast, greater attention is paid by present-day anthropologists to informative comments by the artists themselves, and to their contemplations while they are working on their artifacts (Kasten 2005b; 2012).

For Jochelson, the reason the Koryak make (mostly carved) objects of art lies in the "inter-action of two psychological factors,—the religious and the æsthetic" (Jochelson 1908:668 [698]). He correctly states that it is not easy to ascertain whether an artifact was made solely from a simple desire to imitate nature, or with the additional intention of ceremonial use. With regard to the arrangement of designs in ornaments that were used in sewing and applied to clothing, Jochelson identifies principles of symmetry (ibid.:689, 714–723 [718, 741–750], see also Kasten 2014:102–105). He discerns and investigates various possible origins for geometrical ornaments and those, such as floral motifs, that depict naturalistic images (Jochelson 1908:684–688 [714–717]; see also Kasten 2014:105–108). Where the meaning of ornaments is concerned, however, Jochelson expressed frustration at the answers that he usually got from the seamstresses. This is similar to the responses that modern researchers have received more than 100 years later (ibid.:108f.). "As a general rule," he concludes, "the ornament had no special significance. Even the information as to zigzags [that represent mountains] I obtained only after insistent questioning, which may have stimulated the answer" (Jochelson 1908:685 [715], see also Kasten 2014:109). In most cases, the ornamental designs were borrowed from other peoples just "because of their beauty" (Kasten 2016a:6), but without their meaning, since they had connections to foreign cultural or family traditions. The meaning of such a design is, however, often still preserved among Even families. It may be handed down to the next generation together with the story that accompanies it and that expresses the identity of a particular family (Kasten and Avak 2018:225–245).

Understandably, Jochelson paid scant attention to such performing arts as dance and music. He apparently felt obliged to focus on those arts that expressed themselves in material artifacts for his museum collection. Thus he devotes only a short paragraph to dances (Jochelson 1908:782 [809]) that imitate the movements and sounds of animals, although this represents an extremely rich and informative tradition, especially among coastal Koryaks (Kasten 2016c). It is the same with regard to family songs. Even today, these remain an equally important genre for the Koryaks, among others, and are used to display individual, family, or local identities (especially during festivals), or simply to be enjoyed spontaneously on everyday occasions (Kasten 2004: 16–20). Where songs are concerned, Jochelson concentrates in his recordings and descriptions mainly on incantations used in connection with shamanic healing practices (see below).

Jochelson described such shamanic performances in great detail, although he expressed clear disappointment at what he was shown by the only two "professional" shamans whom he met. He suspected, in fact, that a bit of fakery was involved. In one case, he had to settle on an appropriate remuneration in advance of the séance. On another occasion, the shaman left before daybreak, without waiting to meet with Jochelson (as agreed) to help him transcribe the text of the incantations (Jochelson 1908:50 [87]). A possible reason why Jochelson was unable to obtain a deeper insight into shamanic practices may lie in the inappropriate way that he presented his request. On one occasion, he asked the shaman "to show [him] proof of his shamanistic art" (ibid.:49 [84]).

Jochelson was particularly interested in incantations, which are an important part of shamanic healing practices. This secret knowledge is handed down through generations within the family and was difficult to record, as Jochelson admitted, because it is considered a sin "to sell an incantation to a foreigner" (ibid.:60 [98]). When discussing traditional healing practices with Koryaks today,[12] these formulas are shared with the researcher more freely and spontaneously. They are no longer used in the same sacred way as before and are now regarded more as a recollection of the cultural past.

---

12 Lidiia Chechulina (2015). Archive E.Kasten, AEK15-01-02_5.

Jochelson describes in great detail reconciliation festivals that he observed during his prolonged stay in the coastal Koryak village of Kuel. Involving sacrifices, these aimed at influencing the course of events. He documented a whale festival there that was most likely also conducted in similar ways (and based on the same rationale) in other coastal villages of the Koryak on the northern west coast of Kamchatka, and nowadays with regard to other sea mammals (Kasten 2017a). This was probably the case as well among the Aliutors on the Pacific coast, a people he was unable to visit due to time constraints (see above). As for the festivals of the reindeer herding Koryaks, Jochelson admits that he had to rely on information provided by others. It is surprising, however, that he did not witness and document certain of their most important rituals, which are performed in connection with the birth of reindeer fawns in late spring, since he actually stayed at a reindeer camp at that time (see photo in Jochelson 1908:510). Under Chukchi influence, this festival was held already then, among other Koryak groups, using its Chukchi name, *kilvei*. So Jochelson was told. But the reindeer herder groups from Taigonos insisted that neither their genuine Koryak rituals nor those borrowed from the Chukchi have ever been conducted among them at this important moment in the herd's natural cycle.

The festivals of the coastal and reindeer herding Koryaks (Ololo, Kilvei) are still held today. Even now, they maintain many of their original meanings, which ensure communication with nature. In addition, they are able to incorporate or emphasize new elements, such as those celebrating local or ethnic identities (Kasten and Dürr 2005; Kasten 2015b; 2017b; Plattet 2005).

Further places in the account indicate that Jochelson sometimes relied on what he was told, rather than what he personally observed while participating in the activities involved. Regarding the Koryak kayak (*māto* or *matev*), Jochelson notes: "Sitting in the manhole, the hunter can stretch his feet under the deck of the Kayak" (1908:540 [566]). Although Jochelson describes the construction of this particular kind of boat in great detail, he obviously has never seen one put into practical use. The extremely low design of the frame does not allow one to sit within the *matev*, only to kneel in it. This was apparent from observations in Lesnaya, where the last skin boat of this type was still in use in 2003 (Kasten and Dürr 2005).

As mentioned above, Jochelson was highly critical of Russian colonial policy. However, it is remarkable how rarely he made mention of excessive conduct by Russians in dealing with native people, whereas this was a big issue in the reports of scientists during the proceeding centuries. It its unlikely that relations between Russians and the native peoples were very different from what we know from other parts of Kamchatka. Probably Jochelson's view was biased, since he still trusted in the Russian empire's potential positive influence on the Koryak: "If the country cannot be populated by the Russians, the question arises whether under any conditions it would become possible for the latter to raise the civilization of the natives?" (Jochelson 1908: 805 [831]) Granted that, on a later occasion, during the XXIII International Congress of Americanists in 1928, he underscored the continuity of repression toward native peoples in that area. This had lasted, he asserted, from the first conquest by Russia right up to and including Soviet times. It manifested itself, among other ways, in the Itelmen uprising of the 1730s. However, Jochelson obviously used this argument in opposition to Bogoras's praise of Soviet policy towards native peoples, which was expressed at the same congress.[13]

Likewise, Jochelson did not find evidence in Koryak communities of inherent social inequality or indicators of a class-based society. Yet only three decades later, these alleged features provided the Stalinist justification for the stigmatization of rich reindeer herders as *kulaks*, and their subsequent expropriation and/or elimination. In contrast, Jochelson draws a very clear and detailed picture of entrenched, balanced and shifting property relations among reindeer herding Koryak (Jochelson 1908:747, 765f. [773f., 790f.]). For maritime Koryak, he even claims to perceive "remnants of communal ideas" (ibid.:746 [772]). This is despite the fact that (as shown in tales recorded subsequently in that region) it is clear that when arranging marriages, strategies aimed at establishing dynasties among rich reindeer herders may well have played a role.[14] When exploring the Koryak "idea[s] of ethnic unity" (ibid.:762 [788]), Jochelson was obviously aware of various layers of identity. These, he saw, were expressed by different guardians and charms that "belong each to a family, an individual, and in some cases a whole village" (ibid.:33 [71]). In current discussion, flexible situational strategies in social discourse are often seen as based on such "multiple identities" (Kasten 2005a:247).

Conclusions

To do justice to Jochelson's long-lasting contribution to Siberian anthropology, one should bear in mind Franz Boas's thoughts and specific aims, which underlie the initial conception of the Jesup North Pacific Expedition. Only then can we assess the extent to which Jochelson followed these guidelines. We might ask how well he eventually accomplished this mission. And where was he able to introduce novel research approaches of his own? Some may have been based on his earlier fieldwork experiences during the Sibiriakov Expedition, or were due to the unusually varied background of his early life.

When comparing Jochelson's early German ethnographic publications to his later English ones, some obvious changes in orientation can be recognized (see Kasten 48ff., *this volume*). Boas's ideas clearly affected Jochelson's thinking and approach,

---

13 Cf. Winterschladen, personal communication 24.11.2015. It should be noted that the respective papers were published in the proceedings of the congress side by side (Bogoras and Leonov 1930: 445–450, Jochelson 1930:451–454).

14 Rul'tyneut, Ekaterina 2014. Archive Erich Kasten, AEK-14-22-01.

especially once they entered into close correspondence in 1898 while drafting the program for the Jesup project. According to Boas, "the peculiar interest that attaches to this region is founded on the fact that here the Old World and the New come into close contact. The geographical conditions favor migration along the coastline, and exchange of culture. Have such migrations, has such exchange of culture, taken place?" (Boas 1900:4) Boas did not believe it was only the exchange or the borrowing of cultural elements that induced cultural change. At the same time he was aware that "the acquisition [of a large part of every tribe's culture] only becomes a genuine part of the culture if it fuses with the native perceptions into a comprehensive whole [...] the foreign element in a culture becomes native by being permeated by the spirit or style of the native culture" (Boas 2001:19).

It is clear that Jochelson's monograph on the Koryak came into being, and was in the end largely shaped, both under Boas's personal guidance and through the strong impact of a new discipline, the cultural anthropology. Through Jochelson and Bogoras, the latter exerted a profound influence on Soviet historical ethnography. Nevertheless, it appears that the Russian members of the expedition—together with Lev Shternberg, the third formative authority of the Russian "etnotroika" at that time were still under the influence of Morgan's evolutionism, which is qualified with regard to the latter by Kan (*this volume*). This classified cultures according to their degree of complexity rather than areal similarity (Zgusta 2015:20), which also became part of their legacy to Soviet ethnography.

In spite of the great value of the rich ethnographic data it produced, the Jesup project did not achieve its goal of illuminating historical connections (Zgusta 2015: 359). The generalizations that derived from the project eventually had to be qualified in light of a more likely two-directional flow between Northeast Asia and North America, the so-called "circum-Pacific cultural drift" (de Laguna 1947). Together with the anthropometric data, the comparative analysis of myths were considered crucial in establishing possible historical connections and the dissemination of cultural traits. The results revealed the interconnection of the peoples on both sides of the North Pacific rim, but they were not conclusive as to the kind and direction of migration. Quite recently, this type of argumentation, based on physical anthropological data but also on myths, has enjoyed renewed scholarly interest within a framework of statistical computer models that allow mass comparisons (d'Huy 2013; 2015). At least in the case of mitochondrial and/or chromosomal DNA, the new approach helps to cast new light on prehistoric migration, such as, for example, the settlement of the Americas (Reich et al. 2013; Koppel 2003).

In the wake of Jochelson's work, and other publications related to the Jesup project, one main question remains open: Are the obvious cultural similarities along the North Pacific rim due to historical factors related to migrations? Or do they also—and to what extent—result from adaptations to similar natural environments? As to the latter possibility, it seems that Georg Wilhelm Steller (2013:225) was already quite aware of it. For one thing, he was obviously impressed by the ingenuity of native people. In his deep respect and great admiration for their unique traditional knowledge—in some instances he considered it to be on an equal level with that of contemporary western civilization—he anticipated, 150 years earlier, much of what was to become the foundations of Franz Boas's cultural relativism. In contrast to Steller and other scientists who had traveled through Kamchatka in the 19th century, and also to Jochelson's own earlier reports on the Sibiriakov Expedition, the new academic approach adapted by the Jesup project clearly led to a narrowing of prevailing scientific concepts. Some earlier approaches were considerably broader and, once again, receive greater attention today. Unlike Jochelson's descriptions in *The Koryak*, they often even embraced and closely observed such things as the work processes used in constructing ethnographic items. The same was true for the concrete activities of traditional resource management, such as hunting, fishing and gathering. Nowadays, these are also investigated and interpreted within their more encompassing and important social dimension, as, for example, in expressing sentiments and cultural identities.

As with many other outcomes of the Jesup project, a particular value of Jochelson's monograph on the Koryak lies, however, in the weight that it gives to studying a people's own interpretation of their traditions. For Boas, it "seemed supremely important to document the anthropological material through uncensored accounts of natives in their own words and in their own language, to preserve the original meaning" (Boas 2001:19). This led to the large amount and enormous wealth of texts that Franz Boas and his collaborators collected on the North Pacific rim. Together with additional texts that have been recorded since then on similar topics in the region, those from the North Asian side provide a truly rich database for current and future analysis of important cultural dynamics within and among the peoples of the Russian Far East. Certainly, Jochelson's data on the Yukaghir, and their analysis, can be considered especially complete and accurate. In particular, his multiple visits to that region obviously produced favorable results. By comparison, given the relatively short period of time spent there, it is amazing what he and his wife were able to achieve during their work with the Koryak. Last but not least, we can value the unexpected way in which Jochelson's *The Koryak* provides inspiration to present-day Koryak artists, who derive conceptual ideas for their work from the illustrations of objects in that volume (Kasten 2005b:85).

References

Allen, Joel Asaph 1902. The Hair Seals (family Phocidæ) of the North Pacific Ocean and Bering Sea. In *Bulletin of the American Museum of Natural History* 16: 459–514. New York: American Museum of Natural History.

— 1905. Report on the Birds Collected in Northeastern Siberia by the Jesup North Pacific Expedition, with Field Notes by the Collectors. In *Bulletin of the American*

Museum of Natural History 21: 219–257. New York: American Museum of Natural History.

Allen, Joel Asaph, and Norman G. Buxton 1903. Report on the Mammals Collected in Northeastern Siberia by the Jesup North Pacific Expedition, with Itinerary and Field Notes, by N. G. Buxton. In *Bulletin of the American Museum of Natural History* 19: 101–184. New York: American Museum of Natural History.

Baztan J., Cordier M., Huctin J.-M., Zhu Z., Vanderlinden J-P., 2017. Life on Thin Ice: Insights from Uummannaq, Greenland for Connecting Climate Science with Arctic Communities. In *Polar Science* 13: 100–108.

Boas, Franz 1885. Baffin-Land. *Geographische Ergebnisse einer in den Jahren 1883 und 1884 ausgeführten Forschungsreise.* Ergänzungsheft No. 80 zu Petermanns Mitteilungen. Gotha: Justus Perthes.

— 1895. *Indianische Sagen von der Nord-Pacifischen Küste Amerikas.* Berlin: Asher. [Reprinted 1992: M. Dürr (ed.), Bonn: Holos.]

— 1900. Introduction. In F. Boas, *Facial Paintings of the Indians of Northern British Columbia.* Publications of the Jesup North Pacific Expedition, vol. 1, 1, 3–6. New York: American Museum of Natural History.

— 1916. *Tsimshian Mythology.* 31st Annual Report of the Bureau of American Ethnology. Washington, D.C.: Government Printing Office.

— 1935. *Kwakiutl Culture as Reflected in Mythology.* New York: Stechert.

— 2001. The Results of the Jesup Expedition. In *Gateways. Exploring the Legacy of the Jesup North Pacific Expedition, 1897–1902.* I. Krupnik and W. Fitzhugh (eds.), 17–24. [English translation of: Die Resultate der Jesup Expedition. Verhandlungen des XVI. internationalen Amerikanisten-Kongresses, 1908. Erste Hälfte, 3–18, Wien und Leipzig: Hartleben.]

Bogoras, Waldemar 1902. The Folklore of Northeastern Asia, as Compared with That of Northwestern America. In *American Anthropologist,* New Series, 4: 577–683.

— 1904. The Chukchee. Pt. 1. Material Culture. *The Jesup North Pacific Expedition 7, Memoirs of the American Museum of Natural History* 11. Pt. 1: 1–276. New York. New edition 2017, edited by M. Dürr and E. Kasten. Fürstenberg/Havel: Kulturstiftung Sibirien.

— 1907. The Chukchee. Religion. *The Jesup North Pacific Expedition 7, Memoirs of the American Museum of Natural History* 11. Pt. 2: 277–536. New York. New edition 2017, edited by M. Dürr and E. Kasten. Fürstenberg/Havel: Kulturstiftung Sibirien.

— 1909. The Chukchee. Social Organization. *The Jesup North Pacific Expedition 7, Memoirs of the American Museum of Natural History* 11. Pt. 3: 537–733. New York. New edition 2017, edited by M. Dürr and E. Kasten. Fürstenberg/Havel: Kulturstiftung Sibirien.

— 1904. *The Chukchee.* Publications of the Jesup North Pacific Expedition, vol. 7. New York: American Museum of Natural History. New edition 2017, edited by M. Dürr and E. Kasten. Fürstenberg/Havel: Kulturstiftung Sibirien.

— 1910. Chukchee Mythology. *Jesup North Pacific Expedition* 8, *Memoirs of the American Museum of Natural History* 12. Pt. 1: 1–197. New York. New edition 2016, edited by M. Dürr and E. Kasten. Fürstenberg/Havel: Kulturstiftung Sibirien.

— 1917. *Koryak Texts*. Publications of the American Ethnological Society, 5. Leiden: Brill.

— 1922. Chukchee. In *Handbook of American Indian Languages*. F. Boas (ed.), vol. 2, 631–903. Washington, D.C.: Government Printing Office.

— 1928. Chukchee Tales. In *The Journal of American Folklore* 41: 297–452.

— 2019. Bogoras's Itelmen Note Books. Edited by J. Bobaljik. Fürstenberg/Havel: Kulturstiftung Sibirien (in preparation).

Bogoras, Waldemar, and N. J. Leonov 1930. Cultural Work Among the Lesser Nationalities of the North of the U.S.S.R. In *XXIII International Congress of Americanists*, New York 1928, Proceedings, 445–450. New York: Science Press Printing.

Bogoraz, Vladimir Germanovich 1900. *Materialy po izucheniiu chukotskogo iazyka i fol'klora, sobrannye v Kolymskom okruge*. St. Peterburg. Imperatorskoi Akademiia Nauk.

Brandišauskas, Donatas 2009. Waldemar Jochelson—a Prominent Ethnographer of North-eastern Siberia. In *Acta Orientalia Vilnensia* 10.1–2: 165–179.

Cole, Douglas 1985. *Captured Heritage: The Scramble for Northwest Coast Artifacts*. Vancouver: Douglas and McIntyre.

Dahlmann, Dittmar, Diana Ordubadi, and Matthias Winterschladen (eds.) 2016. *Auf den Spuren der modernen Sozial- und Kulturanthropologie: Die Jesup North Pacific Expedition 1897 bis 1902 in Ostsibirien*. Fürstenberg/Havel: Kulturstiftung Sibirien.

De Laguna, Frederica 1947. *The Prehistory of Northern North America as Seen From the Yukon*. Memoirs of the Society for American Archaeology 3. Menasha, WI: Society of American Archaeology. [Reprinted 1980. New York: AMS Press.]

d'Huy, Julien 2013. Polyphemus (Aa. Th. 1137). A Phylogenetic Reconstruction of a Prehistoric Tale. In *Nouvelle Mythologie Comparée* 1, 2013. http://nouvellemythologiecomparee.hautetort. com/numero-1-no-1-2013/

— 2015. Die Urahnen der großen Mythen. In *Spektrum der Wissenschaft*, 2015, Heft 12: 66–73.

Ditmar, Karl von 2011. *Reisen und Aufenthalt in Kamtschatka*. Erster und zweiter Teil. M. Dürr (ed.). Fürstenberg/Havel: Kulturstiftung Sibirien.

Dürr, Michael 1992. Nachwort. In F. Boas, *Indianische Sagen von der Nord-Pacifischen Küste Amerikas*. M. Dürr (ed.), 389–403. Bonn: Holos.

Fitzhugh, William W., and Aron Crowell (eds.) 1988. *Crossroads of Continents: Cultures of Siberia and Alaska*. Washington D.C.: Arctic Studies Center, National Museum of Natural History, Smithsonian Institution.

Freed, Stanley A., Ruth S. Freed, and Laila Williamson 1988. The American Museum's Jesup North Pacific Expedition. In *Crossroads of Continents: Cultures of Siberia and Alaska*. W. W. Fitzhugh and A. Crowell (eds.), 97–103. Washington, D.C.: Arc-

tic Studies Center, National Museum of Natural History, Smithsonian Institution.
Jakobson, Roman, Gerta Hüttl-Worth, and John Fred Beebe 1957. *Paleosiberian Peoples and Languages. A Bibliographical Guide*. New Haven: Human Relations Area Files.
Jochelson, Waldemar 1899a. In Polargegenden. In *Mutter Erde. Technik, Reisen und nützliche Naturbetrachtung in Haus und Familie*, vol. 1: 261–266, 285–288, 303–308, 325–328, 364–366, 385–388, 453–456, 467–470, 481–485; vol. 2: 207–210, 228–229, 245–247, 261–263, 470–473, 487–490. Berlin / Stuttgart. (See also Jochelson 2017: 91–137)

— 1899b. Die Jukagiren im äussersten Nordosten Asiens. In *Jahresberichte der Geographischen Gesellschaft in Bern*, XVII, 1898–99: 1–48. (See also Jochelson 2017: 42–78)

— 1899c. Über die Sprache und Schrift der Jukagiren. In *Jahresberichte der Geographischen Gesellschaft in Bern*, XVII, 1898–99: 49–63. (See also Jochelson 2017: 79–89)

— 1903. [Anonymus, "Docent"]. Dvulikii Ianus. *Osvobozhdenie*, No. 15, 255–256. (See also Jochelson 2017: 153–158)

— 1904. The Mythology of the Koryak. *American Anthropologist*, New Series, 6: 413–425.

— 1906. Über asiatische und amerikanische Elemente in den Mythen der Koriaken. In *Verhandlungen des Internationalen Amerikanisten-Kongresses, 14. Tagung*, Stuttgart 1904, 1, 119–127. Stuttgart: Kohlhammer. (See also Jochelson 2017: 139–145)

— 1908. The Koryak. *The Jesup North Pacific Expedition* 6, *Memoirs of the American Museum of Natural History* 10, Pt. 1–2. New York. New edition 2016, edited by E. Kasten and M. Dürr. Fürstenberg/Havel: Kulturstiftung Sibirien.

— 1925. *Archaeological Investigations in the Aleutian Islands. Supplement: Archaeological Investigations in Kamchatka*. Washington D.C.: Carnergie Institution.

— 1910–1926. The Yukaghir and Yukaghirized Tungus. *The Jesup North Pacific Expedition* 9, *Memoirs of the American Museum of Natural History* 13; Pt. 1, 1910; Pt. 2, 1924; Pt. 3, 1926. New York. New edition 2018, edited by E. Kasten and M. Dürr. Fürstenberg/Havel: Kulturstiftung Sibirien.

— 1928. *Peoples of Asiatic Russia*. New York: American Museum of Natural History.

— 1930. The Ancient and Present Kamchadal and the Similarities of Their Culture to That of the Northwestern American Indians. In *XXIII International Congress of Americanists*, New York 1928, Proceedings, 451–454. New York: Science Press Printing.

— 1933a. The Yakut. Anthropological Papers of the American Museum of Natural History. New York: The American Museum of Natural History. New edition 2018, edited by M. Dürr and E. Kasten. Fürstenberg/Havel: Kulturstiftung Sibirien.

— 1933b. *History, Ethnology and Anthropology of the Aleut*. Washington D.C.: Carnegie Institution.

— 2017. *Aus dem Fernen Osten Russlands: Deutschsprachige Schriften 1881–1908*. E. Kasten (ed.). Fürstenberg/Havel: Kulturstiftung Sibirien.

Iokhel'son, Vladimir Il'ich 1900. *Materialy po izucheniiu iukagirskogo iazyka i fol'klora.* *Vol. 1: Obraztsy narodnoi slovesnosti iukagirov.* St. Peterburg: Imperatorskoi Akademiia Nauk.

Kan, Sergei 2004. Lev Shternberg (1861–1927). Russian Socialist, Jewish Activist, Anthropologist, in *Biulleten': Antropologiia, men'shinstva, mul'tikul'turalizm* 5: 27–34.

Kasten, Erich 1992. Franz Boas: Ein engagierter Wissenschaftler in der Auseinandersetzung mit seiner Zeit. In *Franz Boas. Ethnologe, Anthropologe und Sprachwissenschaftler. Ein Wegbereiter der modernen Wissenschaft vom Menschen.* M. Dürr, E. Kasten and E. Renner (eds.), 7–37. Berlin: Staatsbibliothek zu Berlin; Wiesbaden: Reichert.

— 1998. *Kinder malen ihre Welt. Kinderzeichnungen aus Sibirien und von der Nordpazifikküste. Mir glazami detei: Detskie risunki iz Sibiri i Severo-tikhookeanskogo poberezh'ia.* Münster / New York: Waxmann.

— 2004. Ways of Owning and Sharing Cultural Property. In *Properties of Culture – Culture as Property. Pathways to Reform in Post-Soviet Siberia.* E. Kasten (ed.), 9–32. Berlin: Dietrich Reimer Verlag.

— 2005a. The Dynamics of Identity Management. In *Rebuilding Identities. Pathways to Reform in Post-Soviet Siberia.* E. Kasten (ed.), 237–260. Berlin: Dietrich Reimer Verlag.

— 2005b. *Rentierhorn und Erlenholz. Schnitzkunst aus Kamtschatka. Olenii rog i ol'kha: resnoe iskusstvo s Kamchatki.* Berlin: Zentral- und Landesbibliothek.

— 2012. *Shamanic Worldviews in Indigenous and Western Art.* DVD. Fürstenberg/ Havel: Kulturstiftung Sibirien.

— 2013a. Steller und die Itelmenen – die Bedeutung seines Werks für die ethnologische Forschung und für indigene Initiativen zum Erhalt von Kulturerbe bei den Itelmenen. In *Georg Wilhelm Steller: Beschreibung von dem Lande Kamtschatka.* E. Kasten and M. Dürr (eds.), 245–267. Fürstenberg/Havel: Kulturstiftung Sibirien.

— (ed.) 2013b. *Reisen an den Rand des Russischen Reiches: Die wissenschaftliche Erschließung der nordpazifischen Küstengebiete im 18. und 19. Jahrhundert.* Fürstenberg/Havel: Kulturstiftung Sibirien.

— 2014. Matematicheskie osnovy pri izgotovlenii odezhdy i v prikladnom iskusstve koriakov: vozmozhnosti ispol'zovaniia traditsionnykh znanii v uchebnykh pro grammakh natsional'nykh shkol na Kamchatke. In *Sibirskii sbornik – 4*, V.N. Davydov and D.V. Arziutov (red.), 96–113. St. Petersburg: MAE RAN.

— 2015a. Schamanische Weltbilder in indigener Kunst im fernen Osten Russlands. In *Kunst & Kontext* 9/2015: 35–42.

— 2015b. *Alkhalalalai. The Fall Festival of the Itelmens in Kamchatka.* DVD. Fürstenberg/ Havel: Kulturstiftung Sibirien.

— 2016a. Challenges and Approaches to Maintaining Cultural Diversity in the Russian Far East. In The *Proceedings of the 30th International Abashiri Symposium [The 30th Anniversary Meeting] Study of Northern Peoples for 30 Years – Progress, Chal-*

lenges and Roles of Museums. Hokkaido Museum of Northern Peoples, 2016: 1–8. Abashiri: Association for the Promotion of Northern Cultures.

— 2016b. Documenting Oral Histories in the Russian Far East: Text Corpora for Multiple Aims and Uses. In *Oral History meets Linguistics*, E. Kasten, K. Roller, and J. Wilbur (eds.), 13–30. Fürstenberg/Havel: Kulturstiftung Sibirien.

— (ed.) 2016c. *Rodovye melodii i tantsy koriakov-nymylanov, s. Lesnaia, Kamchatka/ Songs and Dances, Coastal Koryaks (Nymylans), Lesnaia, Kamchatka*. Fürstenberg/ Havel: Kulturstiftung Sibirien.

— (ed.) 2017a. *Dukhovnaia kul'tura koriakov-nymylanov s. Lesnaia: Mirovozzreniia i ritual'nye prazdniki / Worldviews and Ritual Practice, Coastal Koryaks (Nymylans), Lesnaia, Kamchatka*. Fürstenberg/Havel: Kulturstiftung Sibirien.

— 2017b. Versöhnungsfeste mit der Natur im Nordosten Sibiriens: „Ololo" und „Kilvej" der Korjaken und Čukčen auf Kamtschatka. Mitteilungen der Berliner Gesellschaft für Anthropologie, Ethnologie und Urgeschichte, Bd. 38: 103–122.

— 2019. Georg Wilhelm Steller: Scientist, Humanist and Most Significant Ethnographer for the Itelmens on Kamchatka. In *Writing the Arctic: German Representations of the Far North in the 18th and 19th centuries*. Cambridge: Cambridge Scholars Publishing (forthcoming).

Kasten, Erich, and Michael Dürr 2005. *Feasting with the Seals: Koryaks and Evens in the Russian Far East*. DVD. Berlin: Zentral- und Landesbibliothek Berlin.

Kasten, Erich, and Raisa Avak (eds.) 2018. *Odezhda i prikladnoe iskusstvo evenov Bystrinskogo raiona. Clothing and Decorative Arts, Evens, Kamchatka, Bystrinski district*. Fürstenberg/Havel: Kulturstiftung Sibirien.

Kegel, Johann Karl Ehrenfried 2011. *Forschungsreise nach Kamtschatka*. Werner Friedrich Gülden (ed.). Fürstenberg/Havel: Kulturstiftung Sibirien.

Kendall, Laurel, and Igor Krupnik (eds.) 2003. *Constructing Cultures Then and Now. Celebrating Franz Boas and the Jesup North Pacific Expedition*. Washington, D.C.: Arctic Studies Center, National Museum of Natural History, Smithsonian Institution.

Kendall, Laurel, Barbara Mathé, and Thomas Ross Miller with Stanley A. Freed, Ruth S. Freed, and Laila Williamson (1997). *Drawing Shadows to Stone: The Photography of the Jesup North Pacific Expedition, 1897–1902*. New York: American Museum of Natural History.

Khaloimova Klavdiia, Michael Dürr, and Erich Kasten (eds.) 2014. *Itel'menskie skazki – sobrannye V. I. Iokhel'sonom v 1910–1911 gg*. Fürstenberg/Havel: Kulturstiftung Sibirien.

Kittlitz, Friedrich Heinrich von 2011. *Denkwürdigkeiten einer Reise nach dem russischen Amerika, nach Mikronesien und Kamtschatka. Auszüge aus den Werken*. E. Kasten (ed.). Fürstenberg/Havel: Kulturstiftung Sibirien.

Koester, David, and Erich Kasten (eds.) 2019. *Jochelson's Anthropological Investigations in Kamchatka: Results of the Riabushinsky Expedition*. Fürstenberg/Havel: Kulturstiftung Sibirien. (to be published in 2019)

Koppel, Tom 2003. *Lost World: Rewriting Prehistory. How New Science Is Tracing America's Ice Age Mariners.* New York: Atria Books.

Krauss, Michael E. 2003. The Languages of the North Pacific Rim 1896–1997, and the Jesup Expedition. In *Constructing Cultures Then and Now. Celebrating Franz Boas and the Jesup North Pacific Expedition.* L. Kendall, and I. Krupnik 2003 (eds.), 211–221. Washington, D.C.: National Museum of Natural History and Smithsonian Institution.

Krupnik, Igor, and William Fitzhugh (eds.) 2001. *Gateways. Exploring the Legacy of the Jesup North Pacific Expedition, 1897–1902.* New York, Washington, D.C.: Arctic Studies Center, National Museum of Natural History, Smithsonian Institution.

Krupnik, Igor, and Lyudmila S. Bogoslovskaya 2017. "Our Ice, Snow and Winds": From Knowledge Integration to Co-production in the Russian SIKU Project, 2007–2013. In *Oral History Meets Linguistics.* E. Kasten, K. Roller, and J. Wilbur (eds.), 65–82. Fürstenberg/Havel: Kulturstiftung Sibirien.

Lavrillier, Alexandra, and Semen Gabyshev 2017. *An Arctic Indigenous Knowledge System of Landscape, Climate, and Human Interactions: Evenki Reindeer Herders and Hunters.* Fürstenberg/Havel: Kulturstiftung Sibirien.

Miller, Thomas Ross, and Barbara Mathé 1997. Drawing Shadows to Stone. In *Drawing Shadows to Stone. The Photography of the Jesup North Pacific Expedition,* L. Kendall et al. (eds.), 19–40. New York: American Museum of Natural History.

Müller-Wille, Ludger 2014. *The Franz Boas Enigma. Inuit, Arctic and Sciences.* Montréal: Baraka Books.

Plattet, Patrick 2005. *Le double jeu de la chance. Imitation et substitution dans les rituels chamaniques contemporains de deux populations rurales du Nord-Kamtchatka (Fédération de Russie, Extrême-Orient sibérien): les chasseurs maritimes de Lesnaya et les éleveurs de rennes d'Atchaïvaiam.* PhD Dissertation. Université de Neuchâtel.

Reich, David, Nick Patterson, Desmand Campbell, Arti Tandon, Stéphane Mazieres, Nicolas Ray, and Maria W. Parra 2013. Reconstructing Native American Population History. *Nature* 488: 370–374.

Steller, Georg Wilhelm 2013. *Beschreibung von dem Lande Kamtschatka*, E. Kasten and M. Dürr (eds). Fürstenberg/Havel: Kulturstiftung Sibirien.

Vakhtin, Nikolai 2001. Franz Boas and the Shaping of the Jesup Expedition Siberian Research, 1895–1900. In *Gateways. Exploring the Legacy of the Jesup North Pacific Expedition, 1897–1902.* I. Krupnik and W. Fitzhugh (eds.), 71–89. Washington, D.C.: Arctic Studies Center, National Museum of Natural History, Smithsonian Institution.

— 2004. Nauka i zhizn'. Sud'ba Vladimira Iokhel'sona. (Po materialam ego perepiski 1897–1934 gg.) In *Biulleten': Antropologiia, men'shinstva, mul'tikul'turalizm* 5: 35–49.

Winterschladen, Matthias 2016. Zwischen Revolution und Wissenschaft. Iochel'son, Bogoraz und die Verflechtung von Wissenschaft und Politik – Ein biographischer

Zugang. In *Auf den Spuren der modernen Sozial- und Kulturanthropologie: Die Jesup North Pacific Expedition 1897 bis 1902 in Ostsibirien*. D. Dahlmann, D. Ordubadi, and M. Winterschladen (eds.), 73–110. Fürstenberg/Havel: Kulturstiftung Sibirien.

Worth, Dean Stoddard (ed.) 1961. *Kamchadal Texts, Collected by Waldemar Jochelson*. 'Gravenhage: Mouton.

Zgusta, Richard 2015. *The Peoples of Northeast Asia Through Time: Precolonial Ethnic and Cultural Processes Along the Coast Between Hokkaido and the Bering Strait*. Leiden: Brill.

4 READING THE ETHNOGRAPHIC PAST IN THE PRESENT: WALDEMAR JOCHELSON AND THE YUKAGHIR¹

Thomas Ross Miller

The Yukaghir and Yukaghirized Tungus by Waldemar Jochelson (Vladimir Il'ich Iokhel'son) (1855–1937) is one of those rare books in the history of anthropology: a study of a people so little known or understood, achieved on such a grand scale and in such a comprehensive manner, that it comes to be regarded as the definitive work on the subject. Based on years of fieldwork and collecting, it was written and published in three parts over a period of two and a half decades, years that included the Soviet Revolution and the author's self-imposed exile in America. It was part of the Jesup North Pacific Expedition, to this day perhaps the most ambitious ethnographic collecting enterprise ever undertaken. The journey was made at the border between two centuries, in a historical moment of catastrophic population decline for the Yukaghir people. Salvage anthropology's intervention came at a point of crisis for the survival of the Yukaghir clans, shortly before life in the north was changed irrevocably by revolution, civil war, and collectivization.

Previous expeditionary collecting in Russia had not reached the Yukaghir as much as some neighboring peoples in Siberia. The massive holistic collections Jochelson gathered under Franz Boas's direction for the American Museum of Natural History were driven by an impulse to collect the culture of the past for the science of the future. Anthropologists wanted to document what they considered pre-contact survivals, but they rarely envisioned the long-term survival of peoples and their traditions. With the avowed goal of proving the Bering Strait migration hypothesis regarding the origins of the first Americans, railroad magnate and museum president Morris K. Jesup commissioned the expedition. For five years at the turn of the 20th century, teams of fieldworkers led by Boas scoured the countryside from the interior plateau of British Columbia across the North Pacific as far as central Yakutia, collecting recordings, texts, photographs, human remains, and all manner of material items for the American Museum of Natural History in New York City. The cargo included two previously unclassified small mammal species, including the Kolyma red-backed mouse which was named for Jochelson (*Evotomys Jochelsoni*) (14)². In addition to found objects, a category including most art and artifacts as well as human bones, Jochelson and his team made documentary collections consisting of dictated texts, phonograph records, photographs, and head casts—objects created, at least in part, by and for science.

---

1 This chapter was also published as the foreword to the new edition of Jochelson's *The Yukaghir and Yukaghirized Tungus* [2018]).
2 These numbers refer to the pagination of the main text corpus in Jochelson 2018.

Yukaghir Fire: Land and Language

The Yukaghir are one people in two divisions. The two interrelated but distinct branches are the reindeer herders on the tundra (Wadul) and the hunter-gatherers in the taiga (Odul). The Wadul intermingled more with Even (Tungus) people on the tundra, while the Odul in the taiga were more Russianized. Jochelson, his wife and field partner Dina Brodskaia, and their colleague Waldemar Bogoras coined the hybrid ethnonym "Yukaghirized Tungus" to describe some of the tundra groups. The neologism, suggested by Bogoras, was meant to describe the intermixture of Even (Tungus) and Yukaghir identities and society. Jochelson (16) states that Odul was also a name for Yukaghir people in general, and the people Jochelson and Bogoras named "Yukaghirized Tungus" told Jochelson they too called themselves Odul; but when he told this to the "real" Odul in Kolyma, they were outraged. The Kolyma Odul called the "Yukaghirized Tungus" Alayi-people, which was understood to mean Even (Tungus). The Chuvantsy are a related group whose affiliation was classified in several different ways over the years (see Krupnik 1990).

Jochelson introduced the Yukaghir on the second page of his Memoir as "a tribe insignificant and having no future." The drastic decline in the Yukaghir population during the period of his field collecting left them on the brink of survival. Odul means strong and powerful, and many northern peoples still refer to the stars or the northern lights as "Yukaghir fire." According to oral tradition, the metaphor originated at a time when the Yukaghir were so numerous that their campfires and hearths dotted the night landscape as far as the eye could see. At the beginning of the 17th century there were between 10 000 and 20 000 Yukaghir. By the end of the 19th century, their numbers had declined to some 200. By the turn of the 20th century, they were one of the smallest and poorest of the small-numbered peoples of the north. Soviet census figures reported that the Yukaghir population more than doubled from about 400 in 1959 to 835 in 1979 (Forsyth 1992: 405). By the 1990s, the population of the vast Verkhnekolymsk district was more than 90% ethnically Russian or other non-indigenous people. At the turn of the 21st century, their population was officially reported at between 900 and 1 200. In the complex ethnolinguistic mixture of North Asia, Wadul have more in common with Even (Tungus) culture; the Odul have sometimes been referred to as Russianized Yukaghir, but they have also long been under a strong influence from both Sakha (Yakut) and Even (Tungus).

As the first outsider to cross the Stanovoi mountain range, Jochelson described the Yukaghir terrain as the severest in all Siberia, a region which experiences the coldest winter temperatures of any inhabited part of the earth. "In the Yukaghir country," he writes, "the rivers, as a rule, are long, deep, and carry a large volume of water" (13). Rivers are central places in the topology that includes the Kolyma, Yasachnaia, Rassocha, Indigirka, Omolon, Korkodon, and Shamanikha. The Kolyma region was founded by Russians in 1673 and became a place of banishment, hardship, and death for exiles and prisoners. The many intermixed marriages in this part of Siberia are among the most ethnically complex in northern Asia, but at the end of the 20th century almost all the Yukaghir in the Kolyma settlement of Nelemnoe belonged to one of six intermarried clans. Early and endogamous marriages have resulted in cousin relationships reproduced from generation to generation. They were long under the double domination of Sakha (Yakut) and Russians. Later, under the totalizing force of Soviet living, collectivization and the *kolkhoz* became a way of life, disrupting and reorganizing the patterns of traditional cultures. Despite this, however, remoteness from the administrative center enabled a degree of cultural persistence.

Yukaghir poetry, Jochelson wrote, "is distinguished by an abundance of feeling" (310). The landscape is a frequent motif in Yukaghir songs, as a setting and a metaphor for human longing and separation or as a celebration of the blessings of the earth. Distance in the taiga is more often measured in time than space; a destination is said to be a number of days' journey away rather than a number of kilometers. Hunters and fishermen journeying on the broad rivers of Verkhne Kolyma district leave their fires burning on shore when they break camp so the rising smoke can serve as a beacon of human life, heartening other lonesome travelers passing through the vast uninhabited stretches of wilderness.

The settlement of Nelemnoe sits on a high bank of the Yasachnaia River, deep in the Siberian taiga of the Verkhne Kolyma district in Yakutia (Sakha Republic, Russian Federation). Nelemnoe means "place of many *nelm*" (a white salmon), or according to another theory, of many *nalim* (burbot). Today's settlement is actually the third Nelemnoe; two previous sites were each abandoned when rising flood waters threatened people's houses. The first Nelemnoe, near the mouth of the Rassocha River, was closed in 1931 when the Yukaghir were organized into the "Bright Life" *kolkhoz* (collective farm). The second, on a high bank where there was always a high level of deep water, is now known as Old Nelemnoe. It was evacuated due to rising flood waters between 1956 and 1958 (Vakhtin 1991: 7). Most Odul now live most of the time in Nelemnoe, hunting and fishing along the Yasachnaia and the Kolyma's many tributaries, and in their traditional territory of the Arga-Tas mountains north of Magadan.

The hunter-gatherer taiga Yukaghir (Odul) and the reindeer herding tundra Yukaghir (Wadul) speak cognate but almost mutually unintelligible tongues. Whether Odul and Wadul are two languages or two different dialects of the same language has been the topic of considerable debate by linguists, as has the question of its origins and affiliations. Yukaghir has been classified as an anomalous Paleosiberian language isolate unrelated to neighboring languages, but some modern scholars disagree. Jochelson saw the language as similar to others, but conceded to the isolate classification pending further studies (44; see also Jochelson 1900; 1905). Before Jochelson's research, the language was so little known outside of its native speakers that many thought it was extinct.

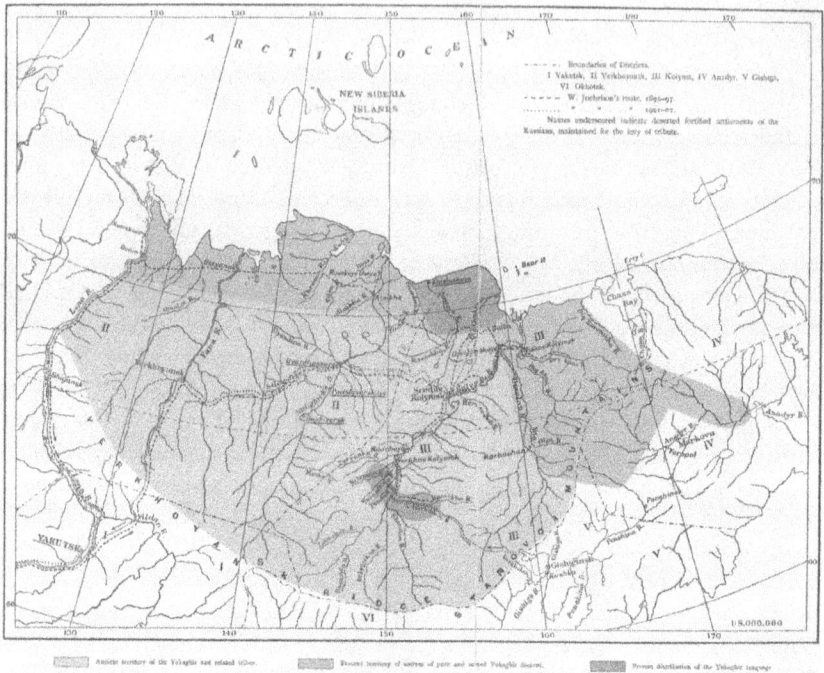

Fig. 1 This map published in Jochelson's memoir shows the loss of Yukaghir territory from the ancient past to the early 20ᵗʰ-century ethnographic present.

Yukaghiric languages were once widely spoken across a vast range between the Lena and Anadyr Rivers across what is today Chukotka, the northeastern Sakha Republic, and northern Magadan Oblast; from the Ural Mountains to the Yenisei River west-east, and from the Arctic circle to southern taiga in Altai. Only two languages or dialects survive, Wadul and Odul. The proper classification of Yukaghir remains contested among linguists. Some still consider the Yukaghiric languages an isolated branch, while others classify them as derived from an ancestral proto-language. Nikolaeva's historical dictionary was an important milestone in Yukaghir linguistics (2006). Based on sound laws, lexical cognates, and glottochronology, Piispanen (2016; 2017) predicts that the Yukaghiric languages will prove to have developed from a Pre-Proto-Uralic language, "perhaps spoken somewhere north of modern Mongolia, close to Manchuria due to typological reasons." The Uralic-Yukaghiric divergence has been dated as far back as 6 600 BC. (see Jochelson 1905; Kreinovich 1958; Nikolaeva 2006).

Of special interest to paleolinguists are the birch-bark maps and letters (*shangar shurele* in Yukaghir) written in signs that are thought to be the remnants of an ancient pictographic writing system (Jochelson 2017: 79–89). Linguists believed the code to have been lost, but at the end of the 20th century some elders were still able to read them from photographs. Some were love letters, while others depicted forests, lakes, and rivers, and crossings. They were used to show good fishing places, to count time, and to predict the return of a hunting party according to the position of the moon. The signs show the story or plot of a song and name the places, but did not indicate the melody. One had to know the signs very well to decode them.

In a section titled "Mental Traits" (42 ff.), Jochelson wrote that although dominated by Russians, the Yukaghir had maintained their dignity. His claim to have never had a single misunderstanding with them (43) probably refers to payments, but it must be taken with a grain of salt as witnessed by numerous incidents including conflict and tension: over love letters addressed to him (65), physical-type photography, the naked anatomical measurements of Yukaghir women, the making of head casts, and his removal of sacred objects including an important *chuchelo* (wooden spirit figure) in the 1890's from a tree that still stands at the mouth of the Shamanikha River. The abduction of the *chuchelo* triggered an outbreak of the nervous disease sometimes referred to as arctic hysteria, causing widespread suffering (see Miller 2004b).

Although his contributions were long erased from the Soviet historical record, northern people have regarded Jochelson's legacy (and that of his fellow Decembrists) quite favorably. Yukaghir people say that he had a good heart and tried to help the people when they had few allies. For his part, he characterized the Yukaghir as especially cheerful and playful: "when the young people begin to dance, one after another—old men and children, healthy and ill, and especially old women—begin to join them, until all the inhabitants of the village have turned out to the dance." Even a sick old woman got up and joined in until she could no longer stand (35). Strong women continue to play a crucial role in maintaining Yukaghir traditions (see Willerslev 2010; Zhukova 1996). Willerslev points out a paradox in the romanticization of the Yukaghir as primitive and remote, a sentiment that made them an icon of small-numbered peoples of the north in the imagination of outsiders: they are sad but cheerful, poor but rich in emotional feeling. Such judgments were based in part on travelers' impressions, including especially Jochelson's canonic tome. The Yukaghir "have thus been in the extraordinary position of being one of the Siberian peoples to whom reference is most often made, but on the basis of data that are now more than a century old" (Willerslev 2004). In fact, the reconstructed traditions of Boasian magisterial ethnography were already at odds with modern realities when they were written.

Collecting on the Edge of Change

The book should be considered in the context of the collection as a whole.[3] The historical moment in which the expedition and collections were made was a period of disastrous population decline for the Yukaghir, who were enduring some of the worst epidemics in Siberian history. Jochelson reported to Boas in 1902 that the Yukaghir had fared worse than any other northeastern Siberian tribe he knew. At the height of the smallpox outbreak Yukaghir were dying at a catastrophic rate. Between 1850 and 1897 the Alaseia (Wadul) clan declined from 99 to 13, most from illness. Among the survivors was Igor Shamanov, clan shaman and grandfather of activist and poet Uluro Ado (Gavril Kurilov). He recorded spirit voices on the phonograph and sold his shaman's coat and drum to Jochelson for the museum.

Waldemar Jochelson's early years as a Jewish revolutionary, exile, and political prisoner have been described elsewhere (see Winterschladen 2016; Kasten 2017; Krupnik and Fitzhugh 2001). As a member of People's Will (*Narodnaia Volia*), he was linked to terrorists and an assassination plot, and like Bogoras he spent years imprisoned in St. Petersburg's infamous Peter and Paul Fortress. His subsequent exile to Yakutia led him to conduct ethnographic research and travel among the Yukaghir and Sakha (Yakut), including collecting for the imperial Sibiriakov Expedition. The Yukaghir treated all Russians as if they were officials; to them, Jochelson and his Cossacks were agents of the state. One Yukaghir elder claimed that "The first researchers who came here, before Jochelson, had rifles; the Yukaghir were afraid of them because the bullets were fast. These researchers thought there were many Yukaghir and that the Yukaghir might kill them, so they put a raft in river and smoke on the raft. They poisoned people to kill them, deliberately."

The imperial bureaucratic state kept Jochelson under suspicion even as it enabled his work (see Jochelson 2017: 153–158). Although his agreement with the museum forbade her getting credit, Dina Brodskaia contributed much of the photography and made anatomical measurements of women. Her charm, personality, and human kindness were important in winning the trust and cooperation of the people; nonetheless, there were great difficulties in taking head casts, anthropometric measurements, and photographs of women's sometimes naked bodies (see Jochelson-Brodsky 1906). While the character of fieldwork Jochelson had to employ with the Koryak because of Boas' instructions differed from his fieldwork with the Yukaghirs, some Koryak women were also terrified by the process (see Kasten 2017: 27).

Fig. 2, 3 Boas directed his field workers to photograph subjects in frontal, side, and three-quarter views for physical-type comparison and classification. Some of the items of clothing and ornaments they wore in the photographs are preserved in the American Museum of Natural History's collection. From Jochelson 2018: Plate I, III.

---

3   https://anthro.amnh.org/jesup_collection; https://anthro.amnh.org/jesup_photos

Yukaghir population decline was caused by environmental conditions, starvation, disease, and the demands of the fur tax and tribute (*iasak*), but the greatest losses came about through absorption into other groups. The rate of depopulation accelerated in the second half of the 19th century. By the time of the Jesup North Pacific Expedition, the combined Yukaghir population of Wadul and Odul had probably declined to around 200 individuals. They judged correctly that smallpox was an alien disease imported by Russians, but their shamans were usually helpless against Russian spirits and illness (see Jochelson 2017: 115–137) where he describes in detail especially how the Yukaghirs dealt with these epidemics).

The stage was thus set for the Boasian salvage ethnology model of collecting at the edge of change, when the old ceremonial artifacts were still in people's houses but their use had declined due to death, assimilation, and what appeared to be a fading out of traditional ceremonial life. Boas instructed his field workers on the Jesup North Pacific Expedition that the cusp of modernity was the best time to collect ritual artifacts, when people still owned them, but would sell them cheaply due to lack of interest.

Shamans and Singing Diseases

The texts by Jochelson and Bogoras on the subject of shamanism, classics in the field, have profoundly influenced western anthropologists' thinking about the subject. Shamans met by Jochelson in Yukaghir country included an old man called Tuliach (Spiridonov) (201); Nelbosh (Samsonov), a Yukaghir shaman from the Korkodon River, was only revealed as a shaman to Jochelson after his death (196). Mashka, an Even Tungus from the Sea of Okhotsk, was Nelbosh's son-in-law. Mashka's movements were wild and loud; but "Nelbosh would sing with deep feeling, but in a low, drawn out voice, as if lulling somebody to sleep, and producing an atmosphere of quiet sadness" (201). The Yukaghir shamans Jochelson recorded in the taiga were actually from the tundra, Wadul whose speech and songs were unknown to the Odul in the area.

Jochelson has been criticized for stating that he encountered few shamans in Siberia, yet constructing an entire ethnographic representation of Siberian shamanism. Field work in the 1990s confirmed that some of his informants were secretly shamans; others went by nicknames or pseudonyms. Was the truth concealed from Jochelson, or did he know this and conceal their true identity rather than reveal it in print? His Yukaghir consultants took part in a tradition of secrecy and covert shamanizing. This tradition has long included the practice of withholding some information from ethnographers in the field, whether at the behest of the spirits or the discretion of the shaman. The negotiation of the informant with the spirits over what esoteric knowledge to reveal and what to conceal from outsiders is a familiar and continuing part of the ethnographic enterprise, a shadow dance of revelation and concealment. Some things are simply not spoken of.

Shamans and shamanizing were fluid, translinguistic, mobile in space as well as between the worlds. Observing that Yukaghir life has always been small scale and lacking in grand public rituals, Willerslev (2007) and some others posit that the Yukaghir were favored by the Soviets as something like primitive communists, and that none of their shamans were persecuted. They were, however, repressed. The source of a Yukaghir shaman's power is ecological, residing in sacred elements of the environment beyond the reach of bureaucrats and *apparatchiki*. One time the authorities came to Nelemnoe and pointed a gun at a great shaman, demanding to be shown the source of his shamanic power. He led them to the river and pointed at a fish. Shamans acted as historical conduits for resistance and provided a secret counter-narrative to Soviet domination.

The outbreaks of "Arctic hysteria" (*emerek* and *emirchanye*) Jochelson witnessed among the Yukaghir during the period of his field work were the most severe and widespread of all documented cases to have occurred in the north. Those stricken, mostly women, exhibited strange behavioral disorders including violent fits, crying out, perseveration, echolalia, compulsive imitation, and speaking in tongues. Some studies have attributed the epidemics to extreme cold, malnutrition, or colonial domination, but few have examined the point of view of the Yukaghir themselves. Outbreaks occurred especially when the clans were without shamans. The worst documented pandemic occurred in the decade around 1900. All accounts agree that Kolyma Yukaghir territory was the epicenter of the epidemics.

S.I. Mitskevich, a Bolshevik physician who later served with Bogoras on the Committee of the North, observed and treated many patients with *emerek*, *menerik*, and related nervous conditions. Victims were frightened of abuse at the hands of Russian exiles. *Tarymta*, also associated with spirits, was a less severe disease that affected women from the onset of puberty by attacking the heart, mouth, and nerves. In several locales he found nearly all persons experienced some type of "domestic hysteria" or cabin fever (1929: 10–23). In the small settlement of Rodchevo, Mitskevich determined that fully 100% of the women had suffered from some type of "psycho-neuropathology," including one *shamanka* (which he considered a type of psychic disturbance).

The *khozain*, masters of taiga and lake, are animal spirits who serve as intermediaries between nature and supernature, acting as shamans' helpers and protectors. But when spirits possess unwitting individuals, the afflicted are powerless against them. Mitskevich documented a widespread epidemic of singing diseases among the Yukaghir in 1929. A patient, he wrote, would "cry, sing rhythmically, beat her head against the wall or shake it from side to side, tear at her hair." Her body cramped and became rigid, and she began to make terrifying noises which built to a crescendo. Others hearing the cries sometimes took up the song in chorus as the nervous illness spread.

Patients "sang in unknown languages and predicted the future; like shamans, they were possessed by spirits and extraordinary powers could appear." The rhythms of their songs were the same as those of shamans' songs, but unlike shamans they could not control their spirits. They usually sang or spoke in Yakut or Russian, and Yukaghir often claimed the affliction was of foreign origin.

Although the pathology of certain nervous and psychic syndromes common to the circumpolar north has been linked to extremes of cold and dark, outbreaks also occurred in summer. They often spread contagiously. Some were attributed to biological epidemics, as among the Verkhne Kolyma Yukaghir and Even in 1899. In Nelemnoe, every night sufferers could be heard crying, singing, and speaking in tongues including Chukchi, which according to Mitskevich was unknown there. Among the Chukchi themselves, the disease was rare. Another outbreak occurred in 1900, when some blamed a shaman from the tundra for bringing the illness (Mitskevich 1929:27–28). The tundra Yukaghir rarely suffered from the affliction. Yukaghir *emiriachki* most often spoke in Sakha or Russian, which might suggest a foreign origin.

Fits of singing disease were associated with the stresses and strains of colonialism, and of the subaltern condition of native women especially. Some of the Cossacks assigned to accompany (and perhaps to spy on) Jochelson were cruel to native women, demanding food, shelter, and sexual favors; some had violent sadistic impulses. One old woman, a *menerik* sufferer, was startled by the crack of Jochelson's camera shutter and rushed at his Cossack Kotelnikoff, cursing and trying to grab his sexual organs. (37) (see Kendall, Mathé and Miller 1997).

Here the erasure of group boundaries was expressed through a vocal repertoire, in this case of a terrifying and uncontrollable variety. Mitskevich proposed attacking the disease by using culture as a weapon. With collectivization and communism, he concluded, the people would come into a natural state of harmony. The doctor's prescription reflected the aims of the Party in the late 1920s to gain control over northern minorities, in line with Bogoras' plan to save native cultures by helping them adapt to the inexorable tide of Communism.

Slow Science

The complete writing up and publication of the Jesup North Pacific Expedition materials took decades of slow science, painstakingly reconstructed by sifting through source materials collected many years earlier. Bogoras' monumental study of the Chukchi, the most widely known in the series, took five years post-fieldwork to be published in full. *The Yukaghir and Yukaghirized Tungus* took far longer; by the time Part III appeared in 1926, some two dozen years had passed since the completion of principal fieldwork. (Jochelson's *The Yakut* took even longer, until 1933.) Jochelson and Boas were using prerevolutionary data to create a canonic description, in the present tense, of a people whose way of life had radically changed by the time the full publication appeared. When is the ethnographic present of the Memoir?

The overarching mission of the Jesup North Pacific Expedition—to accomplish the hypothetical reconstruction of the peopling of the Americas from Siberia, or else obtain definitive evidence to the contrary—through the massive accumulation of holistic fragments always remained in the minds of Jesup, Boas, Jochelson, Bogoras and the others. But the collections and monographs became far more descriptive and focused. They stand as testaments to a legacy of expeditionary fortitude. Boas downplayed the obvious lacuna in his theory of a grand North Pacific culture region: since he collected no evidence from Alaska, the central piece of the geographic puzzle, any hypothetical proof of common origins would remain unresolved. The American Museum of Natural History was already rich in artifacts from Alaska, in particular those purchased from the voluminous collector George Emmons. Instead, Boas concentrated more of the museum's field resources in peripheral areas far from the North Pacific coast, where he already had trained men on the inside: Jochelson (1933) for the Sakha (Yakut) and James Teit on the interior plateau of British Columbia.

In his culture area theory, Boas postulated these regions as transition zones between coastal and interior peoples both in North Asia and North America. This stretched the definition of North Pacific peoples, which was the point of the entire exhaustive endeavor in the first place. In the end it hardly mattered, as the voluminous and richly detailed scope and range of the Jesup collection and monographs continue to inspire artists, scholars, and activists to discover and explore the historic links among indigenous people on both continents (see Fitzhugh and Crowell 1988). While solo fieldwork became standard practice for British and American anthropologists, collecting expeditions remained important in Siberia, where seasonal access to the field remained limited for scholars. For seven decades in the Soviet era, the existence of Siberian collections in New York was hardly known outside of rumors. The reopening of exchanges between Russia and the west in the 1990s allowed indigenous cultural revitalization actors to access and study the Siberian ethnographic collections made by Jochelson and Bogoras, the largest and most significant outside of Russia.

Franz Boas formally separated from the American Museum of Natural History in 1905, but continued to oversee and edit the publication of the complete Jesup North Pacific Expedition Memoirs, including the present work. Unable to come to an agreement with museum administrators over what he saw as a devaluation of scientific research in favor of simplified popular exhibitions, in 1905 he resigned his position as Curator to establish the first department of anthropology in American higher education at Columbia University. Waldemar Jochelson eventually finished the writing during long years of self-imposed exile in New York and the erasure of his legacy in Siberia, while Bogoras became a pre-eminent ethnographer and shaper of official Soviet minorities policy.

Jochelson's writing was interrupted for the Riabushinskii (Riabouschinsky) expedition to Kamchatka and the Aleutian Islands of Alaska, which fulfilled a key part of Boas' unrealized plan for the original Jesup Expedition project. While negotiating the terms of his formal separation from the museum, Boas was asked to outline a program of recommended future research to carry the work of the Jesup North Pacific Expedition further. In a draft memo and budget, he initially assigned top priority to filling in the Alaskan gap in the center of the North Pacific region by mounting a major collecting expedition in the Aleutian Islands, but the cost was prohibitive. His final draft plan instead prioritized Salish collections from the Interior Plateau of British Columbia, where James Teit was already trained and on the scene. Meanwhile, Jochelson sought patrons to fund an Aleutian expedition of his own. In 1907 Boas assisted him by pursuing wealthy collector George Heye, even as he wrote to Jochelson that he "should much prefer to have you finish the Yukaghir manuscript before you take up new researches," but an economic downturn doomed the fundraising effort (APS). When Jochelson then secured sponsorship under the auspices of the Imperial Russian Geographical Society for his Riabushinskii Expedition to Alaska and Kamchatka, Boas remained anxious for him to complete the first part of the Yukaghir manuscript before leaving for the field. While this was not possible, Boas asked him to at least first incorporate into the manuscript Bogoras' material on Yukaghir mythology, and to finish all he had written to that point, so that at least a part of the Memoir could be printed. Torn between the goals of completing the missing Alaskan fieldwork piece of the Jesup Expedition puzzle and completing the publication of the Jesup Expedition Memoirs, Boas had to agree to the interruption. He accepted Jochelson's proposal to print the first six chapters as a stand-alone Part I.

Boas assigned the translation work to anthropologist-activist Alexander Goldenweiser but was frustrated when he received just the first chapter, followed by news of Goldenweiser's arrest in Kiev (it turned out to be a relatively trivial misunderstanding). Finally he asked Jochelson to have the rest translated professionally in London. On the day that he finalized his agreement with the American Museum of Natural History to take over the editing of the Jesup Expedition publication series himself, a jubilant Boas wrote to Jochelson:

> All further relations between yourself and the Jesup Expedition will therefore be directly with me. I am convinced that with this moment our troubles will cease. [...] whatever we do now is to be done between yourself and myself personally, not between you and the Museum. I think it is a matter for congratulation that we do not need to deal with the office now, but that the matter has to be settled among ourselves, who have respect for each other and for our scientific work. (APS)

Jochelson continued to reply to Boas' detailed query letters about the Yukaghir while he and Dina Brodskaia made their way to Unalaska, Atka, and Attu, and Kamchatka over the next few years. In 1913, with Jochelson back in St. Petersburg, Boas finally received the go-ahead from the museum for the completion of the Yukaghir volume. The two anthropologists met in Berlin and agreed that Jochelson would write up the sections on religion, folklore, and material culture in that order. Boas requested a full working out of the material, which he proposed to edit down to the required length and then see to it that the rest got printed elsewhere. Jochelson even bought property in the Ural Mountains, not far from Bogoras, where he worked on the remaining chapters while suffering poor health. When the Russian Revolution and civil war came, Boas lost touch with both Bogoras and Jochelson until 1921. He then secured a small amount of funding from the museum and brought Jochelson to New York to write up the rest of his findings. Part III was finally published by E. J. Brill in Leiden

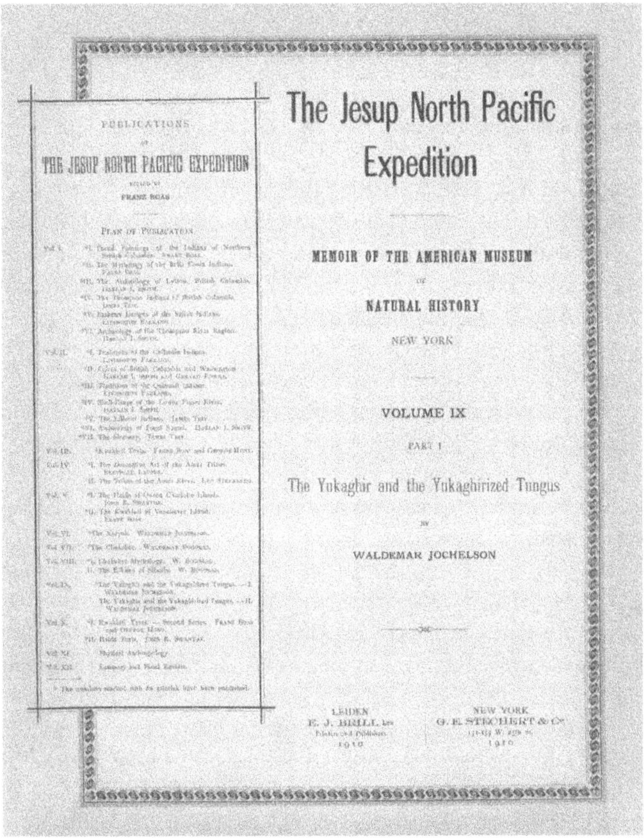

Fig. 4 The Yukaghir and Yukaghirized Tungus was one of the last of the American Museum of Natural History's classic Jesup North Pacific Expedition monographs to be completed. As shown here on the cover of Part 1, series editor Franz Boas eventually published the work in installments.

in 1926, completing the saga. The whereabouts of Jochelson's field notes, if they exist, have remained unknown. The present edition stands as a companion volume to the historic Russian translation of *The Yukaghir and Yukaghirized Tungus* translated and illustrated by native scholars in a years-long collaboration (Jochelson 2005).

While the authorial voice is unmistakably Jochelson's throughout the three parts of the Memoir, the editorial hand of Boas remains firmly in the background. The granular level of ethnographic detail and careful framing of speculative theories adhere to Boas' trademark methodological caution, and yet the ethnographic present of 1901–02 remains in full force despite the total reorganization of Yukaghir life during the Soviet era. The collection itself was curated by Boas to emphasize older material representing pre-contact traditions. Before field work even began, he instructed Jochelson to screen out many modern syncretic realities in order to represent the past (Mathé and Miller 2001).

The Yukaghir in the Long 20th Century

Jochelson called the Yukaghir "a tribe on the eve of extinction" (20), but they have persevered through floods, famine, deadly disease, collectivization, war, dislocation, repression, assimilation, marginalization, and neglect. This volume stands not only as a monumental ethnohistorical record of the Yukaghir, but also a record of a moment in contact history. Collecting was simultaneously part of the removal of tradition and part of its preservation. After the end of the Soviet Union in the early 1990s, the Yukaghir held a gathering of all the clans for the first time in their history. The two main themes that emerged were the importance of preserving their language and their land. Without these, asked poet and activist leader of the Yukaghir *intelligentsia* Uluro Ado (Gavril Kurilov), what is a people?

During the last summer of the 20th century, I stood on the high bank above the river among the abandoned wooden houses being reclaimed by the taiga where Old Nelemnoe once was. In the summer Yukaghirs still use the land for hunting, fishing camps, and smokehouses. My companions lit a fire and we made offerings to the *khozain*, the master spirits of the place. One elder, who was secretly a shaman, said we should eat as if we're eating with the spirits. When the *kolkhoz* was here, he said, there were many cows; they produced their own milk and *kolbasa*. Swans come here in the fall for a short time. (Another man remarked "The czars ate swans, they were a great delicacy.") In summer *nelm*, the white salmon that gave all three settlements their name, swim here against the current from the mouth of Arctic Ocean to spawn. Later in the year, when the river freezes in October and the ice begins to accumulate onshore, *chir* (broad whitefish) come to spawn. In the dead of winter, the ice on the river can reach 2 meters thick, but here the river is shallow, less than two meters deep. People used to sink through the thin ice.

One year before, floods had washed away old houses and the grave of Jochelson's Yukaghir guide Alexander Dolganoff, which had sat on the ground in a small grove on the opposite bank. It is customary for graves to be placed above ground because of the thick hard permafrost, but Dolganoff was buried alone, across the river from Old Nelemnoe and the cemetery. They say it was because he showed Jochelson the *chuchelo* figure whose removal from the tree at the mouth of the Shamanikha River had brought misfortune to the people. This, they say, was probably why Jochelson died destitute in self-imposed exile in America (see Miller 2004b). One year before, the flood waters had risen and washed away Dolganoff's grave, sending his bones into the swollen river to be carried away downstream. His son has been identified in Jochelson's photographs by modern Yukaghirs, and his grandson continued to live with them.

The elders Vakhtin dubbed the "rupture generation" underwent violent erasure of tradition and identity, suffering the displacements of collectivization, purges, famine, and war. Their life histories are suffused with personal memories of events which had a far-reaching impact, historical extensions of colonialism reaching back through three centuries of contact and domination. In deeply personal songs resonating with the collective memory of deprivation and persecution, the narratives of their experience survive the Soviet epoch (see Online Kolyma Documentation Project, Odé 2016a,b; on musical styles and song types, see Sheikin 1996). Three aspects in particular of the Soviet experience are reflected in their songs and narratives: the *kolkhoz* or collective farm, the *Komsomol* (Communist Youth Organization), and the dislocations and deaths of the Great Patriotic War (World War II). The influence of party-run social institutions was overlaid onto, and interwoven with, older cultural strains of Russification with deep folkloric roots going back to the mythology of Old Rus.

Vakhtin has identified three crucial periods during the Soviet epoch in northeast Siberia. During the first, 1920–1927, change came gradually. After Magadan was built as a regional administrative capitol, the prison camps of the vast Stalinist Gulag were hidden throughout Kolyma. As a member of the Committee of the North, Bogoras wrote to Boas around 1930 of their goal to transfer all administration to native languages. But in 1931 the Dalstroi trust brought roads and regional development to Kolyma. The Zyrianka region, built by prisoners, was founded in 1937 as a mining and transport center for coal. The Committee of the North, never highly effective, was soon rendered moot by the hard line emanating from Moscow.

Later, from the Great Patriotic War into the 1950s the principal objective of the state was to develop industry. By the late 1960s, very few villages in the north remained on their original sites. In the late 20th century, in one relatively large port town of 10 000 only 63 were natives, compared to perhaps 40% in smaller towns and villages (Vakhtin 1991). In Nelemnoe, after the Sovkhoz (state farm) was disbanded in 1991, it was replaced by a village cooperative that developed into a self-governing body (Willerslev 2007: 41).

In 1992, members of all the Yukaghir clans gathered in Nelemnoe for the first congress in their history, to unite the people and discuss their future. Speakers emphasized the need to reawaken consciousness, combat alcoholism, teach the Yukaghir language, acquire their own territory, and prioritize environmental preservation and repair. Just surviving in the taiga and the tundra remains a challenge. At the turn of the 20th century, the Kolyma Yukaghir owned no cows. At the turn of the 21st century there were three cows in Nelemnoe, all that were left of two dozen who died when floods killed the hay. The rest were kept alive without heated cow sheds through the Kolyma winter by producing three tons of hay per cow.

Russian 2002 Census figures listed 1509 Yukaghir including 50 Odul speakers and 150 Wadul speakers. By 2009, only an estimated 5–10 Odul speakers and 60–70 Wadul speakers remained, and some linguists have since declared the two languages of Kolyma Yukaghir and tundra Yukaghir "moribund." In 2009 the Tundra Yukaghir project estimated the population of Wadul to be about 700, of whom 50 were mother-tongue speakers. A majority of Wadul Yukaghir now live settled lives in the far northern village Andriushkino in Nizhne Kolymsk. Tundra Yukaghir language is being taught there in school from an early age. In Nelemnoe Jochelson's Memoir, along with drawings and photographs of artifacts from the Jesup collection, have been used as a primary source by teachers to reconstruct and teach traditional designs and stories to schoolchildren (Miller 2004b).

The 20th-century development of the Kolyma River basin negatively impacted indigenous people whose livelihoods depended on fishing. Industrial gold and coal mining operations established in the 1930s, including Dalstroi, depended heavily on prison labor. During the 1950s native people strongly protested the construction of hydroelectric dams. In the early post-Soviet era of the 1990s, several environmental activist groups were formed in Siberia and Kamchatka. One study found nearly 90 percent of indigenous respondents were anxious about pollution and changes in the Kolyma River (Boyakova 2003: 64–65). More recently, in 2018 the government has begun efforts to require environmental preservationist groups in northern Russia who collaborate with international partners to register as foreign agents.

The transition to post-Soviet life in the small hunting, fishing, and gathering society has often been a struggle to persist in the face of shortages of trade goods, food, transportation, and fuel. Yet the Yukaghir activist Gavril Kurilov (Uluro Ado) has maintained that even though they lost their cultural identity during the Soviet period, the October Revolution effectively saved his people from total extinction since they were subsequently supported by the socialist system. He believes the promotion of "culture bases," recognizing the distinctiveness of the *ethnos* and realized partly through the institutions of *kolkhoz* and *Komsomol*, actually kept the thread of continuity alive, making a future Yukaghir renaissance possible. The cultural history of rupture and survival lives on as memory in songs of love, death, and the land transmitted by elders to post-Soviet generations who will come to know their people's past through the melodic poetry of those who lived it.

Through the upheavals of the cataclysmic 20th century, there has remained a continuity of memory and identity. The Yasachnaia River people have been called hare people (*Cholgorodzy*) to distinguish them from other clans. Some consider it a derogatory term used by Russians, while others take pride in the identity. One of the most frequent genres in Yasachnaia Yukaghir folklore involves an old couple and a hare, with countless variants belonging to individual storytellers. An example recorded on wax cylinder in October 1901 by Jochelson was told by Nikolai Sontsev (see English translation on pp. 252–254). In this version, an old woman sends her husband out to hunt for food. He cuts down a willow tree to attract game; eventually a hare comes to eat the willow, but runs away when it sees the old man. Then so many hares come they are "like grains of sand." To punish the old man for felling their tree, they decide to invade his house. The old man beats on his drum as they swarm, then clubs them to death. The old woman scolds him for not leaving her any hares to beat, but there is one last hare hiding under the woodpile. She strikes at it with her kettle hook but misses, just grazing the tip of its ear. This last survivor escapes to become the original progenitor of all living hares, who are its descendants; their black-tipped ears are considered the mark of their ancestor where it was struck by the old woman's kettle hook.

Sontsev's tale can be interpreted as both a comical episode and a metaphorical origin myth for the Yasachnaia Yukaghir people, the *Cholgorodzy* themselves. Once part of a large tribe, then nearly killed off, they are small and few in number; but through cunning and quickness, they have persevered in the face of threatened extinction. At the end of the 20th century, I played a tape copy of the scratchy wax-cylinder recording for elder Akulina Vassilievna Sleptsova. She knew Sontsev's family; the storyteller's grandson, who also had a fine voice, sang for her when she studied Yukaghir children's songs in the local school. Laughing at the words spoken rapidly on the crackling recording, she remarked that while there were many such tales, each is unique:

> This story is primeval, from the longest time ago. Nobody knows these tales; nobody has even heard this one [...]. So this is an old story, almost like it's the first [...]. A Kolymski tale, it truly belongs to Nikolai Sontsev [...]. The family probably sat in the boat and sang [...]. This is pure Yukaghir, without high language. How the words ring out! Only here he speaks quickly: this is a Yukaghir quality. In old times, and even now, Yukaghir people were very joyous. Even when they had no food, they always danced and sang songs. When someone came to the house, even the old women would go down to the club and spend the night. There were young people and old people all together. Actually, I'm astonished it could be like that. Hungry! Yes, without clothes! Hungry children, barefoot children—[I was] barefoot myself, no? People would say, 'What is she dancing and singing for?' It's simply a habit of mine, and has remained so. I myself am amazed at the strength and resilience of the Yukaghir people (personal communication, 1999).

An old metaphorical saying about the Yukaghir holds that "A piece of gold is very small but very precious." Another, more cynical aphorism states that "The Yukaghir are a people sold by weight." As one of the last small hunter-gatherer tribes in the far north, they attract interest from seekers of the exotic and archaic. Akulina Vassilievna worried that she was giving away too much by singing songs and telling the old stories for visiting anthropologists and other latter-day culture hunters. "I'm worse than a fool. Why should I speak? Whenever someone asks me to, I just start telling it to them [...]. Are they telling stories or singing? Then I'll be there. Everyone who passes through asks you to sing, so you sing. They say 'Will you tell a tale?' and I can't refuse. It's too bad for me!" (Miller 2004a: 291–296)

The story of the political purges, repressions, and transformations in the North is still being told. Writer Tekki Odulok (Nikolai Ivanovich Spiridonov, 1906–1938) emerged as a leading intellectual and artist, the first Yukaghir to gain national attention. Although forced to join the Communist Party for show, he was in actuality a powerful advocate for his people and planted the seeds of a nationalist consciousness. As such, he posed a threat to the regime and was executed on false charges of being a Japanese spy. In later years the Kurilov family, especially Gavril (Uluro Ado) and his artist brother Nikolai, has played a key role in the survival and revitalization of Yukaghir culture (see also Odé 2016a,b). A ceremonial arch constructed in Nelemnoe during the 1990s stands as a focal point of ceremonial life and a symbol of perseverance. Jochelson's work, suppressed in the Soviet Union for most of the 20th century, has re-emerged.

Fig. 5 This ceremonial arch, built in the Upper Kolyma settlement of Nelemnoe during the early post-Soviet era of the 1990s, symbolizes the revitalization of Yukaghir tradition for the 21st century. (photo T. Miller)

Reading the ethnographic past in the present raises the question: what kind of story is this Memoir? How should we in the 21st century interpret the ethnographic past of the 19th-century Yukaghir, written over the first third of the 20th century while radical changes took place in Siberia? The Yukaghir's future prospects remain nearly as uncertain as they did more than a century ago. Uluro Ado proposed that if a people loses their land and their language, they are in danger of ceasing to exist as a people. At the turn of the millennium, laws were promoted to protect their land rights, yet it's unclear whether the people are any better off. Meanwhile, through this book Jochelson's work is being used to reconstruct tradition and transmit it to the next generation. Before the elders of the rupture generation died out their children, grandchildren, and great-grandchildren listened carefully to their songs and tales from the past. As folklorist Lyudmila Zhukova (1996b) has remarked, "The old people are dying, but new old people are growing."

References

American Museum of Natural History. Web links to online collections: Division of Anthropology:https://anthro.amnh.org/jesup_collection
https://anthro.amnh.org/jesup_photos
American Philosophical Society (APS). Franz Boas collection. Philadelphia.
Boas, Franz 1905. The Jesup North Pacific Expedition. *Proceedings of the Thirteenth International Congress of Americanists*: 91–100.
Boas, Franz (ed.) 1898–1930. Jesup North Pacific Expedition, Vols. 1–11. *Memoirs of the American Museum of Natural History*. New York: American Museum of Natural History. Leiden: E. J. Brill & Co.
Bogoras, Waldemar 1904–1909. *The Chukchee*. Volume 7 of the Jesup North Pacific Expedition, ed. Franz Boas. Memoirs of the American Museum of Natural History, Vol. 11. 1904 Part 1, the Chukchee: Material Culture. 1907. Part 2, The Chukchee: Religion. 1909. Part 3, the Chukchee: Social Organization. New York: G. E. Stechert and Co. New edition 2017, edited by M. Dürr and E. Kasten. Fürstenberg/Havel: Kulturstiftung Sibirien)
http://www.siberian-studies.org/publications/bogchuk_E.html
Boyakova, Sardana 2003. Traditional Ecological Culture in Yakutia: Transformations in the Twentieth Century. In *Indigenous Ecological Practices and Cultural Traditions in Yakutia: History, Ethnography and Politics*. H. Takakura, Hiroki (ed.), 57–68. Northeast Asian Studies Series 6. Sendai, Japan: Tohoku University Center for Northeast Asian Studies.
Fitzhugh, William W., and Aron Crowell (eds.) 1988. *Crossroads of Continents: Cultures of Siberia and Alaska*. Washington, D.C.: Smithsonian Institution Press.
Forsyth, James 1992. *A History of the Peoples of Siberia: Russia's North Asian Colony*

1581–1990. Cambridge, England: Cambridge University Press.

Jochelson, Waldemar 1910–1926. *The Yukaghir and Yukaghirized Tungus.* Memoirs of the Jesup North Pacific Expedition. Franz Boas, Series Editor. American Museum of Natural History. Leiden: E. J. Brill & Co. (New edition 2018, edited by E. Kasten and M. Dürr. Fürstenberg/Havel: Kulturstiftung Sibirien)
http://www.siberian-studies.org/publications/jochyukaghir_E.html

— 1900. *Materialy po izucheniiu iukagirskogo iazyka i fol'klora, sobrannye v Kolymskom okruge.* St. Peterburg.

— 1905. *Essays on the Grammar of the Yukaghir Language.* Academy of Sciences. Annals March 1905, Bd. XVI, Teil II: 97–152. New York.

— 1908. The Koryak. *The Jesup North Pacific Expedition 6, Memoirs of the American Museum of Natural History* 10, Pt. 1–2. New York. New edition 2016, edited by E. Kasten and M. Dürr. Fürstenberg/Havel: Kulturstiftung Sibirien.

— 1933. The Yakut. In *Anthropological Papers of the American Museum of Natural History,* 37–221. New York: American Museum of Natural History. New edition 2018, edited by M. Dürr and E. Kasten. Fürstenberg/Havel: Kulturstiftung Sibirien.
http://www.siberian-studies.org/publications/jochyakut.html

— 2005. *Iukagiry i Iukagirizovannye Tungusy [The Yukaghir and Yukaghirized Tungus]* (in Russian). With a foreword by Uluro Ado (Gavril Kurilov). Institute for the Problems of the Small Peoples of the North. Novosibirsk: Nauka.

— 2017. *Aus dem Fernen Osten Russlands. Deutschsprachige Schriften (1881–1908).* E. Kasten (ed.). Fürstenberg/Havel: Kulturstiftung Sibirien.
http://www.siberian-studies.org/publications/jochside_E.html

Jochelson-Brodsky, Dina 1906. Zur Topographie des weiblichen Körpers nordostsibirischer Völker. Inaugural-Dissertation. Medizinische Fakultät der Universität Zürich.

Kasten, Erich 2017. Vom politisch Verbannten zum bedeutenden Ethnologen: Waldemar Jochelson und die Sibirjakov-Expedition (1894–1897). In *Waldemar Jochelson. Aus dem Fernen Osten Russlands. Deutschsprachige Schriften (1881–1908).* E. Kasten (ed.), 9–33. Fürstenberg/Havel: Kulturstiftung Sibirien.
http://www.siberian-studies.org/publications/PDF/kasten_jochside.pdf

Kasten, Erich, and Michael Dürr 2016. Jochelson and the Jesup North Pacific Expedition: A New Approch in the Ethnography of the Russian Far East. In *Waldemar Jochelson: The Koryak* (1908). New edition 2016. E. Kasten and M. Dürr (eds.), 9–34. Fürstenberg/Havel: Kulturstiftung Sibirien.
http://www.siberian-studies.org/publications/PDF/jochkoryak_foreword.pdf

Kendall, Laurel, Barbara Mathé, Thomas Ross Miller 1997. *Drawing Shadows to Stone: The Photography of the Jesup North Pacific Expedition, 1897–1902.* New York, Seattle and London: American Museum of Natural History and University of Washington Press.

Kreinovich, E. A. 1979. Iukagirskii Iazyk. *Yazyki Azii i Afriki* (3): 348–369. Moskva.

Krupnik, Igor 1993. *Arctic Adaptations: Native Whalers and Reindeer Herders of Northern Eurasia*. Hanover, New Hampshire and London: University Press of New England.

Krupnik, Igor, and William W. Fitzhugh (eds.) 2001. *Gateways: Exploring the Legacy of the Jesup North Pacific Expedition, 1897–1902*. Washington, D.C.: Arctic Studies Center, National Museum of Natural History, Smithsonian Institution.

Maslova, Elena 2001. *Yukaghir texts*. Tunguso-Sibirica 7. Wiesbaden: Harrassowitz.

Mathé, Barbara, and Thomas R. Miller 2001. Kwazi'nik's Eyes: Vision and Symbol in Boasian Museum Representation. In *Gateways: Exploring the Legacy of the Jesup North Pacific Expedition, 1897–1902*. I. Krupnik and W.W. Fitzhugh (eds.), 106–138. Washington, D.C.: Arctic Studies Center, National Museum of Natural History, Smithsonian Institution.

Miller, Thomas Ross 1999. Mannequins and Spirits: Representation and Resistance of Siberian Shamans. *Anthropology of Consciousness* 10(4): 69–80.

— 2004a. *Songs from the House of the Dead: Sound Shamans, and Collecting in the North Pacific (1900/2000)*. Columbia University doctoral dissertation. Proquest (UMI): Ann Arbor, Michigan.

— 2004b. Object Lessons: Wooden Spirits, Wax Voices, and Collecting the Folk. In *Properties of Culture – Culture as Property. Pathways to* Reform *in Post-Soviet Siberia*, E. Kasten (ed.), 171–201. Berlin: Dietrich Reimer Verlag.
http://www.siberian-studies.org/publications/PDF/cpmiller.pdf

Mitskevich, S. I. 1929. Menerik i emiriachen'e formy isterii v Kolymskom krae [Menerik and Emirchanye, Endemic Forms of Arctic Hysteria in the Kolymsk Country]. *Materialy komissii po izucheniiu Yakutskoi Avtonomnoi Sovetskoi Sotsialisticheskoi Respubliki*, Vypusk 15.

Nikolaeva, Irina 2006. *A Historical Dictionary of Yukaghir*. Berlin: Walter de Gruyter.

Odé, Cecilia (ed.) 2016a. *Il'ia Kurilov: My Life, Songs*. (in Yukaghir, Russian and English). Fürstenberg/Havel: Kulturstiftung Sibirien.
http://www.siberian-studies.org/publications/tyk_E.html

— 2016b. *Akulina Innokent'evna Struchkova: Various Tales, for the Yukaghir Children*. (in Yukaghir, Russian and English). Fürstenberg/Havel: Kulturstiftung Sibirien.
http://www.siberian-studies.org/publications/tys_E.html

Online Kolyma Yukaghir Documentation project. https://www.sgr.fi/yukaghir/

Piispanen, Peter Sauli 2017. *Some Reflections on Late Proto-Yukaghir Reconstructions and Etymologies*. Stockholm: Institutionen för baltiska språk, finska och tyska, Stockholms Universitet.

— 2016. A Prosody-Controlled Semi-Vowel Alternation in Yukaghir. *Journal of Historical Linguistics* 6(2): 247–296.

Sheikin, Yuri Il'ich 1996. *Muzykal'naia kul'tura narodov Severnoi Azii* [Musical cultures of Northern Asian peoples]. Yakutsk: Minsterstvo kul'tury respubliki Sakha (Yakutia).

Slezkine, Yuri 1994. *Arctic Mirrors: Russia and the Small Peoples of the North*. Ithaca, NY and London: Cornell University Press.

Vakhtin, Nikolai 1991. *The Yukaghir Language in Sociolinguistic Perspective*. Steszew: International Institute of Ethnolinguistic and Oriental Studies.

Willerslev, Rane 2010. "Urbanites without a City": Three Generations of Siberian Yukaghir Women. *Acta Boreala* 27(2): 189–207.

— 2007. *Soul Hunters: Hunting, Animism, and Personhood among the Siberian Yukaghirs*. Berkeley: University of California Press.

— 2004. Spirits as 'Ready to Hand': A Phenomenological Analysis of Yukaghir Spiritual Knowledge and Dreaming. *Anthropological Theory* 4(4): 395–418. http://ant.sagepub.com/cgi/content/abstract/4/4/395

Winterschladen, Matthias 2016. Zwischen Revolution und Wissenschaft: Vladimir Iochel'son, Vladimir Bogoraz und die Verflechtung von Wissenschaft und Politik – Ein biographischer Zugang. In *Auf den Spuren der modernen Sozial- und Kulturanthropologie – Die Jesup North Pacific Expedition (1897–1902) im Nordosten Sibiriens*. M. Winterschladen, D. Ordubadi, and D. Dahlmann (eds.), 77–118. Fürstenberg/Havel: Kulturstiftung Sibirien. http://www.siberian-studies.org/publications/PDF/jnpenosibwinterschladen.pdf

Zhukova, Lyudmila 2014. The Odul Folklore: On the Functional Significance of Shamans (trans. Tat'iana Argounova-Low). *Sibirica* 13:2 (Summer): 93–104.

— 1996a. *Odezhda Yukagirov* [Yukaghir Clothing]. Yakutsk: Izdatel'stvo Yakutskii krai.

— 1996b. *Religiia Iukagirov: Iazycheskii Panteon* [Yukaghir Religion: A Linguistic Pantheon]. Yakutsk: Izdatel'stvo yakutskogo gosuniversiteta.

5 WALDEMAR JOCHELSON'S MONOGRAPH *THE YAKUT* AND CONTINUING TRADITIONS OF YSYAKH[1]

Tat'iana Argounova-Low

The beginning

Waldemar Jochelson's monograph *The Yakut* was published in 1933 by The American Museum of Natural History in New York. It is surprising to find out this monumental monograph that contains significant heritage material for the Yakut people, also known as Sakha, was incidental, almost a by-product of the Jesup expedition outputs. It is presumed the monograph is based on data Jochelson collected when participating in two large scientific expeditions, but in reality the collection of data for the monograph started long before.

The collection of data for this volume started in 1888 when Jochelson, a political exile, was sent from the Peter and Paul fortress in St. Petersburg by the Russian Tsarist authorities to Yakutia (Jochelson 1933:197). Here Jochelson would spend nine years, including four years as a prisoner. Like many of his educated and liberally-minded contemporaries, who happened to be in similar situations, Jochelson used such circumstances for studying the culture of the native people living in the area to occupy himself (Vakhtin 2001:79). He was initially sent to Olekminsk and later transferred further to Srednekolymsk, where he immersed himself in the life of the native people from whom he learned the skills of living in the taiga, travelling, fishing and hunting (Ksenofontov 1992:100; Slobodin 2005a:2). In this environment, Jochelson applied his research skills, analytical mind and his writing ability to produce, initially, two papers *The Skoptsi of Olekminsk* (Jochelson 1894) and *Notes on the Population in the Yakut Oblast' in Historic and Geographic Respects* (Jochelson 1895). These works were presented to the Russian Geographical Society and Jochelson was awarded the silver medal of the Society (Slobodin 2005:97). Following these publications, he was invited to take part in the Yakut expedition of the East Siberian branch of the Imperial Geographical Society in 1894–1896, also known as the Sibiriakov (or Sibiryakov) expedition, named after an industrialist and philanthropist who funded the expedition.

In the years Waldemar Jochelson spent in Yakutia, he accumulated abundant material about the native peoples and it is possible that during the Sibiriakov expedition, Jochelson conceived the idea of this separate manuscript dedicated to the Yakut

---

1   This chapter is a slightly abridged version of the foreword to the new edition of Jochelson's *The Yakut* (Jochelson 1933 [2018]).

people. This is apparent from his correspondence to the Russian Geographical Society dated 15 January 1896, where Jochelson reported he "[…] continued conducting measurements and photographing the Yakut, collected more or less full material about the economic situation of the district, economic activities, etc., finally, tried to add to my notes on other issues of the Yakut ethnography." He adds at the end of this reporting letter that "[r]egarding the Yakut, I have the most diverse notes about all aspects of their life" (Sirina and Shinkovoi 2007:353).

However, the material accumulated during Sibiriakov's expedition had to wait for a while, as after this expedition had finished, Jochelson was summoned to participate in another expedition—the Jesup North Pacific in 1897–1902 (see Kasten and Dürr, *this volume*). While working for this expedition Jochelson focused on collecting ethnographic data about the Koryak and the Yukaghir people. But in the process of the Jesup expedition and closer to the end, Jochelson arranged and agreed with Franz Boas the concluding stage of his expedition would be spent among the Yakut people with the purpose of collecting material artifacts. Jochelson feared the culture of the Yakut, who he described as an "interesting tribe", was "disappearing under the influence of climate, Russian contact, and other factors" (Jochelson 1933:197). His task, then, as he recognized it, was to provide a detailed record of specific elements of culture, its rituals, traditions and celebrations. The objects and ethnographic data about the Yakut people collected by Jochelson in the field, although not "an objective of Jesup expedition" as described by Boas (Vakhtin 2001:86), were included in the formidable corpus of data generated by the expedition. Possibly in the process of collecting and organizing the data, it became evident to Jochelson the rich material collected about the Yakut would need to be presented as a separate monograph.

It is most likely that in the process of writing up, Jochelson went back to the collected artifacts which continued to provide him with information. Thus the objects that Jochelson collected: 917 Yakut artifacts, 400 photographs, 225 anthropometric measurements, 20 gypsum masks, 30 phonographic recordings with songs, tales and shamanic rituals, as well as botanical and zoological objects (Ivanov 1999:68), could be considered an integral part of the monograph. Drawings of these objects and high-quality photographs are very important features of the book as well. The black and white photographs taken at various locations are austere and laconic, most of them taken with models in controlled positions, but serve as articulate underpinnings that expand on the descriptive text of Jochelson.

While Waldemar Jochelson was mistaken in his disconsolate prediction about the Yakut culture disappearing, it is due to the scholar's foresight and providence that there is such a rich legacy of objects and ethnographic material held at the American Museum of Natural History (Ivanova-Unarova 2015:2). Importantly, there is a significant volume devoted to Sakha people, their history and culture.

Methods

Involuntary residence and thus an immersion into a different culture gave Jochelson an opportunity to carry out continuous observation and participation. This had resulted in a different kind of qualitative data that was not always obtainable for scholars on a short-term trip (more on his methods, see Kasten, *this volume.*) Jochelson collected information about the Yakut focusing on the historical and geographical data, ethnographic descriptions about dwellings, tools, clothing, food, trades, customs, language and beliefs of the local people. To provide a comprehensive presentation of the region and its environment in his monograph, Jochelson incorporated data related to orography, climate, geography, flora and fauna. He described his pursuits as: "Although my chief objectives were anthropological, I endeavoured to obtain geographical and topographical data, particularly in regions not previously visited. With this end in view I always carried the necessary instruments, compasses, sling thermometers, aneroid barometers, boiling point thermometers, and others, and kept systematic diaries" (Jochelson 1933:66). In this section Jochelson uses a lot of information from other sources, e.g. Wittenburg (1927), but it is obvious from the book he undertook some field trips to remote places to collect the required scientific data. He wrote about climbing mountains matter-of-factly: "according to my travel diary on the eastern slope of the Stanovoi ridge" (ibid.:70). He also mentioned going up 500 meters on the Taigonos Peninsula (currently the Magadan region) to record a type of vegetation (ibid). Jochelson's contribution to the research in fauna has been marked by finding two new species not previously recorded: the Kolyma pike and the Kolyma red-backed mouse that after such discovery was named after Jochelson, *Evotomys Jochelsoni* (ibid.:72).

On ethnographic knowledge and relationship with informants

The anthropological work with indigenous people of that period was often accompanied by a horde of anthropometric data and the photographic images of informants "dressed and undressed, in awkward front and side views, as racial-type data, uncomfortable artifacts of the arrogance of a young science" (Kendall et al. 1997:7). While Jochelson saw himself as a tasked ethnographer and a recorder of various data, it seems for him his informants were not mere models sitting for anthropometric measurements in front of him and his wife, Dina Jochelson-Brodskaia (Kasten and Dürr 2016:19). The native people shared with them the accommodation, food, guided them in their travels, went hunting and fishing, spent leisure time telling jokes and having a good laugh. For Jochelson, having good relationships with the native people was important for work and life. In his letters to Boas he wrote about help he received from local people in various locations, recognizing their indispensable contribution to his work (Ivanova-Unarova 2015:3). He mentioned their names in his letters with an occasional request to send various fishing and hunting gear as a gratitude for their contribution. He acknowledged it would have been impossible to gather such a great collection of objects without the assistance of his friends: "Despite short time that I had to collect the Yakut collection, thanks to my knowledge of the region and my old friends, I guess, this will be the first full ethnographic collection that will leave Yakutsk" (in Ivanov 1999:19). He adds, proudly it seems, he "[…] received 150 items as gifts from my many Sakha friends" (Ivanova-Unarova 2017:89). Indeed, the reference to 'many Sakha friends' demonstrated that Jochelson was not simply an ethnographer and a scholar, but a person with good ties and connections with local people. His considerate attitude to the cultural heritage of the native people, knowledge of the language, and his genuine interest in learning about the native culture earned him respect and deference among the Yakut people in this area.

The structure of the book

Jochelson produced *The Koryak* in 1905 and *The Yukaghir and Yukaghirized Tungus* in 1910. By the time he was putting together the monograph on *The Yakut* he had extensive experience of presenting such rich material and information in a book format. *The Koryak* monograph was a hefty 809 pages and *The Yukaghir* had 458 pages. In comparison with these two volumes *The Yakut*, with only 220 pages, was a much shorter compilation. It nevertheless was aimed at presenting a comprehensive representation of the Yakut people.

The intended broad scope reflected in the structure and wide-ranging aspects of life of the native people are characteristic of the monographs of that period that aimed to present the all-embracing portrayal of the studied peoples. One can easily see parallels between the layout of Jochelson's book and Seroshevskii's[2] serious volume on the Yakut (1896). The structure of the book, again a convention of the time, is similar to the content of *The Yukaghir* and *The Koryak*. This monograph includes important sections on geography, language, anthropology, religion, family and kinship, and material culture. The book opens with history and narratives that go back to the founding legends.

In order to compile a comprehensive coverage in the book and the fullest possible material in various sections, Jochelson built on the works of his predecessors: Fisher, Seroshevskii, Troshchanskii, Berg, Radloff, Pekarskii, Wittenburg, and others. In many sections of the book, Jochelson continues an academic dialogue with these scholars, ethnographers, linguists and natural scientists, who studied the Yakut people prior to him. Such conversations were often presented as a continuous debate or

---

2   Jochelson's spelling is 'Sieroszevski.'

disputation. He wrote, for instance: "His statements concerning the inhabitants of the region are not consistent with the actual facts". And on occasions he was rather categorical: "He believes the Yakut are Mongol and that the Tungus are the aborigines of the country. Actually the Yakut are Turkic. Both tribes are immigrants: The Yakut from the Baikal country and the Tungus from the Amur region, or perhaps from southeastern China" (Jochelson 1933:69). Grounding initial information in the works of his predecessors, Jochelson added new or expanded on the existing knowledge in some sections of the book. What follows are brief highlights of such aspects of knowledge from some sections of the monograph.

Fig. 1, 2 Yakut (Sakha) shaman woman in ceremonial dress, 1902.
Images #1832, 1825. American Museum of Natural History Library.

Two sections of the book *Religion. Pre-Christian Beliefs* and *Shamanism* comprise a logical block on beliefs and their practice and occupy an important place in the book. While the part of the book devoted to the system of beliefs presents the fundamental points succinctly, the following part, *Shamanism,* is remarkable in its detail. Jochelson used the works of his predecessors in this section but a large portion was based on the interviews that Jochelson held in Meginski *ulus* (district), east of the city of Yakutsk, and in Rodchevo village on the Kolyma river, close to Verkhnekolymsk (ibid:116). Jochelson revealed the importance of the shamanic practice and its function through the detailed description of the shaman's dress. Jochelson referred to a Yakut, named Slyeptzov, who sold the shaman dress to him for the museum collection and described the significance of details on the dress. The described shamanic coat served as a transformer—it turned the shaman into a warrior and provided him with an armor to help fight with "hostile shamans and spirits" (ibid.:111). "The fringe around the coat represents feathers", described Jochelson, explaining how the coat turned the shaman into a bird able to fly between many levels of the sky (ibid:118). All details on the shaman's coat are given names in the Yakut language, with an occasional variant in the Tungus, and were dictated by the local people and shamans themselves. The shamanic chants were recorded by Jochelson on his phonograph (ibid:122). From Jochelson's descriptions it is very easy to get a sense the shaman was a very dynamic and mobile figure, who moved and paced all the time on the spot. He also moved in the alternative universe ("the world of spirits") with the help of his drum that appeared to be either a reindeer or a horse, and the drumstick was his whip (ibid.:119). In the related two sections on pottery and metals (blacksmithery and silversmithery) Jochelson analyzed the significant role the smiths played in the Yakut society and commented on the social status of the Yakut blacksmiths, who were ranked as high as a shaman as they were believed to possess supernatural powers. Jochelson makes parallels with the blacksmith practices in Africa and Pamir, making wider connections to explain the phenomena.

In the section *The Family and Kinship,* Jochelson demonstrated very detailed knowledge of the Yakut principles of kinship and provided the reader with the terminology on family ties. The terms are presented as a mini dictionary and are organized in alphabetical order. Most of the terms in this vocabulary are obsolete, but the list serves as more than just a straightforward dictionary. It presents and explains the system of relations between members of the extended family (*Je-usa*, mother's clan or *Aga-usa*, father's clan), as well as values and principles of such organization in the Yakut society. Studying the list, one can learn more about economic relationships between its members, for example "*kulut*—a slave or a servant" (Jochelson 1933:126). The list also contains some rules of behavior, and one such example is the word *kinniti,* described as a "custom of avoidance" by the daughter-in-law. The custom is explained as prohibition of appearing and showing herself or uncovering "her body before the elder male relatives of her husband, particularly her father-in-law" (ibid.:126), thus highlighting modesty, diffidence, and shyness as models of behavior.

The section *Material Culture* includes a significant subsection, *Pottery,* where Jochelson presented the tools used for making clay objects. He pointed out the pottery is an evidence of the southern origin of the Yakut people that could be confirmed by the archaeological findings excavated in the Baikal region (Jochelson 1933:157). While pottery was a very long-term activity of the Yakut, it was of a utilitarian use and never developed into an art form (ibid.:159). Working with metals did turn into an art, as Jochelson demonstrated in a separate subsection on *Metals* (ibid.:163–179). This subsection contains an interesting range of terminology of various metals, tools and products, including the renowned Yakut knives (*bysax*), axe (*sügä*), etc. In this section Jochelson provided a careful description of the objects made of silver. While the Yakut were "mediocre tinsmiths" (ibid.:173), they were excellent blacksmiths and silversmiths, and Jochelson devoted a subsection to the mastery of the Yakut's work with copper and silver.

The subsection *Clothing* contains detailed descriptions of types of dresses, costumes and footwear, well supplemented with drawings and photographs. The section conspicuously lacks descriptions and analysis of the decorative embroidery work which appears in the section on *ysyakh*, written earlier as a separate paper and entitled *The Kumiss Festivals*.

Fig. 3 Yakut bride of prosperous family, 1902.
Image #1773. American Museum of Natural History Library.

Fig. 4 Traditional Sakha costumes at the *ysyakh* festival, 2017. (photo: M. Unarov)

The language section is, as Jochelson admitted, a "brief sketch on the Yakut language" (ibid.:98). This section, predominantly describing the grammar of the Yakut language, is informed by the outstanding work of Böhtlingk, as well as Radloff, Iastremskii, Samoilovich, Pekarskii (ibid.:98–99). While most of this section is built on the works of other scholars, it also highlights Jochelson's outstanding knowledge of spoken Yakut and his great talent as a linguist.

The Kumiss Festivals

This section of the monograph was written by Jochelson as a separate paper for the Boas Anniversary Volume and it occupies a special place in the monograph (Jochelson 1906). The *kumiss*[3] festival, also known as *ysyakh* or *yhyakh*, has always been a major traditional celebration for the Sakha people. There are historical descriptions of this festival written by many explorers and travelers, starting with Ides from his travels in the 17th century with further contributions by Strahlenberg, Messerschmidt, Lindenau, Middendorff and others (Romanova 1994:4–8). The monograph of Seroshevskii on *The Yakut* includes a section about the *ysyakh* with which, undoubtedly, Jochelson was familiar (Seroshevskii 1993 [1896]:445–447). Jochelson's chapter therefore complements the works of his predecessors and fills in several gaps.

Closer to the end of the Jesup expedition and while still up north, Jochelson communicated to Boas his plans of collecting the Yakut material culture objects for the American Museum of Natural History. He decided to go to the *ulus* on the right bank of the Lena River and explained his choice by saying in the eastern ulus "old traditions are preserved better than in western" (Ivanov 1999:67). In order to do so, Jochelson arrived in Yakutsk at the end of April 1902 and, five days later, crossed the Lena River[4] to the Boturusskii *ulus* (Churapcha and Taatta *ulus* presently) where he stayed for three weeks in May (Ivanova-Unarova 2018).

It is apparent from his writing he was in correspondence with his Yakut friends regarding the forthcoming visit and his intention to collect artifacts. In the chapter we read: "I was fortunate enough not only to collect a great number of ancient kumiss vessels in various remote localities, but also to arrange a kumiss festival not far from Yakutsk" (Jochelson 1933:198). While it is not clear what he meant by "to arrange", it is hard to imagine that Jochelson was involved in the organization of the *ysyakh* himself. Zinaida Ivanova-Unarova, who studied Jochelson's archival documents, believes that the *ysyakh* celebration was organized purposefully for Jochelson and in response to his request for assistance (Ivanova-Unarova 2015). We can therefore assume Jochelson

---

3   *Kumiss* is a drink made with slightly fermented mare's milk.
4   At the end of April it becomes impossible to cross the Lena River once the ice starts breaking. Jochelson would have been in a hurry to cross the river. He wrote about it in his letter to Boas five days later (Ivanova-Unarova 2015:3).

meant his visit served as an excuse for organizing a *ysyakh*, confirming the fact *ysyakh* festivals could have been held at different times, not only in the summer (Jochelson 1933:202–203).

The explanation of the significance of the festival is opened with the detailed introduction to the *olonkho,* an epic narrative of the founding legend of the *ysyakh*. This is followed with the description of the main ceremony of the *ysyakh*, the ritual offerings to the gods to thank them for their benevolence. However Jochelson pointed out the celebration was not only about religious significance, it was important for social ties too: "During the summer, in olden times, every rich man arranged a kumiss festival at which all members of the clan assembled and were entertained. Other people, and frequently whole clans, were also invited" (Jochelson 1933:202). Exceptionally hierarchical, the *ysyakh* celebration was a re-confirmation of the social standing, as observed and described by Jochelson precisely: "[...] the boys and girls gave the goblets of sacrificial kumiss to the elder and honored members of the clan, both male and female, who [...] drank from the goblets and passed them on to the less important and the younger people. Behind every honored or aged member of the clan, sat or stood his domestics, less esteemed relatives [...]" (Jochelson 1933:203). However, such hierarchical ladder also inferred some social duties that the honored members of the society had for the poor of their clan and laborers. Indeed, such *ysyakh* celebration was a way to provide some attention and care to them.

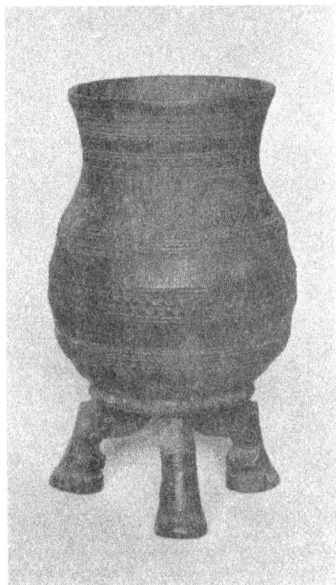

The chapter contains the most detailed description of the important ritual of the *ysyakh*—drinking of the *kumiss*. It also includes the detailed description of the *choron* (carved wooden goblets), utensils and other paraphernalia used specifically for this ritual and the *ysyakh* in general. Jochelson enclosed a detailed explanation of the ornamental motifs on the *choron,* predominantly geometrical straight lines or curved line designs and pointed out people were not depicted on the designs (Jochelson 1933: 209). The section has a record of 17 design patterns used in carving and decorating the wooden dishware and ritual objects. The understanding of ornaments and designs is an important aspect of the contemporary craftsmanship in Sakha where similar research is continued by the local craftsmen (Neustroev 2007).

Fig. 5 Wooden Tripod Goblet used in the *Kumiss* festival (Jochelson 1933:206).

Fig. 6 A ritual of feeding the spirits of the land, 2017. *(*photo: M. Unarov)

Fig. 7 Yakut (Sakha) *Kumiss* feast, 1902.
Image #1795. American Museum of Natural History Library.

On meaning and significance of the book

As a person who immigrated to America, Jochelson turned into an outcast in the Soviet academia and his works were not accepted on the ideological level (Shavrov 1935; Ivanov 1999:68–69; Brandišauskas 2009:176). Only some acknowledged Jochelson's important contribution to the development of the corpus of knowledge about the native people and the Yakut specifically. Gavriil Ksenofontov (1888–1938), a scholar known for his works on the Yakut history and ethnography, wrote about Jochelson's monograph: "Its publication is of great import for the development of scientific Yakutology" (in Ivanova-Unarova 2017:93). Ksenofontov describes Jochelson as a well-known expert on the Yakut: "The latest work by Jochelson *The Yakuts* by its scope is no less significant than *The Yakuts* by V. Seroshevskii and was conceived with the clear purpose to fill the gaps of the latter by writing additionally about the new achievements of the ethnographic knowledge about the Yakut" (Ksenofontov 1992 [1937]:101).

The impact of the Jesup Expedition was far-reaching and helped to shape American anthropology (Darnell 1999:38). Similarly, according to Nikolai Vakhtin, the Jesup expedition helped to shape Russian ethnography and ethnology: "It is a fact the JNPE played an important role in shaping Russian scholarship, especially the development of Russian (and, later, Soviet) research in social anthropology, ethnography, and linguistics of the Siberian Native people [...]. To some extent, to study the roots of Russian northern research after 1897 is to study the history of the JNPE" (Vakhtin 2001:71). The significance of the work produced by Jochelson and his contribution to the anthropological tradition, however, is only now being discovered by the Russian and Sakha audiences, as demonstrated further.

The material collected by Jochelson and photographic images he took are proving to be very important now that the Sakha people are reinstating the importance of the festival. Many elements of this quintessentially Sakha celebration have been lost or heavily modified during the Soviet period. In some places celebrations of the *ysyakh* were not held for decades. There is a huge interest in revitalization of the traditions, re-discovery of the rituals, learning about their meaning and significances. Jochelson's careful description of these rituals serves as a guidebook. The section of the book on the *kumiss* festivals was published in Yakutsk as a separate brochure (Iokhel'son 2015).

In the summer of 2015 my colleagues Alison Brown, Eleanor Peers, and I were working on a project[5] devoted to the *ysyakh* and visited a few *ysyakh* celebrations in the city and other remote places in the region. During that trip we realized the name of Jochelson, his research work in Yakutia and the specific work on *ysyakh* together with the images he took, were well known to many people in Sakha (Yakutia). The

5   We are grateful to the UK AHRC (Arts and Humanities Research Council) for funding the project "Narrative Objects: The Sakha Summer Festival and Cultural Revitalization" which ran from 2015–2018.

section from his book on the *ysyakh* translated into Sakha and Russian was widely distributed. The photographic images taken by Jochelson extensively circulated on the Internet, WhatsApp and other social media. A few times during the interviews, carried out for the project, people would refer either to Jochelson's research or to the images made by him. On one occasion during the *ysyakh* festivities, a friend commenting on the celebration taking place right in front of us, in order to make her

Fig. 8 Yakut dancing at *ysyakh* festival, 1902.
Image #1803. American Museum of Natural History Library.

Fig. 9 *Osuokhai,* a circle dance, brings many people together and can last for hours, 2007.
(photo: M. Unarov)

point clearer, pulled out a cell phone and presented us with an image taken by Jochelson depicting exactly the same aspect, but close up. In a curious juxtaposition of the historical-contemporary and the virtual-actual, one could see two images at once: a black and white image taken by Jochelson on the screen of an electronic gadget and the colorful moving image of the same festival, animated and thriving, 114 years apart.

Conclusion

Jochelson's work *The Yakut* is undeniably a significant contribution to the knowledge about this ethnic group and a key cultural record of the time. It presents an important part in the historic conversation of many scholars engaged in the research devoted to the Yakut over a considerable period.

This monograph, which emerged as an incidental output of the Jesup North Pacific Expedition, today presents a rich legacy for the contemporary Sakha. In the present Republic of Sakha (Yakutia) some people are familiar with the content of the book, which is yet to be fully translated into Sakha and Russian. Some have familiarized themselves with the book through the translated excerpts devoted to the celebration of the *ysyakh*. Some are familiar with the images taken by Jochelson, which seem to live their own life, floating and circulating on the Sakha social media, generating discussion, evoking memories, inspiring new ideas and creative projects.

"The large ornamented wooden kumiss goblets described below are not easily obtained at present. The conical birchbark summer dwelling is no longer used", Jochelson wrote at the opening of the section predicting a decline of the Yakut culture (Jochelson 1933:197). This prediction was to warn about changes in the traditional

Fig. 10 Yakut family and summer house, 1902.
Image #1768. American Museum of Natural History Library.

culture and lifestyle, changes in the purposes and aims of the festival. Jochelson was mistaken in his prophecies of the festival disappearing, yet there might be an element of truth in the sense that the *ysyakh* celebration serves different purposes now. The contemporary *ysyakh* gatherings are about the multifaceted identities of people, the region, and its cultures. They are about political agendas, as well as creativity and ambitions. Jochelson's images and the partially translated text from his book are employed as a point to explore and develop people's own traditions and culture, and, equally, to communicate a sense of proud heritage and a confirmation of authenticity of contemporary celebrations. The existing engagement of people with Jochelson's work and its alignment with contemporary events in Yakutia is a testament to Jochelson's knowledge and the scholastic rigour he applied to document and research Yakut culture.

References

Brandišauskas, Donatas 2009. Waldemar Jochelson – a Prominent Ethnographer of North-Eastern Siberia. *Acta Orientalia Vilnensia* 10 (1–2): 165–179.

Darnell, Regna 1999. Theorizing Americanist Anthropology: Continuities from the B.A.E. to the Boasians. In *Theorizing the Americanist Tradition*. L.P. Valentie and R. Darnell (eds.), 38–51. Toronto: University of Toronto Press.

Iokhel'son, Vladimir I. [Jochelson, Waldemar] 1894. Olekminskie Skoptsy: Istoriko-bytovoi ocherk [The Skoptsi of Olekminsk: A Historical and Lifestyle Account]. *Zhivaia Starina* 2: 161–203.

— 1895. Zametki o naselenii Iakutskoi oblasty v istoriko-geograficheskom otnoshenii [Notes on the Population of the Yakut Oblast' in Historic and Geographic respects]. *Zemlevedenie* 2: 1–37.

— 2015. *Kumysnyi prazdnik i dekorativenoe oformlenie kumysnykh sosudov* [The Kumiss Festival and Decoration of Kumiss Vessels and Their Decoration]. V. Korotov (ed.), V. Solovieva, V. Korotov, N. Pavlov (translation). Yakutsk: SMIK Master.

Ivanov, Vladimir 1999. Vladimir Iokhel'son i ego kniga "Iukagiry i Iukagirizovannye tungusy" [Vladimir Iokhel'son and his book *"The Yukaghir and the Yukaghirized Tungus"*]. *Ilin* 3–4: 18–19.

Ivanova-Unarova, Zinaida I. 2015. Predislovie [Foreword]. In *Kumysnyi prazdnik i dekorativenoe oformlenie kumysnykh sosudov* [V.I. Iokhel'son: The Kumiss Festival and Decoration of Kumiss Vessels and Their Decoration]. V. Korotov (ed.), V. Solovieva, V. Korotov, N. Pavlov (translation), 2–6. Yakutsk: SMIK Master.

— 2017. Sakha (Iakuty) [The Sakha (Yakut)]. In *Material'naia i dukhovnaia kul'tura narodov Iakutii v muzeiakh mira (XVII–nachalo XX vv* [The Material and Spiritual Culture of the Peoples of Yakutia in the Museums of the World (17th–beginning of the 20th centuries]. Vol. 1. Siberian collection in Museums of the USA. Part 1.

American Museum of Natural History, New York. Smithsonian National Museum of Natural History, Washington, D.C. Z.I.. Ivanova-Unarova (ed.), 86–94. Yakutsk: Bichik.

— 2018. Personal electronic communication with the author.

Jochelson, Waldemar [Iokhel'son, Vladimir I.] 1906. Kumiss Festivals of the Yakut and Decoration of Kumiss Vessels. In *Boas Anniversary Volume; Anthropological Papers Written in Honor of Franz Boas, Professor of Anthropology in Columbia University*. B. Laufer and H. Andrews (eds.), 257–271. New York: G. E. Stechert and Co (also in Jochelson 1933a, *The Yakut*. New edition 2018:227–247).

— 1933a. *The Yakut*. Anthropological Papers of the American Museum of Natural History. New York: The American Museum of Natural History. New edition 2018, edited by M. Dürr and E. Kasten. Fürstenberg/Havel: Kulturstiftung Sibirien.

Kasten, Erich, and Michael Dürr 2016. Jochelson and the Jesup North Pacific Expedition: A New Approach in the Ethnography for the Russian Far East. In *W. Jochelson, The Koryak* [1908], new edition 2016. E. Kasten and M. Dürr (eds.), 9–34. Fürstenberg/Havel: Kulturstiftung Sibirien.

Kendall, Laurel, Barbara Mathé, and Thomas Ross Miller with Stanley A. Freed, Ruth S. Freed, and Laila Williamson 1997. *Drawing Shadows to Stone: The Photography of the Jesup North Pacific Expedition, 1897–1902*. New York: American Museum of Natural History.

Krupnik, Igor, and William W. Fitzhugh (eds.) 2001. *Gateways: Exploring the Legacy of the Jesup North Pacific Expedition, 1897–1902*. Washington, D.C.: Arctic Studies Center, National Museum of Natural History, Smithsonian Institution.

Ksenofontov, Gavriil V. 1992 [1937]. *Urangkhai-Sakhalar: Ocherki po dervnei istorii iakutov* [Urangkhai Sakhalar: Essays on the Ancient History of the Yakut]. Yakutsk: National Publishing House.

Neustroev, Boris F. 2007. *Sakha oiuuta-bichige* [The Sakha Design Patterns]. Yakutsk: Bichik.

Romanova, Ekaterina N. 1994. *Iakutskii prazdnik ysyakh: istoki i predstavleniia* [The Yakut Festival Ysyakh: Origins and Ideas]. Novosibirsk: Nauka.

Seroshevskii, Waclaw L. 1993 [1896]. *Iakuty: opyt etnograficheskogo issledovaniia* [The Yakut: An Ethnographic Study]. Moscow: Rosspen.

Shavrov, K.B. 1935. V.I. Iokhel'son [V.I. Jochelson]. *Sovetskaia Etnografiia* 2: 3–15.

Sirina, Anna, and Anatolii Shinkovoi 2007. Neizvestnoe nasledie Sibiriakovskoi (Iakutskoi) ekspeditsii (1894–1896): Pis'ma V.I. Iokhel'sona vo VSOIRGO [Unknown Legacy of the Sibiriakov's (Yakut) Expedition (1894–1896): Letters of V.I. Jochelson to the Siberian Branch of the Russian Geographic Society]. *Rasy i Narody. Ezhegodnik* 33: 331–368.

Slobodin, Sergei B. 2005. Spisok rabot Vladimira Il'icha Iokhel'sona [List of works by Vladimir Il'ich Jochelson]. *Etnograficheskoe Obozrenie Online*. http://journal.iea.ras.ru/online/works/jochelson.pdf. Accessed 16 December, 2017.

— 2005a. Vydaiushchiisia issledovatel' severnykh narodov (k 150-letiiu so dnia rozhdeniia V.I. Iokhel'sona [A Prominent Researcher of the Northern Peoples (to the
150th anniversary of V.I. Jochelson)]. *Etnograficheskoe Obozrenie* 5: 96–115.

Vakhtin, Nikolai 2001. Franz Boas and the Shaping of the Jesup Expedition Siberian
Research, 1895–1900. In *Gateways: Exploring the Legacy of the Jesup North Pacific
Expedition, 1897–1902*. I. Krupnik and W.W. Fitzhugh (eds.), 71–89. Washington,
D.C.: Arctic Studies Center, National Museum of Natural History, Smithsonian
Institution.

Wittenburg, Pavel (ed.) 1927. *Iakutiia* [Yakutia]. Leningrad: Academy of Sciences.

6 WALDEMAR BOGORAS AND THE CHUKCHEE: A MAESTRO AND A CLASSICAL ETHNOGRAPHY¹

Igor Krupnik

Waldemar Bogoras, known in Russian as Vladimir Germanovich Bogoraz or under his pen-name 'Tan-Bogoraz' (1865–1936), was a monumental figure and one of the founding fathers of Russian, and later Soviet, Siberian ethnography. His life story and his many contributions to science, anthropological research and training in Russia, and government policies toward Siberian indigenous people have been related many times (see 'Sources'). *The Chukchee,* his masterpiece of almost 750 pages, was the main outcome of his two formative periods of fieldwork in Siberia, in 1895–1897 and 1900–1901. This work published in three parts in 1904–1909 in the proceedings of the Jesup North Pacific Expedition (hereafter JNPE) by the American Museum of Natural History (hereafter AMNH) in New York soon became a 20th-century ethnographic 'classic' and mandatory reading for many students in anthropology.

Despite its universal acclaim among Russian Siberian specialists and indigenous readers, Bogoras's masterpiece was never thoroughly examined for an English-reading audience. This chapter aims to introduce the life of Bogoras and the story of *The Chukchee* to a new generation of readers. It also seeks to provide much-needed details and additional sources for those, who might become interested in Bogoras, Siberian ethnography, the history of Northern anthropology, and the status of people surveyed by Bogoras more than 100 years ago.

Fig. 1 Waldemar Bogoras, 1900.
Detail from image #338343,
American Museum of Natural History Library.

---

1   This chapter was also published as the foreword to the new edition of Bogoras's *The Chukchee* (Bogoras 1907–1909 [2017]). Here, I keep the original spelling, *The Chukchee,* when referring to Bogoras's publication in the Jesup North Pacific Expedition and citing earlier correspondence of the era. A modern version of the name, 'Chukchi,' is used in all other cases throughout the text. In a similar way, I use the established English version of Bogoras's name ('Waldemar Bogoras') in the text but apply its Cyrillic version ('Vladimir Bogoraz') when citing Russian sources.

Bogoras's Brief Biography

Waldemar Bogoras was born Natan Mendelevich Bogoraz on April 15, 1865,[2] in a Jewish merchant family in the town of Ovruch in today's western Ukraine (then, the Volyn' Province of the Russian Empire). Soon after his birth, the family moved to the port city of Taganrog on the Sea of Azov. In contrast to the backwater Ovruch, Taganrog was more cosmopolitan port city frequented by foreign ships, with the stores of Greek, Italian, and French merchants. It was also home to Russian-speaking middle class and good Russian educational institutions. After graduating from the Taganrog gymnasium (eight-year classical high-school), Bogoras entered St. Petersburg University in 1880, beginning his studies in the Department of Physics and Mathematics and later switching to law.

From his earliest days at the university Bogoras participated in informal student groups studying Marxism, and he later joined socialist-leaning underground organization called the People's Freedom (*Narodnaia volia*). In 1882 he was arrested for his anti-government activities, discharged from the university, and sent back to Taganrog. With barely two years of university behind him and few prospects for a future career, he became a professional 'revolutionary agitator.' He participated in a series of underground actions initiated by the People's Freedom Party until he was arrested again in November 1886. He spent two and a half years in solitary confinement and was sentenced to a ten-year exile in the arctic Kolyma region of northeastern Siberia, where he lived from 1889 until 1898.[3]

Bogoras spent the first years of his Siberian exile in the small town of Srednekolymsk (population 450) on the Kolyma River, at 67° 10′ N, six time zones away from central Russia. Srednekolymsk had a mixed population of Russian Siberian peasants, Cossacks, some settled indigenous families, and scores of exiled anti-government activists—Russians, Poles, and Jews. According to Bogoras's unpublished autobiography (Kolonteeva 1991:13; Mikhailova 2004:98–99), he soon started visiting nearby camps of Native herders and fishermen, as well as recording Russian Siberian lore popular among the Russian residents of the Kolyma River valley. He also began writing poetry. His first literary piece, a short story called "Lame," was published in 1896. In the same year, three Kolyma Russian epics (*bylinas*) from Bogoras's much larger collection of Russian lore appeared in the Russian ethnographic journal *Etnograficheskoe obozrenie* in St. Petersburg (Bogoras 1896).

---

2   The exact date of Bogoras's birth is unknown; he later acknowledged that his father helped him change the date in his personal papers so the boy could enter Russian high-school (gymnasium) at the earliest age possible and then apply to university at age 15 (!). The date of April 15, 1865, is according to the Julian calendar then used in Russia; the date according to the European (Gregorian) calendar is April 27, 1865.

3   For the most detailed coverage of Bogoras's early life, see Mikhailova 2004:95–99.

Bogoras's transformation from an underground political activist into a self-taught ethnographer of Siberian aboriginal people has been thoroughly covered elsewhere (Kan 2006; 2009b; Mikhailova 2004; Sirina 2010; Vakhtin 2001; Kasten, *this volume*). Many of his peers, including Waldemar Jochelson and Lev Shternberg, followed the same transition (see Kan 2009b; Kasten and Dürr 2016b). Unlike Jochelson and Shternberg, however, who upon their return from Siberian exile pursued strict academic careers, Bogoras remained active in politics throughout his life. Shortly after the Bolshevik Revolution of 1917 in Russia, he devoted his immense energy and political standing to developing new Communist government policy and institutions in support of Russian indigenous peoples.

First Fieldwork: Kolyma Area, 1895–1898

Bogoras's entry into the field of Northern ethnography (anthropology) was initiated by another, much older former political exile, Dmitrii Klements (1848–1914), who was by that time an established scholar and executive secretary of the East-Siberian Division of the Russian Geographical Society (RGS). Klements followed on a generous proposal by a Siberian merchant, goldmine owner, and philanthropist, Innokentii Sibiriakov (1860–1901), to finance a three-year survey of the sparsely populated Yakutsk Province of northeastern Russia. A vast area of 3.5 million square kilometers, Yakutsk Province contained a quarter of Russia's Arctic coast and abounded in minerals, furs, and fish but was remarkably short of educated people. As he planned the Sibiriakov Expedition (1895–1897), Klements successfully lobbied the authorities to let him recruit exiled political 'criminals' as field workers in their respective residence areas. Out of 26 members of the expedition, 15 were current or former political exiles, including Bogoras, Waldemar Jochelson, and Klements himself. Bogoras's task during the expedition was to survey the communities of Russian old-settlers in the Kolyma River valley and two local indigenous groups—the Chukchi and the Even, a Tungus-speaking group then known as the 'Lamoot' (Sirina 2010).

According to Bogoras's report on his work for the Sibiriakov Expedition (Bogoras 1899), between February 1895 and October 1897, he covered more than 13,000 km on dog- and reindeer-sleds, boats, and horseback (Fig. 1) and surveyed the lower reaches of the Kolyma River and its eastern tributaries populated by the Reindeer Chukchi and Even. After a long struggle to communicate with the Natives through local interpreters, he became fluent in the Chukchi language and partly fluent in the Even language. His new language skills allowed him to travel on his own and made it possible for him as well to collect language and folklore materials on two aboriginal nations that remained poorly known to scholars and Russian authorities.

Altogether, Bogoras collected more than 200 Chukchi folklore texts, 35 Even texts, and more than 200 texts recorded from the Russian old-settlers (some going back to

Fig. 2 Bogoras in the Kolyma camp.
Image #22402, American Museum of Natural History Library.

the 17th century; see Kolesnitskaia 1971). He kept detailed diaries, compiled preliminary lexicons, and took numerous photographs (currently preserved at the AMNH
in New York). He also learned how to talk, travel, and live with his Native assistants
and hosts. When the funding for the Sibiriakov Expedition expired in 1897, Klements
helped him enlist as a local census taker for the first Russian Population Census of
1897 so that he could continue his fieldwork. This experience was invaluable in making Bogoras an acknowledged expert on the Chukchi people and their home area in
the Kolyma River basin.

Upon completing his surveys in the fall of 1897, Bogoras was allowed to move to
the town of Yakutsk, the administrative hub of the Yakutsk Province, to process his
field records (Raizman 1967:6). In October 1898, he delivered a major presentation
at the headquarters of the East-Siberian Branch of the Russian Geographical Society
in Irkutsk, summarizing his three years of research on the Chukchi. The news of his
successful studies spread rapidly. Impressed by the value of his materials, a group of
members of the Russian Academy of Sciences lobbied the Russian Ministry of Interior
to drop Bogoras's residence restrictions after he completed his 10-year sentence and
to let him return to St. Petersburg 'on a temporary residence permit.' In January 1899
Bogoras arrived in St. Petersburg to continue his work on the Chukchi ethnographic
collections and his language and folklore data (Mikhailova 2004:104–106; Raizman

1967:6). In a single year, he published eight papers in Russian academic journals, produced two books, including a 450-page collection of Chukchi folk tales (Bogoras 1900), and gave public talks to various Russian academic societies. Little did he know that he was soon to travel to Siberia again by his own choice, for his second major period of fieldwork among the Chukchi.

Second Fieldwork: Jesup North Pacific Expedition, 1900–1901

Bogoras was still trekking among the Chukchi herding camps above the Arctic Circle for the Sibiriakov Expedition when a new research program unfolded thousands of miles away at the AMNH in New York. In 1896 Franz Boas, the new assistant curator in the Anthropology Department, lobbied his boss, Frederic W. Putnam, and later the museum director, Morris K. Jesup, to launch a new research and collection venture that Boas called the 'North Pacific Expedition' (Krupnik and Freed 2004; Vakhtin 2001). Boas envisioned a major study on both sides of the North Pacific, in Siberia as well as in Canada and Alaska, to explore cultural relations ('affinities') between the Native people of Northeast Asia and Northwest North America. In 1897 Jesup agreed to finance the entire venture, which was promptly named 'the Jesup North Pacific Expedition' (JNPE).

The JNPE lasted for six years, from 1897 to 1902. Six crews working on two continents eventually surveyed 17 Native nations on the American Northwest Coast and 10 nations in Siberia (Krupnik and Vakhtin 2003:17). Results of the JNPE were briefly summarized by Boas (Boas 1903; also Boas 1910/2001) but mainly appeared in the 11-volume *The Jesup North Pacific Expedition* series published by AMNH in 1897–1930. 100 years later they were revisited in a string of publications under the so-called 'Jesup-2' initiative (Cole 1999, 2001; Krupnik and Fitzhugh 2001; Kendall and Krupnik 2003; Kan 2009b). Several recent papers have explored the Russian portion of the Jesup Expedition and Bogoras's engagement in JNPE in particular (Vakhtin 2001; Mikhailova 2004; Kan 2006; 2009b; Freed 2012; Shentalinskaia 2015). When the first candidate that Boas sought for his planned northeast Siberian fieldwork, a young Austrian scientist named Erwin von Zach, withdrew (Cole 2001:37; Vakhtin 2001:76), Boas contacted his colleague in Russia, Vasilii V. Radloff (1837–1918), then director of the Museum of Anthropology and Ethnology in St. Petersburg. He asked for a 'young man' eager to spend a year or two in northeast Siberia "studying the customs, manners, languages, and physical characteristics of that district" (Vakhtin 2001:77).

Radloff quickly recommended " [...] a gentleman willing to take part in your expedition, a Mr. Jochelson, who has just returned from an expedition to the Yukaghirs and among whom he has lived for two and a half years" (Radloff to Boas, 23 February 1898, AMNH-DA; see Vakhtin 2001:77). Radloff diplomatically omitted that "Mr. Jochelson" was a former political 'criminal,' then 43 years old, who had returned from

Siberia after a 10-year exile. Radloff added that, for the study of the Chukchi people, Jochelson enthusiastically advocated "a friend of his, a Mr. Bogoraz, who has lived two years among them and knows their language. It is my [Radloff's] opinion that you would do well to secure the services of these two gentlemen" (ibid.). To Radloff's credit, he similarly did not say that Jochelson's 'friend' was another 'political criminal,' still serving his exile sentence in northern Siberia. Only when Bogoras returned to St. Petersburg in January 1899 did he and Jochelson started corresponding with Boas, and the plans for the north Siberian portion of the JNPE began to take shape (Vakhtin 2001:82–85).[4]

After much negotiation, Bogoras and Jochelson arrived in New York in late February 1900, received their instructions from Boas, and signed their contracts with Jesup on behalf of the AMNH. In late March 1900 they set out for San Francisco, where they boarded a steamer for Nagasaki and eventually for Vladivostok, their future logistical hub.

The two men had to lead two small crews that were supposed to work independently several thousand kilometers apart. Jochelson, the official leader of the JNPE's joint 'East Siberian party,' could rely on his wife, medical student Dina Jochelson Brodsky (1862–1941), the young American zoologist Norman Buxton from AMNH, and a Russian student assistant, Alexander Axelrod. Bogoras's team originally consisted of him and his wife, Sof'ia Volkova Bogoras (ca. 1870–1921), whom Bogoras married during his exile years in Srednekolymsk (Mikhailova 2004; 2016). Eventually, both Buxton and Axelrod joined Bogoras's party, while Bogoras spent two months with the Jochelsons studying the Reindeer Koryak.

In Vladivostok Bogoras and Jochelson had to wait for several weeks until Dina Brodsky, Sof'ia Bogoras, and Axelrod joined them. Eventually they parted ways; the Bogorases boarded a Russian steamer for Petropavlovsk on June 14. A month later, on July 18, 1900, they arrived at their destination, a small Russian administrative and trade station called Mariinski Post at the mouth of the Anadyr River, near today's city of Anadyr (Fig. 3).

For the next thirteen months that Bogoras spent in northeast Siberia (July 1900–August 1901), he was mostly on the move, traveling by dog- and reindeer-sled and skin boat. Within a year he surveyed an area stretching from the Bering Strait to the Sea of Okhotsk and the Kamchatka Peninsula, a distance roughly equal to the round trip from the Arctic coast of North America to British Columbia (Krupnik 1996:40). To anyone familiar with this rugged terrain, Bogoras's mobility under the traveling conditions of his era is nothing short of staggering.

Upon arriving at Mariinski Post, the Bogorases mostly stayed at or near the station for two months, with a few trips to the nearby Chukchi herding camps, where Bogoras

---

4   By that time, two JNPE researchers—Berthold Laufer and Gerard Fowke—were already working on the Sakhalin Island and in the Lower Amur River area (Cole 2001:36–37).

Fig. 3 Novo-Mariinsk. Image #2347, American Museum of Natural History Library.

Fig. 4 Street in the village of Markovo.
Image #4104, American Museum of Natural History Library.

made his first ethnographic collections for AMNH. As soon as snow hit the ground in mid-October, they moved to the Russian village of Markovo, the main economic and administrative hub of the Anadyr River valley (Fig. 4). A few days later, Bogoras left on another journey to the Koryak village of Kamenskoe on the Sea of Okhotsk in north Kamchatka, where he joined the Jochelsons' winter camp on November 20,

Fig. 5 Bogoras prepares for his sled trip to Ungaziq.
Image #2421, American Museum of Natural History Library.

Fig. 6 Bogoras and his party (summer 1901).
Image #11117, American Museum of Natural History Library.

Fig. 7 Gambell, St. Lawrence Island.
Image #6137, American Museum of Natural History Library.

Fig. 8 Scene in Ungaziq (Indian Point), June 1901.
Image #2563, American Museum of Natural History Library.

1900. He stayed with the Jochelsons and worked with them for a few weeks collecting folklore and ethnographic data among the nearby Reindeer and Coastal Koryak.

In late December 1900, Bogoras once again parted from the Jochelsons (not to see them again until two years later) and went on a two-month survey of the southern Koryak and Itelmen camps across north Kamchatka Peninsula. He visited Native villages of Amanino on January 27–28, 1901, Napana on January 30–February 2; Kavran, Utkholok, Khairiusovo, and Sedanka on February 10–15; and Tigil on February 15–16. He then crossed the Kamchatka Peninsula and reached the Maritime Koryak village of Karaga on the Bering Sea coast by March 4, 1901. From Karaga he returned to Mariinski Post on March 26 via several Koryak and Kerek coastal communities. He was sick and needed time for recovery. Yet barely four weeks later, on April 21, 1901, he left on another long dogsled journey (Fig. 5) from Mariinski Post to the Siberian Yupik village of Ungaziq at Cape Chaplin, accompanied by Axelrod, five Native guides, and a Russian Cossack (Fig. 6). He stayed there for a month (until June 13), during which time he made a short boat trip to nearby St. Lawrence Island, across the Russian-U.S. border. He spent no more than three to four weeks in any of those places.

From Ungaziq, Bogoras returned to Mariinski Post after a four-week trip in an Eskimo skin boat loaded with his field crew, nine dogs, and all of the collections he had acquired. As he wrote to Boas from Vladivostok:

> By good chance, we bought and repaired a large canoe [skin boat – I.K.] and set out for the south [on] June 20th. We were seven of us, Mr. Axelrod and me, one Cossack, three men of Markovo and a Chukchee boy of 16, who assisted Mr. Axelrod as some kind of translator. […] The task was harder than I supposed. This part of sea is very rough and landing places or harbours are scarce […] Two of my improvised crew got seasick and were of no use through the whole journey. Nevertheless, we reached the mouth of Anadyr in 24 days on July 13. (Bogoras to Boas, September 11, 1901; cited in Freed 2012:359)

They had a month to pack the collections (Fig. 9 and 10), before boarding a Russian mail steamer for the return voyage to Vladivostok, from where they traveled to St. Petersburg by train across Siberia.

A seasoned traveler and a man of great energy and physical stamina, Bogoras suffered enormous physical hardship on his yearlong trek. He was seriously sick during a portion of his travels and after his return from fieldwork. Bogoras hardly exaggerated his dire traveling conditions in a letter to Boas in April 1901:

> My journey from the mouth of the Anadyr River through the Gizhiga district to Kamchatka and a long way [back – I.K.] along the sea coast to Anadyr took me five months. During that time I made 4,000 miles with dogs. A considerable part of my way was not made till now by any civilized man. Our journey went through an unpeopled country where we could not find any guide

and had to find our way being guided by the sun and following the rivers. I returned in a very poor state of health. There were a few days when I almost thought I will not be able to reach Anadyr at all (Bogoras to Boas, 1901; see Krupnik 1996:38).

His complete physical recovery took several months after he returned to St. Petersburg. For more than half a year, he was unable to travel to New York to process his field notes and collections at AMNH, or even to stand much physical exercise (Kuz'mina 1993).

The outcomes of his JNPE fieldwork—in terms of ethnological collections, photographs, folklore text, and song recordings—were monumental. Boas proudly cited Bogoras's report in his summary paper on the results of the Jesup Expedition:

> The results of this [Bogoras's – I.K.] work are studies of the ethnography and anthropology of the Chukchee and Asiatic Eskimo, and partly of the Kamchadal and of the Pacific Koryak. These studies are illustrated by extensive collections embracing 5,000 ethnographical objects, 33 plaster casts of faces, 75 skulls and archaeological specimens from abandoned village sites and from the graves. Other material obtained includes 300 tales and traditions, 150 texts in the Chukchee, Koryak, Kamchadal, and Eskimo languages, 95 phonographic records, and measurements of 860 individuals. I also made a zoological collection and kept a meteorological journal during the whole time of my field-work (Boas 1903:115; Krupnik 1996:39).

To that list, we should add almost 700 photographs, now stored at the AMNH in New York, and several dozen field notebooks, now at the Archives of the Russian Academy of Sciences in St. Petersburg. Though Bogoras did not procure all of these items himself (Shentalinskaia 2012, 2015), his remarkable productivity as a field ethnographer and collector was undisputed. Bogoras also took over the collection of the linguistic portion of Jochelson's field materials among the Koryak (at least checking them, as Jochelson himself acknowledged; see Kasten and Dürr 2016:18–19) and recorded language and folklore texts among the Kamchadal (today's *Itelmen* of Kamchatka). His one year of work for the Jesup Expedition eventually resulted in eight monographs: a three-part ethnography of the Chukchi (Bogoras 1904–1909); a volume of Chukchi mythology (Bogoras 1910; Dürr and Kasten 2016); and four volumes on the folklore and languages of other aboriginal Siberian nations: Yupik Eskimo, Koryak, and Russian Creoles (Bogoras 1913; 1917; 1918; 1949); as well as in scores of papers (see list in Krupnik 2001). According to one recent evaluation, no modern anthropologist has ever collected such a diversity of data (Freed et al. 1988:20). By all accounts, Bogoras made an outstanding contribution to the success of the Jesup Expedition and to Siberian anthropology in general.

Fig. 9 Waldemar and Sof'ia Bogoras with the JNPE collections.
Image #1380, American Museum of Natural History Library.

Fig. 10 Bogoras and JNPE collections in Novo-Mariinsk.
Image #22332, American Museum of Natural History Library.

Writing *The Chukchee*

Under their contract with Boas and AMNH, Bogoras and Jochelson were supposed to arrive in New York after completing their fieldwork to process their collections and to write their respective contributions to the JNPE proceedings. Because Bogoras was sick upon his return from Siberia, he had to delay his trip by several months. He arrived in New York accompanied by his wife on April 17, 1902 (Freed 2012:359; Mikhailova 2016:114–115). There he immediately jumped into Boas's operation cataloguing the JNPE collections and the publication of its materials. Waldemar and Dina Jochelson, the last JNPE members to return from the field in spring 1902, joined Bogoras in New York six months later, in November 1902.

Living on a modest AMNH stipend, Bogoras spent a year and half in New York sorting his immense collections of almost 5,000 ethnographic objects, field notes, and photographs. He helped Boas stage a few temporary display cases at AMNH featuring Chukchi clothing and home life (Anonymous 1904a; 1904b)—the precursors of the permanent AMNH Siberian exhibits, still on display some 110 years later. With Boas's assistance, he published two papers based on his Chukchi materials in the *American Anthropologist*, the only professional anthropological journal in the United States at that time (Bogoras 1901, 1902). He started writing a major novel in Russian titled *Eight Tribes* (*Vosem' plemen*), in which he used literary fiction to introduce some of his ethnographic data. But first and foremost, he worked on the chapters for *The Chukchee*, his prime contribution to the JNPE publication series.

Unlike Jochelson and Shternberg, another Russian exile anthropologist whom Boas commissioned to write for the JNPE series (Kan 2001; 2009b), Bogoras had a solid command of English, which he had taught himself during his imprisonment in Russia and his exile in Siberia. It is unclear, however, whether he started writing *The Chukchee* in English, as he claimed years later in its Russian translation. Most certainly, his writing (or translation?) for the JNPE was facilitated by Alexander Goldenweiser (1880–1940), a Russian-Jewish student of Boas at Columbia University, originally from Kiev, who also translated Jochelson's volumes for the JNPE series (Kan 2009a). One way or the other, Bogoras made substantial progress on the first section of *The Chukchee*, 'Material Culture,' which reached almost 300 pages. In late 1903, Bogoras submitted it as Part 1 of his contribution to the JNPE proceedings series (Bogoras 1904). And in fall 1903, after a year and a half at the AMNH, the Bogorases left New York.

Of utmost personal importance to Bogoras was his friendship with Boas and the intellectual bond the two men forged during Bogoras's U.S. sojourn in 1902–1903. The two families even vacationed together in summer 1903 (Cole 2001:41; Mikhailova 2004:112). Bogoras, who had no professional anthropological training, was an avid student, and he came under the strong influence of Boas's personality and his scholarly method of historical particularism, which Bogoras nonetheless never fully accepted (Kan 2006:35). Boas in turn viewed Bogoras positively, as "a man of fine sensitivity, intelligence, and enthusiasm" (Cole 2001:41).

As Bogoras's (and Jochelson's) JNPE funding was running out, Boas had to switch to payments of $150 for each submitted chapter. That meant that Bogoras could write his JNPE contributions anywhere he liked. The Bogorases spent most of 1904 in Europe, where Bogoras attended the 14th International Congress of Americanists in Stuttgart, Germany, that summer. There he delivered a paper on Chukchi religious ideas (Bogoras 1906) and once again met with Boas, as well as with Jochelson and Shternberg. The 1904 paper on Chukchi religious ideas indicated that he was already working on his second issue of the JNPE proceedings on Chukchi religion. When he returned to Russia in September 1904, he was confident he could complete his obligations to Boas and AMNH. Events transpired, however, to put the work on hold for two more years.

The story of Bogoras's involvement in the first Russian Revolution of 1905–1907, of his arrest in November 1905, and of Boas's effort to rescue him and his precious Chukchi manuscripts from prison is well covered in the literature (Cole 2001:41–42; Freed 2012:361–370; Mikhailova 2004:113). As Bogoras jumped wholeheartedly into political activism in Russia, his commitment to Boas and to the AMNH weakened. The famous exchange of letters between him and Boas in April 1905 is a case study in how political activism may interfere with the most careful professional plans. Upon Boas's reminder that no new chapters on the Chukchi had been sent to New York for months, Bogoras responded:

> I am afraid you are right and I feel myself guilty of much neglect to all dear friends in America. But you will understand that an epoch like this happens only once in many centuries for every state and nation and we feel ourselves torn away with the current even against our will.
>
> My work on sociology of the Chukchee [evidently, on the chapters on Social Organization – I.K.] is going on but slowly […] Still I am doing something but little (Bogoras to Boas, April 6, 1905, AMNH, Dept. of Anthropology; cited in Freed 2012:362).

To that message, Boas offered his famous rebuke:

> I fully appreciate the excitement of the present time, and the difficulty in concentrating yourself on scientific work; but if events like the present happen only once in a century, an investigation by Mr. Bogoras of the Chukchee happens only once in eternity, and I think you owe it to science to give us the results of your studies (Boas to Bogoras, April 22, 1905, ibid.; Freed 2012:362–363).

This exchange was followed by Bogoras's arrest on November 27, 1905, in Moscow. He was imprisoned for two weeks and subsequently released, after which the Bogorases, with all the precious field papers, moved safely to Finland, a much quieter place. Bogoras resumed his writing and eventually submitted the missing chapters on Chukchi religion for another issue of the JNPE proceedings (Bogoras 1907) and later delivered the third section on Chukchi social organization (Bogoras 1909). He continued sending his writings to Boas for an issue on Chukchi mythology (Bogoras 1910) and one on Asiatic Eskimo lore (Bogoras 1913). He even offered to write an essay on the Kamchadal (Itelmen) for another Siberian volume in the JNPE series, but that essay never materialized (Krupnik 2001:300).

After Bogoras's death, his massive stock of field notes, language, and folklore data collected during the JNPE years was deposited in the archives of the Russian Academy of Sciences and of the Institute of Oriental Studies in St. Petersburg (Krupnik 2001:307–308). After Bogoras had fulfilled his obligation to Boas and the AMNH, Boas continued helping his Russian colleague publish his materials in the United States for almost 20 years. Collaboration, correspondence, and friendship between the two great men lasted until Bogoras's death in 1936 (Kan 2006).

Bogoras after *The Chukchee*

When Bogoras's last contribution to the JNPE series was released in 1913, he was almost 50 years old. A prolific novelist and publicist, an author of several internationally acclaimed anthropological volumes and papers, and a close partner of Boas, he had no formal training, no scholarly degree or professional position, and little acceptance in Russian academic circles. Like most of Russia's liberal intellectuals, he spent the rest of the decade marked by World War I, two Russian revolutions, and the Civil War in personal and political turmoil, isolation, and dire physical suffering. Boas did his best to support his Russian friends from abroad by offering them money, orders for new papers, and American venues to publish them (Bogoras 1917; 1918; 1922;—see Kan 2001; 2006; 2009b). Yet it was Lev Shternberg, a fellow former political activist and Siberian exile, who helped Bogoras reconstitute his professional standing after Russia's Bolshevik Revolution of 1917 (a revolution neither of them initially accepted).

The story of Shternberg and Bogoras's joint crusade to build a vibrant system of scholarly research, teaching in Northern anthropology, and training cadres for Russia's Arctic minority people has been told several times (Gagen-Torn 1975; Kan 2009b; Liarskaia 2016, see also *this volume*; Vakhtin 2016a; 2016b). It embraced scores of overlapping institutions, short-term initiatives, and ad hoc ventures, and thus required energy and imagination. Bogoras had plenty of both; he was also exceptionally resourceful. Unlike his friend Shternberg, Bogoras enjoyed political power and was comfortable sitting on many committees and being among government bureaucrats. He was one of the founding members in 1924 of the 'Committee on the North' (its full name was 'Committee on Assistance to the Peoples of the Northern Borderlands,' or *Komitet sodeistviia narodnostiam severnykh okrain*, in Russian) under the

Presidium of the Soviet Central Executive Committee, the main legislative body in Communist Russia (Vakhtin 1994). He served as an expert to the Soviet Government's Department on Nationalities and was on many administrative committees dealing with the peoples of the Arctic regions of Russia. He loved wearing many hats, and he skillfully used his new academic and political power to the advantage of his pet projects, students, and public venues, as well as for self-promotion.

Fig. 11 Shternberg, Boas, and Bogoras at the 21st International Congress of Americanists, 1924. Peter the Great Museum of Anthropology and Ethnography/Kunstkamera, St. Petersburg, #И-1371-4. (A slightly different photo is also available in the collection of the American Philosophical Society.)

The period between 1924 and 1932 marked the second peak of Bogoras's scientific productivity and international stature. He published broadly on many general issues, such as the origins of polar cultures, the peopling of North America and the Arctic, the geographic distribution of cultural elements, and the origin of shamanism (Bogoras 1925a; 1925b; 1926; 1928a; 1928b; 1929a). He renewed his communication with Boas and sent him several papers for publication in America. He also traveled widely.[5] He attended the 21st International Congress of Americanists in the Hague

5   In 1924–1927, Bogoras reportedly tried to lure his old friends, Waldemar Jochelson and Dina Jochelson Brodsky, who had emigrated to the United States in 1922, to return to Russia, citing 'good research and financial conditions,' to no avail (Vakhtin 2004:42–44).

and Göteborg (in 1924), where he and Shternberg reunited with Boas after an 18-year break (see Fig. 11), the 22nd Congress in Rome (1926), and the 23rd Congress in New York (1928), where he was hosted by Boas (Krupnik 1998:206–207). After the New York congress, Bogoras participated in a meeting on international research planning in the circumpolar zone attended by such anthropological luminaries as Franz Boas, Clark Wissler, Aleš Hrdlička, Diamond Jenness, Kaj Birket-Smith, William Thalbitzer, and Erland Nordenskiöld on behalf of their respective national institutions. At that meeting, Bogoras officially represented the Russian Academy of Sciences (Bogoras 1929b; Krupnik 1998:216).

Lev Shternberg's death in 1927 was a huge blow to their joint effort to rebuild Russian Siberian anthropology and a devastating personal loss to Bogoras. Soon after, the ideological winds in Soviet Russia turned sour. Ideological intolerance was on the rise, threatening the very fabric of anthropological enterprise that Bogoras and Shternberg aspired to build (Kan 2006:40–44; Krupnik 2008:208; Liarskaia 2016). Bogoras was repeatedly criticized by young radical Marxists for being 'soft,' 'wrong,' or 'not-Marxist enough' in his old writings about the Chukchi, and he had to respond with humiliating self-criticism (Bogoras 1930; 1931; 1934b). Neither he nor his many younger students could submit any new papers to international congresses, and Bogoras's own publications in Western professional journals ceased after 1930. He was not elected to the Russian (then Soviet) Academy of Sciences in 1928 (Kan 2006:40–41) and was not allowed to travel abroad after 1930. He was even forced to denounce his old friend and mentor, Franz Boas, in a humiliating preface to the Russian translation of Boas's paper 'The Aims of Anthropological Research' (Boas 1933) that Bogoras himself arranged for publication in the Russian academic journal *Sovetskaia etnografiia* (Bogoras 1933; Kan 2006).

Fortuitously, at the time of mounting challenges to his scholarly and public standing, the 'Yakut Commission' of the Soviet Academy of Sciences offered to produce a Russian translation of his old JNPE monograph on the Chukchi.[6] The origin of this effort, which Bogoras called an 'authorized (auto-edited) translation' from the original English edition, remains unclear. In his "Author's Introduction" to the first Russian volume of *The Chukchee* written in May 1934, he claimed that:

Throughout 1900–1914, it was impossible to find in Russia a publishing house eager to undertake such a monumental multi-volume publication, with numerous illustrations and Native texts. The possibility of a Russian translation of *The Chukchee* appeared after a twenty-year gap only. The translation

6   According to Elena A. Mikhailova (personal communication, November 9, 2016), the translation was initiated in 1929 by the Soviet Academy of Sciences for a proposed large selection of Bogoras's earlier publications on the Chukchi, both in Russian and in English. According to the original plan, the translated JNPE text of *The Chukchee* was scheduled to appear in *two* volumes ("Material Culture" and "Religion and Social Organization") in 1930–1931, with several other materials in Russian to be added to the venture.

of my monograph was encouraged by the late Karl Ianovich Louks, the critical figure in the field of [Russia's] northern minority people [...] I made this translation, with the assistance of S.N. Stebnitskii and M.L. Stebnitskaia. For the first two chapters, we used the translation by a certain [A.I.] Stepanov that was forwarded to me for correction from the Yakut Commission of the [Soviet] Academy of Sciences. That translation was partially a retelling of the content, so that it could be used by segments only (Bogoras 1934b:xiv).

In fact, Stepanov most probably translated the entire set of *The Chukchee* in 1929–1930. His translation was later checked and corrected by Sergei Stebnitskii (1906–1942), one of Bogoras's anthropology students and once his part-time secretary and his wife, M. Stebnitskaia. Bogoras thoroughly reviewed and edited the final Russian manuscript, now preserved at the Archives of the Russian Academy of Sciences in St. Petersburg with his handwritten remarks (Vdovin 1991a:218; Mikhailova, personal communication, November 2016). Regardless of the identity of the translator, Bogoras's role in organizing the Russian edition was critical. First, he changed the order of the key sections of *The Chukchee*: the first published Russian volume was the section on Social Organization (Bogoras 1934a), which had been Part 3 of the original JNPE set. He also moved the chapter on Chukchi relations with the Russians to the front of the first Russian volume together with three more chapters—'Names and Habitat,' 'General Characteristics,' and 'Trade'—taken from the first JNPE issue, 'Material Culture' (Bogoras 1904). The book also featured a long preface by Ian Al'kor and an extended Russian Introduction written by Bogoras himself (1934b), filled with self-criticism of his old field methods and his 'lack of Marxist vision.' The book was published by the Institute of the Peoples of the North (*Institut narodov Severa*, INS), as Volume 5 of the proceedings of its 'Research Association'; it was poorly printed and lacked the photos and many other illustrations from the 1909 AMNH edition.

Strategically initiating a Russian edition of his master book was a wise decision in the darkening political atmosphere of Soviet anthropology, which was filled with acrimonious discussions on social structures and Marxist interpretation of the laws of social evolution. It was expected that two other translated parts of *The Chukchee* would soon follow. The release of the first volume in Russia in 1934 helped solidify Bogoras's stature as the preeminent Russian Siberian scholar for a while. The celebration of his 70th birthday in 1935 was marked by a major tribute written by Ian Al'kor (1935), the INS director, and a special 250-page issue of the journal *Sovetskaia etnografiia* (Soviet Ethnography) dedicated to Siberian and Arctic research and stocked with papers written primarily by Bogoras's and Shternberg's former students.

Nonetheless, the academic and public niche that Bogoras had carved for himself was rapidly shrinking. That same year, 1935, the Committee on the North was closed and all of its assets were transferred to the State Administration of the Northern Sea Route (*Glavsevmorput'*, see Vakhtin 1994). Another of Bogoras's favorite public spaces, the 'Society of Former Political Convicts and Exiles,' was also shut down that year. Nikolai Matorin (1898–1936), the powerful director of the Leningrad Institute of Ethnography, was dismissed and imprisoned in 1935 (and subsequently executed), a precursor to the purges that would soon decimate the Leningrad academic, professional and administrative elites. Bogoras could not but feel that his days were numbered.

The Chukchee after Bogoras

Bogoras was 'lucky' to die a natural death on May 10, 1936, at age 71. He passed away on the train to Leningrad (St. Petersburg), after visiting his younger brother, surgeon Nikolai Bogoraz, in the southern city of Rostov-on-Don (or on return from a southern vacation; Bogoraz L. 2009:9–10; Gernet 1999:38). He was honored with a high-level funeral ceremony by the Soviet Academy of Sciences, a burial place in the prestigious 'Literary Section' (*Literatorskie mostki*) at the Volkov Cemetery in Leningrad, a memorial festschrift (Meshchaninov 1937), and an obituary by his old friend Franz Boas in *American Anthropologist* (Boas 1937). Yet the system he had built over the last 15 years of his academic career was quick to unravel.

After his death, Bogoras was never officially demoted or disgraced in Soviet Russia, in contrast to many scholars, living or deceased, at the time. Rather, he was marginalized. He was mildly criticized for his 'bourgeois idealistic misgivings' and the lack of a 'proper Marxist' approach in his treatment of the Chukchi and other indigenous people. His favorite students (Nikolai Shnakenburg, Alexander Forshtein, Sergei Stebnitskii, Nikolai Spiridonov, A. K. A. Teki Odulok, and others), whom he personally trained to carry on his research among the Chukchi, Siberian Yupik, Koryak, and Yukaghir, all became victims of the Stalin-era terror or casualties of World War II (Krupnik 1998; 2008). Bogoras was honored by occasional official tributes on the dates of his birth or death (e.g., Ivanov 1946; Vdovin 1957; 1965; 1991b), but his main scholarly publications, though widely cited, were not reprinted in Russia for the next fifty-five years. His fiction writings, similarly, did not appear in new reprints until the 1960s or 1970s (Kolonteeva 1991).[7] For decades after his death, Bogoras remained an honored academic 'elder' of Russian Siberian ethnography but with little following, a truncated legacy, and no true assessment of his contribution (Krupnik 2008).

The second partial installment of the Russian version of *The Chukchee*, 'Religion' (*Religiia*), appeared in 1939, three years after Bogoras's passing. Printed by another publisher (*Glavsevmorput'*), it had another editor and author of an introductory essay,

---

7   Bogoras's monumental 'collected writings' were published in 10 volumes in 1910–1911; this set contained his prose, poetry, and Siberian travel stories. It was reprinted as a condensed four-volume set in 1928–1929 and then reduced to a single volume episodically reissued in the late-Soviet and early post-Soviet era by local Siberian presses (in 1962, 1979, 1987, 1991, etc.).

Iuri P. Frantsov (1903–1969), who replaced Bogoras as the director of the Museum of the History of Atheism and Religion that Bogoras established in 1932. Frantsov's short piece injected a heavy portion of 'Marxist criticism' to Bogoras's masterpiece writing. The shift in tone and publisher was more than symbolic. Ian Al'kor, the author of the introduction to the first Russian volume of *The Chukchee* (Al'kor 1934), was already dead. One of the many victims of Stalin's 'Great Terror,' he was arrested and shot in 1938. Bogoras's treasured Institute of the Peoples of the North (INS) soon followed the fate of its director (Liarskaia 2016:160). Most of its staff members were imprisoned and shot or sent to gulag labor camps to serve terms in much harsher conditions than Bogoras and his peers from the 'People's Freedom" Party ever imagined. The Institute was subordinated to the 'Glavsevmorput' (Northern Sea Route Administration), a quasi-military organization in charge of maritime operations in the Russian Arctic; it was later transformed into a five-year pedagogical college serving Russia's northern regions. Bogoras's and Shternberg's research and educational enterprise came to an end (Liarskaia 2016; Vakhtin 2016b), and the field they created to train their students and indigenous cadres never recovered.

It was another 52 years (!) until the last—actually, the first—section of *The Chukchee*, 'Material Culture,' was published in Russia (Bogoraz 1991). The manuscript was reportedly the portion of the same Russian translation by A.I. Stepanov that Bogoras (and Stebnitskii) edited in the 1930s. The book was printed by Russia's main academic publishing house, 'Nauka' (Science), under the editorship of the leading Russian scholar of the Chukchi, Innokentii S. Vdovin (1907–1996), a former schoolteacher among the Chukchi and a student of Bogoras. Elena A. Mikhailova, a specialist in Chukchi and Yupik ethnology at the Peter the Great Museum of Anthropology and Ethnography, supervised the production of the book, which also contained most of the original illustrations from the AMNH edition of 1904. Unfortunately, the museum never followed up on its plan to publish the full Russian version of *The Chukchee*, as was later done for Jochelson's *Yukaghir* in 2005.

In 2005–2007, aides to then-governor of the Chukotka Area, Roman Abramovich, revived the idea of publishing a full Russian edition of *The Chukchee* simply by collating the three separate Russian volumes of 1934, 1939, and 1991 under a common cover. The plan failed to materialize. To this day Russian readers must rely on three separately published Russian sections of *The Chukchee*. According to online sources, all three were reprinted in 2011–2016 by the Russian press 'Librokom' from their respective earlier editions.

The English (AMNH) version of 1904–1909 remained a three-issue set for almost 70 years. It was widely cited in several publications and used as a course reading for general anthropology curricula in university programs (e.g., Anonymous 1923; Ford 1949; Kroeber and Waterman 1920; Leeds 1965). In 1975, the AMS Press in New York produced facsimile reprints of all of the JNPE publications, so that the three sections of *The Chukchee* finally appeared as one book, according to Boas's original vision. The book is now available at more than 200 libraries on four continents (see the library site www.worldcat.org). Unlike Bogoras's later contribution to the JNPE series, *Chukchi Mythology*, however, the AMS Press's edition of *The Chukchee* in one volume has not been reissued since 1975 and is now out of print. The three issues are accessible separately for free download at the AMNH website (http://digitallibrary.amnh.org/handle/2246/5745), but the complete single volume has not been made available in electronic form. Therefore, this *third* English edition of Bogoras's masterpiece, produced as both printed and on line book for the *Bibliotheca Sibiro-pacifica* series is a long-overdue gift to Northern anthropologists, students, and Siberian/Arctic lovers around the world.

Today's Assessment of *The Chukchee*

The lasting value of *The Chukchee* derives from many factors. Bogoras, like Jochelson, could draw on the experience of two long fieldworks of 1895–1897 and 1900–1901 for his JNPE writings. He personally visited many (though not *all*) regional groups of the Chukchi, and he was the only JNPE researcher, except for James Teit among the Canadian Plateau nations and George Hunt among the Kwakwaka'wakw, who was fluent in local languages, was versed in Native customs, and had first-hand experience of Chukchi daily life. His knowledge of the Chukchi was thorough if uneven—better for the western and southern groups, and rather slim for the eastern divisions, particularly the large Maritime communities of eastern Chukotka. That eventually surfaced in the unequal coverage of Reindeer versus Maritime Chukchi culture in the book.

Bogoras was a self-taught anthropologist, but he was a competent author even after his first fieldwork of 1895–1897. Boas's careful tutorship over the course of the JNPE helped make Bogoras a first-class professional in ethnographic research, and *The Chukchee* an instant classic. By all accounts, Bogoras was a star of JNPE team, second only to Boas himself. As a result, his 750-page overview of the Chukchi culture made one of the best and most solid contributions to the entire 11-volume JNPE series.

He was also an exceptionally prolific writer. Over the 10 years from 1904 to 1913, he published four monograph-size issues on the Chukchi in the JNPE series under the AMNH *Memoirs* (Material Culture, Religion, Social Organization, and Mythology) and a short collection of the Asiatic Eskimo texts (1913). He later supplemented it with an extensive grammatical sketch of the Chukchi language (with some comparative comments on the Koryak and Yukaghir languages) in the Smithsonian *Handbook of American Indian Languages* (Bogoras 1922) and with several works on the folklore of the Koryak, Lamoot (Even), and the Yukaghir.

The Chukchee, when viewed as a single book of 750 pages, made a remarkably comprehensive ethnography of a Siberian indigenous nation poorly known to Western scholars. It was rightly called "the best and the most detailed ever written on this people" (Schweitzer 2005:267). It was illustrated with 302 line drawings and 35 plates made from Bogoras's field photographs and objects he collected for the AMNH. The volume also featured an excellent map of the distribution of Native groups in northeast Siberia (the map also appeared in Jochelson's volume on the Koryak). Bogoras offered a good treatment of available Russian and foreign literature on the Chukchi in a bibliography attached to the first issue of 1904, although he was perhaps too critical of his immediate predecessor, Anadyr district governor and trained anthropologist Nikolai L. Gondatti, the author of several papers on the same area in 1897–1898.

Three factors color our assessment of *The Chukchee* today compared with its reception when it was published a century ago. First, it appeared in *three* individual thematic portions (issues) separated by several years (1904, 1907, and 1909). Though the issues then had a common pagination, it took the library binding—and the later AMS Press reprint in *one* large book of 750 pages—to grasp the overall breadth and value of *The Chukchee*'s original design. To its Russian readers, it is still known in *three* separate books under their individual titles (Bogoraz 1934a; 1939; 1991) and even in a reverse order. Hence, today we may have a clearer view of the strengths and gaps of Bogoras's masterpiece than when it was published.

Second, *The Chukchee* appeared in separate sections within a monumental series of 32 issues, large and small (the shortest were just a dozen pages; the longest, 500 pages) printed over 30 years, between 1898 and 1930, according to a master plan envisioned by Boas. The first issue of *The Chukchee* (Material Culture, 1904) was published during the peak days of the JNPE series and thus received the most attention (see list of reviews in Kagarov 1935). The two latter issues were released when Boas had already left the AMNH for Columbia University and the museum desperately wanted the series to be completed. Of course, the unanticipated factor in the JNPE legacy was the failure by Boas, the expedition's leader, to produce the concluding summary opus on its outcomes. That failure ultimately left each individual volume to stand on its own, a test that *The Chukchee* passed better than any other collated volume in the JNPE series.

The third factor was Boas's well-known intention to make the JNPE volumes comparable to, if not competitive with, the monumental ethnographies (we now call them 'classical ethnographies') of the Bureau of Ethnology, later the Bureau of American Ethnology (BAE) of the Smithsonian Institution in Washington, DC. Boas had ambiguous relations with the Smithsonian; he craved Smithsonian employment in his early years yet was highly critical of the institution's anthropological and museum scholarship. Boas wanted his JNPE volumes to be on a par with the monumental BAE *Annual Reports* that featured many 'classical ethnographies' of Native American groups during the 1880s and 1890s, including Boas's own *Central Eskimo* (Boas 1888; Krupnik 2016b) and other Arctic 'classics', like Murdoch's essay on the Inuit of Point Barrow (Murdoch 1892) and Nelson's (1899) on Western Alaskan Eskimo. Bogoras's *The Chukchee*, as well as Jochelson's *The Koryak* (1908), matched the best BAE publications in terms of breadth and publication quality. These and other elements are important for today's assessment of *The Chukchee*.

As Bogoras returned from his JNPE fieldwork loaded with data and ideas, he was persuaded to accept a Boasian template of 'basic ethnography' for his writings for the JNPE series (Krupnik 1996:46). By modern standards, that template an ambitiously detailed handbook of a Native culture covering its every aspect—from habitat, physical features, and stone lamps to social rites, religion, lore, and mythology. Yet, unlike the independent monographs in the BAE *Annual Reports*, the JNPE proceedings followed a preliminary master plan that has not been intellectually completed. As a result, its individual issues were neither matched to each other nor analyzed according to Boas's original design.

In fact, Boas's monumental scenario for his 'North Pacific Expedition' (Krupnik and Freed 2004) was plagued by ambiguities from its very beginning. On the American Northwest Coast, where some basic coverage of many Native nations was already available (including by Boas himself: Boas 1890, 1891, 1897), JNPE researchers had a freer hand to concentrate on texts, masks, languages, facial paintings, and decorative objects—for the sake of future comparison that never materialized (Krupnik 1996:41). Boas was also careful to avoid overlapping with the areas of interest of the Smithsonian researchers (i.e., west and north Alaska) and with Lt. George T. Emmons's ongoing collecting efforts among the Tlingit and other Native groups in southeastern Alaska.

Siberian crews, in contrast, had to survey less-known ethnic groups, cover much larger areas, and cross extremely harsh terrain. Furthermore, they were given multiple tasks: they were not only to produce 'basic ethnographies' of the surveyed Native nations, but also to secure linguistic, folklore, anthropometric, and other evidence of Siberian-American connections *and* to collect ethnographic and physical specimens for AMNH. To the extent that the lead JNPE scientists in Siberia—Bogoras, Jochelson, and Berthold Laufer—could ever accomplish these tasks, they had to rely on their spouses and other assistants: Dina Jochelson Brodsky for Jochelson, Sof'ia Bogoras and Alexander Axelrod for Bogoras, and Gerald Fowke for Laufer on Sakhalin Island and in the Amur River region.

Under such harsh conditions and mounting pressure from Boas, Laufer mostly failed to deliver on his JNPE assignment, Jochelson endured, and Bogoras excelled. Although his main task from Boas was to collect ethnographic and other materials among his primary group, the Maritime Chukchi, he actually spent more time among other Siberian aboriginal nations: the Maritime Koryak (November 1900–February 1901), Siberian Yupik (May–June 1901), Itelmen (Kamchadal), Kerek, local Russians, and Russian Creoles. That, naturally, moved him toward *comparative* ethnography, in spite of the limitations of the JNPE 'basic ethnography' template (Krupnik 1996). The latter obviously ran against Bogoras's field skills; his personal interests in language, mythology, and lore; and his old populist sensitivities to the issues of economic exploitation, administrative injustice, and colonial treatment of the Siberian Natives.

Therefore, we should view the scope and structure of *The Chukchee* as an intersection of many conflicting forces. It is a book written by an experienced and extremely capable scholar, who was pressured to present his data under an academic template not quite to his personal liking. Bogoras skillfully organized the 750 pages of *The Chukchee* in 23 large chapters in three almost equal sections covering material, spiritual, and social life. He was highly innovative in treating Chukchi material culture by viewing it through the lenses of daily *economic activities* (reindeer herding, dog breeding, hunting, fishing, trade, etc.) rather than as a museum-framed list of respective tools and objects, as in the Smithsonian BAE monographs. Most unusual for a 'basic ethnography' of the era was his last chapter of 50 pages covering Chukchi contacts with the Russians and the structure of Russian administration in the region. That chapter showed Bogoras the historian, former census taker, and populist-socialist at his best.

Yet *The Chukchee* was meant to be a synopsis of a nation that possessed two distinctive types of culture and economy: those of the nomadic reindeer-herders and of the coastal maritime hunters. Overall, the treatment of the two groups differed, often substantially. Whereas the sections on clothing, housing, subsistence implements, and ceremonies were relatively balanced, those on social life were not. A forty-page description of marriage patterns and rituals among the Reindeer Chukchi stood next to a three-page section on the same traditions among the Maritime folk. The book called *The Chukchee* also abounds in randomly injected details and references to neighboring Native groups—the Yupik, the Even (Lamoot), and the Russian Creoles. Here, again, the template of 'basic ethnography' made the gaps and biases in Bogoras's knowledge of the various Native groups he surveyed even more visible (Krupnik 1996).

In spite of these and other shortcomings, *The Chukchee* was an outstanding example of a 'basic ethnography' monograph. That genre of scholarly ethnographic studies dominated the field for about 50 years, from the 1880s to the 1920s (Krupnik 2016a:6). It produced the priceless shelves of anthropological 'classics,' certainly for northern areas, including Alaska (Murdoch 1892; Nelson 1899), Canada (Boas 1888; 1901; Birket-Smith 1929; Jenness 1922; Mathiassen 1928; Stefansson 1919; Turner 1894), Greenland (Birket-Smith 1924; Thalbitzer 1914; 1941), and Arctic Russia (Jochelson 1908; 1910–1926; Seroshevskii 1896). Bogoras's oeuvre on the Chukchi was a prized member of this scholarly cohort. Again, no one said it better than his mentor, Franz Boas (1937:314): „His work on the Chukchee, […] is proof of his deep insight into the life of the people among whom he was compelled to live. The clarity of his description is due to his scientific insight; but no less to his artistic gifts."

'Invisible partners'

Among many controversies that Bogoras inherited from the 'basic ethnography' template was his failure to acknowledge the *collaborative* nature of his fieldwork and collecting among the Chukchi. From the beginning, his party included his wife, Sof'ia Volkova Bogoras, a seasoned Arctic traveler and former midwife during Bogoras's exile years in Sredne-Kolymsk. When Bogoras joined the Jochelsons' camp in November 1900, Jochelson sent his field assistant, Alexander Axelrod, to join forces with Sof'ia Bogoras in Markovo so that the two could complete Bogoras's JNPE assignment. In spring 1901, the two were joined in Markovo by AMNH biologist Norman Buxton, formally another member of the Jochelsons' crew.

One would look in vain for the names of these people in the 750 pages of *The Chukchee* or in many of Bogoras's publications (see a similar comment on Jochelson's *The Koryak*—Kasten and Dürr 2016:18). Also, whereas folklore texts recorded by Bogoras's crew were cited with their storytellers's names, references to specific ethnographic information supplied by particular local informants were all but absent. The text of *The Chukchee* abounds in specific, often individual details, but it bears few Native names—except those of Chukchi female shaman Telpiña, Yupik trader Kuvár (Quwaaren, in today's Yupik transliteration) from Indian Point (Ungaziq; see Fig. 12), and a few others—so the information is hard to connect to particular people and areas.

Fig. 12 Eskimo trader Kuvár (Quwaaren).
Image #1351, American Museum of Natural History Library.

The failure to acknowledge contributions by Sof'ia Bogoras and Alexander Axel-rod to the success of Bogoras's fieldwork looks more systemic. Only recently, thanks to new research by Russian colleagues (Shentalinskaia 2012; 2015; Mikhailova 2016), are we able to grasp Sof'ia Bogoras's true role in collecting ethnographic objects, par-ticularly, musical and folklore texts (almost 200 recordings from Markovo and Novo-Mariinsk), *and* caring for and packing expedition's collections for shipping to AMNH in New York (Fig. 9). Bogoras acknowledged her contribution only in passing, as in his letter to Boas from April 1901:

> My wife and Mr. Axelrod accumulated and packed in 30 large crates a signifi-cant and very precious collection related to the Lamoot and the Russified peo-ple of the Anadyr River valley [that they collected entirely on their own – I.K. (DAA AMNH; cited in Mikhailova 2016:112).

In a similar way, Bogoras ignored Alexander Axelrod's role in taking the bulk of physical measurements and at least 300 photographs listed under Bogoras's name in today's AMNH collection records. We know surprisingly little about Axelrod, both before and after the JNPE. He was a Russian Jewish émigré student from Switzerland whom Jochelson invited to join the expedition. With the Jochelsons and Buxton, he traveled to the town of Gizhiga on the Sea of Okhotsk, and he later accompanied the Jochelsons on their survey of the Penzhina Koryak in September–October 1900. Unlike Jochelson, Bogoras, and Buxton, Axelrod had no previous fieldwork experi-ence in the North. When Jochelson sent him to Markovo to assist Sof'ia Bogoras, he tasked him with taking physical measurements and photographs of Native people and collecting ethnographic objects for the AMNH (Shentalinskaia 2015:153–154), under dire conditions:

> "After leaving the Koryak village of Kamenskoye 11 December [1900], I reached the Russian village [of Markovo] on Anadyr river after 8 days traveling by sled. [...] While waiting for the Chukchi, I worked at increasing the collections, photographing and measuring the inhabitants of Markovo. It was difficult because of the poor light in winter months and because the people didn't want to be measured. [...] I left Markovo 16 Feb. and reached Zeropol (Yeropol – I.K.) late at night on 17th. I photographed, took measurements, made masks [casts] and got artifacts for the Lamoot collection. [...] It is very difficult to work among the Chukchi and the Lamoot during the fair. [...] It is almost impossible to measure them in their yourts; if it is cold, the smoke in there is very thick. In Warkem (?), Markovo or Zeropol I could have taken the mea-surements in Russian houses; but at the Anmanski fair it is impossible because the fair is in the woods on the bank of a small river. [...] Although I arrived a few days earlier, there was hardly any opportunity for taking measurements. I could only photograph and collect artifacts. [...] I left 16 March and after my

Fig. 13 Example of Axelrod anthropological photographs.
Image #1365, American Museum of Natural History Library.

Fig. 14 Alexander Axelrod.
Image #1389, American Museum of Natural History Library.

arrival in Markovo on 17th, I concentrated exclusively in organizing our collections, which were packed in 31 trunks. (Axelrod to Bogoras, April 14, 1901, Mariinski Post; copy at AMNH).

In April 1901, upon his arrival at Mariinski Post, Axelrod took at least 50 more measurements of the local Chukchi, as well as several photographs now attributed to Bogoras. Axelrod later accompanied Bogoras on his trip to Cape Chaplin along the southern shore of the Chukchi Peninsula in April–July 1901, where he took more physical measurements and an unknown number of photographs (Fig. 13) and assisted Bogoras in making ethnographic collections. Yet Bogoras never acknowledged Axelrod's contribution in *The Chukchee* or any of his many other publications. Axelrod appears to be featured in one photograph (Fig. 14) taken at a Chukchi camp near Mariinski Post in July 1901.

From today's perspective, it is hard to grasp the norms of team ethics and data ownership at the time of the JNPE. Axelrod's and Sof'ia Bogoras's service ensured the overall success of Bogoras's party and provided its leader with much-needed time to concentrate on collecting language and folklore material, his prime interest during his JNPE work. Readers should keep the presence of these 'invisible partners' in mind while enjoying the ethnographic riches of Bogoras's seminal book.

Epilogue

I first touched *The Chukchee* as a young Ph.D. student in Siberian anthropology almost 45 years ago, in the library of the then-Institute of Ethnography in Moscow. I remember the awe and trepidation with which I browsed through the three issues of the old AMNH *Memoirs* bound together into a heavy folio-size volume. I have used this book ever since, now in the more practical format of the 1975 reprint. I have another personal copy of that book in my possession, a gift from Frederica de Laguna (1906–2004), another 'maestro' of northern anthropology. I received it shortly before her passing, after I asked her about the role of Bogoras, Boas, and the JNPE in her personal training as an anthropologist, which culminated in her three-volume 'classical ethnography' of the Yakutat Tlingit (de Laguna 1972). That copy of *The Chukchee* forever binds in my mind Bogoras, Boas, and Freddie, the giants of 20th-century ethnology on whose shoulders we stand today.

As I tried to argue in this chapter, Bogoras was perhaps the most talented among the JPNE participants, second only to Boas himself in his energy, his professional skills, and the size of his contribution. *The Chukchee*, Bogoras's masterpiece and the main outcome of his years of research on northeast Siberia, remains the primary source of ethnological information on the Chukchi and other neighboring Siberian nations, despite the fact that it appeared more than 100 years ago. Thanks to its extended sections on the contact history of the Chukchi and other aboriginal groups, it is perhaps the most dynamic and contemporary framed volume in the JNPE series, which remains the monument to the Boasian vision of ethnology and our main pool of knowledge on North Pacific aboriginal nations at the eve of the 20th century.

Nothing of its kind has been produced ever since, certainly not about the Chukchi people, and it makes Bogoras's oeuvre an unchallenged source of ethnographic wealth and the best 'snapshot' of aboriginal culture soon to undergo a rapid transformation. Contemporary readers, particularly indigenous ones, should take this book for what it is—for its breadth of ethnographic material and its user-friendly style and structure, but also for its shortcomings, the products of the JNPE design, Bogoras's self-education in the craft of anthropology, and his penchant for evolutionary theories and non-stop traveling. No one said it better than Boas himself in his stern reminder to Bogoras, then in the fervor of the 1905 Russian Revolution, that " […] an investigation by Mr. Bogoras of the Chukchee happens only once in eternity, and I think you owe it to science to give us the results of your studies." Based on the remarkable combination of Bogoras's personal knowledge and skills, Boasian research design, and Bogoras's deviation from it in search for the 'unknown,' *The Chukchee* is indeed a book that happens once in humanity's time.

Acknowledgements

I am grateful to Erich Kasten for his invitation to write this chapter, first as an introductory essay for a new reprint of *The Chukchee*, a dream of many years. I also thank my colleague at the Smithsonian Institution, William Fitzhugh, who in 1991 introduced me to the idea of a centennial re-visit of the Jesup North Pacific Expedition and invited me to become a partner in the Smithsonian 'Jesup-2' initiative. That ignited my long-held interest in Bogoras and his legacy. Over the years, I benefitted from collaboration and many productive discussions on Bogoras, Boas, and JNPE history with Sergei Kan (Dartmouth College), Nikolai Vakhtin (European University, St. Petersburg), Elena Mikhailova (Museum of Anthropology and Ethnology, St. Petersburg), and Barbara Mathé (American Museum of Natural History, New York), my partners on the 'Jesup-2', to whom I am always grateful. Elena Mikhailova, Sergei Kan, Erich Kasten, Nikolai Vakhtin, and Heidi Fritschel offered valuable comments and added important details to the original draft.

Sources (Further reading)

Peter Schweitzer's (2005) condensed summary of Bogoras's life and his major contributions is perhaps the best current source in English to familiarize the readers with Bogoras's legacy. Other English-language sources include Krader 1968, Cole 1999 and

2001, Vakhtin 2001, and Freed 2012. Elena Mikhailova's detailed essay (2004) is the best contemporary Russian source on Bogoras's life, professional career, and his many public activities. Earlier Russian sources include Al'kor 1935, Zelenin 1937 (from the posthumous festschrift), and several later biographic overviews (Kolonteeva 1991; Vdovin 1991b).

Several lists of Bogoras's publications were compiled at different times (e.g., Vinnikov 1935; Kolonteeva 1991); the one prepared in German by Katharina Gernet (1999) is the most detailed. The most recent online list, compiled by Viacheslav V. Ivanov (available at http://www.kunstkamera.ru:8081/siberia/Bibliorg/Bogoraz.pdf) includes all of Bogoras's published works between 1896 and 1991.

A number of sources cover specific aspects of Bogoras's professional work and legacy. On Bogoras's relations to Boas, see Kan 2006. On Bogoras's (and Shternberg's) formative role in establishing the Russian ethnographic school of Siberian studies, see Kan 2009b, Vakhtin 2016a and 2016b, and Liarskaia 2016, see also *this volume*. Kuznetsova 1957, Vdovin 1977, Shentalinskaia 2015, and Krupnik 1996 discuss specific gaps in Bogoras's coverage of Reindeer Chukchi rituals, Chukchi religion, Native and Russian Siberian folklore, and Siberian Yupik social organization, respectively. On the contemporary situation of the Chukchi and their development under the Soviet power, see Gray 2005, Kerttula 2000, Schweitzer 1999, and Vaté 2005. The best summary of the status of Soviet Arctic minority people, including the role of Bogoras and the 'Committee of the North' is Vakhtin 1994.

References

Al'kor, Ian P. 1934. Predislovie redaktora [Editor's Preface]. In *V.G. Bogoraz: Chukchi*: iii-xii. Leningrad: Nauchno-issledovatel'skaia assotsiatsiia Instituta narodov Severa.

— 1935. V. G. Bogoraz-Tan [W.G. Bogoras]. *Sovetskaia Etnografiia* 4–5: 5–29.

Anonymous 1904a. The Exhibit of Chukchee Clothing. *American Museum Journal* 4(1): 22–24.

— 1904b. The House-Life of the Chukchee in Siberia. *American Museum Journal* 4(2): 35–37.

— 1923. Syllabus and Instructions – Anthropology 1B. *University of California Syllabus Series* 148. Berkeley: University of California Press.

Birket-Smith, Kaj 1924. Ethnography of the Egedesminde District with Aspects of the General Culture of West Greenland. *Meddelelser om Grønland* 66. Copenhagen.

— 1929. The Caribou Eskimos: Material and Social Life and Their Cultural Position. *Report of the Fifth Thule Expedition 1921–24.* Vol. 5(1–2). Copenhagen.

Boas, Franz 1888. The Central Eskimo. *Sixth Annual Report of the Bureau of Ethnology, 1884–1885:* 399–669. Washington, D.C.: Government Printing Office.

— 1890. First General Report on the Indians of British Columbia. In *5ᵗʰ Report on the Northwestern Tribes of Canada. British Association for the Advancement of Sciences*: 5–97. London.

— 1891. Second General Report on the Indians of British Columbia. In *6ᵗʰ Report on the Northwestern Tribes of Canada, British Association for the Advancement of Science*: 10–163. London.

— 1897. The Social Organization and the Secret Societies of the Kwakiutl Indians. In *Report of the United States National Museum for the Year 1895*: 562–715. Washington, D.C.: Government Printing Office.

— 1901. The Eskimo of the Baffin Land and Hudson Bay. *Bulletin of the American Museum of Natural History* 15(1): 1–370. New York.

— 1903. The Jesup North Pacific Expedition. *American Museum Journal* 3(5): 73–119.

— 1910/2001. Die Resultate der Jesup-Expedition. In *Internationaler American-isten-Kongress* 16. Vienna and Leipzig: 3–18. Translated as 'Results of the Jesup Expedition. In *Gateways: Exploring the Legacy of the Jesup North Pacific Expedition, 1897–1902*. I. Krupnik and W.W. Fitzhugh (eds.), 17–24. Washington, D.C.: Arctic Studies Center, National Museum of Natural History, Smithsonian Institution.

— 1933. Zadachi anthropologicheskogo issledovaniia [The Aims of Anthropological Research]. *Sovetskaia Etnografiia* 3–4: 178–189.

— 1937. Waldemar Bogoras (obituary). *American Anthropologist* 39(2): 314–315. Bogoras Obituary.

Bogoraz, Larissa 2009. *Sny pamiati* [Dreams of Memory]. Kharkov: Prava Liudini.

Bogoraz, Vladimir G. [Bogoras, Waldemar] 1896. Novye zapisi bylin v Iakutskoi oblasti [New Recordings of (Russian) Epics From the Yakutsk Province]. *Etnograficheskoe Obozrenie* 2–3: 72–106 (published under the name of Vsevolod Miller, with the reference that the texts were supplied by Bogoras).

— 1899. Kratkii otchet ob issledovanii chukoch Kolymskogo kraia [Brief Report on the Survey of the Chukchi of Kolyma District. With attached map]. *Izvestiia Vostochno-Sibirskogo Otdeleniia Russkogo Geograficheskogo Obshchestva* 30(1): 1–51. Irkutsk.

— 1900. *Materialy po izucheniiu chukotskogo iazyka i fol'klora, sobrannye v Kolymskom okruge* [Materials on the Chukchi Language and Folklore Collected in the Kolyma District]. St. Petersburg: Academy of Sciences.

— 1901. The Chukchi of Northeastern Asia. *American Anthropologist* 3(1): 80–106.

— 1902. The Folklore of Northeastern Asia, as compared with that of Northwestern America. *American Anthropologist* 4(4): 577–683.

— 1904. The Chukchee. Pt. 1. Material Culture. *The Jesup North Pacific Expedition* 7, *Memoirs of the American Museum of Natural History* 11. Pt. 1: 1–276. New York. New edition 2017, edited by M. Dürr and E. Kasten. Fürstenberg/Havel: Kulturstiftung Sibirien.

— 1906. Religious Ideas of Primitive Man, from Chukchi Materials. *XIV Internationaler Amerikanisten-Kongress:* 129–135. Stuttgart.
— 1907. The Chukchee. Religion. *The Jesup North Pacific Expedition 7, Memoirs of the American Museum of Natural History* 11. Pt. 2: 277–536. New York. New edition 2017, edited by M. Dürr and E. Kasten. Fürstenberg/Havel: Kulturstiftung Sibirien.
— 1909. The Chukchee. Social Organization. *The Jesup North Pacific Expedition 7, Memoirs of the American Museum of Natural History* 11. Pt. 3: 537–733. New York. New edition 2017, edited by M. Dürr and E. Kasten. Fürstenberg/Havel: Kulturstiftung Sibirien.
— 1910. Chukchee Mythology. *Jesup North Pacific Expedition 8, Memoirs of the American Museum of Natural History* 12. Pt. 1: 1–197. New York. New edition 2016, edited by M. Dürr and E. Kasten. Fürstenberg/Havel: Kulturstiftung Sibirien.
— 1913. The Eskimo of Siberia. *Jesup North Pacific Expedition 8, Memoirs of the American Museum of Natural History* 12. Pt. 3: 417–456. New York.
— 1917. Koryak Texts. *American Ethnological Society Publication* 5. Leiden and New York.
— 1918. Tales of Yukaghir, Lamut, and Russianized Natives of Eastern Siberia. *Anthropological Papers of the American Museum of Natural History* 20(1): 3–148. New York.
— 1922. Chukchee. In *Handbook of American Indian Languages*. F. Boas (ed.) Pt. 2. *Bureau of American Ethnology Bulletin* 40(2): 631–903. Washington, D.C.
— 1925a. *Early Migrations of Eskimo between Asia and America*. Congrès International des Americanistes. Compte-Rendu de la XXI session: 216–235. Göteborg: Göteborg Museum.
— 1925b. Ideas of Space and Time in the Conception of the Primitive Religion. *American Anthropologist* 27(2): 205–266.
— 1926. Drevnie i traditsionnye pereseleniia narodov v Severnoi Evrazii i Amerike [Ancient and Traditional Population Migration in Northeast Asia and America]. *Sbornik Muzeia antropologii i etnografii Akademii Nauk SSSR* 6: 37–62.
— 1928a. Ethnographical Problems of the Eurasian Arctic. In *Problems of Polar Research. American Geographical Society. Special Publication* 7: 189–207. New York.
— 1928b. *Rasprostranenie kul'tury na Zemle. Osnovy etnogeografii* [The Distribution of Culture on Earth. Introduction to Ethnogeography]. Moscow: Gosudarstvennoe izdatel'stvo.
— 1929a. Elements of the Culture of the Circumpolar Zone. *American Anthropologist* 31(4): 579–601.
— 1929b. Mezhdunarodnoe soveshchanie po planu ustroistva ekspeditsii v poliarnoi zone [International Workshop on the Planning of Field Research in the Polar Zone]. *Etnografiia* 1: 103–107. Leningrad.
— 1930. K voprosu o primenenii marksistskogo metoda k izucheniiu etnograficheskikh iavlenii (na primere chukotskogo folklora) [On the Application of Marx-

ist Methodology to the Study of Ethnographic Phenomena (in the Case of Chukchi Lore)]. *Etnografiia* 1–2: 3–56. Leningrad.

— 1931. Klassovoe rassloenie u chukoch-olenevodov [Class Stratification Among the Reindeer Chukchi]. *Sovetskaia Etnografiia* 1–2: 93–116. Leningrad.

— 1933. Zamechaniia k state Frantsa Boasa [Comments on Franz Boas's article]. *Sovetskaia etnografiia* 3–4: 89–93.

— 1934a. *Chukchi. Sotsial'naia organizatsiia* [The Chukchi. Social Organization]. Leningrad: Institut narodov Severa.

— 1934b. Predislovie avtora k russkomu izdaniiu (Author's Introduction to the Russian Edition). In *Chukchi. Sotsial'naia organizatsiia* [The Chukchi. Social Organization]: xiii–xxx. Leningrad: Institut narodov Severa.

— 1939. *Chukchi. Religiia* [The Chukchi. Religion]. Leningrad: Glavsevmorput'.

— 1949. *Materialy po iazyku aziatskikh eskimosov* [Materials Relating to the Language of the Asiatic Eskimo]. Leningrad: Gosuchpedgiz.

— 1991. *Material'naia kul'tura chukchei* [The Chukchi: Material Culture]. Moscow: Nauka.

Cole, Douglas 1999. *Franz Boas: The Early Years, 1858–1906*. Vancouver and Seattle: Douglas & McIntyre and University of Washington Press.

— 2001. The Greatest Thing Undertaken by Any Museum? Franz Boas, Morris Jesup, and the North Pacific Expedition. In *Gateways: Exploring the Legacy of the Jesup North Pacific Expedition, 1897–1902*. I. Krupnik and W.W. Fitzhugh (eds.), 9–70. Washington, D.C.: Arctic Studies Center, National Museum of Natural History, Smithsonian Institution.

De Laguna, Frederica 1972. Under Mount St. Elias: The History and Culture of the Yakutat Tlingit. *Smithsonian Contributions to Anthropology 7*, Vols. 1–3. Washington, D.C.: Smithsonian Institution.

Dürr, Michael, and Erich Kasten 2016. Preface by the Editors. In *Waldemar Bogoras: Chukchee Mythology*. M. Dürr and E. Kasten (eds.). Fürstenberg/Havel: Kulturstiftung Sibirien.

Ford, Daryll C. 1949. *Habitat, Economy and Society: A Geographical Introduction to Ethnology*. New York: E.P. Dutton.

Frantsov, Iu. 1939. Predislovie redaktora [Editor's Preface]. In *V.G. Bogoraz-Tan: Chukchi. Religiia*, pp. iii–viii. Leningrad: Glavsevmorput'.

Freed, Stanley A. 2012. *Anthropology Unmasked. Museums, Science, and Politics in New York City*. Wilmington, OH: Orange Frazer Press.

Freed, Stanley A., Ruth S. Freed, and Laila Williamson 1988. Capitalist Philanthropy and Russian Revolutionaries: The Jesup North Pacific Expedition (1897–1902). *American Anthropologist* 90(1): 7–24.

Gagen-Torn, Nina I. 1975. *Lev Iakovlevich Shternberg* [Lev Yakovlevich Shternberg]. Moscow: Nauka Publishers.

Gernet, Katharina 1999. Vladimir Germanovich Bogoraz (1865–1936): Eine Bibliographie. *Mitteilungen des Osteuropa-Instituts München* 33. München.

Gray, Patty A. 2005. *The Predicament of Chukotka's Indigenous Movement. Post-Soviet Activism in the Russian Far North.* Cambridge: Cambridge University Press.

Ivanov, Sergei V. 1946. Pamiati Bogoraza [In Memory of (Waldemar) Bogoras]. *Sovetskaia Etnografiia* 3: 3–8. Moscow.

Jenness, Diamond 1922. The Life of the Copper Eskimos. *Report of the Canadian Arctic Expedition 1913–1918.* Vol. 12(A). Ottawa.

Jochelson, Waldemar 1908. The Koryak. *The Jesup North Pacific Expedition 6, Memoirs of the American Museum of Natural History* 10, Pt. 1–2. New York. New edition 2016, edited by E. Kasten and M. Dürr. Fürstenberg/Havel: Kulturstiftung Sibirien.

— 1910–1926. The Yukaghir and Yukaghirized Tungus. *The Jesup North Pacific Expedition 9, Memoirs of the American Museum of Natural History* 13; Pt. 1, 1910; Pt. 2, 1924; Pt. 3, 1926. New York. New edition 2018, edited by E. Kasten and M. Dürr. Fürstenberg/Havel: Kulturstiftung Sibirien.

Kagarov, E. G. 1935. V.G. Bogoraz v zarubezhnoi kritike [W. Bogoras in Foreign Critical Literature]. *Sovetskaia Etnografiia* 4–5: 233–235.

Kan, Sergei A. 2001. The "Russian Bastian" and Boas: Why Shternberg's "The Social organization of the Gilyak" Never Appeared Among the Jesup Expedition Publications. In *Gateways: Exploring the Legacy of the Jesup North Pacific Expedition, 1897–1902.* I. Krupnik and W. W. Fitzhugh (eds.), 217–256. Washington, D.C.: Arctic Studies Center, National Museum of Natural History, Smithsonian Institution.

— 2006. "My Old Friend in a Dead-end of Empiricism and Skepticism." Bogoras, Boas, and the Politics of Soviet Anthropology of the Late 1920s–Early 1930s. *Histories of Anthropology Annual* 2: 33–68. Lincoln and London.

— 2009a. Alexander Goldenweiser's Politics. *History of Anthropology Annual* 5: 182–199.

— 2009b. *Lev Shternberg. Anthropologist, Russian Socialist, Jewish Activist.* Lincoln: University of Nebraska Press.

Kasten, Erich, and Michael Dürr 2016. Jochelson and the Jesup North Pacific Expedition: A New Approach in the Ethnography of the Russian Far East. In *Waldemar Jochelson: The Koryak.* E. Kasten and M. Dürr (eds.), 9–34. Fürstenberg/Havel: Kulturstiftung Sibirien.

Kendall, Laurel, and Igor Krupnik (eds.) 2003. *Constructing Cultures Then and Now. Celebrating Franz Boas and the Jesup North Pacific Expedition. Contributions to Circumpolar Anthropology* 3. Washington, D.C.: Arctic Studies Center, National Museum of Natural History, Smithsonian Institution.

Kerttula, Anna M. 2000. *Antler on the Sea: The Yupik and Chukchi of the Russian Far East.* Ithaca: Cornell University Press.

Kolesnitskaia, I.M. 1971. V.G. Bogoraz – folklorist [Waldemar Bogoras as a Folklorist]. *Ocherki istorii russkoi etnografii i fol'kloristiki* 5. *Trudy Instituta etnografii AN SSSR* 95: 139–159. Moscow.

Kolonteeva, I.V. 1991. *Vladimir Germanovich Bogoraz-Tan i Severo-Vostok. Bibliograficheskii ukazatel'* [Vladimir Germanovich Bogoras-Tan and the Northeast. Bibliography]. Magadan: Magadan Scientific Library.

Krader, Lawrence 1968. Bogoraz, Vladimir G.; Shternberg, Lev Y.; and Jochelson, Vladimir. *International Encyclopedia of the Social Sciences, Vol. 2*. David L. Sills (ed.), 116–119. New York: The Macmillan Company & The Free Press.

Kroeber, Alfred R., and T.T. Waterman 1920. *Source Book in Anthropology*. University of California Syllabus Series 118. Berkeley: University of California Press.

Krupnik, Igor 1996. The 'Bogoras Enigma': Bounds of Culture and Formats of Anthropologists. In *Grasping the Changing World: Anthropological Concepts in the Postmodern Era*. V. Hubinger (ed.), 35–52. London: Routledge.

— 1998. "Jesup Genealogy": Intellectual Partnership and Russian-American Cooperation in Arctic/North Pacific Anthropology. Pt. 1. *Arctic Anthropology* 35(2): 199–226.

— 2001. A Jesup Bibliography. Tracking the Published and Archival Legacy of the Jesup Expedition. In *Gateways: Exploring the Legacy of the Jesup North Pacific Expedition, 1897–1902*. I. Krupnik and W.W. Fitzhugh (eds.), 297–316. Washington, D.C.: Arctic Studies Center, National Museum of Natural History, Smithsonian Institution.

— 2008. V.G. Bogoraz – ego nasledie i ucheniki [V.G. Bogoras: His Legacy and Disciples]. In *Tropoyu Bogoraza: Nauchnye i literaturnye materialy*. L.S. Bogoslovskaia, V.S. Krivoshchekov, and I. Krupnik (eds.), 23–27. Moscow: GEOS.

— 2016a. From Boas to Burch: Eskimology Transitions. In *Early Eskimo Studies: Themes and Transitions, 1850s–1980s*. I. Krupnik (ed.), 1–33. Washington, D.C.: Smithsonian Institution Scholarly Press.

— 2016b. One Field Season and 50-Year Career: Franz Boas and Early Eskimology. In *Early Eskimo Studies: Themes and Transitions, 1850s–1980s*. I. Krupnik (ed.), 73–83. Washington, D.C.: Smithsonian Institution Scholarly Press.

Krupnik, Igor, and William W. Fitzhugh (eds.) 2001. *Gateways: Exploring the Legacy of the Jesup North Pacific Expedition, 1897–1902. Contributions to Circumpolar Anthropology* 1. Washington, D.C.: Arctic Studies Center, National Museum of Natural History, Smithsonian Institution.

Krupnik, Igor, and Stanley Freed 2004. Original Boas Map for the Jesup Expedition Discovered. *ASC Newsletter* 12: 16–17.

Krupnik, Igor, and Nikolai Vakhtin 2003. "The Aim of the Expedition … Has in the Main Been Accomplished." Words, Deeds, and Legacies of the Jesup North Pacific Expedition. In *Constructing Cultures Then and Now. Celebrating Franz Boas and the Jesup North Pacific Expedition*. L. Kendall and I. Krupnik (eds.), 15–31. *Contributions to Circumpolar Anthropology* 3. Washington, D.C.: Arctic Studies Center.

Kuz'mina, Liudmila P. 1993. The Jesup North Pacific Expedition (from the History of Russian-American Cooperation). In *Anthropology of the North Pacific Rim*. W.W.

Fitzhugh and V. Chaussonnet (eds.), 63–77. Washington, D.C.: Smithsonian Institution Press.

Kuznetsova, Varvara G. 1957. Materialy po prazdnikam i obriadam Amguemskikh olennykh chukchei [Materials on Festival and Rites of the Amguema Reindeer Chukchi]. *Sibirskii etnograficheskii sbornik* 2; *Trudy Instituta etnografii AN SSSR* 35: 263–326. Moscow and Leningrad.

Leeds, Anthony 1965. Reindeer Herding and Chukchi Social Institutions. In *Man, Culture, and Animals*. A. Leeds and A. P. Vayda (eds.) *American Association for the Advancement of Science* 78: 87–128. Washington, D.C.

Liarskaia, Elena 2016. "Tkan' Penelopy": 'proekt Bogoraza vo vtoroi polovine 1920-kh–1930-kh gg. ["Penelope's shroud": 'Bogoras's project' in the second half of the 1920s and in the 1930s"]. *Antropologicheskii Forum* 29: 142–186 (see: Penelope's Cloth: "The Bogoras Project" in the Second Half of the 1920s–1930s, this volume).

Mathiassen, Therkel 1928. Material Culture of the Iglulik Eskimos. *Report of the Fifth Thule Expedition 1921–1924*. Vol. VI(1). Copenhagen.

Meshchaninov, Ivan I. (ed.) 1937. *Pamiati Bogoraza (1865–1936). Sbornik statei* [In Memory of (Waldemar) Bogoras, 1865–1936. Memorial Festschrift]. Moscow and Leningrad: USSR Academy of Sciences.

Mikhailova, Elena A. 2004. Vladimir Germanovich Bogoraz: uchenyi, pisatel', obshchestvennyi deiatel' (Vladimir Germanovich Bogoraz: Scientist, Writer, and Public figure). In *Vydaiushchiesia otechestvennye etnologi i antropologi XX veka*. V. Tishkov and D. Tumarkin (eds.), 95–136. Moscow.

— 2016. Sof'ia Konstantinovna Bogoraz (1870–1921): Shtrikhi k portretu Vladimira Germanovicha Bogoraza [Sof'ia Konstantinovna Bogoraz, 1870–1921: Toward a Sketch Portrait of Vladimir Germanovich Bogoraz]. *Antropologicheskii Forum* 29: 109–124. St. Petersburg.

Murdoch, John 1892. Ethnological Results of the Point Barrow Expedition. *Ninth Annual Report of the Bureau of Ethnology, 1887–1888*: 19–441. Washington, D.C.: Government Printing Office.

Nelson, Edward W. 1899. The Eskimo about Bering Strait. *Eighteenth Annual Report of the Bureau of Ethnology, 1896–1897*: 3–518. Washington, D.C.: Government Printing Office.

Raizman, David I. 1967. V.G. Bogoraz-Tan – revolutsioner, pisatel', uchenyi [V.G. Bogoras-Tan: A Revolutionary, Writer, and a Scholar]. *Zapiski Chukotskogo kraevedcheskogo muzeia* 4: 3–10. Magadan.

Schweitzer, Peter P. 1999. The Chukchi and Siberian Yupik of the Chukchi Peninsula, Russia. In *The Cambridge Encyclopedia of Hunters and Gatherers*. R.B. Lee and R. Daly (eds.), 137–140. Cambridge: Cambridge University Press.

— 2005. Bogoraz, Vladimir Germanovich. In *Encyclopedia of the Arctic*. M. Nuttal (ed.), vol. 1: 267–269. New York and London: Routledge.

Seroshevskii [Sieroszewski], Waclaw 1896. *Yakuty. Opyt etnograficheskogo issledo-*

vaniia [The Yakut. An Ethnographic Study]. Vol. 1. St. Petersburg: Russian Geographical Society.

Shentalinskaia, Tat'iana S. 2012. Sof'ia Bogoraz – avtor zapisei russkogo fol'klora na Chukotke [Sof'ia Bogoraz: The Author of Russian Folklore Recordings in Chukotka]. *Etnograficheskoe obozrenie* 1: 110–120. Moscow.

— 2015. Fonozapisi sibirskogo folklora iz amerikanskikh arkhivov [Siberian Folklore Phonographic Recordings at the American Archives]. In *Folklore – rannie zapisi.* V.M. Gatsak and V.A. Bakhtina (comps.), 145–271. Moscow: IMLI RAN.

Sirina, Anna A. 2010. Pis'ma V.G. Bogoraza iz Sibiriakovskoi ekspeditsii [V.G. Bogoras's letters from the Sibiriakov Expedition]. *Etnograficheskoe Obozrenie* 2: 138–149. Moscow.

Stefánsson, Vilhjalmur 1919. The Stefánsson-Anderson Arctic Expedition of the American Museum: Preliminary Ethnological Report. *Anthropological Papers of the American Museum of Natural History* 14(1). New York.

Thalbitzer, William (ed.) 1914. The Ammassalik Eskimo. Contributions to the Ethnology of the East Greenland Natives. Pt. 1. *Meddelelser om Grønland* 39. Copenhagen.

Turner, Lucien M. 1894. Ethnology of the Ungava District, Hudson Bay Territory. *Bureau of Ethnology, Smithsonian Institution, 11th Annual Report:* 159–350. Washington, D.C.

Vakhtin, Nikolai B. 1994. Native Peoples of the Russian Far North. In *Polar Peoples. Self-Determination and Development:* 29–80 London: Minority Rights Publications.

— 2001. Franz Boas and the Shaping of the Jesup Expedition Siberian Research, 1895–1900. In *Gateways: Exploring the Legacy of the Jesup North Pacific Expedition, 1897–1902.* I. Krupnik and W.W. Fitzhugh (eds.), 71–89. Washington, D.C.: Arctic Studies Center, National Museum of Natural History, Smithsonian Institution.

— 2004. "Nauka i zhizn'". Sud'ba Vladimira Iokhel'sona (po materialam ego perepisi 1897–1934 gg.) ["Science and Life". The Destiny of Waldemar Jochelson (based on His Correspondences between 1897–1934)]. In *Biulleten'. Antropologiia, men'shinstva, mul'tikul'turalizm* 5: 35–49.

— 2016a. "Proekt Bogoraza": borba za ogon' [The Bogoras's Project: The Quest for Fire]. *Antropologicheskii Forum* 29: 125–141.

— 2016b. Bogoras Project and Yupik Eskimo Linguistics in Russia. In *Early Eskimo Studies: Themes and Transitions, 1850s–1980s.* I. Krupnik (ed.), 193–218. Washington, D.C.: Smithsonian Institution Scholarly Press.

Vaté, Virginie 2005. Chukchi. In *Encyclopedia of the Arctic.* Mark Nuttal (ed.). Vol. 1: 335–338. New York and London: Routledge.

Vdovin, Innokentii S. 1957. V.G. Bogoraz kak issledovatel' iazykov i kul'tury narodov Severo-Vostoka [Waldemar Bogoras as a Scholar of Languages and Culture of the Northeast]. *Na Severe Dal'nem* 6: 174–188.

— 1965. V. G. Bogoraz – issledovatel' iazykov i kul'tury narodov severo-vostoka Sibiri

[Waldemar Bogoras: A scholar of Siberian languages and cultures]. *Sovetskaia Etnografiia* 3: 70–78.

— 1977. Religioznye kul'ty chukchei [Chukchi Religious Practices and Beliefs]. In *Pamiatniki kul'tury narodov Sibiri i Severa (2-ia polovina XIX–nachalo XX v.).* I.S. Vdovin (ed.), *Sbornik Muzeia antropologii i etnografii* 33: 117–171. Leningrad.

— 1991a. Posleslovie [Afterword]. In *V.G. Bogoraz – Material'naia kul'tura chukchei*: 211–222. Moscow: Nauka.

— 1991b. V.G. Bogoraz – uchenyi, pisatel', obshchestvennyi deiatel' (K 125-letiiu so dnia rozhdeniia) [W. Bogoras: A Scholar, Writer, and a Public Figure (To the 125th Anniversary of his Birth). *Sovetskaia Etnografiia* 2: 82–92.

Vinnikov, Isaac N. 1935. Bibliografiia etnograficheskikh i lingvisticheskikh rabot V.G. Bogoraza [Bibliography of W. Bogoras's ethnographic and linguistic publications]. *Sovetskaia Etnografiia* 4–5: 235–241.

Zelenin, Dmitrii K. 1937. V.G. Bogoraz – etnograf i folklorist [W. Bogoras as Ethnograph and Folklorist]. In *Pamiati V.G. Bogoraza.* I.I. Meshchaninov (ed.), v–xviii. Moscow: Academy of Sciences.

Zhornitskaia, Maria Ia. 1994. Chukchee. In *Russia and Eurasia/China. Vol. VI. Encyclopedia of World Cultures.* P. Friedrich and N. Diamond (eds.), 76–79. New York: G.K. Hall & Company.

7 „PENELOPE'S CLOTH": „THE BOGORAS PROJECT" IN THE SECOND HALF OF THE 1920s-1930s

Elena Liarskaya

Introduction

The history of Soviet ethnography, the Leningrad ethnographic school and the Northern Studies inseparably connected with it in the period of 1920–1930s have attracted the researchers' attention[1] for quiet a long time. They are interested in the figures of the founding fathers of the Leningrad school L.Ia. Shternberg and V.G. Bogoras,[2] and the fates of those whom they taught.[3]

It is known that the Leningrad Northern Science of that time was not limited to the University and the Academy of Sciences, but rather incorporated other institutions designed to study the North, such as the Institute of the Peoples of the North (hereinafter INS) and Pedagogical Institute named after A.I. Herzen (further LGPI). A number of individual studies[4] have been devoted to them, but most often these institutions and people working in them are described separately and in different contexts. In some cases the history of science, the academic life of Leningrad University and the Academy of Sciences of the USSR would fall into the focus of the researchers, and then the graduates of the ethnographic department of Leningrad State University, who studied with Bogoras and Shternberg, get into the center of attention, and other institutions go to the background, beginning to get confused and merge almost to the point of merging.[5] In others, the attention is focused on the work of training of the national *intelligentsia*; in such cases the researchers are interested only in the history of INS, and everything else becomes the background (Smirnova 2012).

---

1 See Slezkine 1993; 1994; Solovei 1998; 2001; Kozmin 2009; Arziutov and Kan 2013; Alymov and Arziutov 2014.
2 For example: Mikhailova 2004; Kan 2005; Krupnik 2008; Krupnik and Mikhailova 2008; Kan 2009, and others.
3 For example, the work by A.M. Reshetov (see the bibliography of his works: <http://kunstkamera. ru/files/lib/978-5-02-025593-7/978-5-02-025593-7_02.pdf>), and also the collection Repressed Ethnographers (2002; 2003) and others.
4 For example, Northern Studies 2003; Smirnova 2012.
5 Even in such carefully performed work as Alymov and Arziutov 2014, the northern branch of LGPI and the northern faculty of the Institute of Living Oriental Languages named after Yenukidze are confused (ibid.:83).

In this article the focus of analysis is transferred from individuals or organizations to a system of relationships that existed between some of them. I consider it important that such institutions as the ethnographic department of the geographical faculty of Leningrad State University, INS (with all its predecessors) and the northern branch of LGPI existed at the same time in the same place not by mere chance but by the will of their creators; that certain general principles formed the basis of their activities; that they acted not independently of each other but in close collaboration. Each of these institutions had to solve its own tasks, but they were united in a single structure created by the will of V.G. Bogoras and his associates, who complemented each other, created a special research and educational environment, which allowed to solve problems that each of these institutions separately would not be able to.

Different areas of training were being formed in constant interaction with each other, matched each other and were complementary. Scientists taught at INS and simultaneously learned from their students; languages came first; future teachers participated in the development of grammars of the languages on which they were to teach; future Soviet workers from the indigenous peoples, while comprehending the basics of the Soviet government, simultaneously learned to translate and edit texts in their native languages and acted as consultants for a variety of specialists studying the North. This is how a special personal and scientific environment arose, which allowed to solve questions on complex study and development of the North.

The purpose of this article is to describe the institutions that the history of Soviet northern studies began from as a purposefully created system. I will call this system the "Bogoras project".[6] My task also includes integration and some preliminary regularization of the data on the work of the organizations that were parts of this system: information about them is scattered over various, sometimes hard-to-access sources, which makes it difficult to see the overall picture.

One of the features of northern studies (and ethnography in general) in the 1920–1930s is an inseparable link between theoretical study of the North and solution of practical problems of transforming life in this region. This feature is well-known to modern researchers, it is regularly mentioned in their works, but the consequences of this order of things elude their attention and do not have a serious impact on the analysis of the situation. Apparently, it is due to the habit of modern rigid separation into academic science and cultural (or applied) work, which prevents them from accepting, problematizing and analyzing the consequences of the division relevant for a different epoch.

---

6   This is the conventional name I chose paying tribute to the memory of the person, whose will and great efforts made it possible to implement the project. At the same time, it must be remembered that he alone would have never been able to create this structure, and in his work he relied on his colleagues and students of the Leningrad ethnographic school created by them together with L.Ia. Shternberg. Since most of the events described in the article occurred after the death of L.Ia. Shternberg, the conventional name of the "project" contains only the name of V.G. Bogoras.

The sources for the article include archival materials (primarily relating to the organization of training and the work of institutions) stored in St. Petersburg Central Archives and other archives of St. Petersburg, texts published in the journals *Etnograf-issledovatel', Sovetskaia Etnografiia, Taiga i Tundra, Sovetskii sever* and other periodicals of 1920–1930s. Another important source of information is the collection (Enlightenment 1958), which contains generalizing articles devoted to the problems in the focus of our interest; many of the texts were written by direct participants in the events, Bogoras's students V.I. Tsintsius (1958), G.M. Vasilevich (1958), F.F. Krongauz (1958), etc.. Among them, of great interest is the article by M.G. Voskoboinikov (1958) *On the preparation of pedagogical personnel for the schools of the peoples of the Far North*: its author recalls the smallest details concerning the organization of training in this or that institution. Another important source is the electronic catalog of the Russian National Library. It allows searching through the texts of bibliographic cards of pre-war books that helps to identify publications relevant to institutions of our interest.

The first part of the article is devoted to a brief survey of the history of these institutions as elements of a single structure. The second part analyzes the relationships between the individual components of this structure. The final section will deal with the fate and significance the "Bogoras project".

The "Bogoras project": elements

The 1920s

The first element of the "project" was the ethnographic department (at the beginning of the Higher Geographical Courses, then of the Faculty of Geography of Leningrad State University, then—ethno-department) that arose in 1916. I will not dwell on this in detail, referring the reader to N.B. Vakhtin (2016).[7] Let me remind you only the basic principles of the organization of student training, important for this topic.

Firstly, the connection of students' studies with practical work was important: students went on long expeditions and 'in the field' performing a variety of tasks, some being far from just academic. Bogoras formulated this as the preference of the stationary method of investigation to the expeditionary one.[8] Secondly, it was considered obligatory to study the language of those people with whom it would be necessary to work, and the language was interesting not as such, but rather as a tool that allowed to remove intermediaries between the ethnographer and the informant, as a means to penetrate into the world of images and representations of non-literate peoples. In addition, the task was set to organize the training of the inhabitants of the North in

---

7   See also Ratner-Shternberg, 1935; Solovei 1998.
8   For a discussion of this topic and many examples of this kind of work, see Alymov and Arziutov 2014.

their native languages, and in solving this problem the students of Shternberg and Bogoras also considered it necessary to participate.

The second element of the "project" was the predecessors of the INS—*Rabfak* (workers' faculty) and *Sevfak* (faculty for representatives of northern peoples). INS history is rather well described: in 1925 a northern *Rabfak* was opened at Leningrad State University, which in 1926 became the northern *Rabfak*[9] of the Institute of Living Oriental Languages (LIZHVYA), and in 1927 was reorganized into the Northern faculty of the same institute (Salatkin 1933; Voskoboinikov 1958:51), which existed until the end of December 1929 (Voskoboinikov 1958:50–53),[10] and then was transformed into the Institute of the Peoples of the North (see below).

The main task of these organizations was to train future members of national *intelligentsia*. The training was attended by representatives of the northern outskirts, sometimes not only unable to read and write, but also not knowing the Russian language at all. Classes were very intensive: students had to go through the preparatory department courses, i.e. the curriculum of ordinary *Rabfak*s, at an accelerated pace.

Let me note that, contrary to the popular belief, not only the representatives of the peoples who were later included in the list of indigenous small peoples of the North, but also those who at that time were called "the peoples of the East"[11] were trained at the *Rabfak*, as well as later at the *Sevfak*. The article devoted to the third anniversary of INS said that when the Northern Faculty of LIZHVYA was established in 1927 it had two branches: the northern and the eastern ones (Salatkin 1933:7). This fact is worthy of special mentioning, since it allows us to stop considering the *Rabfak* for the northerners something unique and makes it possible to compare the educational practices for the "peoples of the North" with those for the "peoples of the East", which existed at that time.

---

9 Part of the archive of the Northern Workers' Union of Leningrad State University was preserved in the Central State Archive (CSA) of St. Petersburg (fund 6951, inventories 1–2), the materials of the *Sevfak* LIZHVYA were preserved in the fund 7222 of the same archive.

10 The places where these institutions were located were very colorful: first the northerners, who had just come from taiga and tundra and sometimes did not speak Russian at all, were accommodated right in the Catherine Palace (in *Tzarskoe,* at that time *Detskoe Selo*). Later the department found a more suitable place in the same *Detskoe Selo*. When the *Rabfak* was transformed into *Sevfak*, it moved to Leningrad, where for the entire subsequent history (both of *Sevfak* and INS) it was located in the building of the Theological Seminary of the Alexander Nevsky Lavra (Obvodny Canal Embankment, 17). The same building during the Civil War hosted a receiver-distributor for "morally defective" children, the most formidable institution for homeless children of that time in Petrograd. Apparently, the meetings of the northerners and street children did take place, at least, they are reflected in short novel by Bogoras "The Risen Tribe" (Bogoras-Tan 1935).

11 The list of the *Sevfak* students of 1929 includes Kirghiz, Kurd, Uzbek, Mongol, Buryat, Tadzhik, Tibetan, Baluchi, Ossetian, Turkmen, etc. A significant group (24 from the list of 289 people) were Todinsk Tuvan (I'd like to remind that at that moment Tuva was not a part of the USSR) (CSA SPb. Fund 7222. Inv. 10. File. 7-a. Aid. 1–100b).

The purpose of these institutions was not to provide a small group of "natives" with a more or less decent education, but to train cadres for the North,[12] so that the graduates would return home and be able to work in local institutions. For this purpose, an important mechanism was designed and used: the students had to go home annually (and the inhabitants of Chukotka biannually) for externship. In fact, this was the embodiment of the same idea of the need for regular field expeditions and stationary field work, which was laid down by Bogoras in the system of ethnographers' training (Voskoboinikov 1958:52,60; Vakhtin 2016). Vacation trips solved several tasks at once: they allowed students not to break away from their native places and keep in touch with them, as well as gave the chance, at least for a while, to provide local institutions with relatively competent personnel, the need for whom was extreme. In addition, native society saw the results of the training and heard stories about life in Leningrad, and, while working, students understood what they did not yet know and what they needed to learn.

From the very beginning, the ethno-department of Leningrad State University and the *Rabfak* (and then the Northern faculty of LIZHVYA) were not isolated from each other. On the contrary, the connection between Bogoras's students from the north and other students of ethnography arose very quickly: the ethnographers studied live languages directly with the native speakers, conducting linguistic and other scientific research. With the help of the *Sevfak* students conducted was approbation of field expedition programs, folklore record, etc. (Seleznev 1928).

Bogoras's organization in Leningrad of an institution for teaching illiterate northerners, some of whom had never been outside their homes, caused a very mixed reaction in the society. It is known the *Sevfak* worked under the patronage of the Committee of the North at the All-Russian Central Executive Committee,[13] and in 1927 the People's Commissar of Education A.V. Lunacharskii gave a positive review of the *Sevfak* (1927:20–21). However, not only in the government, but also among the colleagues and pupils of Bogoras there were those who thought that the system invented by him was too cruel: the children of taiga and tundra, torn from their environment, could barely endure the damp Leningrad climate and adapted poorly – which was confirmed by rather a high mortality among the students (Gagen-Torn 2002: 318–319). The archive of the *Sevfak* has preserved the materials[14] that indicate

---

12 The list of students of 1929 allows us to figure out the social composition of the students. The total was 289, from who the majority was recorded as hunters—112 people, 40 people are designated as fishermen and 8—as fishermen-hunters, 49 peasants also appear on the lists. Especially noteworthy in this context is the number of reindeer herders—there are only 9 of them (4 "Lopar" and 5 "Samoyed"). In addition, there were 30 farm laborers (18 of them were representatives of the northern outskirts) (CSA SPb. Fund. 7222 Inv. 10, File 7-a. Aid. 1–100b).

13 For example, when the students of the Northern faculty began to publish their own magazine *Taiga i Tundra*, they received an official greeting from the Chairman of the Committee of the North, P.G. Smidovich (1928:1).

14 See an interesting document—a denunciation, written in mid-March 1928, two and a half

that its existence was not cloudless. There were people in LIZHVYA who did not only doubt the meaningfulness of this enterprise, but also wrote letters denouncing them to different instances, trying to prove that the northern branch was just "professorial fun", a waste of state money: students did not study there, but only "got spoiled", and the *Sevfak* must immediately be disbanded.[15] Nevertheless, Bogoras and his associates managed to convince the country's leadership of the prospects of this enterprise, and the northern branch not only survived, but rather turned into an independent educational institution — the Institute of the Peoples of the North,[16] which began its existence in January 1930.

---

years after the first students arrived in Leningrad. Its author is the head of the political enlightenment work department of LIZHVYA, a certain Potopov (orthography and punctuation of the original showed a certain level of ignorance):

The Northern Faculty in connection with the tasks of cultural construction in the North.
[...] The Northern Faculty duplicates residential schools with some significant minuses. The question is: who and for what purpose needs a bad duplication with wasting 3–4 times more money than any school for the locals. The conclusion is clear: only the "Northern patriots" want to duplicate it, want it badly and protect it. What was the Northern Faculty doing for more than two years? It was eliminating illiteracy among Northerners and Easterners. And wasn't it better to do it on the spot? Of course it was. But maybe we have a lot of scientific forces of the northern people who can reorganize this matter and subsequently prepare a frame of good workers on the spot. The trouble is, we do not have these scientific forces. There are two people, one professor Bogoras-Tan, who adversely affects students with a rude [so!] patronage-like approach to the tasks of nurturing the natives. And in general, Professor Bogoras-Tan is known among students as a hero of the liberation of the northern nationalities, and all the others, together with existing organizations, do nothing. His student Ia.P. Koshkin, the head of the Northern Club, the club that goes far beyond the limits of local history, maintains that "as a result of the October Revolution, the Jews and the northern peoples have a harder life than they had before the revolution" (See the protocol of the Bureau of the Party Cell from 1/ 3–28). The Northern Club boosts nationalism by discussing the issue of the relocation of non-native people from the native territories, restrictions on hunting and fishing areas, and so on for non-natives, and the fact that the national strife among the students has intensified is indisputable. As noted in the resolution of the Bureau of the Cell from 1 / 3–28 [...] all this is in favor of the fact that the two existing northerners, one young, the other old, can not bring the necessary benefits to the educational institution. It turns out that we have no specialists in northern studies of the kind that the Party and the Soviet power wants. [...] The conclusion can be only one: the existence of the Northern Faculty in Leningrad is not advisable. It must be disbanded, otherwise we will waste enormous sums of money with no benefit. [...] allowing the existence of the *Sevfak* for the elimination of illiteracy and experiments of prof. Bogoras-Tan is impossible. (Head of political education, Potopov). March 14, 1928. In: CSA St. Petersburg Fund. 7222. Inv. 9. File 44. Aid. 3–4).

15	Conflicts at the *Sevfak* are also mentioned in Slezkine (1994:189).
16	Order on LIZHVYA No. 36 on the conversion of the *Sevfak* into INS from December 30, 1929 (CSA SPb. Fund. 7222. Inv. 10. File 4. Aid. 38). It is interesting that the tenth anniversary of INS was celebrated in 1935, because the count was started from the date of the *Rabfak* creation, and further transformations were considered as a history of its continuous development (Voskoboinikov 1958:58).

The 1930s

1930 was in many respects crucial for the whole "Bogoras project". On the one hand, a serious blow was struck on the preparation of ethnographers: this year, as a result of another "restructuring and optimization", ethno-department ended its independent existence.[17] At the same time, the Leningrad Institute of Linguistics and History (LILI, also LIFLI—Institute of History, Philosophy and Linguistics)[18] was separated from the Leningrad State University where teaching of some northern languages was preserved. It is known that "in 1932, at the request of the leading bodies of the Far East at LIFLI, the northern branch was launched with two linguistic courses: the Tungus-Manchurian and the Paleo-Asiatic" (Voskoboinikov 1958:65). LILI (LIFLI) was graduated by many northeastern scholars who began their studies at Leningrad State University, but this institution did not produce a large number of new scholars (not connected with studies at Leningrad State University),[19] the training of ethnographers at the university was interrupted and, in fact, LSU actually fell out of the "Bogoras project".[20]

In 1930, as already mentioned, dues to the efforts of Bogoras and his associates, the *Sevfak* was transformed into the Institute of the Peoples of the North, whose rector was K.Ia. Luks. The Institute had a special status of an "Institute at the Central Executive Committee of the USSR", which meant that it was not subordinated to the People's Commissariat for Education, but directly to the government of the country.

In the same year, a new element of the "project" appeared, which had no analogue in the 1920s,—the Research Institute, engaged in the study of the North and the training graduate students in humanities specializing on the northern topics. It was established at INS and was named the Scientific Research Association of the Institute of the Peoples of the North (NIA INS). Over time, this organization brings together

---

17 Order of Leningrad State University № 24 from January 10, 1930 on the creation of a commission on transferring ethno-department into the structure of the Historical and Linguistic Faculty (Balashov et al. 1999:67).

18 Unfortunately, the archives of this institute still can not be found in the Central State Archive of St. Petersburg,

19 Such as V.A. Avrorin, G.F. Verbov, S.B. Okun, and others.

20 LIFLI existed for 7 years (until 1937), then was re-reunited with LSU (Universities 1935:40; Voskoboinikov 1958:65). An attempt to return ethnography to Leningrad State University was made before the war: in 1938, the Dean of the Geographical Faculty asked for restoration of some departments at the Faculty, including that of Ethnography (Balashov et al. 1999: 67). The Ethno-Department was reborn again at Leningrad State University in 1939–1940, this time combined with philology. In 1939, the Nenets and Koryak languages were taught there, and in 1940, the Tungus language was also added. Bogoras's students worked there, but they did not manage to achieve any results because of the war. After the war, the northern branch was restored at the Oriental Faculty of Leningrad State University, where ethnographic students who had entered Leningrad State University before the war completed their studies (Vinnikov 1939; Voskoboinikov 1958:66).

a large number of specialists in various northern fields (from archeology and history up to economics, linguistics and school organization).

Then another new element of the system appears—LGPI, named after Herzen, begins training teachers for northern schools. This institute proved to be important for the entire structure of the "project", since it trained not only educators, but also researchers of the North, partially replenishing the loss of ethno-department of Leningrad State University. Let us consider each of these elements in more detail.

The Institute of the Peoples of the North (INS)

The INS[21] had the following structure:[22]

1 *Preparatory Department* (the successor of the *Rabfak*), which had 8–12 differentiated groups, depending on the students' general level.
2 *The Main Department* (of the level of a technical school), which initially had six branches and later three (Soviet-Party, pedagogical, cooperative-collective farm [later: economic]).
3 *North-Asian Seminar*—a university level unit.

In 1934, 155 people studied at the Preparatory Department, with 221 students at the main one. The last branch was the smallest: in 1931 only 6 people managed to get enrolled there, by 1934 this number had grown to 16 (Dorovin 1932:51; Voskoboinikov 1958:58). Thus, in 1934 there were 392 students at INS.[23] It is noteworthy that of the 155 participants in the Preparatory Department only 40 were women: at that time among the northerners education was clearly a masculine affair.

In addition to the three above-named permanent training departments, various courses (from 6 to 12 months) for the peoples of the North were periodically organized at INS, where workers from Soviet organizations, cooperatives, hunting specialists, livestock experts and bookkeepers were trained (Voskoboinikov 1958:56). In the first years several workshops successfully operated at INS: carpenter's, locksmith's, sewing, wood and bone carving, a small currying factory (ibid: 54).

The life of this institution proceeded in a peculiar atmosphere, because the students lived and worked in one large building (Obvodny Canal Embankment, 17), where there were bedrooms, classes, workshops, laundry, a hairdresser, club rooms, and other services.

---

21 Materials of INS have been scattered across different archives and funds. Some of them are kept in the Central State Archive of St. Petersburg, mainly in the fund 9471, part of the scientific and organizational materials is stored in the SPF ARAN, fund 1025, some of the information can be found in the same archive in the Bogoras Foundation (fund 250). The most important part of the heritage of INS is stored in the Archive of the MAE (K-II fund, inventory 1 "Field materials, manuscripts of books, articles, dissertations of INS employees for 1929–1941").
22 See Dorovin (1932:51); Voskoboinikov (1858:54).
23 Cf. eight years before, in 1926, 74 people were studying at the northern *Rabfak* (Voskoboinikov 1958:58).

It is important to bear in mind the following:

- although INS has the word "institute" in its title, not all students had to receive higher education: the main department gave education at the level of a technical school (college);
- the task of the INS was to train not only teachers, but also various workers for the northern outskirts from the indigenous peoples of the North, i.e. the national *intelligentsia*. This is a serious difference between INS of this period and its reformed successors;
- all students of INS were involved in the work on alphabets and writing, working closely with the students of LGPI and helping to train researchers in the colloquial language of their people.

The Research Association of the Institute of the Peoples of the North[24]

This research institute was launched practically simultaneously with the INS. Although NIA INS and INS itself had similar names, they were located at the same address and were closely related to each other in terms of level and tasks, they were two completely different organizations. INS was an institution that trained the *intelligentsia* from among the peoples of the North (not always providing them with higher education), and NIA INS was a research institute that united people who studied the North and its population.

The academic staff of NIA INS (as it was written at that time) was divided into three main categories: researchers, post-graduate students and their lecturers. The Central State Archive of St. Petersburg stores the lists of NIA employees for several years. For example, in 1933 the staff included: 31 researchers (among them Bogoras himself, his students who had different specialties, as well as the leading specialists in the economy of the North, people engaged in the history of the North or teaching problems); 14 lecturers for post-graduate studies (some of them were at the same time employed as researchers, some were external, invited, visiting lecturers, for example,

---

24　The main published sources of information about the organization of NIA INS work are the already mentioned article by Voskoboinikov (1958) and the texts on the current life of NIA INS published in *Sovetskaia Etnografiia* in the section *Khronika*: in 1934 (short essay), 1935 (detailed description) and 1936 years. (A review of expeditions and business trips). The data presented by Voskoboinikov are systematic and complete, but they have one peculiarity: he analyzes the work of NIA INS primarily from the point of view of its importance for the organization of school instruction, and not from the position of contribution to the academic study of the North. Sources of academic life are to a large extent the materials of the *Khronika* in *Sovetskaia Etnografiia*, and especially the archival materials stored in St. Petersburg CSA and Archive of the Museum of Anthropology and Ethnography of the Academy of Sciences of the Russian Academy of Sciences (fund K-II), and data from the electronic catalog of Russian National Library.

L.V. Shcherba was the professor of experimental phonetics); 42 (!) post-graduate students.[25]

In addition to the people on the lists, "permanently and actively participating" in the work of the association were members of other research institutions and universities of Leningrad and Moscow (Khronika 1934:108; 1935:228).

Structure

The NIA INS was divided into large sections, within which separate directions were allocated. At first there were three sections, since 1933 their number increased to four (Khronika 1934:108; Voskoboinikov 1958:55).

1. *Linguistic Section.* The largest section by the number of participants: in 1934 there were 36 people in it (Khronika 1935:228). The tasks of the section included: study of the languages of the peoples of the North, scientific development of language construction matters in the North, creation of educational, popular political- and fiction literature in the northern languages. In 1934, the linguistic section was divided into four subgroups: Finno-Ugric-Nenets, Tungus-Manchurian, Paleo-Asiatic and the group for studying the folklore of the peoples of the North. The section was preparing to publish volumes dedicated to different language groups, as well as works on individual languages and linguistic problems. Almost all NIA linguists were simultaneously teachers of northern languages at INS and other institutions of the city, as well as authors or co-authors of the first ABC-books and textbooks.

2. *Historical and Ethnographic Section* (in 1934—12 people). The main task of the section was to study the history of the peoples of the North: their social structure in the tribal period and their history in the era of colonization of the territory.[26] In addi-

---

25 In 1934 there were 43 research associates and 37 graduate students in the NIA INS (Khronika 1935:228), in 1936–36 post-graduate students (Zelenin 1938:19). Already the very number of graduate students testifies the scale of this scientific institution.

26 Topics for research in 1934–1935. (Khronika 1935:229): "Ancestral order among the Evenk", "The Social System of the Transbaikal Evenk", "The Khasovo nights", "Nenets names", "Vogul and Ostiak principalities in the 17th century", "Penetration of commercial Capital into Yakutia in the 17th century", "Colonial policy of tsarism in Kamchatka and Chukotka in the 18th century", "Enfeebling of the Nenets in the 18th century", "Yasak and the liberation struggle of the Nenets in the 17th and 18th centuries", "The Voivodeship administration in Yakutia", 'The Evenk liberation movement in the 18th century". A special place in the work of the section was given to the study of archival materials of the Yakut and Tiumen funds. In addition, the historical-ethnographic section set two more tasks for itself: 1) preparing for printing of a number of works on the peoples of the North (respectively processed and commented) by various travelers of the 16th-18th centuries (Krasheninnikov, Steller, Castrén, Miller, etc.) and research in the history of the studying certain nations of the North (Khronika 1935:230; CSA St. Petersburg. Fund. 9471. Inv. 2. File. 35. Aid. 8–10a); 2) preparation of a textbook on the history of the peoples of the North (in 1935 they wrote the chapters *Siberia under the Mongolian power, The*

tion, the section worked on preparation of textbooks, teaching aids and programs for schools in the Far North.

3. *Cultural and Educational Section* (later Pedagogical). The staff of this section (in 1934—9 people) studied the specifics of northern children, provided courses on teaching techniques and the history of teaching, and developed individual teaching methods. In 1935 the section performed its work in two directions:

– Research—the study of *natsmen*[27] children and the experience of northern schools,[28] including such topics as "An Evenk child's system of views", "Development of a methodological study of a northern child intellectual development", "Family education in Gilyak[29] culture", "Children of the peoples of the North in ethnographic literature", "Localization of teaching in the northern national school", "The work of a northern school: INS materials", "The Russian language among the peoples of the North", "Pedagogical experiment as a method of studying the teaching process in a northern school", "Missionary schools among the peoples of the North";

– Methodological and pedagogical assistance to teachers built around three main topics: "The Study and development of methods in separate subjects schools and ethnic schools", "Theory of teaching and education in schools in the far north" and "Organization of school affairs in the North" (Khronika 1935:230).

4. *Economic and Geographical Section* (1934—12 people). It worked on the preparation of economic monographs on the northern ethnical districts and areas and studied certain branches of the northern economy.[30] Its tasks also included study of "socialist reconstruction of the economy of the peoples of the North". Like all the other sections, it was engaged in development of textbooks and manuals for the schools of the North. Employees of the Ethnographic and Economical-Geographical Department conducted local history work among the students. Section staff participated in the preparation of the new circumpolar census, which was planned to be held in early 1930s (Sergeev 1933).[31]

Conquest of Siberia, Siberia in the 17th century).

27 *Natsmen* is a short for members of ethnic minorities.

28 This was before the crackdown of pedology. A list of articles published at that time on this topic is contained in Iasnitskii (2013).

29 Gilyak are now named Nivkh.

30 In 1935, economic monographs were prepared for Taimyr National District, the Northern (Okhotsk) districts of the Lower Amur Region, Vitimo-Olekminsk National District and the Turukhansk District (Khronika 1935:230).

31 In 1935, according to the curriculum, the following subjects were studied: "Next tasks for further study of the Koryak economy", "Hunting of the Novaia Zemlia", "Salmon fishery in the Far North and the participation of the peoples of the North in it", "Hunting in the budget of the Far North population", "Passive samplers in the hunting of the peoples of the North" (part 1 of

In addition to the sections in NIA INS, there were two other scientific offices and two commissions (Khronika 1935).[32] The *Anthropological Chair* (three employees) conducted anthropometric and biochemical studies of INS students; *The Ethnic Physical Education Chair* organized methodological events and conducted researches (including: "Physiological and hygienic assessment of household postures of the peoples of the North", "Functional tests of the cardiovascular system of INS Students", "Collection of materials on ethnic types of sport games and dances", etc.). The *Commission on History of Religion and Anti-Religious Work*, in addition to its own anti-religious work, studied the religiosity of INS students, collected exhibits on the religion of the peoples of the North, made a bibliographical file on the history of religion and anti-religious work in the North. In 1935, a publication on the history of Tungus religion was being prepared for publication. The *Commission on National Art* (in 1934—8 people) was dealing with two types of tasks: theoretical—the study of all types of national arts of the peoples of the North, and practical—research of its development problems. The commission was divided into sectors of painting and drawing, sculpture, national theater, national music.[33]

NIA conducted a great expeditionary work: only in 1933 20 expeditions were organized to different parts of the North (Khronika 1934:108).[34]

The *Khronika* of 1935 emphasizes that at that time the NIA INS had expanded considerably and strengthened the communication (mainly through the literature exchange) with a number of foreign scientific institutions (mainly in the USA, France,

---

the monograph *The Peoples of the North; Technology of Hunting for Animals*), *Soviet Trade in Ostiako-Vogulskii National District* (Khronika 1935:230)

32   The same publication reports on the ongoing work on shooting of a full-length film, the purpose of which is to show the peoples of the North and the giant socialist construction in the Far North under the conditional title "Bolsheviks of the North". The picture is mainly based on the existing film material, but with the additional shooting of missing coherency moments both in INS itself and on site by one of the expeditions of the NIA. Over the past period, a lot of work has been done on viewing of more than 100 paintings, annotations have been compiled, the latter being are made out in the form of a special work "Northern Films" (Khronika 1935:232); See also Arziutov (2016).

33   One of the tasks of this commission was to popularize the art of the peoples of the North, arranging exhibitions in the USSR and abroad, preparing albums, books, reproductions for printing, "promoting the reproduction of sculpture in materials: terracotta, plaster, majolica, bronze, wood, bone and stone" (Khronika 1935:231). In addition, the commission conducted experiments with new material for northerners, collaborated with Leningrad Porcelain Factory, for which INS students created product designs and sculptural models. It worked on the illustration and design of publications of national literature. For more details on the work of the artistic part of the commission, see Musiankova (2012). The same commission studied musical instruments and musical folklore of the peoples of the North and was engaged in creation and development of a Nanai theater group, on the basis of which they planned to create second (Evenk) theater group soon.

34   Expeditions were predominantly linguistic, but their participants also collected ethnographic materials (Khronika 1934:108).

Austria, Estonia, Latvia, etc). This connection was realized both directly and through VOKS[35] (Khronika 1935:229). Just at this time (1934–1937) a German Communist scientist, a specialist in Ugric languages, the future vice-president of GDR Academy of Sciences, W. Steinitz, worked at NIA INS (CSA St. Petersburg F. 9471. Inv 2. Case 88 [160], Khronika 1936:157).

Publishing

Almost all the works devoted to INS mention that it published a periodic collection of *Taiga and Tundra* implemented by the northerners—the most famous (and unusual) publication by INS.[36] However, in scientific terms it was far from the most important: in the early 1930s, NIA INS conducted huge publishing work. The first was the series *Proceedings of NIA INS* published in 1932–1933 (5 issues). It was in this series that the book by P.E. Terletskii *Population of the Far North According to the Census Data* was published (1932), as well as a study by M.O. Kosvena devoted to Morgan (1933), and the work by E.A. Kreinovich about Gilyak numerals (1932). Then, instead of a single *Proceedings*, several series began to appear: *Works on Economics, Works on History, Works on Ethnography, Works on Linguistics* and *Works on Folklore*. In addition to them, in 1935–1936 10 more issues of the *Izvestiia of NIA INS* series were published. Besides all the series, about 20 books were published also devoted to various aspects of modern study of the North. In addition, from 1934 to 1936, the series *Materials on Ethnography* was published, which contained classical ethnographic works (two volumes of L.G. Morgan's works, two volumes of works by L.Ia. Shternberg and the first volume of Bogoras's *The Chukchee*.[37] INS was active in publication work: it is known that the works by Castrén, Steller, Krasheninnikov, Shirokogoroff were translated and prepared for publication, Miller's *Siberian History* was being prepared for revised publication, annotated indexes of literature on the peoples of the North were compiled and prepared for publication (CSA SPb. F. 9471. Inv. 2. Case. 35. Aid. 8)—but these planned publications did never appear.[38]

The largest number of works published under the stamp of NIA INS was associated with the languages of the peoples of the North. They included works on grammar, dialectology, the language of folklore, experimental phonetics, dictionaries, and self-tutorials. In addition, there were numerous works devoted to creation of written language, textbooks, self-instruction manuals, methodological recommendations for

---

35 All-Union Organization for Cultural Relations with Foreign Countries.
36 In fact, the collection *Taiga i Tundra* was born at the *Sevfak*: the first issue was published in 1928, and the last one, No. 2 (5), in 1933.
37 The series ceased to exist in 1936, and the second volume of *The Chukchee* was published outside this series after the author's death (1939), but still under the stamp of NIA INS.
38 For additional information on the INS publications see appendices in the Russian edition of this article in Antropologicheskii Forum 2016 (29): 37–42.

teachers, analysis of possible educational difficulties in learning the language.[39] Literature in the northern languages was written, translated and prepared for publication.

Even a brief review of the structure of NIA INS, the number of its staff and graduate students, the directions of their researches, publications prepared there show that this was a large scientific institution that seriously influenced the state of affairs in the northern studies. At the same time, in modern works devoted to the history of Russian ethnography in the 1920s–1930s, the activities of NIA INS not just fail to be considered, but rather are hardly ever mentioned: it is believed that the Institute of the Peoples of the North was engaged solely in training the "native" students.

LGPI named after A.I. Herzen: Northern Branch and Northern Courses

The purpose of this institution was to train teachers for northern schools and workers for national northern technical training colleges. I would like to underline that not just elementary school teachers were trained there, but teachers of senior classes and "key specialists", i.e. those who, having returned back, would themselves be able to train teachers for local schools.

Unlike INS, this institution accepted people regardless of their ethnic background, only secondary education was required. Forms of training at the Institute were very different, for example, they provided a short-term or one-year further vocational training courses for teachers who came from the North, or courses for the teacher training for junior or senior undergraduates of various faculties of LGPI and other pedagogical institutions wishing to work in northern schools. The essence of this training was that students *in addition to* their specialty were taught national languages and did northern studies, receiving the right to teach in national schools or pedagogical schools. Another important form of training, which existed at the teacher's college, was a special Northern Department, which was administered separately. More than the half of the graduate students by the time they entered LGPI had already had experience of work in northern schools (Voskoboinikov 1958:62). The Northern Branch more or less constantly worked at the Philological Faculty; occasionally it recruited a group of "northerners" from the Historical and Geographical Faculties. In all cases, students studied special northern courses in addition to their main curriculum.

As a side note, in the early 1930s teachers were trained at LGPI for work not only in the North, but also in other regions, for example, the archive has retained curricula of 1934 for the department of the western section of the "*natsmen* division" for the Poles, Finns, Estonians and Latvians (CSA St. Petersburg, 4331. Inv. 11. F. 443.) Thus, the northern direction in the LGPI was again (as in LIZHI), although important, but not unique and exceptional.

---

39 There were 7 issues in the series "Teacher's Aid for Ethnic Elementary Schools in the Far North".

LGPI graduates worked directly at northern schools, taught at pedagogical colleges, became "leading workers in the field of education" in Siberia, the Far East and the regions of the Far North. Before the war more than 200 people had been trained (Voskoboinikov 1958:64).

As already mentioned, training of northern teachers began at Leningrad State Pedagogical Institute in 1930, i.e. just when the Ethnographic Department of Leningrad State University ceased to exist. In the archive of the CSA SPb (Fund 4331), some northern courses for different types of training, curricula and reports were preserved, based on which one can get an idea of who taught there, what subjects they taught and in what scope. Considerable attention was paid to training future teachers in the field of northern languages, which was a specific feature of the northern branch. It is known that from 1932 to 1934 the Chukchi language was taught by Bogoras, the Inuit by Forstein, the Tungus by Vasilevich, the Nenets by Prokofiev, Verbov, Almazova, the Ostiak by Karger, the Vogul by Chernetsov, and the introduction to the study of northern languages was taught by prof. Bubrich. In addition to language training, future teachers were given courses in the history of the peoples of the North[40] and in the economy of the North,[41] in physical and economic geography of the North (lecturer A.V. Korolev). We know nothing about the existence of any courses in common ethnography and ethnography of the northern peoples, but programs by prof. Bogoras devoted to religion and anti-religious work in the North included topics traditional for ethnographers.[42]

The northern branch of LGPI was closely associated with Bogoras and his students. Beginning in 1932, the same logic in teaching began to be applied at the Teacher's College as at the Ethno-Department: after the second year students majoring in the North were sent to the North for a long practice, after which they could return and finish their studies.[43] (In 1934, the training in the northern section became five-year-long, in contrast to the four-year-curriculum for the rest of the institute). These students, together with Bogoras's pupils of the past and graduates of LILI, participated in creating textbooks and writing for the peoples of the North, while the best students were engaged in teaching the languages at short-term teacher-training courses (Voskoboinikov 1958:63).[44]

---

40 Unfortunately, in the available curriculum the author of the course is not listed.

41 The course "On the reconstruction of the Northern economy" was delivered by A.F. Bruchanov.

42 It is known that at the annual courses for teachers in 1937 ethnography was delivered as a separate subject.

43 The courses were called "Lectures on the history of beliefs" (14 hours) and "Religion and anti-religious work among small ethnic groups of the North for third-year students" (20 lectures).

44 Voskoboinikov writes about this (1958:61). Unfortunately, neither memories nor archival materials give us an opportunity to imagine how widely this practice was used and for how long it was preserved.

The Northern Branch of LGPI, although it was an independent organization with its own goals and objectives, was in fact an integral part of the unified structure created by Bogoras and his colleagues, centered in the first half of the 1930s around NIA INS. It was not just an overlap in the teaching staff—there was a close and deep structural connection between these institutions. As an illustration, I will cite a few quotes from the current plans and reports of the early 1930s preserved in LGPI funds:

1   From the minutes of the meeting devoted to the situation in the northern branch of Herzen Institute, 1932: "When undergoing pedagogical practice, establish contacts with INS in order to conduct, in addition to practical classes in model schools in Leningrad, classes with ethnic contingent of the students of the Institute" (CSA SPb F. 4331. Inv. 11. F. 217. Aid. 1).

2   From the working plan of the northern department for 1933–1934 academic year, 2nd spring semester: "P. 20 [...] the research work of the students of the department is to be done in INS" (CSA St. Petersburg F. 4331. Inv. 11. F. 388. Aid. 7).

3   From the report on the work of the northern branch in 1933–1934 academic year: "The research club did not work this year, but some students took part in compiling textbooks for northern languages (the Chukotka section, the entire Nenets section) and in the critical analysis of the published textbooks (the Eskimo section)" (CSA SPb F. 4331. Inv. 11. F. 388. Aid. 1). (The preparation of textbooks was conducted at INS.)

4   From the work plan of the Department of Northern Languages of the Institute named after A.I. Herzen for the second semester of 1933–1934 academic year:
    "Despite the considerable staff of the department, all employees except two are the full-time employees of the Institution of the People of the North. The department staff includes 3 professors, 2 assistant professors, 10 assistants, 2 laboratory assistants (part-time workers who work half-time)" (CSA SPb F. 4331. Inv. 11. F. 388. Aid. 12);
    "There is a cabinet of Northern languages at the Chair, and there are two laboratory assistants in the office on the part-time contract. The overall management of the cabinet is led by the Head of the Department, Vasilevich, who works on the volunteer basis. The Cabinet is an educational and auxiliary institution. In the current year, the Cabinet will work on methodological assistance to the mass school, while the plan of this work in the second half of the year will be correlated with the work of the method section of NIA INS" (CSA SPb F. 4331. Inv. 11. F. 388. Aid. 12rev.). "There are no post-graduate courses at the department. Students who graduated from the department remain as graduate students at NIA INS" (CSA SPb F. 4331. Inv. 11. F. 388. Aid. 13).

It is not surprising that having such close ties with NIA INS, LGPI, which was supposed to train primarily teachers, also trained specialists in northern studies, who in fact belonged to the same Leningrad ethnographic school as the graduates of Leningrad State University. Among LGPI graduates there were I.S. Vdovin, N.M. Tereshchenko, E.S. Rubtsova, G.A. Menovshchikov. Apparently, many courses studied by majors in northern studies in Leningrad State Pedagogical University and students of the Ethno-Department of Leningrad State University were close to each other, and all these students considered themselves as belonging to the Leningrad ethnographic school.[45]

The second half of 1930s

In the mid-1930s the "project" launched by Bogoras and his colleagues worked very productively: graduates of the Ethno-Department, who formed the backbone of teachers in both universities and most of the staff of NIA INS, participated in the research, taught new students (including those who did not belong to the peoples of the North), published their works, went on expeditions. But the general situation in the country and, as a consequence, the situation in academic life could not but affect their work.

On May 10, 1936 suddenly, in the train to Rostov-on-Don, dies professor Bogoras. After his death, his "project" goes through a series of reorganizations and eventually ceases to exist.

In 1936 INS was transferred to the *Glavsevmorput*[46] system—an organization not much interested in INS. At this time it was focused on the water, that is on the waterway of the Northern Sea Route (NSR), and loses interest in the land adjacent to the NSR and its peoples' (Evladov 2008:257).

In 1937, started the so-called case of INS (Roon and Sirina 2003:61–62): first, arrested was a graduate of NIA INS, a writer, an employee of *Detgiz* publishing house N.I. Spiridonov, followed closely by INS director Ia.P. Alkor (Koshkin), then by employees and graduate students of INS A.F. Bruchanov, N.F. Prytkova, V.I. Tsintsius, A.S. Forstein, E.A. Kreinovich, editor of *Detgiz* K.B. Shavrov, V.T. Peresvet-Saltan, and many others. "Most part of the cohort of young scientists, born at the Ethnographic Department of Leningrad University under the direction of L.Ia. Shternberg and V.G. Bogoras in the 1920s and at the Institute of the Peoples of the North in the

---

45 I have a feeling that Hertzen students were more inclined to study languages than ethnography in the broadest sense. Perhaps this is due to the fact that in the 1930s because of the need for urgent development of written language and textbooks it was the languages that were the focus of attention.

46 A state organization established in 1932 for the national economic development of the Arctic and ensuring navigation along the Northern Sea Route or GUSMP, the Main Directorate of the Northern Sea Route.

1930s, was annihilated or permanently expelled from academic work during Stalin's repressions [...] The works of these scholars were not reprinted, the remaining manuscripts were not printed, and their names were forgotten," writes I.I. Krupnik. And then he continues: "Almost all the staff of researchers and teachers of the Institute of the Peoples of the North were arrested and repressed in 1937, and the institution was disbanded" (Krupnik 2008:19,20).

Indeed, on October 1, 1939, INS was reassigned to the People's Commissariat of Education of the RSFSR (*Narkompros*). This reorganization was not a formal reassignment to a different structure, but a radical change in the entire organization of INS: from that moment INS was turning into the Pedagogical Institute of the Peoples of the North, whose task was just to provide higher education. INS had now two subdivisions: the Pedagogical Institute (with a five-year course) and the Teachers' Institute (3-year course).

All citizens of the USSR could enter the new INS regardless of their ethnic belonging, although some privileges for the natives of the North were not lost when taking the Russian language exam. In 1940, a new allotment for districts and ethnic groups was made (Voskoboinikov 1958:60).

	Terms of education	Faculties	Specialization
Preparatory Department	No enrolment any longer		
Teacher's Institute	3 years	3 faculties: Historical; Science and Geography; of Northern Languages and the Russian language and Literature	Teachers of incomplete secondary schools
Pedagogical Institute	5 years	1 faculty: of Northern Languages and the Russian Language and Literature	Teachers of complete secondary schools and national teacher's colleges

Table 1. The structure of INS in the late 1930s (Voskoboinikov 1958:59).

Since this moment, INS was training only teachers, and not the "national *intelligentsia*" in various specialties. In addition, as a result of the transformation in Leningrad, there were now two educational institutions that trained the staff for northern schools: LGPI and the reorganized INS. *Narkompros* could not tolerate such duplication and saught to remedy the situation: the first attempt was to transfer students from

LGPI to INS (CSA SPb. F. 4331. Inv. 34. F. 124. Aid. 39), and after some time INS was eliminated and its students were transferred to LGPI.[47]

As a result of the repressions and reorganization of the late 1930s, active publishing work of INS and NIA INS was curtailed, most of the publication plans remained incomplete, almost all the series, with the exception of linguistic ones, were interrupted, and only works on the languages of the peoples of the North continued to be published for some time.

The "Bogoras project": correlations

How, why, and for what purpose was all this network of institutions described above united into a single whole, referred to here as the "Bogoras project"? Let us start with a rather unusual document—almost a denunciation (March 1928), written by Bogoras's LIZHVYA colleague, prof. (sic!) Kamenshchikov.[48]

Comments on some pedagogical contradictions observed in the work of *Sevfak*, dated by March 15, 28 [addressed to the assistant to the *Sevfak* rector A.E. Smyk – E.L.].

1   A student for comparatively a long time (for 4–5 years) tears (sic!) himself away from his native situation, from the environment, is weaned from local conditions of life, becomes declassed. All this, of course, can not be considered useful from the state point of view.

2   Complete absence of textbooks. There are not even ABCs and books for teaching arithmetic. Available textbooks in Russian are intended for adult working class or peasant audience, for our students they are completely inappropriate. Compiling any textbooks for our students here in Leningrad or Moscow, being far from the local conditions of life, is impossible. […]

3   […] From the pedagogical point of view it is more useful (sic!) to organize native schools for each ethnic group separately. In these schools, teachers should be those who know the local way of life and language of a given group. […]

4   […] The *Sevfak* should be a school of a higher type (underlined by Kamenshchikov). It can exist in Leningrad only as a school for training of highly skilled workers

---

47   The order of the *Narkompros* No. 699 from September 29, 1941 on closing of Leningrad Pedagogical Institute of the Peoples of the North, see: CSA SPb. Fund. 4331. Inv. 31. File. 603. Aid. 28. By this time many students and teachers of INS had already gone to the battles of the WWII.

48   The text is kept in the same folder as the above-quoted denunciation—see footnote 13 (CSA SPb. Fund. 7222. Inv. 9. File. 44. Aid. 1–2). (Orthography and punctuation of the original showed a certain level of ignorance).

for the North. Workers of average qualification must be prepared by indigenous schools on the spot. Then, graduates of these local schools should work on the spot for 2–3 years and the best of them are sent to Leningrad or Moscow to receive higher qualification from such specialists who are not there on the ground.

Prof. Kamenshchikov

Let's look at this letter not only as at a denunciation. It precisely articulates the problems that the "Bogoras project" was to solve. Prof. Kamenshchikov is certainly right: from the pedagogical point of view, it is much better to teach children "on the spot", using textbooks, and it is better if teachers know their pupils' native language, and it is better to train in Leningrad only highly qualified personnel. Most likely, Bogoras would agree with this, but the problem was that there were no textbooks or teachers in 1928, while the question of where they would come from and how much time it would take did not bother prof. Kamenshchikov. Meanwhile, it was these issues that were central for prof. Bogoras when he began to build his own construction.

Of course, if you have enough time and money, you first need to train specialists, then wait until they conduct the necessary studies and then write grammars for the languages, create textbooks and prepare teachers capable of teaching with these textbooks; then carry out approbation of these programs in local schools, train educated natives in these schools; after that start teaching them at a university in Leningrad; and only then can we expect that these people will take part in the modernization processes. This path is logically impeccable, but it can stretch out for several decades. The task was to complete it as soon as possible—from the point of view of Bogoras (and the Committee of the North), it was impossible to wait.

The whole design, created by Bogoras, was aimed at combining scientific research with practical activities and, at the expense of this, to solve the tasks as quickly as possible. Already in the early 1920s, together with Shternberg, he started preparing students who were closely acquainted with the life of the studied peoples and were part-time "missionaries of a new culture" (Bogoras-Tan 1925:48) and who immediately began working on the spot, creating schools and programs, participating in alphabetization and teaching northern languages. In this case the newly-created *Rabfak* (and its successors) not only trained the national *intelligentsia*, settling "illiterate natives" in a large European city and forcing them to learn a lot in a very short time, but immediately turned into a "living ethnographic laboratory" (Seleznev 1928:13) for ethnographic students who studied here a living language and who received, directly in Leningrad, the information about the culture, economy and life of the northern regions. A few years later, when both specialists in the North and experience in organizing work with the northerners were in place, the development of the project reached a new level: a special institution was created that dealt only with the North.

The new institution was still based on the same principle of complementarity: INS as an educational institution acted as the base for INS as a research institute. The fact that such an organization would make it possible to solve issues of alphabetization and training personnel for the northern regions faster and at higher level, was predicted by K.Ya. Luks, the director of INS, already in the first year of its existence: "It is possible to organize a solid study of the language problem only in a centralized manner and with the direct participation of the natives themselves. All northern indigenous schools need their own central laboratory to test local experience. INS can and should become, under certain conditions, such laboratory" (Luks 1930:135). Engaging future teachers of northern schools into alphabetization and study of the North also became a logical continuation of the project.

Prof. Kamenshchikov in the quoted letter against Bogoras "experiments" argued that "it is impossible to write any textbooks for our students here in Leningrad or Moscow, far from the local conditions of life". As the results of the Bogoras's project showed, with proper organization of work, it is possible. At the same time, the northerners who came to the capital, albeit poorly literate, played a significant role in the success: a great contribution to their work was made by the presence in Leningrad of the people with whom they could learn the basics of linguistics, check the texts, edit publications in their native languages, who could be involved in preparing of textbooks and grammars and in the common cause of alphabetization and writing literary work. So it was for a good reason that, at one of the sessions on the "localization" of schools, the creators of textbooks complained that they had difficulties with verifying texts in the Nenets language, because students who studied Nenets in INS mainly spoke Komi (AMAE RAS. F. K-II. Inv. 1. F. 273. Aid. 101). Actually, INS as a laboratory is precisely the "Professor Bogoras's experiments", which irritated Mr. Potopov so fiercely (see footnote 14).

At the same time, NIA INS staff and LGPI students were researchers who used knowledge of the northerners and their teachers: they not only wrote textbooks, but also directly formed the national *intelligentsia*. This interaction is a striking feature of the project: a bunch of "researchers and the future *intelligentsia* of the North" was formed from the very beginning of the creation of the northern *Rabfak*.[49]

Needless to say, a significant part of NIA INS employees were students of Bogoras and Shternberg. According to Mr. Potopov, in 1928 there were only two northern scholars in Leningrad, "the old and the young", Bogoras and Koshkin. In 1933 (only five years later!) in the INS graduate school, as already mentioned, there were 42 people (35 of them belonged directly to the school of Bogoras and Shternberg: 29 people

---

49 The role of this community of students and researchers was clearly recognized and highly appreciated by contemporaries. Thus, the propaganda book "Miraculous Chum" by M. Rokhman, devoted to INS, said: "It's them, the *employees* of the Institute of NIA under the leadership of the party and the director Ia.P. Alkor (Koshkin) [...] who, *together with students*, provided for the literacy of the peoples of the Far North in 15 languages, created the first ABCs and first books for primary schools in these languages, *continuing simultaneously teaching each other and learning from each other*" (Rokhman 1935: 23; — italics: E.L.). This is another reason for discussing the relations of informants and researchers in the early Soviet period; cf. Alymov and Arziutov (2014:83).

graduated from the ethnographic departments of LSU or LILI (LIFLI), the other six were graduates of LGPI).[50]

We have already spoken about the place of LGPI in this whole structure: the team of the NIA INS staff taught northern languages and northern disciplines at the Pedagogical Institute (Ratner-Shternberg 1935:148); the students of the Institute (like the students of Ethno-Department of the Faculty of Geography before) learnt their native language from the students of INS, and were involved in the research work and scientific life of NIA INS. It can be seen that in LGPI students used the same logic and tactics in organization of the training as in the Ethno-Department.

The core of this system was, apparently, scientific work, which required scientific personnel. The system trained such personnel, set tasks for them and acted as an employer for them, providing opportunities for field research, comprehensive humanitarian study of Siberia and the North, creating scripts, textbooks, etc. At the same time, the tasks of training teachers and the national *intelligentsia* were being solved.

Thus, all of the above-mentioned formally different institutions supplemented each other in functions, and were closely related logically, structurally and in composition, which allowed them to solve problems facing academy and society better and faster. It is obvious that these institutions and the connections between them were not formed spontaneously, but were the result of creative thought, tireless energy and the enviable perseverance of the creators and project managers. All this structure becomes obvious if we consider these institutions not in isolation, but in their interrelation with each other.[51]

Is Ethnography in a knockdown?

If we trace the history of the "Bogoras project" step by step, it becomes obvious that, although the ideas behind the project were both well-balanced and logical, the structure itself was organizationally shaky and fragile. Sometimes it is not clear at all how Bogoras and his comrades managed to achieve at least any results. What the Leningrad ethnographic school achieved in the study of the North in the 1920s–1930s, it achieved in many respects *contrary* to the actions of the authorities and the events

---

50 In fact, Potopov was wrong about 1928. By that time quite a lot of students had already been prepared, a considerable part of whom were engaged in research of the North. Several of them were in the field after graduation from the university (for example, G.N. and E.D. Prokof'evs), while others were on expeditions, having not yet completed the course (as N.K Karger, V.I. Chernetsov, N.A. Kotovshchikova, and others). A few years later they began to return and, thanks to the establishment of Bogoras's NIA INS, they had the possibility to process the collected materials and apply their knowledge.

51 In fact, there were more institutions associated with the name of Bogoras and with the exploration of the North: students of Bogoras worked in the Museum of Anthropology and Ethnography, and in the Museum of the History of Religion and Atheism, and in other places, but in the center the structure was as described above.

that the era brought down on people. Analyzing the archival materials, one can realize how much the existence of the whole complex and its functioning were not due to "the support of the Soviet power" but to the will and energy of Bogoras (before 1927— Bogoras and Shternberg), his disciples and associates.

At first, the authorities were re-subordinating the ethnographic department non-stop, then they liquidated it completely. It would seem that everything was lost, but under the slogan of the need for quality education of school teachers,[52] Bogoras and his colleagues managed to transfer the more or less full-fledged training of specialists in the northeastern studies to Herzen Institute. At the same time, they tried to save at least some of the devastated ethnographic schools in LILI, where the students of the closed Ethno-Department came to: after a couple of years they even managed to start teaching certain northern languages (Voskoboinikov 1958:65). Thus, Bogoras's structure was maintained and began to bear fruit. But the state machine was inexorable: the transfer of INS together with the NIA under the leadership of the *Glavsevmorput*, repressions against INS staff, sudden transferring in 1937 of the writing of the northern languages from Latin alphabet to Cyrillic, abolition of the subject and ethnic specifics of INS and its transformation into a pedagogical institute for everybody —all this at last led to the destruction of such a painstakingly and diligently developed structure, finally completed in the years of the Second World war. One can't but recall the words said once by Bogoras about the plans for another reorganization of Ethno-Department: "It looks like a fatal circle, something like Penelope's cloth—no matter how much you weave it, an idle person comes and unweaves everything' (SPF ARAN. F. 250. Inv. 3. F. 167. Aid. 516 rev).[53]

I will also note the ambiguous position of the Leningrad northern studies. On the one hand, it was assessed as "professorial experiments" and existed despite administrative arbitrariness and extra-academic pressure, and sometimes direct violence by the authorities. At the same time the results of the work subsequently were attributed by the state to itself as "the merits of Soviet power". On the other hand, this situation once again demonstrates how difficult it is to understand who defined the state policy and represented the interests of the state. In a certain sense, Bogoras and his disciples were "Soviet power",[54] acting in the same hypostasis that was inspired by the pathos of modernization and worked to transform the country.

---

52 The requirement to introduce teaching of ethnography into the curriculum of pedagogical universities was recorded in the resolution based on the reports at the same meeting of ethnographers in 1929. (Meeting in 1929).

53 The letter of Bogoras to D.B. Riazantsev at the Marx and Engels Institute with a request to help in the fight against the People's Commissariat for Education, *Narkompros*.

54 Let us recall that INS was subordinated not to the People's Commissariat for Education, but directly to the government of the USSR. According to T.D. Solovei (1998:211), this did not so much boost the state control (it could be implemented with the help of the ministry), but rather increased the status of the institution and freed it from unnecessary coordination and delay. INS, therefore, was directly integrated into the Soviet state apparatus.

The historiographical fate of Bogoras's project is paradoxical. In the academic world there is a certain consensus that the 1930s were the hardest time for the national ethnography, as evidenced by the titles of the works and their sections devoted to this period: *Life After Death* (Solovei 2001:117), *Soviet Ethnography in a Knockdown* (Slezkine 1993). In such studies, NIA INS is at best only mentioned; more often, it just goes unnoticed. At the same time, the available sources convincingly demonstrate that NIA INS in the first half of the 1930s was a big academic institute with a large number of post-graduate students, with broad range of scientific topics, performing a huge expeditionary, editing and publishing work. NIA INS was in the center of a well-thought-out and (with all the reserves) effective system of training people for working in the North—in various fields of science, production, education and administration. The question arises: how fair is our idea of a "knockdown", which happened in Soviet ethnography (at least—with the northern studies) after 1929? What we know about NIA INS, conflicts with the assessment of this time in the scientific literature.

Why does the modern history of ethnography see neither the integrity of the project, nor the significance of the INS? The reasons for this "invisibility" lie both in the objective circumstances, and in our ideas about what ethnography is and what is included in its history. We imagine the meaning and purpose of our studies in a different way now than did Leningrad ethnographers of the 1920s–1930s.

Not seeing the scale of NIA INS work was due to quite serious external reasons. First, after the case of INS, the termination of the work of NIA INS, the Great Patriotic War and a new wave of repression of the late 1940s, the participants in the events were reluctant to recall their prewar work and did not themselves publish any studies with scientific analysis of the work done (compare, for example: Voskoboinikov 1958; Gagen-Torn 1971; Antropova 1972).[55] Secondly, some of the materials of NIA INS were lost, some were divided between different archives, and the researchers had nothing to rely on when studying the history of this institution. Thirdly, the publications made under the NIA INS stamp are mostly known to researchers, but they have never been collected in one place. Only recently, after significant improvement of the work of the Russian National Library electronic catalog, it became possible to identify most of NIA's publications by keyword and collect them in one list, which allows us to evaluate the publishing activity and understand the scale of the work done in the 1930s.

However, in my opinion, not only the lack of materials prevents researchers from "seeing" the structure created by Bogoras. There are other reasons connected both with the entrenched historiographic tradition and with the tradition of interdisciplinary barriers in the humanities. First of all, historiography, cultivated in rigid institutional and disciplinary boundaries, "does not see" some elements of the "Bogoras

---

55 It is known that V.V. Antropova studied materials relating to the expeditions of the 1920s in the archives, and N.I. Gagen-Torn began to write a book dedicated to the ethnographers of the 1920s–1930s, but did not have time to complete it (Gagen-Torn 2002:335–336).

project": NIA INS is not a classical university, not an academic institution, it does not belong entirely to any of the known institutions and therefore falls out of the habitual world structure, thus seemingly getting into another dimension for the researchers studying primarily academic life. At the same time, as it was already said, in modern historiography, NIA INS and INS are hardly distinguishable: they are perceived as one institution, in the definition and description of which the main feature is teaching semi-literate northerners in the capital city (the assessment of this fact depends on the author's position: it is either "fine" if the article is devoted to the history of education in the North, or a "professorial fun", or "the whim of Soviet power"). The scientific work of NIA INS is in the shadows; at best, it is mentioned that writing for the northern languages was being developed there.

Another mechanism of "non-seeing", in my opinion, is created by the discrepancy between today's and yesterday's ideas about what ethnography should be engaged in, first of all, in the area of the relationship between theory and practice. When modern ethnographers or anthropologists write their history, they easily delegate to other specialties what the north-easterners of those days were doing: alphabetization and grammar turns out to be the history of linguistics,[56] the study of the past of Siberia and the position of its population under the tsarist ('colonial') administration is history, excavations in the north of Yamal belong to archeology, the study of the specifics of art and the artistic language of the northerners is art criticism, the study of the diversity of the world perception, of child's formation of concepts is referred to as pedology (today, apparently, it is cognitive science).

Let me give a quote from Yuri Slezkine's article (mentioned above) *Soviet Ethnography in a Knockdown*: "Ethnographers were disorientated, and the pre-industrial peoples of the USSR became an easy prey for pedologists [...] Pedologists discovered the causes of various manifestations of backwardness were in the environment, and gave recommendations on their fastest eradication" (Slezkine 1993:118). Further, the author says that after the defeat of pedology, this work passed to "practicing teachers". It is impossible not to notice that today's contrasting ethnographers, pedologists and teachers contradict the principles of that time, in particular, the principles of the "Bogoras project" which was based on synthesis. Bogoras's approach combined ethnographic, anthropological, linguistic, art and pedological studies based on the northern material: these directions coexisted and interacted within the same institution, often the same people were engaged in it.[57] We are discussing this era from the point of view

---

56 And this is despite the obvious fact that most of the 'linguists' of NIA INS considered themselves ethnographers, and that Shternberg 's motto "ethnographer must be a linguist and a linguist must be an ethnographer" (Ratner-Shternberg 1935:152) was one of the cornerstones of the Leningrad ethnographic school.

57 Such an approach inevitably puts contemporary historians of science in a difficult situation: the material resists such violence, sometimes there are not enough grounds to unambiguously refer a person or his/her research to a particular branch. How, for example, should one attribute V.N. Cherentsov, who was one of the creators of the Mansi writing, the author of ethno-

of today's disciplinary boundaries (which in many respects arose as a consequence of the catastrophes of the Soviet era). This approach assumes that there were ethnographers studying peoples and groups, linguists who compiled grammars, pedologists who studied children and their living conditions, art historians and archaeologists, historians who were sitting in their department, as in modern institutes, attributed to different branches.[58]

From the point of view of dividing ethnographic research into theory and applied work, the situation is even more revealing. After the notorious meetings of 1929 and 1932, there took place an official narrowing of the ethnographic subject field: its academic status was lowered to an auxiliary historical discipline. However, at the meeting of ethnographers in 1929, both in reports and in resolutions, the importance of the ethnographers' practical work in the matter of socialist construction was stressed repeatedly and persistently. Actually, this was one of the central themes in the speeches made by the representatives of the Leningrad ethnographic school, in particular. Ethnographers saw the opportunity to serve the public interest not only in classification of peoples and definition of the boundaries of their residence (see, for example, Anderson 1998:77–97), but also in direct active participation in the transformations of the North and in socialist construction. It should be understood that these words were not just a forced rhetorical gimmick (Yurchak 2014): most representatives of the Leningrad school really worked part of their lives in taiga and tundra in practical positions, saw the need for transformations and felt it necessary to participate in them. As Bogoras (Bogoras-Tan 1925:50) had envisaged, they were "missionaries of the new culture". The young generation of the ethnographers of that time were simultaneously *Narodniks'*[59] pupils and *Narodniks'* children, and in many ways acted as continuators of their work.[60]

As far as I know, the need for the practical participation of ethnographers in socialist construction was never questioned (disputed were only the forms of this

---

graphic research on the peoples of Western Siberia and an archaeologist; or G.N. Prokof'ev, the author of the Selkup grammar, an ethnographer, whose methodology of school teaching to indigenous children attracted the attention of N.K. Krupskaia; or N.K. Karger, the academic secretary of NIA INS, who conducted research on the peoples of the Amur region, who studied the interaction of the Podkamennaia Tunguska population with credit organizations, who taught the Khanty language, who created the Ket alphabet? Should the research by A.M. Schubert about the Evenki children, published under the stamp of NIA INS, be attributed to ethnography or to pedology?

58 It is significant that in her detailed work on the transformation of Soviet ethnography, T.D. Solovei while highlighting the activities of NIA INS, mentions only the activities of the historical-ethnographic section.

59 The *Narodniks* was a movement and ideology that was active in the Russian Empire in 1860-1910. It was based on the idea of the *intelligentsia* being indebted to the common people.

60 They were very sensitive to the "sight of people's miseries": descriptions of the situation on the ground and suggestions for change took a lot of place in the letters written by young ethnographers to Bogoras from expeditions (SPF ARAN, fund 250).

participation). Perhaps that is why when in the early 1930s any open theoretical discussions and work in universities and the Academy of Sciences proved to be hindered, NIA INS created outside the old academic framework and arranged so that each of its sections had obvious practical, "applied" significance, managed to become a research center where the living academic life continued. Practical work in the North required opening of schools and alphabetization—NIA INS had a section that studied grammar, phonetics, folklore, etc. To open schools we need methods of teaching, knowledge of how the concepts and perception of the world are formed in children of the northerners, we need to study the experience of predecessors and new schools—a section of pedagogy was opened at NIA INS, which dealt with manifold studies of children and education. We need textbooks in which the history of the North and its peoples would be reflected—a section of history appeared. It is necessary to understand how the economy and crafts are organized—the economy and its changes, technologies, crafts are being studied, survey programs are being created, etc. We need to study the health of the northerners, explore, develop and promote their art, fight against religion—and this becomes the object of attention of NIA INS staff.

As a result, within this structure it was possible to conduct scientific work on the broadest topics—from physical anthropology to cognitive research, from studying hunting economy to research on experimental phonetics, from the peculiarities of perception of space and color by Evenki children to the history of colonization of Yakutia. At the same time, each section created an applied product; therefore, in the list of NIA INS works a significant part was made up by textbooks, methodological materials, manuals and programs. On the one hand, these applied results were really necessary for the ongoing transformations, on the other hand, they and their practical significance turned out to be the screen that could cover up or even disguise researchers' theoretical, scientific interests. In itself, this mimicry is not surprising—it's amazing how convincing it was even for descendants who still see only the applied side and do not notice NIA INS's scientific work.

The research interests of the north-easterners of that time included not only the past of Siberia and its peoples, but also their present day. This continued, if one is guided by what is known about NIA INS, until about 1936, after which the study of modernity came to naught (which later became a problem for Russian ethnography (see Vakhtin and Sirina 2003:144). The reasons for this, naturally, lay outside science: the research of modernity in that era turned out to be inappropriate in principle. This is true not only for ethnography; about the same time other sciences that studied modernity were faced with serious problems: pedology was destroyed, so were demography, sociology and psychology. As it was precisely noted by E.M. Balashov in his work on the history of pedology, "in a society of illusions being built in the Soviet Russia, there was no place for any real investigation of this society, as well as for studying the personality of a real person" (Balashov 2012:184). It was from this moment that researches of modernity in the USSR were indeed in a deep knockdown, and it took them very long to recover.[61]

Returning to the question of why the "Bogoras project" and the work of NIA INS have so far remained "invisible" for historiography, I want to emphasize once again that the reasons for this are that modern researchers are transferring their ideas about the object and subject of ethnography onto the past without noticing the studies that "simulated" being practical. Using this approach, the conclusion about the catastrophe in northern studies, which occurred at the turn of the 1920s and 1930s, is inevitable. It seems that the sources managed to deceive the researchers.

We are thinking about knockdown of Soviet ethnography because we believe the USSR ethnography to be embodied in the boring scholasticism of journal *Sovetskaia Etnografiia* of those years, generated by ideological interference in scientific work. The Leningrad northern studies in the late 1920's—the first half of the 1930's invented a form of existence that could suit the Soviet power, a form of practically oriented scientific and educational programs and institutions. This helped the science survive until ideology finally forced out all manifestations of living science—and while Bogoras was alive.

Unfortunately, time is ruthless both to people and to science: Penelope's cloth was eventually unweaved. Nevertheless, even in the hardest times for science we find evidence of the success of the "Bogoras project". Here is a quote from a speech delivered in 1936 by A.I. Mineev—a polar explorer, who worked for a long time in *Glavsevmorput,* the Main Directorate of the Northern Sea Route, and at that time had just become

---

61 The situation in the USSR in these branches of science, which are completely different at first glance, is described by researchers in a singularly uniform way: flourishing in the 1920s and early 1930s, a turning point in the mid-1930s, which led to devastation, stagnation, degradation of scientific discussions, empty scholasticism. Here are some examples. Psychology: "Instead of an empirically oriented, relatively independent science, aimed at studying the universal laws that would apply to the social life of people, psychology turned into a relatively anti-empirical, applied science forced to subordinate theory to the demands of practice" (Bauer 1952:4–5; quoted by Iasnitskii and Zakreshneva 2009:14). Demography: "A quarter of a century—from the beginning of the 1930s to the mid-1950s—was wasted for Soviet demography, leaving behind no significant studies or new names. Moreover, it was precisely during these years that a new direction emerged in the Soviet science, which denied not only the very existence of demography, but also any specific problems of population that are not reducible to the problems of the economy. The place of researches was occupied by scholastic theoretical exercises, for example on the theme of 'socialist population law'" (Vishnevskii 2005:461). Pedagogy: "Ideology-driven pedagogy, contrary to the decision of the Central Committee, proclaiming the creation of the 'Marxist science of children', turned into a set of dogmatic provisions based on lacking of a real content commandments on communist morality and socialist discipline" (Balashov 2012:184). It is interesting that if researchers associate the problems of ethnography with its inability, due to rapid development in 1920s, to stand on the "Marxist rails" (Slezkine 1993; Solovei 2001), then psychology, by contrast, as early as the 1920s considered itself Marxist (Iasnitskii and Zapshneva 2009). However, in the 1930s their destinies were surprisingly similar, regardless of their commitment to the teachings of Marx.

the director of INS, which was reassigned to it. Having familiarized with his new enterprise, he speaks at a meeting on the scientific study of the North in *Glavsevmorput* and in his speech compares the work of INS and other research organizations:

We at the Institute of the Peoples of the North have those who have an academic title: 1 full member, 5 senior scientific researchers, 4 candidates of science, 10 in total. But there are only 25 people in the scientific organization of INS, so their specific weight is solid. […] We do not have a research institution, so to speak, where scientists would be trained. *INS has only post-graduate course, but it prepares people who work exclusively on the spot among people. It trains linguists, economists, historians and ethnographers. And who teaches geologists? And who teaches land-surveyors? Nobody!* So far, the Hydrological Department of the Arctic Institute has had two graduate students! These two graduate students study on the side, they will defend their thesis and there will be two new scientists. This is not enough! (AMAE RAS. F. K-II. Inv. 1. F. 221. Aid. 333; —italics: E.L.).

This passage allows not only to assess the path covered by the "Bogoras project", but also to take a fresh look at the amount of the work done. Just eight years before (according to the science's terms, the time is very short) Potopov argued that there were no "cadres" to work with the northerners (see footnote 13), but now INS set an example for geologists and land-surveyors.

Would Bogoras himself have wished his efforts to bring such fruits? It is not clear, but under the conditions in which he had to exist and act, it was an unquestionable victory.

List of Abbreviations

AMAE RAS — Archive of the Museum of Anthropology and Ethnography of Russian Academy of Science
GUSMP — the Main Directorate of the Northern Sea Route
INS — the Institute of the Peoples of the North
NIA INS — Academic Research Association of the Institute of the Peoples of the North
LGPI — Leningrad State Pedagogical Institute named after A.I. Herzen
LIZHVYA — Leningrad Institute of Living Oriental Languages
LILI (LIFLI) — Leningrad Institute of Linguistics and History, later — Institute of History, Philosophy and Linguistics
SPF ARAS — St. Petersburg Branch of the Archive of Russian Academy of Science
CSA SPb — Central State Archive of St. Petersburg

Archive materials

SPF ARAS. Fund. K-II. Inv 1. File 221. Stenographical materials of the meeting on "Sovershchaniia po snabzheniiu" of the Far North held at *Glavsevmorput* in 1936.

SPF ARAS. Fund. K-II. Inv.1. File 273. Preparatory materials to the stenograph on "localization policy" to the All-Union meeting of the teachers from schools of the Far North, 1940–1941.

SPF ARAS. Fund. 250. Inv 3. File 167. Materials on teaching activities at Geographical Institute, 1923–1925.

CSA SPb. Fund. 4331. Inv 11. File 217. Minutes of the meeting on the situation in the Northern Dept. of Pedagogical Institute named after A.I. Herzen, 1932.

CSA SPb. Fund. 4331. Inv 11. File 388. Minutes, production plans and reports of the Northern department for 1933/34 ac. year.

CSA SPb. Fund. 4331. Inv 11. File 443. Programs of *natsmen* department for 1933/34 ac. year.

CSA SPb. Fund. 4331. Inv. 31. File 603. Inner institute instructions and correspondence with different people, 1941.

CSA SPb. Fund. 4331. Inv 34. File 124. Correspondence between the RSFSR People's Commissariat for Education, Byelorussian People's Commissariat for Education and the Head Department for Higher Educational Institutions of the RSFSR People's Commissariat for Education, 1939.

CSA SPb. Fund. 7222. Inv 9. File 44. A memorandum about some pedagogical contradictions in the work and the place of the Northern faculty in the system of cultural enlightenment among the Northern nationalities, 1928.

CSA SPb. Fund.7222. Inv 10. File 4. The order book on the economic activities, 1929–1930.

CSA SPb. Fund. 7222. Inv 10. File 7-a. List of student staff for 1929 and lecturers for 1938.

CSA SPb. Fund. 9471. Inv 2. File 35. Personal cases, 1933–1934.

CSA SPb. Fund. 9471. Inv 2. File 88 (160). Worklist of Steinitz, Wolfgang Kurtovich. 1934.

References

Alymov, S.S., and Arziutov, D.V. 2014. Marksistskaia etnografiia za sem' dnei: sovershchanie etnografov Moskvy i Leningrada i diskussii v sovetskikh sotsial'nykh naukakh v 1920-1930-e gg. [Marxist Ethnography in 7 Days: The Meeting of Ethnographers from Moscow and Leningrad and Discussions on Soviet Social Sciences in the 1920s–1930s]. *Ot klassikov k marksizmu: Stenogramma soveshchaniia etnografov Moskvy i Leningrada (5–11 apreliia 1929)*, 21–90. St. Petersburg: Museum of Anthropology and Ethnography Press.

Anderson, D.G. 1998. *Tundroviki: ekologiia i samosoznanie khantaikskikh evenkov* [Tundra Residents: Ecology and Self-Identification of Khantai Evenki People]. Novosibirsk: SO RAN.

— 2000. *Identity and Ecology in Arctic Siberia.* Oxford: Oxford University Press.

Antropova, V.V. 1972. Uchastie etnografov v prakticheskom osushchestvlenii leninskoi natsional'noi politiki na Krainem Severe (1920–1930 gg.) [Participation of Ethnographers in Implementing Leninist National Policy in the Far North]. *Sovetskaia Etnografiia* 6: 19–27.

Arziutov, D. 2016. Etnograf s kinokameroi v rukakh: Prokof'evy i nachalo visual'noi antropologii samodiitsev. [Ethnographer with a Movie Camera: The Prokof'evs and the Beginning of Visual Anthropology of Samoyed]. *Antropologicheskii Forum* 29: 187–219.

Arziutov, D.V., and S. Kan 2013. Kontseptsiia polia i polevoi raboty v rannei sovetskoi etnografii. [The Concept of the Field and Fieldwork in Early Soviet Ethnography.] *Etnograficheskoe Obozrenie* 6: 45–68.

Balashov, E.M. 2012. *Pedologiia v Rossii v pervoi treti XX veka* ["Pedology" in Russia in the First Third of the 20th Century]. St. Petersburg: Nestor-Istoriia.

Balashov, E.M., M.Iu. Evsevev, and N.Iu. Cherepenina 1999. *Materialy po istorii Sankt Peterburgskogo universiteta 1917–1965. Obzor arkhivnykh dokumentov.* [Materials on the History of St Petersburg University, 1917–1965. A Review of Archival Documents]. St. Petersburg: St. Petersburg State University Press.

Bauer, R.A. 1952. *The New Man in Soviet Psychology.* Cambridge, MA: Harvard University Press.

Bogoras-Tan, V.G. 1925. Podgotovitel'nye mery k organizatsii malykh narodnostei [Preparatory Measures for Organizing National Minorities]. *Severnaia Aziia* 3: 40–50.

— 1935. *Vockresshee plemia* [Resurrected Tribe]. Moskva: Khudozhestvennaia literatura.

Dorovin, G. 1932. Rabota INS [INS Activities]. *Taiga i Tundra* 2: 50–51.

Evladov, V.P. 2008. *Polarnaia iamal'skaia zimovka: Severo-Obskaia ikhtiologicheskaia ekspeditsiia Vsesoiuznogo articheskogo instituta 1935–1936 gg.* [Wintering in Polar Yamal: Ichthyological Expedition of All-Russian Arctic Institute in North Ob Region, 1935–1936]. Ekaterinburg: Ural'skii rabochii.

Gagen-Torn, N.I. 1971. Leningradskaia etnograficheskaia shkola v dvadtsatye gody (u istokov sovetskoi etnografii) [The Leningrad Ethnographic School in the 1920s (at the Origins of Soviet Ethnography]. *Sovetskaia Etnografiia* 2: 134–145.

Gagen-Torn, G.Iu. 2002. Nina Ivanova Gagen-Torn—uchenyi, pisatel', poet [N.I. Gagen-Torn. Scholar, Author, Poet.]. In *Repressirovannye etnografy*, vol. 1, 2nd edition. D.D. Tumarkin (comp.), 308–341. Moscow: Vostochnaia literatura.

Iasnitskii, A. 2013. Bibliografiia osnovnykh sovetskikh rabot po kross-kulturnoi psikhonevrologii i psikhologii natsional'nykh menshinstv v period kollektivizatsii industrializatsii i kulturnoi revoliutsii (1928–1932) [Bibliography of the Main Soviet Publications on Psychoneurology and Psychology of Ethnic Minorities during Collectivization, Industrialization, and Cultural Revolution (1928–1932)]. *Dubna Psychological Journal* 3: 97–113. <http://psyanima.su/journal/2013/3/2013n3a6/2013n3a6.pdf>.

Iasnitskii, A., and E. Zavershneva 2009. Ob arkhetipe sovetskoi psikhologii kak nauchnoi distsipliny i sotsial'noi praktiki [On the Archetype of the Soviet Psychology as an Academic Discipline and Social Practice]. *Novoe Literaturnoe Obozrenie* 100: 334–354.

Kan, S. 2007. "Moi drug v tupike empirizma i skepsisa": Vladimir Bogoras, Franz Boas i politicheskii kontekst sovetskoi etnologii v kontse 1920-kh – nachale 1930-kh gg. ["My Old Friend in a Dead-End of Empiricism and Scepticism": Boas, Bogoras, and the Politics of Soviet Anthropology of the late 1920s – early 1930s]. *Antropologicheskii Forum* 7: 191–230.

— 2009. *Lev Shternberg: Anthropologist, Russian Socialist, Jewish Activist.* Lincoln: University of Nebraska Press.

Khronika 1934. Danilin A.G.—Nauchno-issledovatel'skaia assotsiatsiia pri Institute narodov Severa [Scientific and Research Association at the Institute of the Peoples of the North]. *Sovetskaia Etnografiia* 3: 108–109.

— 1935. Petrov G.N., Rakhmanin G.E.—V nauchno-issledovatel'skoi assotsiatsii pri Institute narodov Severa [At the Scientific and Research Association at the Institute of the Peoples of the North]. *Sovetskaia Etnografiia* 4–5: 229–232.

— 1936. Petrov G.N.—Ekspeditsiia i nauchnye komandirovki Instituta narodov Severa TSIK SSSR [Expeditions and Research Trips at the Institute of the Peoples of the North, Central Executive Committee of the USSR]. *Sovetskaia Etnografiia* 1: 157–158.

Kosven, M.O. 1933. Morgan. Zhizn i uchenie [Life and Science]. *Trudy NIA INS TSIK SSSR*, Vol. 4–5, Leningrad: In-t narodov Severa TSIK SSSR.

Kozmin, V.A. 2009. Iz istorii etnograficheskogo obrazovaniia v Leningradskom / Sankt Petersburgskom universitete [From the History of Ethnographical Education in Leningrad / St. Petersburg University]. *Etnograficheskoe Obozrenie* 4: 109–117.

Kreinovich, E.A. 1932. Giliatskie chislitelnye [Giliat Numerals]. *Trudy NIA INS TSIK SSSR*, Vol. 3, Leningrad: Komintern.

Krongauz, F.F. 1958. V istorii shkoly na Krainem Severe. Prosveshchenie na sovetskom Krainem Severe [On the History of School in the Far North. Education in the Soviet Far North]. Vyp. 8: 37–47. Leningrad: Uchpedgiz.

Krupnik, I.I. 2008. V.G. Bogoraz, ego nasledie i ucheniki [V.G. Bogoras, his Legacy and Disciples]. In *Tropoiu Bogoraza: Nauchnye i literaturnye materialy.* L.S. Bogoslovskaia, V.S. Krivoshchekov, and I. Krupnik (eds.), 17–22. Moscow: Heritage Institute GEOS.

Krupnik, I.I., and E.A. Mikhailova 2008. Eskimolog Aleksandr Forstein (1904–1968)

[Eskimologist Aleksandr Forstein (1904–1968)]. In *Tropoiu Bogoraza: Nauchnye i literaturnye materialy*. L.S. Bogoslovskaia, V.S. Krivoshchekov, and I. Krupnik (eds.), 32–43. Moscow: Heritage Institute GEOS.

Luks, K.Ia. 1930. Institut narodov Severa, ego mesto i zadachi [The Institute of the Peoples of the North, its Place and Tasks]. *Sovetskii Sever* 1: 130–136.

Lunacharskii, A.V. 1927. Zadachi Narkomprossa na Krainem Severe [The Tasks of People's Commissariat for Education in the Far North]. *Severnaia Aziia* 3: 18–22.

Mikhailova, E.A. 2004. Vladimir Germanovich Bogoraz. Uchenyi, pisatel', obshche-stvennyi deiatel' [Waldemar Bogoras. Scientist, Writer, Social Activist]. In *Vydaiu-shchiesia otechestvennye etnologi i antropologi XX veka* [Outstanding Russian Ethnologists and Anthropologists of the 20th Century]. V.A. Tishkov and D.D. Tumarkin (eds.), 95–136, Moscow: Nauka.

Musiankova, N.A. 2012. Liubiteli i professionaly: khudozhestvennaia studiia Insti-tuta narodov Severa (1926–1941) [Amateurs and Professionals: Artistic Studio of the Institute of the Peoples of the North]. *Khudozhestvennaia kultura* 5. <http://sias.ru/publications/magazines/kultura/vypusk-5-2012/prikladnaya-kultur-ologiya/779.html>.

Ratner-Shternberg, S.A. 1935. L.Ia. Shternberg i leningradskaia etnograficheskaia shkola 1904–1927. [L.Ia. Shternberg and the Leningrad Ethnographic School in 1904–1927]. *Sovetskaia Etnografiia* 2: 134–154.

Rokhman, M. 1935. Chudesnyi chum (Povest' o Institute narodov Severa) [Miraculous Chum. The story about the Institute of the Peoples of the North]. E.M. Tager (Lit. red.). Leningrad: INS TSIK SSSR.

Roon, T.P., and A.A. Sirina 2003. E.A. Kreinovich: zhizn' i sud'ba uchenogo. [E.A. Kreinovich: Life and Destiny of a Scholar]. In *Repressirovannye etnografy*, Vol. 2. D.D. Tumarkin (comp.), 47–77. Moscow: Vostochnaia literatura.

Salatkin, N. 1933. Trekhletie INSa. [INS' Third Anniversary]. *Taiga i Tundra* 2(5): 7–8.

Seleznev, A. 1928. Sviazi i vzaimootnosheniia severno fakul'teta LVII etnootdeleniia geofaka [Connections and Interrelations of the Northern Faculty at the Depart-ment of Geography, LVII]. *Etnograf-issledovatel'* 2–3: 12–14.

Sergeev, M.A. 1933. K voprosu o narodo-choziaistnennoi perepisi Krainego Severa [On the Issue of the National and Economic Census in the Far North]. *Sovetskaia Etnografiia* 3–4: 9–28.

Severovedenie v Gertsenovskom universitete. Institut narodov Severa 2003. [North-ern Studies in Herzen University]. G.A. Bordovskii (Nauch. red.). Sankt Peter-burg: Asterion.

Slezkine, Iu. 1993. Sovetskaia etnografiia v nokdaune: 1928–1938 [Soviet Ethnography in a Knockdown]. *Etnograficheskoe Obozrenie* 2: 113–125.

— 1994. *Arctic Mirrors: Russia and the Small Peoples of the North*. Ithaca NY, London: Cornell University Press.

Smidovich, P.G. 1928. Privetstvie [Welcoming Speech]. *Taiga i Tundra* 1: 1.

Smirnova, T.M. 2012. Institut narodov Severa v Leningrade—uchebnoe zavedenie novogo tipa [The Institute of People of the North in Leningrad as an Educational Institution of a New Type]. *Vestnik LGU* 2: 51–65. <http://cyberleninka.ru/article/n/institut-narodov-severa-v-leningrade-uchebnoe-zavedenie-novogo-tipa>.

Solovei, T.D. 1998. Ot *"burzhuaznoi" etnologii k "sovetskoi" etnografii: Istoriia otechestvennoi etnologii pervoi treti XX veka* [From "Bourgeois" Ethnology to "Soviet" Ethnography: History of Native Ethnology in the First Third of the 20th Century]. Moscow: Institute of Ethnology and Anthropology Press.

— 2001. "Korennoi perelom" v otechestvennoi etnografii (Diskussiia o predmete etnologicheskoi nauki konets 1920 nachalo 1930 gg) ["Radical Turn" in the Soviet Ethnography: late 1920s – early 1930s]. *Etnograficheskoe Obozrenie* 3: 101–121.

Soveshchanie 1929. Soveshchanie etnografov Moskvy i Leningrada (5/IV–11/IV 1929). [Meeting of Moscow and Leningrad Ethnographers]. *Etnografiia* 2: 110–144.

Terletskii, P.E. 1932. Naselenie Krainego Severa (po dannym perepisi 1926–27 gg), *Trudy NIA INS TSIK SSSR*, Vol. 1–2. Leningrad: In-t narodov Severa TSIK SSSR.

Tsintsius, V.I. 1958. Rodnoi iazyk v nachal'nykh shkolakh narodov Krainego Severa. Prosveshchenie na sovetskom Krainem Severe [Native Language in Primary Schools of the Peoples of the Far North. Education in the Far North]. Vyp. 8: 76–89. Leningrad: Uchpedgiz.

Tumarkin, D.D. (comp.) 2002. *Repressirovannye etnografy* [Ethnographers—Victims of Political Repressions]. Moscow: Vostochnaia literatura.

Universitety 1935. *Universitety i nauchnye uchrezhdeniia RSFSR* [Universities and Scientific Institutions in the RSFSR]. Moskva/Leningrad: Ob"edinennoe nauch.-tekh. izd-vo.

Vakhtin, N.B. 2016. "Proekt Bogoraza": borba za ogon' [The Bogoras's Project: The Quest for Fire]. *Antropologicheskii Forum* 29: 125–141.

Vakhtin, N.B., and A.A. Sirina 2003. Razmyshleniia posle mezhdunarodnogo seminara "Komu prinadlezhit sibirskaia etnografiia?" [Thoughts after the International Seminar "Who Owns Siberian Ethnography?"]. *Etnograficheskoe Obozrenie* 3: 141–148.

Vasil'evich, G.M. 1958. Ob intelligentsii malykh narodov sovetskogo Krainego Severa. [On the *Intelligentsia* of the National Minorities in the Soviet Far North]. *Prosveshchenie na sovetskom Krainem Severe*. Vyp. 8: 207–227. Leningrad: Uchpedgiz.

Vinnikov, I. 1939. Vnov' organizuemoe etnograficheskoe otdelenie na filologicheskom fakul'tete LGU [Newly Organized Ethnographical Department at the Philological Faculty, LSU]. *Sovetskaia Etnografiia*: 232–233.

Vishnevskii, A.G. (ed.). 2005, *Demograficheskaia modernizatsiia Rossii, 1900–2000* [Demographic Modernization of Russia, 1900–2000]. Moscow: Novoe izdatel'stvo.

Voskoboinikov, M.G. 1958. Podgotovka v Leningrade pedagogicheskikh kadrov dlia shkol narodov Krainego Severa [Training Teaching Staff for the Schools in the Far North in Leningrad]. *Prosveshchenie na sovetskom Krainem Severe*. Vyp. 8: 48–77 Leningrad: Uchpedgiz.

Yurchak, A. 2005. *Everything Was Forever, Until It Was No More: The Last Soviet Generation*. Princeton, NJ: Princeton University Press.

Zelenin, D.K. 1938. Narody Severa posle oktiabr'skoi revoliutsii [Peoples of the North after the October Revolution]. *Sovetskaia Etnografiia*: 12–54.

8 LEV IAKOVLEVICH SHTERNBERG: AT THE OUTSET OF SOVIET ETHNOGRAPHY[1]

Anna A. Sirina and Tat'iana P. Roon

Introduction

The works of Lev Iakovlevich Shternberg, the eminent Russian and Soviet scientist, accomplished theoretical evolutionist, professor, and corresponding member of the Soviet Academy of Sciences (from 1924), are well known by present day historians, ethnographers and anthropologists. An active public figure, he was engaged in the ethnography of the peoples of the Russian Far East and in Jewish ethnography. His acquaintance through correspondence with Friedrich Engels played a not insignificant role in his prominence: Engels wrote to Shternberg, having become acquainted with his discovery of group marriages amongst the Gilyak (or Nivkh) people (Shternberg et al. 1933; Shternberg 1933b: xvii-xix; see also Marx and Engels 1962, vol. 22:364–367). This "discovery," as with his description of other features of the Nivkh (Gilyak) social order, made on the Island of Sakhalin, was the beginning of his scientific activities. Over the period of his eight-year administrative exile he gathered unique field material on the language, folklore and social and religious life of the Nivkh. The results of his research were published in Russia beginning as early as 1893 (Shternberg 1893a; 1895; 1896).

A considerable amount has been written on Lev Shternberg: obituaries, including ones in foreign journals,[2] articles by ethnographers, archeologists, museologists and historians of science.[3] Of particular interest is an absorbing book by Nina Gagen-Torn who, on the basis of personal recollections and archival documents, gives a vivid and emotional account of her teacher—the revolutionary and founder of the Leningrad School of Ethnography (Gagen-Torn 1971; 1975). Renewed interest abroad in Shternberg's works in historiography was linked to the 100th anniversary of the famous Jesup North Pacific Expedition (Kan 2000; Shternberg 1999; Krupnik 1998). In the process of unearthing why Shternberg's book on the Gilyak was not published in the

---

1   This article had first been published in Russian (Sirina and Roon 2004:49–94) and was trans-
    lated from that edition into English by J. M. Sutton.
2   Ol'denburg 1927; Kleinman 1928; Jochelson 1928; Kagarov 1929; Azadovskii and Vinogradov 1928;
    Arsen'ev 1966; Vinnikov 1928.
3   Bogoras 1927; 1928; 1930; Krol' 1929; Alkor 1930; Edel'shtein 1930; Ivanov 1930; Ratner-Shtern-
    berg 1930; 1935; Samoilovich 1930; Vinnikov 1930; Okladnikov 1963; Staniukovich 1986; Shul-
    gina 1989; Khasanova 2000; and more.

transactions of the expedition, Shternberg's biographer, Sergei Kan, rehabilitated the scientist's life and, in particular detail, the period after his acquaintance with Boas. (Kan 2001) Shternberg's book "The Social Organization of the Gilyak" was published in the USA in 1999, appropriately in time for the anniversary of the Jesup Expedition (Smoliak and Sirina 2002). The American anthropologist Bruce Grant, who had conducted ethnographic studies on Sakhalin at the beginning of the 1990s, became the book's editor and author of its substantial introduction and epilogue (Grant 1999 a,b).

What has driven us to write an article on a scientist about whom, it would seem, a considerable amount has already been written? What has stimulated this undiminished interest?

The history of Russia's ethnographic research is still full of gaps, amongst which the early period of the development of Soviet ethnography stands out.[4] It was at this particular time that Lev Sternberg's work as an educator flourished. His main works are notable for their theoretical generalizations within the framework of evolutionary theory, broad comparative parallels and the use of extensive factual material. Shternberg's approach outlined the direction of research in Soviet ethnography and determined its particular interest in the history of primitive societies, questions of ethnogenesis and ethnic history, social organization and religion.

Shternberg's archives opened up for us unique materials, the analysis of which made it possible to understand more deeply, not only his personality, but also his preparation of the first generation of Soviet scientists, the sources of the scientific resourcefulness of his followers and students who worked in the mid and second half of the 20th century.

A significant amount of ethnographic and linguistic material on the peoples of the Far East was gathered and interesting books and articles published during the period 1930–1960s.[5] At the same time our forerunners enlarged the source base of the subject under study considerably.[6] This opens up the possibility of tracing the fate of Shternberg's ideas and hypotheses and assess his contribution to the development of ethnography.

The present article is based on both published works and on archival materials from Shternberg's personal collection (St. Petersburg Branch of the Russian Academy of Sciences Archives), E.A. Kreinovich's personal collection (Sakhalin Museum

---

4   Chronologically this period was the first, but in fact it was transitional, the prerevolutionary to the new, Soviet ethnography. As it happens, the present-day situation of transition from Soviet ethnography to post-Soviet ethnology is, in some sense, similar to the situation in the 1920s, but with a different vector of development, and it helps, if not to understand, at least to feel the processes that were taking place in the earlier transition period. See in more detail: Tumarkin 1999 (1):4–5.

5   See, for example, Zolotarev 1933; 1934; 1937; 1939; 1964; Levin 1958; Kreinovich 1973; Ostrovskii 1997; Smoliak 1975; 1974; 1990; Taksami 1975; Shternberg 2001a,b; Dudarets 2004.

6   Pilsudski 1996; Khasanova 2001; Shternberg 2001c, Vakhtin 2001; Roon and Sirina 2002; Reshetov 2003.

of Regional Studies) and the anthropological section of the American Museum of Natural History in New York.[7]

Haim (Lev) Shternberg was born on May 4th (old style April 21st) 1861 in the remote provincial city of Zhitomir. His parents, especially his mother, dreamed of seeing him an eminent rabbi. At five he was sent to a heder, a religious school, where the teacher taught Hebrew and the children studied the Torah, the Prophets and the Talmud from early morning until late in the evening. From the age of eleven Haim went to a rabbinical school and from 1873 to the Zhitomir classical gymnasium. He studied well, played little and spent a lot of time reading. "We were indoctrinated with a mixture of Judaism and mysticism from early childhood," as Shternberg's childhood friend, Moses Krol' [Moisei Krol'], recollected. "We were wholly in the power of these beliefs until that new world of ideas, that the Jewish religion judges to be heretical, began to open up before us" (Krol' 1929:217–218). Gradually his horizons widened and his outlook was enriched by new ideals, by his reading of Russian and west European classical literature translations which began to appear in Russia in the 1870s, and by the works of the revolutionary *Narodniks* (PF ARAN 282/1/195:100–101, 165).[8]

Already as a student Shternberg began to participate in conspiratorial circles. He graduated from the gymnasium in 1881 and entered the physics and mathematics faculty at St. Petersburg University. In the same year, the future scientist became a member of the illegal revolutionary organization *Narodnaia Volia* (People's Will) that called for the abolishment of the monarchy including by means of violence and terror.[9] The organization was comprised in the main by *raznochintsy* (people of miscellaneous rank); in some regions of Russia up to a quarter of its members were young Jews (Grant 1999a:xxviii). Not having significant support amongst the majority of the population of Russia, its members tried to overthrow the autocracy by themselves. In March 1881, they successfully assassinated Tsar Alexander II. However, this act of terrorism not only failed to bring them the desired results but led to harsh repression that drained the resources of *Narodnaia Volia* and caused an ideological and organizational crisis. For all the selflessness and self-sacrifice of the *narodovol'tsy*, their endeavor to bring freedom and a better fate to the people, as the present day historian G.S. Kan believes, the fruits of their actions were "bitter to the extreme: from the lib-

---

7 A.A. Sirina is grateful to the staff of the St. Petersburg branch of the Archive of RAN (PF ARAN), especially N.S. Prokhorenko and M. Mandrik, for their great assistance. The authors are thankful for the literature made available, the consultation and discussion of the draft version of the article by E.P. Akbalian, I.I. Krupnik, V.M. Latyshev, A.V. Smoliak, and M.M. Khasanova.

8 This archive material is a manuscript, which was prepared for printing by the scientist's widow.

9 On the revolutionary activities of L.Ia. Shternberg in the party *Narodnaia Volia*, see also: Krol' 1929; Gagen-Torn 1975; Grant 1999a; Kan 2000; 2001. See also the article of Mikhailova (2004) on W. Bogoras.

eral point of view, having brought about years of reaction while, from the conservative point of view, having wounded Russia's prestige" (Kan 1997:153).

For his revolutionary activities, organization and participation in a student demonstration and for writing and publishing a pamphlet "Political Terror in Russia" Shternberg was expelled from university, arrested and exiled from the capital. After having enrolled in the Faculty of Law at the Novorossiisk University in Odessa in 1883 he continued conspiratorial activities. Shternberg participated in attempts to revive *Narodnaia Volia*: he was one of the leaders of the convention of *narodovoltsy* of southern provinces held in 1885 in Ekaterinoslav and edited the last issue of the newspaper *Narodnaia Volia*. In 1886, during the university's final examinations, he was arrested a second time and spent three years in solitary confinement in Odessa's central prison. As his diaries show, this was a painful time of profound self-analysis. But his years in prison were not wasted: here he began to study European languages and read philosophical and literary works, including Milton, Machiavelli, Shakespeare and Defoe, in the original.[10] In 1889, Lev (at what time he had changed his name from Haim to Lev we were unable to ascertain) was sent for ten years' administrative exile to the Russian Far East on the Island of Sakhalin, which had become a place of exile and hard labor in the second half of the 19th century.

Political exiles, especially the *narodniki*, played a substantial role in the development of Russian ethnography. It was exiles who made up the backbone of the participants of Siberiakov's Expedition of 1894–1896, which was equipped to study the way of life of Siberian peoples in connection with the development of gold mining. Particularly large numbers of settler-exiles—ethnographers and linguists of necessity, and brilliant ones at that!—were to be found in the Yakutsk region. Suffice it to name Waldemar Bogoras, Vladimir Zenzinov, Waldemar Jochelson, Dmitrii Klements, Sergei Kovalik, Ivan Mainov, Waclaw Seroshevskii, Vasilii Troshchanskii, and Ivan Khoudiakov. In the conditions of Siberian exile their revolutionary activity, directed at the overthrow of the "old world" gradually transformed into a fertile channel of scientific studies and produced impressive fruit. So, what happened to Shternberg at the distant outposts of Russia? And what role did the Sakhalin period (1889–1897) play in his life?

Sakhalin penal servitude is a mixture of criminal and political prisoners and exile-settlers, prisons, the arbitrariness of overseers, grueling work in coal mines, logging, and road building. But even here, the end of the earth had a life of its own. In a letter to his childhood friend Moses Krol', who had been sent to Zabaikal'e for his revolutionary activities in the same *Narodnaia Volia*, Lev described his first days on the island.

---

10   In historiography the opinion has come about that L.Ia. Shternberg read the work of Engels for the first time in prison. S. Kan, referring to archival sources, thinks that Shternberg was acquainted for the first time with the work of Engels (1884) on Sakhalin in 1889. See Kan 2001: 221, 244.

"On Sakhalin we arrived on 19th May, on a warm, sunny day and my first impressions were very pleasant. The head of the district, who met us on the deck, was courteous and informed us about the monthly allowance of 11 roubles 50 kopeks, and that we could have works in the offices and lessons [...] I won't describe all the joy and cordiality with which we were met by the large Sakhalin colony of convicts. Except that over the first days I was inebriated by the joyous welcome."[11]

Shternberg tried to find himself in these new conditions and to occupy himself with some undertaking. The status of administrative exile eased his life somewhat and increased his rights: he could travel around the island and correspondence was "free from supervision". He got to know local "politicals," and kept in contact with his comrades I.F. Suvorov, A.I. Aleksandrin and N.L. Perlashkevich.[12]

Soon the ways and order of penal servitude gave rise to protest in Shternberg. He confided to his friend, "The hardest thing is to live side by side with convicts [...] with people deprived of all rights. It is this closeness, it seems, that will drive me to some wild corner of Sakhalin, [where there will be] close communion with bears and the primitive people of the taiga."[13]

In March 1890, the island authorities transferred him to the Viakhtu cordon for his active defense of political prisoners who were subjected to lashing. It is possible that Shternberg's transfer had been guided by another factor: that summer, Anton Chekhov had arrived on the island to study penal servitude and the population census. He tried to meet political exiles. Knowing Shternberg's character, it is possible that the authorities sent him to Viakhtu in good time so that he would not be able to say too much (Gagen-Torn 1975:28–30).

The Viakhtu cordon was a stage station of five log houses on the post road to the mainland and Nikolaevsk-on-Amur. The cordon gave Shternberg the oppressive impression of a "lonely, deserted grave standing in an uninhabited taiga on the shores of the Tartar Strait," as he wrote (in Taksami 1961:109). The exile was accommodated in a screened off corner of one of the houses where three guards from amongst the criminals that had served their time and a soldier overseer also lived. But special premises were later arranged for him for work and accommodation. In a letter to Krol', Shternberg described his quarters in this way:

"It has, as it were, two halves, a bedroom and study-come-living room-kitchen [sic]. They made me a divan, two tables, a bed, cabinets, and, apart from all this, the admin[istration] has sent me a large box with medicaments, because

---

11 Shternberg. Letter to M. Krol' of 16th August 1889. In Dudarets 2004:112.

12 In the personal archive of L.Ia. Shternberg in the PF ARAN are letters of comrades of the Sakhalin exile: I. Manucharov, I.P. Iuvachev, B.O. Pilsudski, G. Gostkevich, N. Perlashkevich, and also photographs of some exiles. See Dudarets 2004:106, 113.

13 Shternberg. Letter to M. Krol' of 2nd March 1890. In Dudarets 2004:113.

I am treating settlers and native people. I carry out the treatment conscien-
tiously [...] In these new premises (where there are pictures of friends on the
walls, your picture is on the table in a frame, where I am by myself [...]), obviously, I feel better than before, and this is where, with God's help, I intend at
last to write and read [...] at the moment I am reading Weber's "History of
Greece", not long ago I read Wegele's research on Dante, and read the entire
Italian library. When I feel the need to see someone, I call the virtuous guard,
a big fellow who had killed his wife, and talk with him about God and people
and lofty matters in general. In order to satisfy my need to teach someone,
I instruct the big oaf of an overseer in grammar, arithmetic and philosophy.
But I do have more interesting society: I am frequently visited by sons of the
taiga—Tungus, Gilyaki [Nivkh–A.S., T.R.], Orochens, and settlers—on one
question or another."[14]

Two kilometers to the south there was a Nivkh camp. Evenk reindeer herdsmen
visited the cordon and the Nivkh, taking the post to the mainland and back, and
stopping over. The young man had the chance to see local inhabitants at close quarters and converse with them. At that time there were two places of residence for the
"politicals" on the island: the Aleksandrovskii station and the settlement of Rykovskoe
(now Kirovskoe) in the middle reaches of the River Tym (Pilsudski 1996:14). Life at
the Viakhtu cordon was relatively free: as he wrote in his letter, Shternberg made a few
excursions of 100 *versts* on foot to Aleksandrovskii where he met friends. One such
event was for the New Year holidays of 1891. At the beginning of January, he and his
companion Suvorov went off for 10 days to Rykovskoe to stay for a while in order to
get acquainted with other 'politicals' (Dudarets 2004:115).

Of all the new acquaintances in Rykovskoe, Shternberg singled out the exile Bronislav Osipovich Pilsudski. He had turned up on Sakhalin two years before Shternberg
in connection with the case of 1st March 1887 (the attempt to assassinate Tsar Aleksander III). In exile, Pilsudski became acquainted with the indigenous people of the
island and took down a few Nivkh texts. It is possible that Shternberg's choice to study
Sakhalin's indigenous peoples was finally determined after his meeting with Pilsudski
(Iuvachev 1927; Kreinovich 1968).

On Shternberg's return to the Viakhtu cordon, the district administration proposed that he take part in a census of the people in the Nivkh encampments of Northern Sakhalin. Their original cultural identity had been poorly studied at the end of the
19th century. It is not surprising that the young man jumped at this work straight away.

On 7th February 1891, Shternberg set off to the north on dog sleighs together with
Nivkh guides. Far out in the snows of the Ten'gi, Muzmvo and other settlements, for
the first time, the future scientist plunged deep into the world of the living Nivkh
culture that hitherto he had only observed from the outside in Aleksandrovskii and

---

14 Shternberg. Letter to M. Krol', January 1891. In Dudarets 2004:114–115.

at Viakhtu. In carrying out the census he acted in accordance with the instructions of the island's administration. Its questions were quite detailed, so the material obtained proved to be unique.

> "Over the month of my stay in the iurtas I had the opportunity to make intimate acquaintance with their customs, live their life with them, as it were, and could ascertain that a lot of what the 'primitive' people venerated was far from being as utopian as it may seem [...] I discovered their terms for relationships and family and clan institutions, identical to those of the Iroquois and in the famous Punalua-family (on the Sandwich islands). In a word, the remains of that form of marriage on which Morgan based his theory and which serves as the first point in Marx and Engels' pamphlet on the origins of the family, private property and the state."[15]

In June of the same year, 1891, Shternberg continued his study of the Nivkh of the River Tym and the Okhotsk coast where, apart from the Nivkh, there were Evenki and Uilta (Oroki). Together with Uilta herders, Shternberg continued the journey on reindeer from the mouth of the River Tym to distant places around the bays on the north-eastern coast of the island. The journey by dugout along the Tym up to Niiskii Bay and further south along the eastern shores to the Cape De l'Isle de la Croyère lasted from 22ⁿᵈ June until 17ᵗʰ July. During this time, Shternberg visited Nivkh seasonal camps in the Tym valley and got to know their way of life. Despite fatigue, the harassment of mosquitoes and midges, and other hardships, he never failed to keep up his traveler's diary. As a rule, the events and impressions of the day were recorded late in the evening, after having settled down by the campfire (Shternberg 2001a).

After his return to Aleksandrovskii, Shternberg processed the journey's materials, wrote articles and gave lessons to children. His position as a citizen showed itself particularly vividly during the years of the "Onor case" when, during road construction on the island, as a result of the brutal treatment of convicts, some one hundred of them died or went missing without a trace over a period of three months. There appeared a series of articles in the *Vladivostok* newspaper under the headline "Sakhalin Conversations", written by Shternberg under the pseudonym Verus; they were received fervently by the entire colony (See Latyshev 1996:17–18, 289).

> "My present life (personal, in the narrow sense) is devoid of difficulties. I have an agreeable room [...] eat well, comrades are devoted, once or twice a week I mix with society, where I am very talkative, even jovial, at times making everyone laugh. Relations with the administration are peaceful, I receive 30 roubles a month and not long ago even had the extremely disagreeable satisfaction of sending my parents a hundred roubles at their request [...]."[16]

---

15 Shternberg. Letter to M. Krol', 19ᵗʰ May 1891. In Dudarets 2004:117–118.
16 Shternberg. Letter to M. Krol', 10ᵗʰ November 1892. In Dudarets 2004:123.

In the summer of 1892, Shternberg set off for South Sakhalin along the River Poro-nai in order to record the Sakhalin Ainu people and buy items of women's tools for an exhibition in Chicago. He visited both east and west coasts, acquainted himself with the life of the Ainu, took advantage of the hospitality of Japanese fishermen, and got the feel of the rhythm of life over the southern part of the island.

"In the summer, the indigenous people live in the work yards of the Japanese, whose fishing stations are scattered over a distance of 2–3–5 and more versts," Shternberg wrote, "one has to stop at each depot, enter each of the temporary huts [...] there are corners where large-scale trade is undertaken, whose prod-ucts are loaded onto large steamships, where Americans, who have lived on the island many years, do the managing [...] there is a place called Mauko on the western shore of Sakhalin, where Ainu, Chinese and Koreans, settlers under the management of the merchant Semenov and the American Damby, harvest seaweed [...] The American is married to a Japanese woman, the Japanese live with Ainu women, the Ainu have Winchesters and American watches, eat Jap-anese spice cakes, smoke American pipes and feed on rice."[17]

In August 1893, Shternberg left post Aleksandrovskii for a short while to travel south to Sortunai, to the Nivkh and Ainu. This time he surveyed a section of the north-western shore. The survey of this coast took Shternberg almost three weeks. The weather was against him; there were storms and south-westerly winds. Apart from that, an epidemic of intestinal influenza in one of the Nivkh settlements kept him longer than expected. He gave medical assistance to those in need and left medi-cine with one Nivkh, having instructed him how to recognize the symptoms of some illnesses. In the Agnevo, Pil'vo, Soia, Sokh and other settlements he carried out a cen-sus of the Nivkh living there by name (Roon and Prokof'ev 2001). It struck the young man that the area had been abandoned by Ainu not long before.

"Most of the inhabitants have Ainu blood in them. There are clans that consider themselves to be Ainu-Gilyaki. In the settlement of Pil'vo, the whole population, including women and children, speak Ainu fluently" (Shternberg 2001b:285).

Shternberg registered cases of the migration of Nivkh to this area from other parts of Sakhalin and from the mainland. During his journey he collected a herbarium and minerals, and for the first time in the history of North Sakhalin he undertook arche-ological excavations.

Once again, in 1893 and 1894, Shternberg journeyed along the north-western coast of Sakhalin in order to collect new material and check his old records taken in 1891. It was important to catch the changes in the natural movements of the Nivkh popu-lation over the previous years and compare them with the results of earlier records.

---

17   Shternberg. Letter to M. Krol', 10th November 1892. In Dudarets 2004:123–124.

In the first stages of independent work, Shternberg did not have any professional training in the undertaking of fieldwork. In many ways he acted on intuition, sometimes according to the instructions of the administration (for the first census of the Nivkh). From his diaries and early field reports it is clear that Lev Shternberg determined the methods of study himself: observation, daily descriptions of field situations, rarely by full interviews, more often by exposition of a conversation. Such an approach limited the subject and depth of the research somewhat. The content of Shternberg's early diaries is fragmentary, often there are no dates, no names of settlements where the records were made, they lack the necessary information on the informant and those being interviewed and also other important and essential data for further processing of the field material. Unfortunately, Shternberg's handwriting was far from ideal and many handwritten texts from his notebooks are practically unintelligible.

The language barrier hampered communication and understanding of the subtleties of the other culture. The Nivkh guides did not always know Russian well and spoke with an accent. The structure of the Nivkh language differed from that of Russian, and it was difficult to "access". So, Sternberg decided to learn Nivkh. He was the first to begin research into the Nivkh language.

There have long ceased to be Ainu and Nivkh camps in the majority of areas Shternberg visited. The Ainu moved to Japan from south Sakhalin after World War II. Nivkh live in mixed settlements or in towns and their culture has changed considerably. The diary descriptions of Shternberg's first journeys have become valuable ethnographic sources. From them one can see the formation of the scholar's personality and his search for methods for fieldwork.

No less important is Shternberg's activity as a collector who made a significant contribution to the establishment of the first museum on Sakhalin at the post Aleksandrovskii. In the order of the military governor of the Island of Sakhalin, Major-General V.D. Merkazin, of 6th December 1896, on the opening of the museum, Pilsudski and Shternberg are mentioned in the list of persons whose "participation furthered the acquisition, compilation and arrangement of the museum's collection, contributing various gifts."[18] It is a rare case in the history of penal servitude that political exiles are noted in the order of a military governor for their achievements for the good of society together with military personnel and civil servants! Collections of items of Ainu, Nivkh and Evenk culture were exhibited in the ethnographic section of the first Sakhalin museum. A few collections gathered by Shternberg for demonstration at an exhibition in Chicago 'settled' in America, but without the name of the collector, they were 'dissolved' into the museums, probably, part of them kept in the Field Museum and private collections.[19]

---

18 Order of the military Governor of the island of Sakhalin, December 6th 1896 Nr. 226, signed by Major-General Merkazin (in Kostanov 1996:7–9).

19 Shternberg 1900:388; Shternberg. Letter to F. Boas 11th July 1905. American Museum of

In 1895, with the permission of the authorities, Shternberg visited the mainland, going to Vladivostok and Blagoveshensk. He was able to work around the Lower Amur amongst the Nivkh, Oroch, and Ulch peoples. This page of his journeys is perhaps the most enigmatic: documents witnessing to the permission to leave Sakhalin and the financing of the episode are yet to be uncovered. The well-known American anthropologist, Franz Boas, in a letter to Berthold Laufer (1898) who was working on Sakhalin 1898–1899 as part of the Jesup project, mentioned the funding of Siberian expeditions in Russia at the expense of the benefactor Sibiriakov: "He paid the expenses of Shternberg, who went to the Amur, and two gentlemen who visited the Yukaghir and Chukchi."[20] This made it possible for Shternberg to expand the geography of his research and collect comparative material after which he returned to Sakhalin. Two years later, in 1897, he received amnesty and left the island ahead of time.

Ivan Iuvachev, political exile and Shternberg's acquaintance from Sakhalin, thinking over everything that had happened to him, wrote to his close relatives: "Don't grieve: we often don't suspect what will serve us well" (Iuvachev 2001). Sakhalin served as a turning point in Shternberg's life. Here, for the first time, he tried himself as a linguist and field researcher-ethnologist; here he thought over his first scientific works and dreamed of his future activities in Russia. As a result of his long exile to the far reaches of Russia, Shternberg's revolutionary activity of necessity gave way to a passion for the history and culture of indigenous peoples, and later became his profession. But he did not renounce the ideals of his youth. In the midst of the peoples of his studies, and later in the society of students, he continued to spread the ideas of equality and brotherhood, progress and social justice. 'Primitive' peoples, their social structure and beliefs became a 'model' to illustrate the ideas of progress and the unity of the cultural development of humankind.

———————

In 1898, having returned from exile to his native Zhitomir, Shternberg became acquainted with Sarah Ratner, who before long became his wife. She had returned to Zhitomir after having graduated from the St. Petersburg Bestuzhev Women's Pedagogical Courses and become the director of a college for women. The history of their relationship is very important for an understanding of Shternberg's scientific work.

Lev Shternberg was very happy in his private life, always surrounded by the love of those close to him and friends. Sarah had three sisters and a brother. "When I turned ten years of age," she recollected, " [...] my elder sister and I were consigned to the family of our uncle, to his large disorderly family where I was given little attention"

Natural History, Anthropology Department Archive. Shternberg Correspondence, acc.# 9/26/1903-9/12/1906.

20 Letter from F. Boas to B. Laufer, 10th October 1898. American Museum of Natural History, Anthropology Department Archive, Correspondence acc. #1900–12.

(PF ARAN 282/4/18:11 rev.). Sarah was left to herself and often felt lonely, forgotten and unhappy. At 12 years of age she finished four years at a boarding school, and later went to St. Petersburg to study. Sarah's diary of her student years shows her to be a complex person in whom intellect, education, a passion for the beautiful and at the same time a "high degree of self-esteem," and lack of confidence in herself were combined. This was a time when the spirit of Bazarov had possessed peoples' minds and the specter of imminent social upheaval was hovering in the air. "I had long lost the god, to whom I had so sincerely, so fervently prayed in childhood; instead of him I acquired another god, another faith, a belief in progress, in happiness [...]" (PF ARAN 282/4/18:13 rev.). The female students underwent good practica in various educational establishments of St. Petersburg, for example, in the Abramov school that was famous in those times. In the summer, the girls earned some money at the *dachas* (summer cottages) of the well-to-do, by giving lessons to their children. Judging from her diary, Sarah did not aim to return home to Zhitomir, but wanted to gain the right to live in St. Petersburg (PF ARAN 282/4/18:28 rev.).

The young people found each other—a fortunate instance of love and mutual consent. They needed each other—Lev, an ardent, passionate, open-minded person, and Sarah—cautious, somewhat cold, very clever in a conventional way, but constantly needing support and approval. That was the very talent Shternberg had: he could encourage a person with a couple of words and make them believe in themselves. "You easily slip into pessimism when you are far from me," he wrote to her in 1900, when they had to live separately, she in Zhitomir, he in St. Petersburg, having gained a residence permit there in order to prepare his scientific works for publication.[21] Sarah established good relations with Shternberg's parents straight away, for which he was very grateful: "My sister writes that they (his parents–A.S., T.P.) have come to love you like their own daughter" (PF ARAN 282/2/361:17).

When Shternberg left on an academic trip, expedition or spa (where they, actually, frequently went together), they still kept in contact. They wrote letters to each other. As Shternberg traveled more often, most of the letters were from him, and Sarah kept them all carefully. One of the letters was written in 1900 when they had still not long been married: "You say I forget you [...] No, my dearest, I can forget myself, but you never, never" (PF ARAN 282/2/361:27). Shternberg shared everything with her: day-to-day things, scientific, museum, and anything else; there were no secrets between them, it appears, all the more so because, from about 1914, Sarah Ratner-Shternberg began work in the Museum of Anthropology and Ethnography in the ethnology of North America section. It is no exaggeration to say that Sarah lived the life of her husband: his successes and setbacks; his career was her career.

In the autumn of 1901, the Shternberg's son was born. Much loved by his parents, he was given a good education. At home he went by the family name Adia. Arcady

---

21   These letters are now in the personal archive of L.Ia. Shternberg: PF ARAN 282/2/361:15.

graduated from the Military-Medical Academy and became a doctor. It would appear he shared more interests with his uncles: Abram, Aaron and David Iakovlevich Shternberg, who were also doctors. Lev always maintained close relations with his relatives.[22]

Throughout their lives, Shternberg's childhood friends remained his closest friends: Moses Krol' [Moisei Krol'], Waldemar Bogoras [Vladimir Bogoraz], and Waldemar Jochelson [Vladimir Iokhel'son]; people with the same ethnic, social roots, the same mindset and experience of life as revolutionary *narodniks*. They were sent into exile at the same time: Shternberg to Sakhalin, Bogoras—to Srednekolymsk in the Yakutsk region, and Krol' to Selenginsk (Zabaikal'e) (Bogoras 1927:275–276). Throughout their exile, the friends kept in touch with each other. Here is an extract from a letter from Bogoras of 4th November 1895:

> "May the biggest devil they've got in hell take you. On what grounds are you celebrating the name day of your heart and inviting me, in absentia, to try the pie. 'I am leaving, you are leaving, he is leaving.' All your letters are filled with the conjugation of this verb. Leave, then, 'for god's sake, go' as a Jewish girl I know says. I myself am not leaving and have nothing to be joyful about. If only you knew, Lev, what vicious mockery your words about [my] garb and retirement garb, about the need to cheer up, about future activity in Russia and so on, when I have to 'be on duty' another three years in Kolymsk at God's will, by order of major-general Otchaiannyi!" (PF ARAN 282/2/34:7).

However, Bogoras went to St. Petersburg in 1898, before Shternberg. He took part in the Jesup Expedition, and got to know Boas well. Bogoras (and Jochelson) were the first "stages" on the way to Shternberg's relations with C.G. Salemann and V.V. Radloff, and they recommended him to Boas as the third Russian participant of the Jesup project. Bogoras together with Krol' furthered Shternberg's transfer from Zhitomir to St. Petersburg.

According to the laws of the Russian Empire of that time, Jews could not settle beyond the Pale of Settlement. In order to transfer to St. Petersburg, one had to have higher education (officially Shternberg gained that only in 1902), or accept Christianity, or find a valid reason for living in the capital. Shternberg's reason was the necessity to work on a book about the language and folklore of the Gilyak and consultations with the well-known linguists Carl Salemann and Vasilii Radloff.

By that time, "thanks to some degree of impudence," Bogoras had already moved, " 'with flying colors'" to St. Petersburg, "and after some negotiations stayed there on a temporary basis. And since temporary arrangements in Russia are the most lasting, I don't feel disheartened […] my temples have gone quite white and fur on my brow

----

22 Some 400 items of family correspondence are kept in PF ARAN (F 282).

somewhat tarnished, but, on the whole, it seems, I have only aged a little" (Gagen-Torn 1975:115). The first to solicit for Shternberg's transfer to St. Petersburg before Radloff was Krol' (Kan 2001:223). A little later, Bogoras did the same.

> "I was at Radloff's today and tempted him with your collection [...] and he promised to solicit your transfer to Petersburg in order to process your collection, which will be given over to the museum." Furthermore he advised him to, "Boast a little with restraint, but with weight [...] that there is material on the Gilyak language that should be handed over to the Academy, it is with academician Salemann [...] and that you need the consultation of competent people in order to process it and ask for permission to come to Petersburg for half a year [...] Radloff promises not only to solicit permission, but even to give you an allowance to process the collection and material [...] The academicians can be activated only if you motivate them. It follows that this will depend on your work" (PF ARAN 282/2/34:10–11. See extracts in Vakhtin 2001:80).

Shternberg moved to St. Petersburg in June 1899. Permission to stay in St. Petersburg for three months was received from the Minister of Interior, and at the suggestion of Salemann it was decided to take advantage of this from September 1900, as everyone spent the summer at their *dacha*. Shternberg settled down in Perkjärvi; Salemann spent the summer at a *dacha* in Usikirki, not far away (Gagen-Torn 1975:118). Shternberg wrote home, "Petersburg didn't give me the depressive impression that could have been expected. On the contrary, I felt quite at ease when I plunged into this vast place [...] But the *dachas* [...] are real Sakhalin" (PF ARAN 282/2/361: 34 rev.).

The materials on the Gilyak language and folklore were finally prepared for publication over the summer of 1900. Shternberg took the system of the Russian linguistic alphabet (the so-called academic alphabet) from Salemann and Radloff in order to transcribe the sounds of the Gilyak (Nivkh) languages. He received the proofs of his work at the end of September, and worked tirelessly for ten hours every day until he completed them. Shternberg wrote his work like a "pass" into St. Petersburg, into a different life; it was for this reason that it was finished so quickly. Undoubtedly, his wife insisted on this as well. Shternberg was missing her and searched actively for lodgings: "I am sure that with you my works will be twice as auspicious" (PF ARAN 282/2/361:54–54 rev).

In 1900, the young scientist became the editor of the ethnographic section of the most popular encyclopedic dictionary in Russia—Brockhaus and Efron. He wrote some 40 articles for this encyclopedia on various questions of ethnography and religious studies.[23]

In St. Petersburg, Shternberg lived at the lodgings of Krol', who was practicing law. Usually, before tea, he would take a bath; he loved water and swam well, walked every

---

23 Those articles concerning religion were republished in Shternberg 1936.

day and occasionally cycled around Marsovo Pole. Radloff offered Shternberg work at
the museum and promised to solicit for his acceptance after the three-month period
of registration. Salemann himself took the proofs of Shternberg's manuscript to the
printers, which "moved" its author considerably. In general, it was at this time that
Shternberg felt "very happy" (PF ARAN 282/2/361:1 ov., 16, 22 rev.).

———————

Of all the organizations at the beginning of the 20th century that dealt with ethnographic research, the Imperial Russian Geographical Society (IRGO), in which there
were ethnographical sections and regional branches in different places, was the most
important. There was an ethnographic department at the Imperial Society of Natural History, Anthropology and Ethnography (OLEAE) at Moscow State University, as
well. Ethnography was developed in museums also, in particular in the Museum of
Anthropology and Ethnology (MAE) of the Academy of Sciences, and since 1902 at
the Russian Museum of the Emperor Alexander III.

   Shternberg came to the MAE in 1901 and worked there till the end of his life. He
began as an unpaid volunteer; in 1902, when he had officially received higher education, having taken examinations at the faculty of law (*Jewish Encyclopedia* 1991:108),
he was accepted on the staff in the position of junior ethnographer. In 1904, he
became a senior ethnographer at the MAE—the second person after the director of
the museum, V.V. Radloff.

   It is difficult to imagine that at the beginning of the 20th century there were only
four researchers, including the director, working at the MAE. Today, the museum is
the largest research, exhibition and educational center in Russia, where more than 100
researchers work in 12 departments. The museum has some 2 million exhibits including 27 000 from the main assemblage of Siberian collections. More than a million and
a half people visit the main ethnographic museum every year (Taksami 2000: 16–18).
Work in the museum is always diverse, and includes scientific, educational, collections and arrangement of exhibitions. Shternberg was involved in all of these activities. At the beginning of the 20th century, attempts were made to stimulate scientific
research, including that concerning museums. In 1903, at the initiative of Ol'denburg
and Radloff, the Russian committee was set up for the study of Central and East Asia,
under the Ministry of Foreign Affairs. The Chairman of the Committee was Radloff, and the secretary—Shternberg. The task of the committee was to give financial
support to researchers in different countries who were undertaking their study in
Siberia and East Asia. Funds were given out annually for carrying out ethnographic
and archeological expeditions. These also included individual annual scholarships
for researchers who were completing their scientific work (Ratner-Shternberg 1928
:35). Exhibits collected on such expeditions would have to go to Russian museums. In
Shternberg's opinion, the Russian committee was a "special ethnographic organization at the Academy of Sciences" (Shternberg 1925:61). The committee operated until

1918 and made a significant contribution to scientific research. Most attention in the museum was given to the acquisition of collections of items relating to natural history and ethnography that comprised the foundation of its existence. At the same time, work was devoted to the scientific identification and attribution of existing items. For the establishment of the main collections of the museum, and especially its Siberian collection, credit is due, to no small degree, to Shternberg.

Stock came from different sources. First and foremost, collections were brought from expeditions by members of staff. In 1910, after a long pause, Shternberg went on an expedition to the Far East. Over three summer months, together with students, I.I. Zarubin[24] and I.N. Anshel's, he worked with the Gold (Nanai) people on the Amur, and with the Oroch and Negidal of the River Amgun', and also on Sakhalin.

Officially the expedition began on the last day of May in Vladivostok, with the visit to the Governor General in order to receive permission to undertake excavations, meetings with comrades of exile, and making the acquaintance of local regional historians. The members of the expedition spent four days in Khabarovsk. Here, they visited the Grodekovskii museum, where they met Vladimir Arsen'ev, and arranged with him the dispatch of ethnographic items to St. Petersburg (Tarasova 1985:22). The steamboat left on its run down the Amur on 9th June. The first stop for expeditionary work was at the settlement of Viatskoe, in the vicinity of which they examined Amur petroglyphs. Unfortunately their main part happened to be under water because of a flood. On 19th June, after two weeks of work in the Nanai settlement of Sakachi-Alian (where they had been surprised, because the settlement had become Russified, to meet two shamans), they reached the Troitskoe settlement by steamboat and later Nanai settlements located in the area. They traveled by boat along the Amgun' River to the Negidal. There they had planned to stay a week, but remained for two. They arrived at Nikolaevsk-on-Amur on 25th August, and from there went on to Sakhalin. On the way out of the mouth of the Amur they got stuck on sandbanks twice, and Sakhalin greeted them with unprecedented torrential rain that had swept away all the bridges and washed away roads. Shternberg was overwhelmed with melancholy, although the Governor General came to visit him and everyone recognized him. He visited the graves of his comrades and was left with " [...] only one desire—to get away from Sakhalin as fast as possible" (PF ARAN 282/2/361: 73, 73 rev.).

Shternberg, together with his students, carried out ethnographic and anthropometric studies, took photographs and bought exhibits for the museum. From the 1910 expedition he brought back not only linguistic, anthropological, archeological and folklore material, but also four large ethnographic collections, and phonographic cylinders with recordings of folklore texts. A scrupulous analysis of these ethnographic collections was undertaken by Marina Khasanova (Khasanova 2000:85–97).

---

24 Later Zarubin come on the staff of the MAE, professor of Leningrad University, expert on the languages of the peoples of the Pamirs.

The Nanai collection is the largest: 362 storage units. Shternberg acquired the Nanai items in the Torgon, Sakhachi-Alian (later Sikhachi-Alian), Dada, Chol'chi and other settlements; amongst the items are things collected from the small Udege group of the Anui River. The majority of the items characterize the spiritual culture of the Nanai and their beliefs (representations of spirits, hunting amulets, talismans, shaman clothes and belongings). It was at this time that Shternberg made an Amur and Sakhalin Nivkh collection of 175 storage units. He gathered the Negidal collection (127 storage units) mainly along the Amur in the area where the River Amgun joins the Amur. Until then it was only possible to see very few Negidal items in the MAE.

As V.I. D'iachenko was able to ascertain, the stock of photographs of the peoples of Siberia and the Far East that had been taking shape at MAE since 1880, contained over 800 photographs from Shternberg's expedition of 1910. His collection of photographs of the Nanai and Nivkh includes 217 negatives; prints of them make up separate collections. Another photographic collection is dedicated to the Nanai, Negidal and Oroch. Thematically, they include anthropological types of the population and objects of their spiritual culture relating to shamanism, funeral rites and musical instruments (D'iachenko 2000:180). The museum lacked the means to equip the expedition and purchase exhibits so, on the initiative of Radloff and Shternberg, a Council of Trustees was set up to find funds for the museum. Well-to-do people, including well-known industrialists and manufacturers, joined the Council. The fact should not be omitted that the activities of this Council, at the beginning of the 20th century, were linked to a scandal known as the "Adler affair" that caused great harm to the prestige of the MAE. A.I. Teriukov was the first to make the materials of the case public (Teriukov 1993). A member of MAE staff (later a professor at Kazan' University), Bruno Adler raised the question of unethical actions on the part of V.V. Radloff and senior ethnographer Shternberg in relation to the collection of A.V. Zhuravskii. One of the members of the Council of Trustees, the St. Petersburg merchant E.I. Aleksander, with the knowledge of the museum's leadership and for the achievement of material benefits, manipulated the collections gathered by Zhuravskii in the north of Russia. Although the leadership of the Academy of Sciences did everything they could not to let the scandal leave its walls, it had to take some measures; the case was considered by a court of arbitration and became the subject of special proceedings in the Academy, leading to a revision of the work of the MAE. Keppen, who was charged with the preliminary investigations by the President of the Academy, was obliged to come to the following conclusion: "The affair made a painful impression on me and gives grounds to acknowledge actions on the part of the administration (MAE–A.S., T.R.) as not being worthy of the Academy of Sciences" (Teriukov 1993:259). Although in the course of investigations no selfish aims on the part of Radloff and Shternberg had been revealed, it made everyone involved very anxious. The Academy tightened its control of funds entering the museum's Council of Trustees (Teriukov 1993).

On Radloff's initiative, a Committee of Assistance for the museum was set up. The geography of the collections covered most of the world, which reflected the economic and political standing of Russia in the world. In 1914, expeditions were equipped to go to South America, Inner Asia (Zabaikal'e, Manchuria and the Amur region); and in the same year to India and Ceylon (Karmysheva 2002; Sirina 2003; Revunenkova and Reshetov 2003).

Collections were made by devotees as well. Shternberg actively formed a network of such "correspondents", and drew colleagues, friends and acquaintances into gathering exhibits, their sale or donation. Amongst the people who made an enormous contribution to the formation of the MAE ethnographic collections were, in particular, Bronislav Pilsudski and Vladimir Arsen'ev, who worked with the museum through Shternberg.

Credit for developing the Ainu ethnographic collection at the MAE is due to Bronislav Pilsudski. Today it is one of the largest and most complete Ainu collections in the world, and includes 1890 objects of which Pilsudski collected more than a thousand. In all, he contributed nine sets of Ainu, Nivkh and Orok (Khasanova 2001:415) items and one collection of photographs to the MAE. Pilsudski had received funds via the MAE and the Academy for trips, mainly expeditionary, for the collection of exhibits. From 1902 to 1905, Pilsudski worked in South Sakhalin, and in 1903, together with V. Seroshevskii traveled to the Ainu of south Sakhalin and Hokkaido Island. The museum received rich collections of objects of ethnographic interest, including photographs and sketches. In 1907 and 1909, the MAE bought collections on Nivkh ethnography and a collection of photographs. All Pilsudski's collections were registered by Shternberg and some, written by him, exist to this day.

Vladimir Arsen'ev began acquiring ethnographic collections for the MAE in 1910. Shternberg was constantly making orders for such collections, asking him to gather "everything possible," since extra items could be exchanged for others. "Now I have a special request," he wrote in 1925. "I am very much in need of a small Gol'dy collection comprising ornamented fish-skin clothes, birch bark ornamented tableware, and wooden, grass and other religious figures. I'll send you the expenses […] With your connections with the Goldy, this will be easy to fulfill. I need this collection urgently" (in Tarasova 1979:73).

At last, the exchange of duplicates from collections was being made with museums of the world or the purchase of exhibits abroad. It was this that Shternberg dealt with energetically on his trips abroad, and his personal contacts and connections played a considerable role in it. For the first time, in 1904, he went to Berlin and Stockholm in order to arrange for a museum exchange. In 1908, after the congress of Americanists in Vienna, he dropped into Prague to buy ethnographic collections, and in 1911, he visited Stockholm. In 1924, after a congress of Americanists, Shternberg worked in Stockholm once again, selecting some 500 exhibits for the MAE. He was assisted by the Swedish traveler and President of the Swedish Academy Sven Hedin (PF ARAN 282/2/361:188).

Apart from his museum and scientific activities, Lev Shternberg took an active part in public and political affairs and journalism, which took up a great deal of his time and energy. Sergei Kan ascertained that it was this that was one of the reasons why the book "The Social Organization of the Gilyak" was not completed on time and consequently did not appear in the transactions of the Jesup Expedition (Kan 2001). Shternberg took part in the legal and illegal Jewish movement in Russia in the period between the 1905 and 1917 revolutions. Their aim was to overthrow the monarchy and set up a democratic government in which all Jews would receive all citizens' rights. During his first trip to America in 1905 he contacted especially Jewish emigrants from Russia. Shternberg was one of the organizers and ideologists of the Jewish People's Group (1906–1907), an association of Jewish public figures who did not share the idea of Zionism. He went in for journalism and editing, published articles and items for periodicals, and gave lectures on the Jewish question (Shternberg 1907b). In 1910, he was one of the consultants to the State Duma on this range of questions (Kan 2001:228, 231). In 1915, Shternberg visited the front as a delegate of the Committee of Assistance to Jewish Refugees (Grant 1999a: xiii).

———————

Shternberg was a fortunate combination of good field worker and erudite scientific theoretician. He never had an ethnographical education; everything he achieved in ethnography, he achieved through self-education. His mind aspired to large generalizations and new resounding discoveries. He understood the main shortcoming of ethnographical research in Russia at that time: the lack of a theoretical foundation. Shternberg went down in the history of science as a consistent advocate of evolutionism. He adhered to the formational approach to the development of human society. At the same time, he aimed his students towards the concrete and comprehensive study of separate cultures, which drew his approach closer towards the American school of the historical ethnography of Franz Boas.[25]

Ethnography became not only a profession but the focus of Shternberg's life. He aspired to raise ethnography in public opinion and in politics (sometimes by way of excessive idealization) up to the level of a separate field of science, and at he same time important and necessary for society from a practical point of view.

Shternberg considered ethnography to be a science of an undivided humanity. He called it now ethnography, now ethnology, but the latter term he used in relation to research abroad (Shternberg 1926d). He understood culture to be common life experience, which forms recollections that unite people into one historic whole. Regarding the development of culture from the point of view of progress and along an ascending line, Shternberg proposed bold hypotheses and, using examples of the cultures of different peoples of the world, drew wide comparative parallels. He was aiming to

———————

25   According to the recollections of Z. Cherniakov, Bogoras and Shternberg considered themselves
      to be the students of Boas (see Grant 1999b:248).

show that humanity develops according to a single set of laws. Each phenomenon was regarded by him as the direct expression of a common historical necessity; from the point of view of evolutionism, with the help of examples from the most diverse parts of the world, even torn from their interconnections and concrete context, it is possible to reconstruct the course of the progressive development of humanity.

The main object of Shternberg's studies were the peoples of the Russian Far East, first and foremost, the Nivkh. Apart from this, he studied the Ainu, Oroch, Nanai and Negidal. He did not avoid even the least significant problem connected with the ethnography of these peoples. He followed Schrenck [Shrenk], one of the most outstanding researchers into the peoples of the Far East in the 19th century, subjecting to reexamination and raising doubt about the main scientific hypotheses put forward by his forerunner (Shrenk 1883; 1892; 1903).

Shternberg was a talented linguist, describing the grammatical, phonetical, and lexical structures of the Nivkh language for the first time. He wrote over 100 works on ethnography and linguistics.[26]

Lev Shternberg had a particular interest in questions of social organization and religious faith. One gets the impression that he proceeded not so much from the analysis of concrete facts in coming to the construction of a hypothesis and theory, as from a concrete evolutionistic theory to the collection of facts "to fit it" (at least in his study of social organization). The latter interested Shternberg from the point of view of the development of family and marriage institutions; here, one should think, he was attempting to understand (especially having got acquainted with the relevant literature) the sources of the present-day state of society and possible paths of its future development. An interest in religion had been established in him in early childhood, while an interest in questions of customary law is natural for a person who had almost completed a course in law.

Shternberg began writing his first works while in exile; they came to the attention of the head of the island of Sakhalin, Merkazin. "He has taken my notes and wants to talk with the governor-general about them," he wrote in 1893, "the latter, judging from the papers, is a widely educated person and sympathises with the study of the region."[27] With the light hand of officials, Shternberg's articles began to be printed in well-known scientific journals.

The first publication was Shternberg's communication about the Sakhalin Nivkh that appeared in the newspaper *Russkie Vedomosti*, on the 14th October 1892. It contained brief notes on the social organization of the Nivkh, registered by him in terms of kinship during the undertaking of the census in February and March 1891. It was this article that drew the attention of Friedrich Engels. In his opinion, the author of the report "not only establishes the existence of group marriages, i.e. the right to

---

26 For a detailed bibliography of the works of Shternberg: see Shternberg 1933a:709–714; Ol'denburg and Samoilovich 1930b:7–19.

27 Shternberg. Letter to Krol', 21st November 1893. In Dudarets 2004:125.

mutual sexual relations between a number of men and women, but gives examples of such a form that closely borders on the punalual marriage of Hawaiians, on the most developed and classical phase of group marriage" (Engels 1892–1893:364). During the census he got to know the Nivkh terms for relationships and about "free" relationships between men and women in Nivkh society by comparison with the European counterpart. He interpreted the material he collected as the existence of "group marriages" amongst the Nivkh of Sakhalin. However, Shternberg was not pleased with the German publication. In a letter to a friend he wrote, "I received another letter from Rakhil [...] she sent me a cutting from a German newspaper with a review and translation from "Russkie Vedomosti" of a report on my article by Friedrich Engels. For all that I am not happy that it got into print prematurely. Now it will be necessary to make a lot of changes."[28] Shternberg's article "Sakhalin Giliaki" (1893), "Journey to the Far North of Sakhalin" (1895), "Orochi of the Tatarskii Strait" (1896), relating to the period of exile on the island, appeared in *Etnograficheskoe Obozrenie* (Ethnographical Reviews), *Tiuremnii vestnik (*Prison bulletin) and in the newspaper *Vladivostok*.[29] They were noted and praised highly.

Nivkh linguistics and the collection of folklore occupied a significant place in Shternberg's early creative works. He studied the language for six years, having to acquaint himself with the living language that was unknown to science.

"At first it was particularly difficult [...] in Viakhtu settlement there was not even one Gilyak with any knowledge of Russian whatsoever. My attempts at learning the language by ear through conversations [...] were quite unsuccessful. I decided [...] to approach the task the longer way—through theoretical study. Surrounding myself with [...] a few young Gilyaki, I started to write down short texts, seeking phrase analysis [...] At first work was extremely difficult as my teachers did not realize that phrases consist of separate words, and [...] stunned me with long sentences, which I was hardly able to jot down in the least perfect form. On top of that, painstaking questioning quickly bored them and our sessions moved on with long intervals" (Shternberg 1908: viii-ix).

One of Shternberg's more important works is still little called for and underestimated by those studying Siberia, "Materials on the study of the Gilyak and their folklore." This rich collection of mythological texts on the Nivkh, recorded in two languages, came from the printers in 1908 (see also Shternberg 1900:387–434). "There is nothing easier than to have the chance to listen to a Gilyak story-teller, but to take it down is extremely difficult. Gilyak speak very quickly. Furthermore, the language of a story-teller is archaic, different from conversational and even for the Gilyak them-

---

28 Ibid.
29 Shternberg 1893a; 1893b. Between 1893–1896 L.Ia. Shternberg published several articles in the weekly bulletin *Vladivostok* on issues relating to local life, satirical essays, travel articles and stories.

selves is not fully understood" (Shternberg 1908:x). Shternberg recollected. For the first time an outline was given in this work of the phonetics of the Nivkh language; folklore texts (in west and east Sakhalin dialects) with a translation into Russian were published for the first time ("literally a word-for-word translation"). These texts were recorded both by the author himself in the Rykovskoe settlement in 1897, and by Bronislav Pilsudski from the Nivkh, Churka, Pletunka and other Nivkh, and passed on to Shternberg for publication.[30] Shternberg proposed detailed commentary to the texts, and also the first classification of Nivkh folklore; he gave a characterization of the story-teller and singer, and for the first time noted the mutual influence of the Nivkh and Tunguso-Manchurian epic.

Shternberg believed that the Gilyak language was genetically close to American Indian languages; however, he later agreed with Leopold von Schrenck's opinion than the Gilyak language is part of an isolated group of "paleo-Asiatic" languages. The expert in the Nivkh language, Erukhim Kreinovich appraised his teacher's contribution at its true worth, pointing out at the same time, however, some of Shternberg's mistaken conclusions in the numeral system, phonetic system and others (Kreinovich 1968). Shternberg's great service was in the fact that for the first time he placed the Nivkh language into linguistic terms of reference, though he failed to complete this work; the Nivkh-Russian dictionary remained unpublished, as did his outline of Nivkh grammar.

Sternberg kept and developed his interest in questions, traditional in Russian ethnography, of ethnogenesis and ethno-history. Active studies into ethnogenesis were being undertaken in Siberia, since it was the nature of the Siberian "field" that archaic cultures were passing into history and even those observable in the present gave grounds for such investigations and permitted significant results to be achieved. That this later became a dominant subject in Soviet ethnography was not by chance (Tokarev 1949).

The Far East, Primor'e and Priamur'e [Outer Manchuria] have been regions of intensive inter-ethnic and cultural contacts since ancient times. Shternberg tried to investigate the most complex, many-layered and intertwined peoples and cultures, drawing on, as in the case of the Ainu, all possible sources: linguistic, archeological, ethnographic and anthropological. It was his last work on the Ainu that was noted by Maksim Levin as being an example methodologically "of the complex approach to research into questions of ethnogenesis" (Levin 1958:232). Such an approach allowed Shternberg to state, and for the first time argue most fully, the hypothesis of a southern, Austronesian origin of the Ainu, which, although it still required further refining, was actually proven by him (Shternberg 1929). Shternberg created a new method of studying ethnogenesis by identification of the formation and genesis of each clan comprising the people being studied. This method came to be widely used by Soviet scientists (Smoliak 1975).

---

30 Folklore texts in the Nivkh language, collected by B. Pilsudski during his exile on Sakhalin, partly published by Shternberg 1908:ix, xxii.

Contemplating questions of the classification of peoples of the Far East, Shternberg came to the conclusion that the main classification must be the ethnonym of the people. Based on this proposition, he drew the conclusion that the Tungus-Manchurian peoples of the Amur and Sakhalin—the Orok (Uilta), Oroch, Mangun (Ulchi), and Gold (Nanai), make up one tribe, i.e. people, since they all call themselves in the same way: *nani* (Shternberg 1933a:6–10, 396–398.). In this he did not agree with Schrenck. Although the ethnic proximity of the above peoples is beyond doubt, all the same they differ from each other linguistically and culturally. Shternberg, like the majority of scientists of his time, thought that Oroch and Udege (the latter he mistakenly called Kekari) were one and the same people. There were other points of view: Sergei Brailovskii was the first to use the ethnonym *Udikhe*, that corresponded with the ethnonym of these people; Vladimir Arsen'ev and Innokentii Lopatin supposed, on the basis of an analysis of the languages, that the Oroch and Udege were different peoples (Brailovskii 1901; Lopatin 1912; Brailovskii 1923; Arsen'ev 1926; 1947). The latest research has shown that it is their point of view that is correct. The theory on the tribal unity of the Tungus language peoples of the Lower Amur and Sakhalin based on the unity of their ethnonym turned out to be insufficiently validated (Smoliak 1975:43–44).

Shternberg, as opposed to Schrenck, thought that the ancestral home of the Nivkh was on the mainland; having analyzed the construction of their dwellings and type of dog breeding, he put forward the hypothesis of their northern origin. The hypothesis has not been confirmed by the latest research (Levin 1958:119–120). Another of Shternberg's hypotheses on the genetic link of Nivkh with Native Americans that arose at the peak of popularity of cross-cultural studies of North-West North America and the North-East of Russia at the end of the 19th beginning of the 20th centuries, was also later acknowledged to be unsatisfactory (Levin 1958:297).

Shternberg, arguing with Schrenck, believed that the Oroch moved to the Amur from the north. He pointed to the mixed character of Oroch descendants, noting that up to three-quarters of Oroch clans come from peoples living to the north of the Oroch. The latest research confirmed the heterogeneous ethnic composition of the Oroch, the main role in the formation of which, in the opinions of Valentin Avrorin and Elena Lebedeva, was played by the Nanai-Ulch component (Avrorin and Lebedeva 1966:7–8).

Shternberg took an interest in the question of the determination of the ethnic origin of the ancient population of Sakhalin, but the lack of archeological data prevented him from making any substantial deductions. The latest research has confirmed that the Ainu came to Sakhalin quite late (Kozyreva 1967:117–118).

In connection with the ethnogenesis of the peoples of the Far East, the question remains of the indigenous substrate in the culture of the Amur peoples. Analysis of the bear festival plays a considerable role in determining the answer. Shternberg put forward the hypothesis that the bear festival, when a bear is kept in captivity, was taken by the peoples of the Amur from the Ainu. This hypothesis was accepted by the majority of scholars of the time. However, Anna Smoliak in one of her works showed that the bear festival, with the bear captive in a cage and with its later killing, has even more ancient roots with the peoples of the Lower Amur than with the Ainu (Smoliak 1961:337–344). She considered the influence of the Ainu in Priamur'e had been highly exaggerated, drawing attention to Manchurian and Chinese influence.

As can be seen, many of Shternberg's hypotheses have not been confirmed. However, the very fact of the posing of general questions, the analysis of materials accumulated, the breakthrough to the level of major and bold generalizations were, from the point of view of the development of the science, very productive. Many years had passed since the time of observations of the phenomena by the scientist, and new interesting work devoted to the ethnography of the Nivkh and other peoples of the Far East had appeared. These works clarify and complement his observations, and in some areas diverge from them.[31] The question of the ethnogenesis of the peoples of the Far East is still far from being settled.

———

In studying the social organization of the Nivkh, Shternberg "discovered" amongst them, and later amongst other peoples of the Far East, "vestiges" of group marriage. Already a few of his contemporaries were skeptical about the hypothesis of group marriage. In particular, Aleksander Maksimov wrote that all the examples of marriage institutions that are usually referred to reinforce it, in actual fact are not group marriages in the full sense of this term, but are purely local, unique cases, which are not genetically interconnected; apart from that, the terms of the relationship do not correspond with systems of relationships. Nevertheless, in the Soviet period the approach, according to which systems of classifying relationships cannot be explained in any way other than by the existence of group marriages in the past, was widespread (Maksimov 1997).

Nowadays the concept of group marriages is no longer so invulnerable, as in Morgan's and post-Morgan times (Kriukov 1972; Artemova 2000).

In his book on the social organization of the Gilyak (Nivkh), which, as noted above, was published posthumously in English in 1999, Shternberg described and analyzed the system of relationships of the Nivkh and in addition to previous works drew analogies with the social organization of other peoples, first of all of the northeast of Russia and north-west of North America. There is nothing essentially new in the book by comparison with already published works. However, despite the sometimes word for word repetition of a book published in 1904, from the point of view of interpretation and theoretical generalizations it is a somewhat different work. It

———

31 See, for example: Kreinovich 1973; Ostrovskii 1997; Smoliak 1975; 1974; 1990; Taksami 1975; Black 1973.

is more up to date from a theoretical point of view than the works of Bogoras and Jochelson (see Kan 2001:218).

Shternberg devoted a number of works to the social organization of the Nivkh, which include a classical analysis of the clan organization and family-clan relations within this people. He looked deeply into the many and various family and social bonds that tie a Nivkh to his clan, considering the main indications of a clan to be notions of the singleness of origin, of a common fire, exogamy, common religious norms and ceremonies, the existence of one and the same clan from which all the members of this particular clan take wives, and also the existence of a common, third clan where all members of the clan give their women in marriage (the so-called three-clan union) (Shternberg 1933a:210–214). In the opinion of Smoliak, the "three-clan phratry," about which Shternberg wrote a great deal, is not discernible in investigations undertaken after him (Smoliak 1974:170–217; 1975). This was possibly caused by the fact that, already at the end of the 19th and the beginning of the 20th century, marriages on the basis of three-clan unions were no longer being concluded, rather mutual marriages between two clans were being practiced. Relatively recently the marriage bonds of minority ethnic groups of North Asia were studied in an article by G.M. Afanasieva and Iu.B. Simchenko. They expressed the opinion that the existence of three-clan marriage phratry (which in Shternberg's constructions were important components of Nivkh social organization) in a numerically small group was impossible (Afanasieva and Simchenko 1981). In old editions of his work, describing marriage customs of the Nivkh, Shternberg demonstrated such ties without indicating specific clans: clan A takes women from clan B, B from C, and C from A (Shternberg 1933a). However, in a later page the author wrote that different "real-life conflicts did not always permit" the realization of these rules, there were exceptions and fourth clans appeared, and a three-clan phratry turned into a four-clan union. Shternberg's last work, published in English, vividly demonstrates both the three-clan and the more complex, four-clan (and even five-clan) phratry: clan A – clan B – clan C – clan D and back again (Shternberg 1999:31–38).

Shternberg wrote that some clans of this people were "flourishing," others were "dying out": "a clan is a living organism." Indeed, materials in the archive of Niko-laevsk-on-Amur, which relate to the first quarter of the 20th century and include a list of Nivkh clans of the Amur and Sakhalin and their representatives who entered into marriage, show that this indigenous people had more than 70 clans (Smoliak 1970; 1974; 1975).

Shternberg himself never wrote about the clan make-up of the Sakhalin Nivkh. Data of 1910 on clans of the Amur Nivkh that had settled in the lower reaches of the river and in the estuary were taken from his notebooks and put into scientific circulation in 1933 in his posthumously published books. On the basis of field and archive studies, Smoliak ascertained that absolutely all Nivkh clans at the end of the 19th and the beginning of the 20th century lived each in his or her own clan community, but the composition of the settlement was multi-clan, and sometimes multi-national. Shternberg did not single out the Nivkh community, the unit of which is the settlement, as an independent social unit. In V.R. Kabo's opinion, "the settlement as it stands out in the works of Shternberg and other authors should be seen as a heterogenic or indigenous-clan community. The latter was an economic unit in Nivkh society" (Kabo 1981:206). The old position on the clan as an economic unit that L.G Morgan and other researchers adhered to (Shternberg was strongly influenced by his idea), is not found with the Nivkh. The same is true for the neighbors of Nivkh along the Amur (Smoliak 1974; 1975). If the wide extent of the areas occupied by the Nivkh and the small numbers of this people are taken into account, then there were no grounds for setting apart separate clan hunting grounds. For this reason, representatives of different clans did not come into conflict and, on the contrary, were happy when outsiders turned up, inviting them into the settlement. The commonality of clan territory was observed only with a new, recently formed clan (Shternberg 1933a:175). Returning to the question of the territorial property rights of the Nivkh, we would stress that Shternberg's assessments in this area were inconsistent, which can be explained by the complex structure of land holding relations with the Nivkh.

Shternberg's works, having marked out the direction of further research, at the same time objectively played the role of a "brake" in the study of questions of kinship. The elaboration of this area in Soviet ethnography right up to the period of the 1950–1960s went along the course constructed by Morgan and Engels. Within the framework of the structuralist and post-modernist theoretical approaches many of the propositions of evolutionism and Marxism appear to be mistaken.

———

At Leningrad University Shternberg taught a course "The History of Religious Beliefs," that was taken down in shorthand by his students and published by them in 1936 (Shternberg 1936). Shternberg defined religion as one form of the struggle for existence. He came to that conclusion on the basis of his own field materials, as he was still not acquainted with the work of Edward Tylor (Ratner-Shternberg 1933:99). But he saw in the idea of the soul not a primary concept, but the product of long development. Shternberg marked out three stages in the development of animism: animatism, primary spiritualism, personification of nature, and the concept of the soul (Shternberg 1936:2–12). He underlined the importance of the psychology of a primitive person when studying early forms of the development of religion, and in these approaches we see some closeness of his to the French sociological school of Emile Durkheim.

———

A large place in the scientific work of Shternberg was devoted to the study of different religious phenomena. He paid special attention to the study of the evolution of religious beliefs using examples of different religious phenomena that are widespread amongst different peoples, sometimes far from each other in location, language, culture and place in history. He especially made a deep study of the cults of the eagle and twins amongst the peoples of Siberia, the cult of *inau* with the Ainu, and religious 'chosenness'.

Shternberg introduced the term "cult of twins" into circulation and proposed another interpretation for it that differed from the concept of the mythological school. In his opinion, twinned gods reflect the mythology of a real phenomenon in religious practice: the twin cult. He drew the conclusion that "the twin cult is only one type of cult of deified people-kinsmen." Later, Aleksander Zolotarev and Sergei Tolstov pointed to another basis for the twin cult, that is, the archaic dualistic organization of society and corresponding world-view (see Basilov 1993b:34–37).

Shternberg devoted his article "Divine election in religion" to the question of shamanism and the inheritance of the shamanic gift (Shternberg 1927a). He thought it was possible to become a shaman through the will of the spirits (but not obtain the shamanic gift by human action, although that was possible), and the "shamanic sickness", being overcome, opens the way to shamanic practice. On the expedition of 1910, he put forward for the first time (which is very important), on the basis of several conversations with a young Nanai shaman in the settlement of Sikhachi-Alian, the hypothesis that a sexual element is one of the main reasons for the belief that a shaman is chosen. Shternberg assumed that shamanism represents the primary, early stage of selection on the sex motif, and the same motif is common to a number of other religious phenomena. He understood the lack of factual material for the basis of a pattern for this phenomenon for all humankind. For this reason he set his students the task of collecting such material. Some of his followers, having become interested in the new hypothesis, took another look at their field material and found evidence to support it.[32] However, the hypothesis has not been confirmed to this day, though neither has it been refuted. Scientific opinion was divided on the question.[33] The well-known investigator into shamanism, Vladimir Basilov, thought that the concept of somebody 'being chosen' was one of the "significant religious conceptions of humanity, but cannot be fully accepted today [...] the role of the sex motif in the concept of somebody 'being chosen' was unjustifiably exaggerated by Shternberg; this relates both to shamanism and to later cults and institutions" (Basilov 1993a: 95).

---

32 Such information can be found in the letters of Nevskii to Shternberg (PF ARAN 282/2/211), and in letters from Prokofiev to Shternberg (PF ARAN 282/2/242:1, 5 rev.).

33 See, for example: Smoliak 1994 (3):174–175; Kharitonova 2000:312–338. In the opinion of M.M. Khasanova the sex motif in devine election in the religious views of the Nanai, Ulch, and Oroch is present, without doubt, but the question remains: what is its place amongst other motifs and to what extent is it characteristic of other peoples of the world? (personal communication–A.S.).

Whereas, on the whole, he was highly critical of Freudianism, amongst his positive groundwork Shternberg noted the role of the unconscious factor in religion, and also the abnormal psyche of a concrete individual in the formation of religious ideas. He thought that Siberian shamanism originated in a single south Asian center, possibly in India (Ratner-Shternberg 1930:120).

Historiographic research and the study of Jewish ethnography occupied a specific place in Shternberg's scientific work and heritage.

At the beginning of the 1900s, Shternberg actively published reviews of books, the list of which indicates the variety and wide breadth of his interests: G. Mortillet—"The Prehistoric World," L. Krzhivitskii—"Mental Races," N. Kharuzin—"Ethnography," L. Sokolovskii—"The Study of Human Nature," H. George—"The Works of Henry George," S. Kotliarevskii—"Present Day Catholicism," W. Bogoras—"The Chukchee" and others. Apart from that, he wrote a number of small essays on the life and work of V.V. Radloff, G. Miller, V. Bartold, D.N. Anuchin, M.A. Castrén: the majority of whom were timed for anniversary dates (Shternberg 1907; 1909; 1913a; 1916; 1926; 1925; 1927c; 1928a). Shternberg paid a great deal of attention to tendencies abroad in sciences relating to humans (Sternberg 1926b).

That side of Shternberg's life and scientific work concerning Jewish ethnography is still little known and requires special study. He was not a specialist in this field but he gave it considerable attention. Throughout life he maintained an interest in his native culture, which apparently urged him to read lectures on the Jewish question and engage in Jewish ethnography. In Petrograd, in 1919, an Institute of Higher Jewish Knowledge (later to be named the Petrograd Jewish University and later still the Leningrad Institute of Jewish History and Literature) was established with the aim of producing different specialists; Sternberg was one of its lecturers (Sobolev and Anfert'eva 1995[2]:7–8, 6).

Shternberg collaborated with a number of organizations engaged in the study of Jewish culture. He was chairman of the committee administering the work of the Jewish History and Ethnographical Society. It had been set up on 16th November 1908 with the aim of furthering the "study and research into all areas of Jewish history and ethnology." There were a number of sections in the Society, an archive and museum with exhibits on the history and ethnography of Jews. In 1923, Shternberg became the editor of the journal *Evreiskaia Starina* [Jewish antiquity], in which he published several articles on Jewish ethnography (Shternberg 1913b; 1912; 1924a; 1924b;1924c; 1928b; Anskii 1914). The most interesting of these is the article "Issues of Jewish National Psychology," in which the author emphasizes an "inborn complex" of the Jewish people. "The most surprising in the mentality of a Jew," Shternberg notes, "is a combination of extreme rationalism with intense emotionality and activity" (Shternberg 1928b:32). This "inborn complex" was a feature of the scientist himself to the whole.

Shternberg became a field ethnographer 'against his will'. One can safely say that without that eight-year exile on Sakhalin there would not have been that Shternberg who is well known as an investigator into the peoples of the Far East. Field ethnography did not interest Shternberg until he was impelled to engage in it in exile, in that vacuum of spiritual life that existed on Sakhalin for an active person overflowing with energy: "Occupation with ethnography," his wife recollected, "raised his spirits and filled his solitary life with a living interest" (PF ARAN 282/2/195:121). The same, however, applies to the colleague with whom he had endless professional arguments and a time-tested friendship—Waldemar Bogoras. And it is also true that Shternberg, unlike Bogoras, was prepared deep down for these investigations from the point of view of his interest in the history of the development of society and the state (Kan 2000:21).

And from the very beginning he was interested in the history of the development of marriage and the family in ethnography, and also the history and evolution of religious beliefs, from the study of which he did not stray.

The years of life on Sakhalin were indeed that period when young Shternberg could undertake intensive field studies. True, it was not participant observations that were dominant in his methods, as they were, for example, with Pilsudski or Bogoras, who, in 1895 wrote to Shternberg from Srednekolymsk: "I am now entangled in ethnography. Traveled around the district, moving from place to place for seven months with the Chukchi, the devil take them, rode on reindeer, rafted down rivers [...]" (PF ARAN 282/2/34:6 rev.; in Vakhtin 2001:71–89), but by the method of interviews, including in-depth interviews, during the taking of the census in 1891, in the northeast of the island. He worked mainly in the summer. Shternberg's diaries, 1892–1896, were published not long ago in Iuzhno-Sakhalinsk (Shternberg 2001a,b; Roon and Prokof'ev 2001:211–215). Criticizing some foreign theories, among other things, Shternberg used as his strongest argument the fact that they were written by scientists, not conversant with the real life of the peoples being investigated, in their "studies."

Strictly speaking, no one taught Shternberg the method of field studies. One can risk saying that he actually had no method. Does anyone teach a shaman how to become a shaman and perform the rituals? Here too it was a sort of intuition based on his inherent ability and knowledge, experience of life and convictions. He showed his interviewee books with pictures, calling forth their reaction to the cultural life of other peoples, and he was quite provocative in relation to places that were, for the Nivkh, forbidden, and then getting their explanations, he painstakingly worked with his interviewees to learn the language, terms for relationships and beliefs (Shternberg 1904:30).

In general, on the basis of his first experience of work, Shternberg came to the conclusion that it was essential to learn the language and, despite all the difficulties, he did this.

One gets the impression that Shternberg did not like long periods of fieldwork. His mind was of a different mold: analytical, hypothesizing, discerning general patterns in language and culture. Before us is an example, quite rare in the Russian ethnographical community, of a person with an alert analytical mind and at the same time an interest in concrete ethnographical facts. As an evolutionist, he asserted the singleness of human culture, considered that it develops in one direction, and put forward unexpected parallels from different aspects of Nivkh culture with those of the German, Slavic, Jewish and other peoples (Shternberg 1893a:10, 13, 28).

More often than not the conversation began with a discussion of the history of things that interviewees sold or gave to the museum. This was one of the most productive methods of gathering information in conditions of limited time that continues to be used successfully today, especially by museum scholars. Shternberg was present at shamanistic rituals also (Shternberg 1927a:11–16).

In 1914, Shternberg published "A Short Course in Ethnography (with regard to the mode of life of peoples of the north)," in which he shared his practical experience as a field ethnographer: it is necessary to learn how to observe, know the language or at least have a basic vocabulary of the people under study, keep a daily diary and, already "in the field" to systematize the data obtained. He briefly outlined different elements of culture and ways of their investigation. Most space in his course was given to questions of "social culture" (clan, terms for relationships and marriage), and there was a section on "beliefs" (including shamanism) (Shternberg 1914; 1933a:715–737).

Shternberg did not only collect material on indigenous peoples, but propagated ideas of better social organization, equality and brotherhood. K.M. Mylnikova and V.I. Tsintsius, working in 1926 amongst Negidal on the River Amgun, passed on the reminiscences of the older people about Shternberg: "Lev Iakovlevich did not only relate to them as equal to equals, but told them that, it turns out, all people were equal, and that there would be a time when they won't be exploited. He also tried to develop in them a sense of national identity or, as they say, 'asked them to take care of their old law'"—"But now that good time has come that Lev Iakovlevich told us about," (PF ARAN 282/1/110: 79) in that way they summed up their reminiscences. Shternberg did the same amongst young teachers, workers, and students with whom he came into contact in one way or another throughout his life.

Science is moved by ordinary people. Their interactions with each other, temporary or permanent coalitions, sympathies and antipathies play a big role in the intra-scientific life, determine the vectors of further research, speed them up for a time or, on the contrary, hold back the development of particular areas of science, ideas and works. In connection with this, we would like to sketch out the interrelations of Shternberg with some of his colleagues and friends.[34]

---

34 The scholar's archive contains a wide correspondence both with Russian and foreign colleagues. Shternberg's main correspondents at different times were F. Boas, C.V. Hartman, J. Ambrosetti, W. Bogoras, W. Jochelson, B.O. Pilsudski, S.M. Shirokogoroff, V.K. Arsen'ev and E.A. Kreinovich.

A significant role in Shternberg's scientific career was played by his relationship with the American scientist Franz Boas (1858–1942), the founder of the "American school of cultural anthropology." If Boas had not ordered Shternberg's manuscript of his book on Gilyak, who knows, it is possible that even the work "Family and Clan of the Peoples of North-East Asia" of 1933 would not have come into being. Boas thought Shternberg to be the "Russian Bastian"[35] and spoke highly of him (posthumously) as an outstanding anthropologist and scientific theorist, and he also underlined his personal friendship with him (see also Kan 2001).

This relationship, built up on a professional basis, grew into many-sided cooperation. The point was that Boas, like Shternberg, was a passionate champion of human rights, individual freedom, advocate of equality, and enemy of racism, ethnocentrism and chauvinism (Lewis 2001). Both scientists were highly acknowledged in scientific circles and had many students and followers.

Correspondence between Shternberg and Boas began in 1905. At that time, the question of Shternberg's visit to the American Natural History Museum for work with its collection from the Amur region was being discussed. Boas wanted Shternberg to meet Dr. Laufer, one of the participants of the Jesup Expedition who had worked in the Amur region and gathered an ethnographic collection at the end of the 19th century (PF ARAN 282/2/29:2). Shternberg arrived in America at the beginning of May 1905 and spent two and a half months there, which were full of impressions, meetings and journeys (see also Kan 2001). During this time he wrote three and a half pages of texts with explanations of some items, indicated by the manuscript of the scholar himself, and visited the Chicago museum in order to learn about the fate of the collection he had made that had been sent to America at the beginning of the 1890s (Roon 2000:141). Boas made Shternberg a proposal of cooperation in a project on the preparation of a manuscript and publication of the transactions of the Jesup Expedition. During meetings, discussions and in letters the subject of Shternberg's book was crystallized: "The Gilyak and their Neighbors," which in the following was narrowed down to "Social Organization of the Gilyak." However, for different reasons the manuscript was published only at the end of the 20th century.

Boas drew Shternberg, and Bogoras and Jochelson also, into participating in the congresses of Americanists: in Stuttgart (1904), Quebec (1906), Vienna (1908), Buenos-Aires (1910), and London (1912). Shternberg gave papers at the congresses on theoretical questions of ethnology, and specifically on questions that were being devel-

---

The limited length of the article and in some instances lack of materials does not permit us to illustrate the relations of Shternberg with W. Jochelson, M. Krol', A. and L. Mervart and some others of his colleagues and friends.

35   Adolf Bastian (1826–1905) was one of the founders of German ethnology. He produced numerous works on the peoples of the world. He put forward the hypothesis of the psychological concurrence of humankind, and recognized the possibility of different paths of evolutionary development.

oped by participants of the Jesup Expedition headed by Boas (Krupnik 1998:205). In 1912, Shternberg wrote to his wife from London: "Famous scientists have gathered here. It was here that I had the pleasure of making the acquaintance of the eminent Frazer and had a long conversation with him. He had come, I am able to say, to a large extent because of me." London made an "enchanting impression" on Shternberg: "[...] a city with charming architecture, gardens, courteous people on the streets, and everything marked with the imprint of the strength of taste and coziness." It was then too that he met Boas: "We had a very pleasant and friendly conversation [...]" (PF ARAN 282/2/361:132, 132 rev.).

The history of relations between Shternberg and Bronislav Pilsudski (1866–1918) has been the subject of attention of a number of scientists and local historians both in Russia and abroad in recent years (Pilsudski 1996; Khasanova 2001; Reshetov 2000; Latyshev 2008). A surprising friendship of two people, their identical "starting point" in penal servitude on Sakhalin, similar interests in the sphere of ethnography, and such different fortunes in life! But with time everything falls into place and, not having received due acknowledgement in his lifetime, Pilsudski "is returning" in triumph into the history of science first and foremost as a brilliant field linguist and ethnologist (Inoue 2003:135–163).

Pilsudski was very fond of Shternberg. "You [...] have bestowed a living stream of interests, a will to live," he wrote to him in 1897, "I have become so used to sharing my anxiety and apprehensions with you. But, most of all, it is so interesting with you! It's difficult to part, but I am happy for you [...] Very happy" (in Gagen-Torn 1975:103–104).

Only one side of the correspondence between Pilsudski and Shternberg has been preserved: to date Sternberg's letters to Pilsudski have not been found, but Pilsudski's letters to Shternberg have been published by V.M. Latyshev (Pilsudski 1996).

Pilsudski shared his field materials and folklore texts with Shternberg, and part of the latter (according to one source, four texts, but to another—eleven texts) were included in his book on folklore (Shternberg 1908, Vol. 1. Part 1). Shternberg needed Pilsudski as a person who had worked a great deal with the Ainu and Gilyak, knew the Far East well and could be the gatherer and conveyer of collections to the museum and a correspondent. Shternberg never forgot his Sakhalin comrade and from time to time helped him with friendly advice, arrangement of an expedition or purchase of collections.

Sergei Mikhailovich Shirokogoroff (1887–1937) began working at the MAE in 1910 (Revunenkova and Reshetov 2003). It was Shternberg who advised him, a person never having visited Siberia, to choose Zabaikal'e, where Tungus were living, as a region for research. An expedition in 1912 was the first expedition that he went on together with his wife. He wrote to St. Petersburg: "Both Elizaveta Nikolaevna and I are enchanted with the nature of Zabaikal'e and of Siberia in general. We like the Tungus and they like us too, it seems [...] they are very trusting. I am very, very grateful to you, much appreciated Lev Iakovlevich, for your prompting me to go to the Tungus" (PF ARAN 282/2/319: 1 rev.).

The expedition was successful: new collections were made and scientific material gathered. It would appear that Shirokogoroff at that time was close to Shternberg in his political views, as he received the news of the revolution of February 1917 enthusiastically. But soon the Shirokogoroff couple experienced the consequences of the disturbances in the normal course of life directly. Mongolians in Hailar were in a state of trepidation and areas close to the border in the Far East were unsettled: bands of Chinese were terrorizing the populace. Everyone was caught up in it: travelers, local inhabitants and the Tungus. On the road from Blagoveshensk, where Shirokogoroff had been translating texts with the help of an Oroch, to Chita, the couple and people accompanying them were arrested and "[...] found themselves in a dreadful situation [...] All these circumstances: arrest, difficulties in travel, literal robbery of people who found themselves forced to use other people's services, and these muddle-headed Mongolians have exhausted us completely both morally and physically" (PF ARAN 282/2/319:16).

In August 1917, Sergei Shirokogoroff was in Ekaterinodar, where he was resting with his wife at the isolated farmstead of her parents after the Manchurian expedition. He wrote to Shternberg about his uncertain situation. From China, where Shirokogoroff had emigrated, he informed Shternberg that he had completed his work on the subject "Ethos and Ethnography:" "By my calculations, I thought I would crawl out with them much later, but my unnatural exercises in the university [...] forced me to begin writing. I am aware that a great deal in the work is unfinished [...] but I don't want to put it off till an unknown future, but put these questions, at least in order that everyone criticized severely, it is good for the future" (PF ARAN 282/2/319:25 rev.)[36]

For personal and ideological reasons (towards the end of his life Shirokogoroff became a monarchist) their scientific and personal communications broke off completely. Evidently, it was not by chance that after the mid-1920s Shirokogoroff himself never referred to Shternberg amongst those who had had any kind of influence on his scientific destiny. The early correspondence is evidence of the opposite. Bogoras once called Shirokogoroff "the most capable of Shternberg's older students" (Bogoras 1928:8; see also Reshetov 2003b:188). Shternberg's relations with Vladimir Arsen'ev (1872–1930), an outstanding researcher into the Far East, took a different shape (Luganskii 1997). These were people of quite opposite descent, outlook, education and experience of life.

In 1910, Arsen'ev became acquainted with Shternberg and accompanied him for a period of time on his journey along the Amur (PF ARAN 282/1/110:25). At that time, Bruno Adler invited Arsen'ev to participate in an All-Russian ethnographic exhibition organized at the Russian Museum in St. Petersburg. Arsen'ev gave a collection to the

---

36 In Shternberg's archive there are 11 letters from Shirokogoroff for 1912–1924, the last of which posted from Hailar and Shanghai.

museum for which he was awarded a small silver medal of the Geographical Society (Polevoi and Reshetov 1972).

Shternberg, because of the above-mentioned "arbitration tribunal," was in poor relations with Adler and, it would appear, he all but transferred these relations to Arsen'ev. Feeling this, the latter wrote to Shternberg: "B.F. Adler has an account to settle with you—this is his and your affair! But there is no misunderstanding between us and therefore there should not be strained relations between us. Then (in St. Petersburg) I said to myself, 'The duty of every decent person is not to enflame enmity between others, but on the contrary to try to put it out!' And for this reason your quarrel with Adler could not influence me [...]." Arsen'ev always had a respectful, courteous and friendly disposition towards Shternberg. "Remember my words at the I.R.G.O. [Imperial Russian Geographical Society] during the lecture (the paper "Orochi-Udehe," read by Arsen'ev 18ᵗʰ March 1911–A.S., T.R.) I officially and publicly announced that I would listen to your objection with pleasure (although it was very strongly worded) and that I am ready to have further conversations and discourse with you," (PF ARAN 282/2/20: 3 rev., 4) he wrote to Shternberg in 1913.

"Lev Shternberg was a very serious critic of other people's work. He was not shy to speak his mind," Arsen'ev recalled in his public speech devoted to Shternberg's memory. He spoke about the kind of comments the scientist made on the pages of his work: "Nonsense. What you are venturing is not serious. [...] Everything needs to be started afresh." But gradually the tone of his remarks changed: "Your book has disturbed me. It has revived in my memory that past time when I was young and began work on ethnography for the first time and had direct contact with indigenous people. You have written little on ethnography recently, but what you are communicating now are real masterpieces" (PF ARAN 282/1/110:23, see also Arsen'ev 1966).

At Shternberg's request, Arsen'ev was collecting information on terms used for relationships and norms of marriage, arranging and dispatching ethnographical collections, and taking care of his students and colleagues for him. Shternberg helped Arsen'ev also and, in times that were difficult for him, he invited him to work in Leningrad. Shternberg's scientific, social and political authority helped Arsen'ev parry the attacks of his ill-wishers in the early post-revolutionary years.[37]

Shternberg had close ties with Bernhard Petri (1887–1937). The son of the well-known anthropologist Edward Petri, the young Petri, remaining at an early age without his father, fell under the guardianship of Radloff and Shternberg. In 1910, after graduating from St. Petersburg University, Petri began work at the MAE where he remained in the position of junior ethnographer until 1917. The scientific interests of a number of the staff of the MAE were connected with Siberia, and Petri also chose the region of western Pribaikal'e, where Buryat live, for his research. Both the region and the subject of research, family and clan of western Buryat and their religious beliefs,

---

37 Letters of L.Ia. Shternberg to V.K. Arsen'ev: 76, 80; PF ARAN 282/2/20.

it appears, were suggested by Shternberg. Over the years at the MAE, Petri went on three lengthy expeditions in Pribaikal'e (1912, 1913, 1916), which were financed by the Russian Committee for the study of Central and East Asia. Over the course of the expeditions he maintained a correspondence with Shternberg.

After the October Revolution, Petri decided to remain in Irkutsk for an indefinite period, and in 1923 he settled permanently in Siberia: "My plan is closely linked with personal ties and the sympathy and interest which local people have in my research," he wrote to Shternberg in 1922, "I cannot bring myself to give all this up and leave for Petersburg, as you insist [...] I ask you to keep for me the high title of ethnographer of the Academy of Sciences that I have born so far and of which I am proud [...]" (PF ARAN 282/2/227:15,16).

In the 1920s, professor Petri, together with other Siberian scientists set up the Irkutsk School of Archeology and Ethnography, whose students are well-known in the history of Soviet science: A.P. Okladnikov, M.M. Gerasimov, and G.F. Debets (Sirina 2003:57–80).

The October Revolution rocked and overturned the whole of Russia—civil war, intervention, emigration. At the same time for many people it opened up new possibilities. Amongst them was Lev Shternberg. In the post-revolutionary confusion he was arrested for a short time, but then released.

After Radloff's death in 1918, Shternberg began to carry out the duties of director of the MAE. The First World War and the Russian Revolution had upset established connections and new concerns presented themselves. Shternberg had to arrange for the export of collections gathered by Liudmila and Aleksander Mervart in India. Not until the beginning of 1920 were collections on Greenland Inuit, ordered way back in 1914, brought out of Denmark.

The former staff of the museum had become sorely depleted in post-revolutionary years: some staff failed to return after work on expeditions, remaining in Siberia and north China, like Petri and Shirokogoroff; others returned but were later repressed, others still, like Jochelson, chose to emigrate from what was by then the USSR (Sirina 2003:64–65; Revunenkova and Reshetov 2003; Vigasin 2003).

New people came to the museum, whose director was now Efim Karskii. One of them was Dmitrii Ol'derogge, later to become a corresponding member of the Academy of Sciences, one of the founders of the Russian school of Africanists. After finishing the department of linguistics and literature in the faculty of social sciences at Leningrad University in 1925, Ol'derogge began working at the MAE, where he attended Shternberg's seminars. Shternberg compiled lists of literature for Ol'derogge and, remaining in his study in the evening, had long conversations with him on the theory of culture circles and the views of Fritz Graebner and Heinrich Schurtz, imperceptibly directing his research towards African Studies. In 1927, on Shternberg's initiative, Dmitrii Ol'derogge was sent to Germany on an official assignment for half a year in order to study African collections and languages; the trip turned out to be very fruitful (Osnitskaia 1993; Popov 2004).

Shternberg helped A.B. Piotrovskii, the uncle of the future director of the Hermitage, outstanding expert on Oceania, and a gentle, considerate, outwardly unobtrusive person, not embarrassed by his handicap of deafness (Zhmoida 1999:146).

"The ease with which Lev Iakovlevich talked with me, in a way (exclusively in writing) that troubled many other people so much, his ability to encourage a person, fill him with a belief in his own powers, and readiness to assist at all times with his colossal erudition were an invaluable service to me," Piotrovskii recollected. "For me meeting Lev Iakovlevich was a salvation in the full sense of the word, only thanks to this did my life gain content and meaning" (PF ARAN 282/1/110:114).

Shternberg was nurturing the idea of arranging a section in the museum for the evolution and typology of culture that would reflect his theoretical preferences. The setting up of such a section began in 1925, but after his death the shaping of the section was discontinued, and the idea itself was forgotten.

The Soviet state showed a particular interest in the development of ethnography and regional studies and allocated considerable funds to this end. Shternberg was one of the editors of the journal *Etnografiia* (Ethnography) 1926–1930), the forerunner of the present *Etnograficheskoe Obozrenie* (Ethnographical Review), editor of *Chelovek* (The Human) (1927). Together with Bogoras he also conducted scientific and practical work as a member of the Committee for assistance for the Peoples of the North in the Presidium of the All-Russian Central Executive Committee.

The country's leaders needed detailed information on the population: numbers, languages, details of life, and also specialists. Shternberg suited the role of teacher for the new, Soviet social and economic structure better than anyone else. Even before the revolution he had used every chance to expound his ideas of the unity of cultural development and human progress, and called for a fair social structure of society. Shternberg's experience and multifaceted abilities were required by the Soviet authorities that regarded the peoples of the north the most oppressed and backward in social and economic development and, for that reason, requiring particular state paternalism. Shternberg received a unique possibility to teach first in the Institute of Geography set up in 1918 (he was the dean of the ethnographical section), and then, in 1925, after the reorganization of the Institute and its merging with the university, within the walls of Leningrad State University [LGU], in the ethnographical department of the Geography faculty (Staniukovich 1971). These educational institutions became the basis for the preparation of a new generation of Soviet ethnographers, and the school itself received the name "the Leningrad school" (see Liarskaia, *this volume*). It was the graduates of this school that had the outstanding role of solving the practical tasks of eliminating illiteracy and forming a national *intelligentsia* from amongst the peoples of the North, which, indeed, they fulfilled. It was not out of nothing that the "school" arose: through Bogoras and Shternberg the traditions of Russian ethnography, field station research, knowledge of the language, and the humanistic orientation of research were passed on to a new generation of students.

Student ethnographers received multifaceted knowledge in different spheres of science: the history of world culture was taught by well-known scholars: V.M. Alekseev, N.I. Kareev, V.V. Struve, I.V. Frank-Kamenetskii; the theory and practice of linguistics by B.V. Vladimirtsev, L.Ia. Shternberg and W. Bogoras; and statistics by F.F. Kaufman. Students were also taught the natural sciences, the knowledge of the basics of which could prove useful during fieldwork: botany, zoology, soil science, geology and others. Theoretical groundwork was combined with museological and expeditionary practice. To prepare students for the "field" they were taught the skills of work with cameras, map-making, outlining, and the basics of drawing. (On the "Leningrad ethnographic school" see also: Ratner-Shternberg 1935; Gagen-Torn 1971; Staniukovich 1971)

At the University, Shternberg taught courses in "An introduction to ethnography," the "Evolution of material culture," "Evolution of religious beliefs" and the "Evolution of social culture." One of the first of Shternberg's students recalled that in 1921 the professor read lectures in the enormous hall of the main University building, where only 2 or 3 electric lamps cast a stingy light on the figures of students crouched-up from the cold (PF ARAN 282/1/110:15).

"A thin, elderly man, shriveled up as if by internal combustion," Nina Gagen-Torn recounts in her memoirs, "spread out stacks of scribbled cards and raised his eyes; looked intently at us for a while through his glasses, and then began to speak:

> "Many people don't have the slightest idea that, without ethnography, without its data, classifications and generalizations there would be no science of man, his culture, space, and time. To put it more simply, the discipline called history is impossible, and the same for the discipline of sociology [...] The greatest service of ethnography is in the fact that for the first time it established the concrete notion of humanity en masse. If one can put it like this, is it that for the first time made a roll call of all the peoples of the planet [...]
>
> He bent down to his stack of cards so as to make a quotation that would prove his thought. Brought them close up to his glasses, read, and coughed a little, shuffling the cards. He was no orator, he even stuttered slightly. It was not easy to listen to him, or to make notes.
>
> I was surprised: what had brought all these students here? Why were they listening to the strained and matter-of-fact speech of Shternberg? And soon I understood that what we were witnessing was not an academic lecture, but the pith of this man's life. He was infusing his whole will and passion into ethnography. This was felt by everyone and could not but enflame [...]" (Gagen-Torn 1994: 50–51).

After the lectures students would fairly often see Shternberg home (he lived not far from the university) and converse along the way, arguing on one topic or another, about philosophy, or history, and this informal dialogue conveyed no less than the formal classes (Grant 1999b:247–248, 252). One of his students recalled: "Lev Iakovlevich had an original manner of behaving in conversations that was peculiar to himself, he would listen carefully, put in questions, elucidate and argue without advancing his own superiority, as an equal with equals, without irony [...]" (PF ARAN 282/1/110:134).

Those around him were attracted by his inner charisma as a leader, his ability to stand up for his convictions and interests, and also to inspire his collocutor with a faith in his own abilities.

Shternberg was able to interest young people in science, and together with Bogoras, he demanded knowledge of the language of the peoples being investigated as well as "being in the field" no less than one or two years, that is, participatory observation. Both scientists taught students the basics of the Nivkh, Chukchi and Evenk languages. Bogoras, a person with a quick temperament, sociable, full of life, open and explosive, often became distracted at lectures, answered questions, laughed together with the students and made jokes. Shternberg, according to the recollections of his students, was a complex, reserved person, who they loved but were somewhat afraid of for his sharp judgments, strictness, sternness and seriousness (Grant 1999b:247).

Many of the students of Shternberg and Bogoras eventually became outstanding scientists, organizers of the scientific process, compilers of alphabets and dictionaries for peoples formerly having no written language. But first there were expeditions; for the majority, scientific work was combined with administrative work or teaching.

It is appropriate at this point to recall the "Ten Commandments of the Ethnographer" compiled by Shternberg, presumably by analogy with the Biblical Ten Commandments. We give them here in full (Gagen-Torn 1971:142–143):

1. Ethnography is the crown of the humanitarian [social–A.S., T.R.] sciences, for it makes comprehensive studies of all peoples in the past and present.

2. Do not idolize your own people, own religion or own culture. Know that all people are potentially equal: There is neither Hellen [Greek–A.S., T.R.], nor Jew, nor white, nor colored. He, who knows one people, knows none, he, who knows one religion, one culture, knows none.

3. Do not profane science, nor defile ethnography by careerism: the real ethnographer can only be the one that fosters enthusiasm towards the science, love for humankind and for people.

4. Work for six days, and on the seventh sum up the results. Remember your duty before society and science.

5. Honor great forbears, and teachers in scientific and public life, in order that you be honored according to your services.

6. Do not destroy science with the falsification of facts, superficial, inaccurate observations, or quick conclusions.
7. Do not change the once chosen subject of ethnography. He, who has started along the path of ethnography, should not stray from it.
8. Do not commit plagiarism.
9. Do not bear false witness against your neighbor, against other peoples, their character, customs, practices etc. Love your neighbor more than yourself.
10. Do not force your own culture onto the people you study: approach it with regard and care, with love and attention, no matter at what stage of culture it is, and it will aspire to rise to the level of a higher culture itself.

This "moral code" of the first generation of Soviet ethnographers was born on the wave of post-revolutionary enthusiasm and was by no means a "flippant code" as Nina Gagen-Torn believed (Gagen-Torn 2002:318).

In a distinctive form, Shternberg's fundamental theoretical, methodological and ethical views are reflected in it. Romanticism and maximalism, the idealization of the science of peoples are characteristic of the "Commandments": not to betray ethnography, ethnography being the crown of all the humanitarian (social) sciences, all peoples are equal, he, who knows one culture, knows none. The humanistic traditions of Russian ethnography were also reflected in the "Commandments." Although they speak of the potential equality of peoples and cultures, Shternberg, in accordance with the evolutionist paradigm, actually "arranged" peoples along "stages of culture," stressing that the people being studied would "itself aspire to rise to the level of higher cultures."

But in practice not everything was unequivocal. The process of including the peoples of the North and Far East into the Soviet state framework was being forced through without restraint, especially in the 1930s. Unfortunately, almost no one amongst the researchers paid attention to the incongruence of the noble goals and the rushed methods as if the end justifies the means. Severed from their usual surroundings and living conditions, many students of the Institute of Peoples of the North (INS) fell ill, and dropped out, as A.P. Koshkina-Alkora expressed it, "the inevitable percentage of the debilitated." Those who like Nina Gagen-Torn expressed openly their doubts about these kinds of method were in the end obliged to give up teaching (Gagen-Torn 2002:142).

Shternberg, Bogoras and other teachers of the ethnographic section of the Geography faculty of the Leningrad State University prepared a whole *pleiad* of students who continued the work of their teachers in a worthy manner.

Sergei Vasil'evich Ivanov (1895–1986), having become an eminent ethnographer and art historian, was a student at Leningrad University in 1922. He attended one of Shternberg's lectures by chance and was so carried away that he later wrote:

"As for my main subject now, I can say that its choice is due exclusively to L[ev] Y[akovlevich]. Before I became acquainted with him I was mainly interested in modern European and Russian art (and leftist currents in art at that) [...] Thanks to lectures and conversations with L[ev] Y[akovlevich]. I turned my attention in quite the opposite direction – to the art of the other peoples" (PF ARAN 282/2/97:5).

At Shternberg's suggestion, Ivanov began to study this art based on the materials at the MAE and literature. In 1922 he studied the ornamentation of the headdresses of the Aleuts from the evolutionary point of view. On Shternberg's proposal, Ivanov became a junior assistant in the ethnographic section at the Leningrad University in his department and at the same time a trainee at the MAE. Ivanov and Karger wrote to Shternberg from their expedition in the Far East in 1926–1927: "In Boktor, we were present at the shamanistic ritual (*kamlanie*) and took part in the driving out of a devil. We become friends with the indigenous people very quickly [...] Both of us feel well. We work for days on end" (PF ARAN 282/2/97:12). Ivanov worked under Shternberg's guidance for five years, right up to the death of his favorite professor, gaining the necessary experience.

Erukhim (Iurii) Abramovich Kreinovich (1906–1985) was, without exaggeration, Shternberg's favorite student, on whom he placed special hope. Iurii Kreinovich graduated from LGU (Shternberg himself taught him the basics of the Nivkh language) and in 1926 on the recommendation of his teacher he went to Sakhalin where he remained for two years authorized by the Sakhalin Soviets to deal with indigenous affairs.[38] Despite being busy with work, Shternberg quickly responded to his student's requests, helped him with advice and informed him about university news. Persistently and patiently he reminded the young intern about what would seem to be commonplace truths, but, without doubt, important parts of ethnographical investigations. "When you take down words and texts, note without fail who his mother is, if she spoke like the Gilyak of the Tangi settlement, or the Ada-tymy, or the Tro. This is very important, because children speak the language of their mother. I implore you to take down everyday language, make them speak in Gilyak about ordinary things from everyday life. Epics and such things go without saying [...] I would like to give you millions of instructions and questions, but first learn the language and write down as many texts as you can."[39]

During the first days after his arrival on Sakhalin Kreinovich, at Shternberg's request, sought out his friends in exile who remained alive, the graves of his comrades and also former interviewees. He found then even the Nivkh, Churka, Shternberg's

---

38　Letters that Kreinovich wrote to the professor are kept in Shternberg's personal archive (PF ARAN 282/2/154:17 rev.).

39　Letter of L.Ia. Shternberg to E.A. Kreinovich. Sakhalinskii oblastnoi kraevedcheskii muzei, # 6473-188 a,b; Shternberg 2001c:203.

kind old acquaintance. It was at his place that Shternberg, while traveling around the island at the beginning of the 1890s, made his first notes of the texts of Nivkh folktales. Kreinovich repeated the fate of his teacher, as an exile, but even in the camps of Kolyma he survived as a linguist and ethnographer, leaving a notable trace on Nivkh and Ket linguistics and ethnography (Roon and Sirina 2003).

Vera Ivanovna Tsintsius (1903–1984) went down in the history of science as an outstanding linguist, professor, and dean of the Faculty of Peoples of the Far North at the Leningrad State Pedagogical Institute (LGPI) named after Herzen.

In 1926, the fourth-year student of the ethnographic department of the Geography Faculty at the LGU, Vera Tsintsius and Klara Mylnikova broke off their education and left for a year for the Far East, to the Negidal (Khasanova and Pevnov 2003:230). They wrote to their teacher: "Now, just at the time of our arrival, the humpback salmon and summer chum harvest began. And the Negidal, out of sheer joy, start ring dances: hand in hand, they dance rhythmically to shouts [...] They converse with us very willingly. And although we, with the long road and all the fuss of an unscientific kind, had decidedly forgotten the language, all the same they say that we know the Tungus language well, and perhaps for this reason they trustfully tell us about the *alarinki* (the place where the ritual of presenting gifts to the spirits is held–A.S., T.R.) [...] We are absolutely enchanted with the Amur [...]" (PF ARAN 282/2/307: 2, 1 rev., 3).

After Shternberg's death the girls recalled: "[...] they (the Negidal–A.S., T.R.) without any hesitation, only a week after our arrival, took us to their place of prayer and sacrifice, where women are not permitted to go, and where they are hardly likely to have taken us with such willingness, had it not been for the fact that we are Lev Iakovlevich's students" (PF ARAN 282/1/110:79).

In 1927, Vera Tsintsius began teaching Tungus-Manchurian languages in the Institute of Peoples of the North [INS] in Leningrad. Tsintsius and Mylnikova made a considerable contribution to the posthumously published works of their teacher. It was they who prepared almost all his archive materials concerning the languages and cultures of the Tungus-Manchurian peoples (see also Khasanova 2000; Kishinev 2002:101)

Back in 1925, V.L. Kotvich wrote to Shternberg that "somehow the Tungus materials are unlucky—a great deal was taken, but little has come out of it as a result. Perhaps someone from amongst your students will have more luck. It will not be easy to begin [...]" (PF ARAN 282/2/152:3). Vera Tsintsius, like Glafira Vasilevich (1895–1971), another outstanding student of Shternberg, made a scientific breakthrough in the study of the Tungus-Manchurian languages: she was the editor of the Comparative Dictionary of the Tungus-Manchurian languages, (Tsintsius 1975–77) and did much for the development of questions of the language, folklore, and ethnography of the Tungus-Manchurian peoples.[40] Marina M. Khasanova, having worked amongst the

---

40 See more about V.I. Tsintsius in: Bulatova and Charekov (eds.) 2003.

Negidal at the end of the 20th century, noted that amongst them "[...] to this day, stories about the two astonishing Russian girls, Vera and Klava, who spoke the Negidal language beautifully and took down folk tales and legends are still alive" (Khasanova 2000:102).[41]

Georgii Nikolaevich Prokof'ev (1897–1942), a talented ethnographer and expert on Siberia. In 1925, the Committee for the North in the All-Russian Central Executive Committee (VTsIK) Presidium sent him on an assignment to the Tazovskii tundra to study the economic and cultural situation with the Ket and Samoyed. He went together with his wife, Ekaterina Prokof'eva. There he worked for three years as head of the boarding school and teacher in the settlement of Ianov Stan (from July 1925 until July 1928).

A few letters from Prokof'ev that he wrote from his Taimyr expedition (1925–1927) have been kept in Shternberg's archive. "Fate has brought me to Ianov Stan, where I was given the position of head of the boarding school: the place is very busy; this is the center of the Tazovskii tundra; all the indigenous peoples of the district gather here." Prokof'ev began studying the Selkup and Nenets languages straight away and ran into a number of difficulties: his language materials in some cases diverged from those of Castrén. He compiled, for the first time, a Nenets alphabetical primary on the basis of the Latin, and then the Russian alphabet, wrote the first teach-yourself manual of the Nenets language, the first grammatical outlines of Nenets, Selkup, Enets and Nganasan languages, and worked vigorously on the questions of the ethnogenesis of the Samoyed peoples. Prokof'ev consulted Shternberg on questions of Ostyako-Samoyed shamanism and systems of relationships: "I feel an urgent need to receive the necessary instructions from you for my further investigations" (PF ARAN 282/2/242: 1,5 rev.).

Andrei Aleksandrovich Popov (1902–1960), a remarkable ethnographer and expert on Siberia, was engaged in ethnography even before receiving higher education. Popov was born into the family of a priest in Yakutia and was proficient in the Yakut language from childhood. In 1925, *Narkompros* [People's Committee for Education] sent him to study in the Geography Faculty at the LGU. It should be mentioned that both Shternberg and Bogoras thought the participation of Siberians themselves in the study of Siberia most advantageous. Popov was 35 penniless and carried out work under contract, receiving little for it (Gracheva 1993:408). He recalled:

"Although I was with Lev Iakovlevich for only two years, I nevertheless got to know him well and his uplifting image will stay in my memory forever [...] At

---

41 The fate of Vera Tsintsius was quite fortunate, though Klara Myl'nikova (married name Forshtein) was unable to continue her work on linguistics and folklore, although she was not less talented than Tsintsius: on her first expedition she recorded a large number of texts (M.M. Khasanova, personal communication—A.S.).

the first meeting I had with Lev Iakovlevich I was amazed at his trustful attitude towards me, a person quite unknown to him, his sincere desire to help on
seeing my difficult circumstances, without inquiring about who I was [...] The
person writing these lines had been in quite onerous material conditions that
had forced him to forgo higher education. But Lev Iakovlevich did not permit
it: for two whole years he supported me, finding various ways for me to make
some earnings [...]" (PF ARAN 282/1/110:115–116).

Popov left valuable work on the ethnography and folklore of the Dolgan, Yakut,
and Nganasan peoples and contributed considerably to the study of the worldview of
these peoples. (Popov 1966; 1976; 1984)[42]

Leonid Pavlovich Potapov (1905–2000), outstanding investigator into peoples of
South Siberia, professor, many years heading the Leningrad part of the Institute of
Ethnography, recalled that Shternberg had played an appreciable role in his life having
interested him deeply in "indigenous religions."

Potapov had come from the Altai to Leningrad and entered the ethnographic
department of the LGU. The "green" first-year student of the ethnographic department gave a paper on the nut trade amongst the Altai people. After this there was a
very critical discussion and Potapov became depressed, having taken the criticism as
a personal fiasco and tragedy. "I needed support very much but was completely alone."
Then he went to his little-known professor Shternberg. "With a heavy heart I ascended
the narrow stone stairs, where L.Y. lived. He came out to me and we went through to
his study. A warm, conveniently arranged room full of books, and a comfortable arm-
chair where L.Y. invited me to sit, and finally his gentle question: 'Tell me what has
brought you to me,' discharged my state of mind and from the first words of my story
I felt how large tears were rolling down from my eyes" (PF ARAN 282/1/110:111–112).
Shternberg encouraged the student, gave different kinds of advice and spoke of the
role of enthusiasm in science.

Once, late in the autumn, Potapov was preparing for an expedition to the Shor.
"It hurts me to send you off deep into the taiga where you must study the everyday
life and beliefs of hunters and sleep with them on the snow," Potapov recalled Shternberg's words. "I feel that I am taking upon myself a grave responsibility, sending
you out into such conditions, but you are young and love ethnography, if you feel
quite fit, only in such a case will I accept your concurrence,"—these were his additional words. Hearing that Potapov had no means to pay for treatment of his ailing
teeth, Shternberg gave him some (D'iakonova and Reshetov 2002:125–130; PF ARAN
282/1/110:110–113).

---

42 For more works of A.A. Popov see: Gruppa tovarishchei 1961(2):139–140.

Since 1924, Shternberg's health had gradually begun to deteriorate, becoming particularly noticeable in 1926. At the insistence of his doctor-brother, Shternberg went to Kislovodsk. In November of the same year he took part in the Third Pacific Science Congress held in Tokyo. As a representative of the USSR Academy of Sciences, whose corresponding member he had become in 1924, Shternberg informed Congress participants about the book, published in English, "Russian Scientific Research in the Pacific," for which he had written the section on "Ethnography" (Shternberg 1926c:160–188). The scientist also read a paper on the question of the origins of the Ainu, who he had made observations of during his exile in the south of the island of Sakhalin. Before this he had published an article on the Inau cult of the Ainu (Shternberg 1905 [vol 1, pt.4]:289–308). This "enigmatic" people had interested him because their language and culture clearly differed from the cultures of other Sakhalin peoples.

Shternberg followed the course of the Congress attentively and later wrote an article on it that was published in the journal *Etnografiia* (Ethnography) (Shternberg 1927b:327–336). Every day was loaded with sessions and receptions. Shternberg gave a lecture in the USSR embassy in Tokyo to which Japanese with knowledge of the Russian language were invited. After the Congress he wanted to stay for another week: "I would like to visit the Ainu, at least for a couple of days," he wrote to his wife, "then devote another couple of days to conversations with local scientists that are particularly interesting for me but were not at the Congress, and later purchase various things for the Museum [...] I have found experts on Japan here who have assisted me greatly" (PF ARAN 282/2/361:2). He also met N.A. Nevskii who was living then in Japan. A correspondence was established between the scientists, although not for long. In one of the letters, Nevskii put forward his etymology of the word *inau*: *inu*—"listen to the end," *hay*—"talking, speaking, listening (to people's words and requests) and telling (about this to the gods) (PF ARAN 282/ 2/211: 4).[43]

An excursion around the country took place within the framework of the Congress. Delegates visited Kyoto, former capital, and had the honor of meeting the Emperor. The nature and culture of Japan made a significant impression on Shternberg and made him forget his ailment for a time: "[...] what is particularly delightful here are the gardens and especially the gardens of ancient mansions (7th or 8th century, at every step here). This is indescribable beauty in the combination of colors, and incomparable views [...] in the beauty of each tree, which is tended as one would a child [...]." And everywhere the refrain is repeated: "I am very homesick [...] I so want to leave for home" (PF ARAN 282/2/361:218–218 rev., 215 rev.). He returned to Leningrad already seriously ill.

Sergei Stebnitskii was one of the last students to see Shternberg less than a month before his death. Stebnitskii dropped in to Shternberg's *dacha* at Duderhof before leaving for Kamchatka in July 1927. Despite his sick condition, the professor had a

---

43   Shternberg's version: ni—"tree" + au—"tongue."

long conversation with Sergei, and helped him to make up a concrete program of research, the value of which his student realized properly only "in the field." Later Stebnitskii recalled:

"It was two versts to the station, Lev Iakovlevich took his hat and a stick and set off to accompany me. He took me along his favorite road—over the hill. He kept stopping. Narrowing his eyes at the setting sun, he showed me the sea: 'Look!' The evening was a rare one. 'Now look at this pine!' He almost ran up to the enormous forked pine and knocked it with his stick. The pine's appearance was indeed quite fantastic. And Lev Iakovlevich stood beneath it lithe, joyous and, I could even say, full of life. I had never seen him like that and couldn't even imagine it. 'I run down this road every day to bathe.' ('Run!') 'You swim?'—'And what did you think? I'm not such an old man!'- 'Well, let's go,' he walked on, all the time drawing attention now to some odd branch, now to a flower poking out amongst the grass. That's how I remembered him—in the forest, at sunset, light and hungrily breathing in the pure evening air" (PF ARAN 282/1/110:11–12).

Shternberg died on 14th August 1927 at his *dacha* in Duderhof. "He was delirious over his last hours and came to himself just before his death," Bogoras related, "He couldn't speak, and wrote with his finger in the air: 'I am dying'" (Bogoras 1927:282). His civil funeral took place on 16th August in the Society of Political Exiles. The next day, accompanied by a large gathering of people, Lev Shternberg was buried in the Jewish Preobrazhenskii graveyard in Leningrad, opposite the grave of the famous sculptor Aleksander Antokolskii. On the upper part of his gravestone the words of the scientist are clearly seen: "All humankind is one" (PF ARAN 282/1/195:176).

News of Shternberg's death found many of his students on expeditions. Sergei Stebnitskii heard of his teacher's death only half a year later:

"Late in the evening in winter the post arrived on dogs at the Koryak settlement of Kichiga. A lot of people were crowded in my cramped little room at the indigenous school, sorting out the bundles and packets. I was given a few envelopes, amongst them one that had been typed with the stamp of the Ethnography Museum. I tore the envelope open. A photograph of Lev Iakovlevich fell out and onto the table. His intent familiar eyes, as if in life, were looking at me. I could barely read the attached notification. I put it on the table, turned and rushed out into the cold dark classroom. I stood there for a long time, running my finger over the misted glass. Before me the flat snowed-over tundra was lit up by the moon" (PF ARAN 282/1/110:11–12).

After Shternberg's death, his widow, students and unfinished works were left behind. "Years have passed, but no, my friend, there is no oblivion, and the pain is sharp, as in the terrible moment of parting," Sarah Ratner-Shternberg wrote a few years after the death of her husband (PF ARAN 282/ 4/116:10). She collected reminiscences of his students, former students, scientists and friends of her husband. It is thanks to her efforts that a collection of reminiscences of Shternberg was prepared for printing (Ol'denburg and Samoilovich 1930). On the initiative of his widow a Commission was set up for the publication of his works under the chair of I.I. Meshchaninov. It was supposed that the collected works of Shternberg would be published in five volumes. At the same time it was planned to write and publish a book about Shternberg in the series "The Lives of Outstanding People" (PF ARAN 282/4/20:147–151). In 1936 the manuscript of the collected works was sent to the printers, then sent for completion and, finally, with the change of the director of the MAE, withdrawal of D.K. Zelenin and I.N. Vinnikov from the editorial board, arrest and execution by firing squad of Y.P. Koshkin-Alkor, and arrest of E.A. Kreinovich, it was delayed and set aside.

Nevertheless, the majority of Shternberg's main works: the book "Sem'ia i rod u narodov Severo-Vostochnoi Azii" [Family and Clan of the Peoples of North-East Asia] (1933), "Giliaki, Orochi, Goldi, Negidals and Ainu. Articles and Materials" (1933); the collection "Pervobytnaia religiia v svete etnograficheskogo issledovaniia" [Indigenous Religion in the Light of Ethnographic Research] (1936), and the book "The Social Organization of the Gilyak" (1999), were published posthumously. At the same time, "Sem'ia i rod u narodov Severo-Vostochnoi Azii" and "The Social Organization of the Gilyak" are very close in content. More than half the book "Gilyaki, Orochi, Goldi, Negidals and Ainu," published in Khabarovsk, is comprised of articles and materials that had previously been published by Shternberg. For the first time Shternberg's lectures, on the transcripts of which he had worked in his last years, were published in a collection in 1936. The other half of the book's text was made up of Shternberg's articles on questions of religion that had already been published.

A meeting of ethnographers of Moscow and Leningrad (April 1929) changed the alignment of forces in ethnography. New approaches to the discipline of history were taking shape, programs in higher education were being revised and criticism of "bourgeois specialists" was unfolding. Y.P. Koshkin (Alkor), understanding full well the changing situation, supplied Shternberg's works, already prepared for reissue, with introductions including criticism of the views of his teacher. He was accused of underestimating the role of the means of production in human history, and of over-emphasizing the psychological element in his analysis of religious beliefs. But it was too late to save many "young Marxists": the flywheel of repression had already been launched.

Lev Shternberg lived and worked at turning points in the history of Russia. He began as a revolutionary of the *narodnik* kind, and was an active participant in the social reorganization of life. Gradually, under the influence of scientific, museum and teaching activities, he moved away from revolutionary methods of action. "He was one of the lucky ones in his generation," Bogoras believed, "being able to switch his revolutionary ardor over and away from the sharp chasms of politics towards the wider and calmer course of science" (Bogoras 1927:271). Shternberg's evolutionism was not only the methodology of his research: he believed deeply and sincerely in the progressive development of humankind and was an opponent of racism, chauvinism, and national exclusiveness.

The results of social revolutions are often unpredictable. The revolution lifted Shternberg up high, he was in demand, but it could have cast him into hell. History showed how this can happen a little later [...]. Lev Shternberg, fortunately, did not live to see this. His widow died of hunger in 1942 in the Leningrad blockade, having given her husband's telescope for the needs of the front not long before her death (Vologdina 1994:181).

The charisma of a leader moved Shternberg through life, giving it a special meaning. Three years of solitary confinement and later exile to Sakhalin, that forced him to concentrate in the main on ethnography, linguistics and folklore, played the role of a compressed spring.[44] When released, it brought into action an enormous inner energy. This energy fulfilled itself in Shternberg's multifaceted activity: ethnography, linguistics, museology, social and political activist, teacher and journalist.

Science does not stop in its development, and it is natural that a number of Shternberg's hypotheses, discoveries and methods have been revised with time. All the same, in the history of Russian science he will always remain an outstanding scientist and wonderful teacher who stood at the source of the highs and lows of Soviet ethnography.

References

PF ARAN – St. Petersburg Branch of the Archive of Russian Academy of Sciences.

Afanasieva, G.M., and Iu.V. Simchenko 1981. O brachnykh sistemakh avtokhtonnykh narodov Severnoi Azii [About Marriage Systems of the Indigenous People of North Asia]. *Sovetskaia Etnografiia* 4: 39–52.

Alkor, Ia.P. [Koshkin] 1930. L.Ia. Shternberg kak tungusoved [L.Ia.Shternberg as Researcher of the Tungus]. In *Pamiati L.Ia. Shternberga (1861–1927)*. S.F. Ol'den-

---

44 In 1895, Bogoras, in a letter to Shternberg from Srednekolymsk, where he was in exile, expressed this thought like this: "I am so hungry, I have been so hellishly, cadaverously, unbearably hungry over these 3650 eternities [...] that if I could get hold of a chunk of life [...]. I am ready to get my teeth into it and tear at it like a rabid dog" (PF ARAN 282/2/34:6).

burg and A.N. Samoilovich (eds.), 137–158. Leningrad: Akademiia nauk SSSR.

Anskii, S.A. (comp.) 1914. *Programma po etnografii evreev. Part 1: Chelovek* [Human Being] (Compiled under close supervision of L.Ia. Shternberg). St. Petersburg.

Arsen'ev, V.K. 1926. Tazy i udege [The Tazy and the Udege]. *Statisticheskii biulleten'* 1(16): 0–26. Khabarovsk.

— 1947. Lesnye liudi udegeitsy [The Udege Forest People]. *Sbornik Soch.* 5: 137–188. Vladivostok.

— 1966. Pamiati L.Ia. Shternberga [Memories of L.Ia.Shternberg]. *Zapiski Primorskogo filiala Geograficheskogo obshchestva USSR* 25: 103–108. Vladivostok.

Artemova, O.Iu. 2000. V ocherednoi raz o teorii 'rodovogo byta' i ob 'avstraliiskoi kontroverze' [One More Time About the Theory of 'Clan's Everyday Life' and 'an Australian Controversy']. In *Rannie formy sotsialnoi organizatsii: Genezis, Funktsionirovanie, istoricheskaia dinamika*. V.A. Popov (ed.), 25–50. St. Petersburg: MAE RAN.

Avrorin, V.A., and E.P. Lebedeva (comp.) 1966. *Orochskie skazki i mify* [Tales and Myths of the Oroch]. Novosibirsk: Nauka.

Azadovskii, M.K., and G.S. Vinogradov (eds.) 1928. Pamiati L.Ia. Shternberga (14 avg. 1927 g.) [In Memory of L.Ia. Shternberg (14. Aug. 1927)]. *Sibirskaia Zhivaia Starina* 7: 3–8.

Basilov, B.N. 1993a. Izbrannichestvo [Divine Election]. In *Religioznye verovaniia: Svod etnograficheskikh poniatii i terminov* 5. V.N. Basilov and I. Vinkelman (eds.), 94–95. Moscow: Nauka.

— 1993b. Bliznetsov kult [Cult of Twins]. *Religioznye verovaniia: Svod etnograficheskikh poniatii i terminov* 5: 34–37. Moscow.

Black, L. 1973. The Nivkh (Gilyak) of Sakhalin and the Lower Amur. *Arctic Anthropology* 10(1): 1–110.

Bogoras, W. [Bogoraz-Tan, V.G.] [1927. L.Ia. Shternberg kak chelovek i uchenyi [L.Ia. Shternberg as a person and scholar]. *Etnografiia* 2: 269–282.

— 1928. L.Ia. Shternberg kak etnograf [L.Ia. Shternberg as Ethnographer]. In *Sbornik Museia Antropologii i Etnografii*. E. Karskii (ed.), (7): 4–30. Leningrad: Akademiia nauk SSSR.

— 1930. L.Ia.Shternberg kak fol'klorist [Shternberg as Folklorist]. In *Pamiati L.Ia. Shternberga*. S.F. Ol'denburg and A.N. Samoilovich (eds.), 85–96. Leningrad: Akademiia nauk SSSR.

Brailovskii, S.N. 1901. Tazy ili udikhe. Opyt etnograficheskogo issledovaniia [The Tazy or the Udege. Experience of the Ethnographic Research]. *Zhivaia Starina* (2): 129–216; (3–4): 323–455.

Bulatova N.Ia., and S.L. Charekov (eds.) 2003. *Materialy konferentsii, posviashchennoi 100-letiiu so dnia rozhdeniia professora Very Ivanovny Tsintsius (13–14 Oktiabria 2003 g.).* [Proceedings of the Conference Dedicated to the 100th Anniversary of the Birth of Professor Vera Ivanovna Tsintsius (13–14 October 2003)]. St. Petersburg:

Nauka.

D'iachenko, V.I. 2000. Fotoilliustrirovannye kollektsii Otdela Sibiri. [Photo Collections of the Siberian Department]. In *285 years Peterburgskoi Kunstkamere: Materialy itogovoi konferentsii MAE RAN, posviashchennoi 285-letiiu Kunstkamery.* Ch.M. Taksami (ed.), 178–184. St. Petersburg.

D'iakonova, V.P., and A.M. Reshetov 2002. O Leonide Pavloviche Potapove [About Leonid Pavlovich Potapov]. *Etnograficheskoe Obozrenie* 2: 125–130.

Dudarets, G.I. 2004. Epistolyarnoe nasledie uznikov sakhalinskoi katorgi (po pis'mam L.Ia. Shternberga, I.P. Uvacheva i drugikh politicheskih ssyl'nykh). (Epistolary Heritage of Sakhalin Penal Convicts (on the Base of the Letters of L. Shternberg, I. Iuvachev and Other Political Exiles). *Izvestiia Instituta Naslediia Bronislava Pilsudskogo pri Sakhalinskom Gosudarstvennom Oblastnom Kraevedcheskom Muzee* 8: 105–130. Iuzhno-Sakhalinsk.

Edel'shtein, Y.S. 1930. L.Ia. Shternberg i ego rol' v sozdanii etnograficheskoi shkoly [L.Ia. Shternberg and his Role in the Foundation of the Ethnographic School]. In *Pamiati L.Ia. Shternberga 1861–1927.* S.F. Ol'denburg and A.N. Samoilovich (eds.), 29–35. Leningrad: Akademiia nauk SSSR.

Engels, F. 1884. *Der Ursprung der Familie, des Privateigenthums und des Staats.* Hottingen-Zürich: Verlag der Schweizerischen Volksbuchhandlung.

— 1962. Vnov' otkrytyi primer gruppovogo braka [Once again an Example of Group Marriage]. In *Sochineniia [Writings]* Marx, K. and Engels F., vol. 22: 364–67. Moscow: Gosudarstvennoe izdatel'stvo politicheskoi literatury.

Ermolova, N.V. 2003. Tungusoved Glafira Makar'evna Vasilevich [Glafira Makar'evna Vasilevich—Specialist in the Tungus]. In *Repressirovannye etnografy*, vol. 2. D.D. Tumarkin (comp.), 10–46. Moscow: Vostochnaia literatura.

Gagen-Torn, G.Iu. 2002. Nina Ivanova Gagen-Torn—uchenyi, pisatel', poet [Nina Ivanovna Gagen-Torn as Scholar, Poet and Writer]. In *Repressirovannye etnografy*, vol. 1, 2nd edition. D.D. Tumarkin (comp.), 308–341. Moscow: Vostochnaia literatura.

Gagen-Torn, N.I. 1994. *Memoria.* G.Iu. Gagen-Torn (comp.). Moscow: Vozvrashchenie.

— 1971. Leningradskaia etnograficheskaia shkola v dvadtsatye gody (u istokov sovetskoi etnografii) [The Leningrad Ethnographic School in the Twenties (at the Beginning of Soviet Ethnography)]. *Sovetskaia Etnografiia* 2: 134–145.

— 1975. Lev Iakovlevich Shternberg. Moscow: Nauka.

Gracheva, G.N. 1993. Etnograf po prizvaniu: K 90-letiiu A.A. Popova.[Ethnographer as Vocation: To the 90th Anniversary of A.A. Popov]. *Kunstkamera: Etnograficheskie tetradi* 2–3. St. Petersburg: 406–421.

Grant, B. 1995. *In the Soviet House of Culture: A Century of Perestroikas.* Princeton NJ: Princeton University Press.

— 1999a. Foreword. *In The Social Organization of the Gilyak by Lev Shternberg. Anthropological Papers of the American Museum of Natural History* 82: xxiii–lvi.

— 1999b. Appendix B. An Interview with Zakharii Efimovich Cherniakov. In *The*

Social Organization of the Gilyak by Lev Shternberg. Anthropological Papers of the American Museum of Natural History 82: 245–255.

Gruppa tovarishchei 1961. Pamiati Andreia Aleksandrovicha Popova [In Memory of Anderei Aleksandrovich Popov]. *Sovetskaia Etnografiia* 2: 137–140.

Inoue, K. 2003. Franz Boas and an "Unfinished Jesup" on Sakhalin Island: Shedding New Light on Berthold Laufer and Bronislav Pilsudski. In *Constructing Cultures Then and Now. Celebrating Franz Boas and the Centenary of the Jesup North Pacific Expedition 1897–1902*. L. Kendall and I. Krupnik (eds.), 135–163. Washington D.C.: Arctic Studies Center, National Museum of Natural History, Smithsonian Institution.

Iuvachev, I.P. 2001. Pis'ma s Sakhalina. I.A. Tsupenkovoi (comp.). [Letters from Sakhalin]. *Izvestiia Instituta Naslediia Bronislava Pilsudskogo pri Sakhalinskom gosudarstvennom Oblastnom Kraevedcheskom Muzee* 5: 176–195.

Ivanov, S.V. 1930. L.Ia. Shternberg i primitivnoe iskusstvo [L.Ia. Shternberg and Primitive Art]. In *Pamiati L.Ia. Shternberga 1861–1927*. S.F. Ol'denburg and A.N. Samoilovich (eds.), 159–172. Leningrad: Akademiia nauk SSSR.

Jewish Encyclopedia by Brockhaus and Jefron, 1991. Reprint, 16th edition. St. Petersburg: Terra.

Jochelson, W. 1928. Leo Sternberg. *American Anthropologist* 30(1): 180–181.

Kabo, V.R. 1981. Obshchina i rod u nivkhov [The Nivkh's Clan and Community]. In *Puti razvitiia Avstralii i Okeanii: istoriia, ekonomika, etnografiia*. K.V. Malakhovskii (ed.), 198–219. Moscow: Nauka.

Kagarov, E. 1929. Leo Sternberg. *American Anthropologist* 31(3): 568–571.

Kan, S. 1997. *"Narodnaia Volia": ideologiia i lidery* ["Peoples' Will": Ideology and Leaders]. Moscow: Probel.

— 2000. The Mystery of the Missing Monograph: Or Why Shternberg's "The Social Organization of the Gilyak" Never Appeared Among the Jesup Expedition Publications. *European Review of Native American Studies* 14(2): 19–38.

— 2001. The Russian "Bastian" and Boas: Why Shternberg's The Social Organization of the Gilyak Never Appeared Among the Jesup Expedition Publications. In *Gateways. Exploring the Legacy of the Jesup North Pacific Expedition, 1897–1902*. I. Krupnik and W.W. Fitzhugh (eds.), 217–248. Washington, D.C.: Arctic Studies Center, National Museum of Natural history, Smithsonian Institution.

Karmysheva, B.Kh. 2002. Ot tropicheskikh lesov Amazonki do tsentral'noasiatskikh stepei: zhiznennyi put' F.A. Fiel'strupa [From the Amazon Tropical Forests to the Central Asian Steppe: F.A.Fielstrup's Journey Through Life]. In *Repressirovannye etnografy*, vol. 1, 2nd edition. D.D. Tumarkin (comp.), 152–163. Moscow: Vostochnaia literatura.

Kharitonova, V.I. 2000. "Ne v vole cheloveka stat' shamanom?" ["Is it not in Human Power to Become a Shaman?"] In *Shamanskii dar: K 80-letiiu doktora istoricheskykh nauk Anny Vasil'evny Smoliak* [The Shaman's Gift: Devoted to the 80th Jubilee

of Anna Vasil'evna Smoliak, Doctor of Historical Sciences]. Etnologicheskie issledovaniia po shamanstvu i inym traditsionnym verovaniiam i praktikam, vol. 6.
V.I. Kharitonova (ed.), 312–338. Moscow: IEA RAN.

Khasanova, M.M. 2000. Negidal'skaia kollektsia L.Ia. Shternberga v sobraniiakh MAE.
[The Negidal Collection of L.Ia. Shternberg in the MAE Fond] In *285 let Peterburgskoi Kunstkamere: Materialy itogovoi nauchnoi konferentsii MAE RAN, posviashchennoi 285-letiiu Kunstkamery*. Ch.M. Taksami (ed.), 85–97. St. Petersburg: Nauka.

—   2001. B.O. Pilsudski i L.Ia. Shternberg [B.O. Pilsudski and L.Ia. Shternberg]. In
*Bronislav Pilsudski and Futabatei Shimei—an Excellent Chapter in the History
of Polish-Japanese Relations*. A. Majewicz and T. Wicherkiewicz (eds.), 413–420.
Poznan. Wydawnictwo UAM, Poland.

Khasanova, M., and A. Pevnov 2003. *Mify i skazki negidal'tsev* [Myths and Tales of the
Negidal]. Publications on Tungus Languages and Cultures, vol. 21. Kyoto: Nakan-
ishi Printing.

Kleinman, I.A. 1928. L.Ia. Shternberg. *Evreiskaia Starina* 12: 7–10.

Kostanov A.I. 1996. Yubilei Sakhalinskogo muzeia [Jubilee of the Sakhalin Museum].
Vestnik Sakhalinskogo Muzeia 3: 3–20. Iuzhno-Sakhalinsk.

Kozyreva, R.V. 1967. *Drevnii Sakhalin* [Ancient Sakhalin]. Leningrad: Nauka.

Kreinovich, E.A. 1968. *Istoriia moego otnoshcheniia k arkhivu L.Ia. Shternberga* [His-
tory of my Relation to the L.Ia. Shternberg Archive]. Manuscript. Sakhalinskii
oblastnoi kraevedcheskii muzei, #6473.

—   1973. *Nivkhgu. Zagadochnye obitateli Sakhalina i Amura* [The Nivkh. The Enigmatic Inhabitants of Sakhalin and the Amur River]. Moscow: Nauka.

Kriukov, M.V. 1972. *Sistema rodstva kitaitsev (evoliutsiia i zakonomernosti)* [System of
Chinese Kinship]. Moscow: Nauka.

Krol', M.A. 1929. Vospominaniia o L.Ia. Shternberge [Memories on L.Ia. Shternberg].
Katorga i Ssylka 57–58: 214–236.

Krupnik, I. 1998. Jesup Genealogy: Intellectual Partnership and Russian-American
Cooperation in Arctic/North Pacific Anthropology. *Arctic Anthropology* 35(2):
199–226.

Latyshev, V.M. 1996. Sakhalinskie universitety [Sakhalin's Universities] In *Pilsudski
B.O. "Dorogoi Lev Iakovlevich" (Pis'ma L.Ia. Shternbergu. 1893–1917)* [Pilsudskii
B.O. "Dear Lev Iakovlevich" (Letters to L.Ia. Shternberg. 1893–1917)]. V.M. Latyshev (comp.): 5–28. Iuzhno-Sakhalinsk: Sakhalinskii oblastnoi kraevedcheskii
musei.

Levin, M.G. 1958. *Etnicheskaia antropologiia i problemy etnogeneza narodov Dal'nego
Vostoka* [Ethnic Anthropology and Issues of Ethnogenesis of Indigenous Peoples
in the Russian Far East]. Trudy Instituta etnografii Akademii Nauk SSSR, new
series, vol. 36. Moscow: Nauka.

Lewis, H.S. 2001. The Passion of Franz Boas. *American Anthropologist* 103(2): 447–467.

Lopatin, I.A. 1912. *Leto sredi orochei i gol'dov* [A Summer Among the Oroch and the

Gold]. Vladivostok: Dal'ekaia okraina.

— 1923. Etnografiia Primoriia. In *Primor'e, ego priroda i khozaistvo*. A.N. Krishtofo-vich (ed.), 141–155. Vladivostok: Dal'nevostochaiia Goskniga.

Luganskii, Iu. (comp.) 1997. V.K. Arsen'ev: Biografiia v fotografiiakh, vospominani-iakh druzei, svidetel'stvakh epokhi [V.K. Arsen'ev: Biography in Photographs, Memories of Friends, Evidences of an Epoch]. Vladivostok: Ussuri.

Maksimov, A.N. 1997. Gruppovoi brak [Group Marriage]. *Izbrannye Trudy*. O.U. Artemova (comp.), 49–87. Moscow: Vostochnaia Literatura.

Mikhailova, E.A. 2004. Vladimir Germanovich Bogoras: uchenyi, pisatel', obshchest-vennyi deiatel' [Vladimir Germanovich Bogoras: Scholar, Writer, and Public Fig-ure]. In *Vydaiushchiesia otechestvennye etnologi i antropologi XX veka*. V. Tishkov and D. Tumarkin (eds.), 95–136. Moscow: Nauka.

Okladnikov, A.P. 1963. Znachenie rabot L.Ia. Shternberga dlia arkheologii Dal'nego Vostoka. [The Significance of L.Ia. Shternberg's Works for the Archaeology of the Far East]. *Ocherki Istorii Russkoi Etnografii, Fol'kloristiki i Antropologii* (2): 259–267. Moscow: Akademiia nauk SSSR.

Ol'denburg, S.F. 1927. Pamiati L'va Iakovlevicha Shternberga [In Memoriam Lev Iakovlevich Shternberg]. *Etnografiia* 2: 267–268.

— 1930. L.Ia. Shternberg uchenyi i chelovek [L.Ia. Shternberg as Scholar and Person]. In *Pamiati L.Ia. Shternberga 1861–1927*. S.F. Ol'denburg and A.N. Samoilovich (eds.), 21–28. Leningrad: Akademiia nauk SSSR.

Ol'denburg, S.F., and A.N. Samoilovich (eds.) 1930a. *Pamiati L.Ia. Shternberga 1861–1930*. Leningrad: Akademiia Nauk SSSR.

— 1930b. Lev Iakovlevich Shternberg: Vazhneishie biograficheskie daty Spisok nauchnykh trudov. [Important Biographical Dates. List of Scientific works]. In *Pamiati L.Ia. Shternberga (1861–1927)*. S.F. Ol'denburg and A.N. Samoilovich (eds.), 7–11. Leningrad: Akademiia nauk SSSR.

Osnitskaia, I.A. 1993. *Shestdesiat let v Kunstkamere: K 90-letiiu D.A. Ol'derogge* [60 Years in the Kunstkamera Museum: To the 90th Anniversary of D.A. Ol'derogge]. Kunstkamera. Etnograficheskie tetradi. St. Petersburg.

Ostrovskii, A.B. 1997. *Mifologiia i verovaniia nivkhov* [Mythology and Beliefs of the Nivkh]. St. Petersburg: Peterburgskoe vostokovedenie.

Pilsudski, B.O. 1996. "Dorogoi Lev Iakovlevich…" (Pis'ma L.Ia. Shternbergu, 1893-1917) ["Dear Lev Iakovlevich…" (Letters to L.Ia. Shternberg, 1893–1917)]. V.M. Latyshev (comp.). Iuzhno-Sakhalinsk: Sakhalinskii oblastnoi kraevedcheskii musei.

Polevoi, B.P., and A.M. Reshetov. 1972. V.K. Arsen'ev kak etnograf [Arsen'ev as Ethno-grapher]. *Etnograficheskoe Obozrenie* (4): 74–87.

Popov, A.A. 1966. *The Nganasan. The Material Culture of the Tavgi Samoyeds*. Bloom-ington: Indiana University Publications.

— 1976. Dusha i smert' po vozzpeniiam nganasanov [Soul and Death in Nganasan Beliefs]. In *Priroda i chelovek v religioznykh predstavleniiakh narodov Sibiri i Sev-*

era. I.S. Vdovin (ed.), 31–43. Leningrad: Nauka.

— 1984 *Nganasany: sotsial'noe ustroistvo i verovaniia* [The Nganasan: Social Structure and Beliefs]. Leningrad: Nauka.

Popov, V.A. 2004. Dmitrii Alekseevich Ol'derogge: shef otechesvennoi afrikanistiki [Dmitrii Alekseevich Ol'derogge: Chief of Domestic African Studies]. *Vydaiushchiesia otechestvennye etnologi i antropologi XX veka*. V. Tishkov and D. Tumarkin (eds.), 450–474. Moscow: Nauka.

Ratner-Shternberg, S.A. 1930. L. Ia. Shternberg kak issledovatel' religii [L.Ia. Shternberg as Researcher of Religion]. *Pamiati L.Ia. Shternberga 1861–1927*. S.F. Oldenburg and A.N. Samoilovich (eds.), 97–136. Leningrad: Akademiia nauk SSSR.

— 1928. L.Ia. Shternberg i Muzei antropologii i etnografii Akademii nauk. Po lichnom vospominaniam, literaturnym i archivnym dannym. [L.Ia. Shternberg and the Museum of Anthropology and Ethnography of the Academy of Sciences. According to Personal Memories, Literary and Archival Data]. In *Sbornik Museia Antropologii i Etnografii*. S.F. Ol'denburg and A.N. Samoilovich (eds.) 7: 31–69. Leningrad: Akademiia nauk SSSR.

— 1935. L.Ia. Shternberg i Leningradskaia etnograficheskaia shkola 1904–1927 [L.Ia. Shternberg and the Leningrad Ethnographic School, 1904–1927]. (From Personal Recollections and Archive Data). *Sovetskaia Etnografiia* 2: 134–156.

Reshetov, A.M. 2000. Dva pis'ma B. Pilsudskogo k L.Ia. Shternbergu (1903). [Two Letters of B. Pilsudski to L.Ia. Shternberg (1903)]. *Izvestiia Instituta Naslediia Bronislava Pilsudskogo pri Sakhalinskom Gosudarstvennom Oblastnom Kraevedcheskom Muzee*, 4: 62–64.

— 2003a. L.Ia. Shternberg i S.M. Shirokogorov: kem oni byli drug dlia druga. (Na material ikh perepiski 1912–1924). [Shternberg and Shirokogoroff: How they Interrelated to Each Other (On the Material of Their Correspondence 1912–1924)]. In *Narody i kul'tury Dal'nego Vostoka: vzgliad iz XXI veka. Sbornik statei*. T. Roon and M. Prokof'ev (eds.), 57–64. Iuzhno-Sakhalinsk: Sakhalinskoe Knizhnoe Izdatel'stvo.

— 2003b. S.M. Shirokogoroff: kitaiskii period zhizni i deiatel'nosti (1922–1939). [S.M. Shirokogoroff: Chinese Period of Live and Activity]. In *Zarubezhnaia Rossiia, 1917–1939*, vol. 2. I.Iu. Cherniaev (ed.), 183–189. St. Petersburg: Liki Rossii.

Revunenkova, E.V., and A.M. Reshetov 2003. Sergei Mikhailovich Shirokogoroff. *Etnograficheskoe Obozrenie* 3: 100–119.

Roon, T.P. 2000. Kollektsii narodov Amuro-Sakhalinskogo regiona v muzeiakh SShA. [Ethnographic Collections from the Amur-Sakhalin Region in U.S. Museums]. *Izvestiia Instituta Naslediia Bronislava Pilsudskogo pri Sakhalinskom Gosudarstvennom Oblastnom Kraevedcheskom Muzee* 4, 139–157.

Roon, T.P., and M.M. Prokof'ev. 2001. Pervye puteshestvie L.Ia. Shternberga po Sakhalinu v 1891 i 1893 godakh [Shternberg's first journeys on Sakhalin in 1891 and 1893]. *Izvestiia Instituta Naslediia Bronislava Pilsudskogo pri Sakhalinskom Gosu-*

darstvennom Oblastnom Kraevedcheskom Muzee 5, 211–216.

Roon, T.P., and A.A. Sirina 2002. Narody i kul'tury: vzgliad iz XXI veka: Konferentsiia, posviashchennaia 140-letiiu so dnia rozhdeniia L.Ia. Shternberga [Peoples and Cultures: View from XXI Century. Conference Devoted to L.Shternberg's 140 Anniversary]. *Etnograficheskoe Obozrenie* 6: 153–157.

— 2003. E.A. Kreinovich: zhizn i sud'ba uchenego [E.A. Kreinovich: The Life and the Fate of a Scholar]. In *Repressirovannye etnografy*, vol. 2. D.D. Tumarkin (comp.), 47–77. Moscow: Vostochnaia literatura.

Samoilovich, A.N. 1930. L.Ia. Shternberg i tiurkologiia. [Shternberg and the Turkology]. In *Pamiati L.Ia. Shternberga 1861–1927*. S.F. Ol'denburg and A.N. Samoilovich (eds.), 173–176. Leningrad: Akademiia nauk SSSR.

Shrenk, L.I. [Leopold von Schrenck] 1883–1903. *Ob inorodtsakh Amurskogo kraia* [On the Natives of the Amur Region], 3 vols. St. Petersburg: Iz. Imperatorskoi Akademii Nauk.

Shternberg, L.Ia. 1893a. Sakhalinskie Giliaki [The Gilyak of Sakhalin]. *Etnograficheskoe Obozrenie* 2: 1–46.

— 1893b. Zametki o sakhalinskikh giliakakh [Article on the Sakhalin Gilyak]. *Tiuremny Vestnik* 9: 342–361; 10: 390–412.

— 1895. Puteshestvie na krainyi sever o. Sakhalina [Journey to the Far North of the Island of Sakhalin]. In *Sakhalinskii Kalendar'*: 16–53.

— 1900. Obraztsy materialov po izucheniiu giliatskogo iazyka i fol'klora, sobrannye na ostrove Sakhaline i v nizoviakh Amura [Samples of the Materials for the Study of the Gilyak Language and Folklore]. *Izvestiia Imperatorskoi Akademii Nauk* 13(4), 387–434.

— 1904. *Giliaki*. [The Gilyak]. *Etnograficheskoe Obozrenie* 60: 1–42; 61: 19–55.

— 1905. Kul't inau u plemeni ainu [The Inau Cult of the Ainu]. In *Ezhegodnik Russkogo Antropologicheskogo Obshchestva pri St. Peterburgskom Universitete*, vol. 1, part 4: 289–308.

— 1906. Tragediia shestimillionnogo naroda [The Tragedy of a People Numbering Six Million]. In *Nakanunie probuzhdeniia: Sbornik statei po evreiskomu voprosu*. I.V. Gessen et al. (eds.), 163–187. St. Petersburg: A.G. Rozen.

— 1907a. Muzei antropologii i etnografii za 12 let upravleniia V.V. Radlova. K dniu 70-letiia V.V. Radlova [The Museum of Anthropology and Ethnography During 12 Years of V.V. Radloff's Administration. To the 70th Anniversary of V.V. Radloff]. St. Petersburg: Imperatorskaia Akademiia nauk.

— 1907b. Natsional'nye techeniia v russkom evreistve [National Trends in Russian Jewry]. *Svobodo i Ravenstvo* 5: 2–6.

— 1908. *Materialy po izucheniiu giliatskogo iazyka i fol'klora*, vol. 1 [Materials for the Study of the Gilyak Language and Folklore]. Obraztsy narodnoi slovesnosti. Chast' Pervaia: Epos. St. Petersburg: Imperatorskaia Akademiia nauk.

— 1909. Iz zhizni i deiatel'nosti V.V. Radlova: berlinskii, altaiskii i kazanskii periody [From V.V. Radloff 's Life and Activity: His Berlin, Altai and Kazan' Times]. *Zhivaia Starina* 2–3: 1-25.

— 1912. Noveishie raboty po antropologii evreev [Recent Works on the Physical Anthropology of the Jews]. *Evreiskaia Starina* 3: 3–30.

— 1913a. V.F. Miller kak etnograf [V.F. Miller as Ethnographer]. *Zhivaia Starina* 22: 417–425.

— 1913b. Zabytoe kladbishche [A Forgotten Cemetery]. *Kolos'ia* 3: 37–45; 5: 85–95.

— 1914. Kratkaia programma po etnografii (primenitel'no k bytu severnykh inorodtsev) [A Brief Program for Collecting Ethnographic Data on Northern Peoples]. In *Sbornik instruktsii i programm dlia uchastnikov ekskursii v Sibir'*. S.A. An-skii, (comp.), 212–255). St. Petersburg: Fototipiia i tipografiia A.F. Dresslera.

— 1916. I.T. Savenkov 1846–1914 (Obituary). *Sbornik MAE* 3: 1–14.

— 1924a. Problema evreiskoi natsional'noi psikhologii [Issues in Jewish National Psychology]. *Evreiskaia Starina* 11: 5–44.

— 1924b. Review of Fritz Kohn F. Die Juden als Rasse und Kulturvolk. *Evreiskaia Starina* 1: 378–380.

— 1924c. Rol' sokhraneniia imion v evreiskom levirate [The Role of the Preservation of Names in the Jewish Levirate]. *Evreiskaia Starina* 11: 177–179.

— 1925. Dvukhvekovoi iubilei russkoi etnografii i etnograficheskikh muzeev [Two Centuries Jubilee of Russian Ethnography and Ethnographic Museums]. *Priroda* 7–9: 46–66.

— 1926a. D.N. Anuchin kak etnograf [D. Anuchin as Ethnographer]. *Etnografiia* 1–2: 7–13.

— 1926b. Sovremennaia etnologiia. Noveishie uspekhi, nauchnye techeniia i metody [Contemporary Ethnology. Latest Success, Scientific Trends and Methods]. *Etnografiia* 1–2: 15–43.

— 1926c. Etnografiia. Tikhii okean [Ethnography. The Pacific Ocean]. In *Russkie nauchnye issledovaniia*, 147–172. Leningrad: Soviet Academy of Sciences.

— 1927a Izbrannichestvo v religii [Divine Election in Religion]. *Etnografiia* 1: 1–56.

— 1927b Etnografiia na III Vsetikhookeanskom nauchnom kongresse v Tokyo v Noiabre 1926. [Ethnography on the 3th Pacific Congress in Tokyo in November 1926]. *Etnografiia* 2: 327–336.

— 1927c. Kastren: altaist i etnograf. *Pamiati M.A. Kastrena* [Kastren (Castrén): Altaist and Ethnograph]. E.F. Karskii (ed.): 35–56. St. Petersburg: Akademiia nauk SSSR.

— 1928a. Petr Karlovich Dombrovskii. *Katorga i Ssylka:* 20–21.

— 1928b. Problema evreiskoi etnografii [Issues in Jewish Ethnography]. *Evreiskaia Starina* 12: 11–16.

— 1929. Ainskaia problema [The Ainu Issue]. In *Sbornik MAE*, vol. 8: 334–374.

— 1933a. *Giliaki, orochi, gol'dy, negidal'tsy, ainy* [The Gilyak, the Orochen, the Gold, the Negidal, and the Ainu]. Ia.P. Al'kor (Koshkin) (ed.). Khabarovsk: Dal'nevostochnoe knizhnoe izdatel'stvo.

— 1933b. *Sem'ia i rod u narodov Severo-Vostochnoi Azii* [Family and Clan with the Peoples of North-East Asia]. Ia.P. Al'kor (Koshkin) (ed.). Leningrad: Institut Narodov Severa.

— 1936. *Pervobytnaia religiia v svete etnografii* [Primitive Religion in Light of Ethnography]. Leningrad: Institut Narodov Severa.

— 1999. The Social Organization of the Gilyak. Edited, and with a foreword and afterword by B. Grant. *Anthropological Papers of the American Museum of Natural History,* 82: 3–183.

— 2001a. Dnevnik puteshetviia k vostochnym giliakam i orokam [A Diary of the Journey to the Eastern Gilyak and the Orok]. *Izvestiia Instituta Naslediia Bronislava Pilsudskogo pri Sakhalinskom Gosudarstvennom Oblastnom Kraevedcheskom Muzee* 5: 217–283.

— 2001b. Puteshestvie ot Aleksandrovska do Sortunaia: Kratkii predvaritel'nyi otchet [A Journey from Aleksandrovsk to Sortunai: A Brief Preliminary Report]. *Izvestiia Instituta Naslediia Bronislava Pilsudskogo pri Sakhalinskom Gosudarstvennom Oblastnom Kraevedcheskom Muzee* 5: 283–290.

— 2001c. *Pis'ma k E.A. Kreinovichu. Pis'mo k nivkhu Shurka. Pis'mo nivkha Pletun.* [Letters to E.A. Kreynovich. Letter to the Nivkh Shurka. Letter of the nivkh Pletun.] *Izvestiia Instituta Naslediia Bronislava Pilsudskogo pri Sakhalinskom Gosudarstvennom Oblastnom Kraevedcheskom Muzee* 5: 203–211. Yuzhno-Sakhalinsk.

Shternberg, L.Ia., F. Engels, and Ia.P. Al'kor 1933. *Sem'ia i rod u narodov Severo-Vostochnoi Azii: S prilozheniem stat'i Fr. Engel'sa "Vnov'otkrytyi sluchai gruppogo braka"* [Family and Clan Among the Peoples of Northeastern Asia: With Attached Article by F. Engels "Once Again a Case of Group Marriage Has Been Discovered"]. Leningrad: Izdatel'stvo In-ta narodov Severa Tsik SSSR.

Shul'gina, T.S. 1989. *Russkie issledovateli kul'tury i byta malykh narodov Amura i Sakhalina, (konets XIX – nachalo XX veka)* [Russian Researchers of the Culture and Life of the Small Peoples of Amur and Sakhalin, (From the End of 19th – Early 20th Century)]. Vladivostok: Dal'nevostochnyi Universitet.

Sirina, A.A. 2003. Zabytye stranitsy sibirskoi etnografii: B.E. Petri [Forgotten Pages of Siberian Ethnography: B.E. Petri] In *Repressirovannye etnografy,* vol. 1, 2nd edition. D.D. Tumarkin (comp.), 57–80. Moscow: Vostochnaia literatura.

Sirina A.A., and T.P. Roon 2004. Lev Iakovlevich Shternberg: u istokov sovetskoi etnografii. [Lev Iakovlevich Shternberg: The Beginning of Soviet Ethnography]. In *Vydaiushchiesia otechestvennye etnologi i antropologi XX veka.* V. Tishkov and D. Tumarkin (eds.), 49–94. Moscow: Nauka.

Smoliak, A.V. 1961. Nekotorye voprosy proiskhozhdeniia narodov Nizhnego Amura (o tak nazyvaemom ainskom komponente v medvezhem prazdnike amurskogo tipa. [Some Questions of the Origin of the Low Amur River Peoples. (About the So-called Ainu Component in the Bear Festival of the Amur Type]. In *Voprosy istorii Sibiri i Dal'nego Vostoka.* Shun'kov V. (ed.), 337–344. Novosibirsk: Nauka

— 1970. Sotsial'naia organizatsiia narodov nizhnego Amura i Sakhalina v XIX–nachale XX v. (novye materialy o nivkhakh) [Social Organization of the Peoples of Amur and Sakhalin in the 19th–Early 20th Century (New Materials on the Nivkh)]. In *Obshchestvennyi stroi u narodov Severnoi Sibiri*. I.S. Gurvich and B.O. Dolgikh (eds.), 264–299. Moscow: Nauka.

— 1974. Rodovoi sostav nivkhov v kontse XIX–nachale XX v. [Clan Structure of the Nivkh at the End of 19th–Early 20th Century]. In *Sotsial'naia organisatsiia i kul'tura narodov Severa*. I.S. Gurvich (ed.), 176–217. Moscow: Akademiia nauk.

— 1975a. O vzaimnykh kul'turnykh vliianiiakh narodov Sakhalina i nekotorykh problemakh etnogeneza [About Mutual Cultural Influences Among the Peoples of Sakhalin and Some Issues About Their Ethnogenesis]. In *Etnogenez i etnicheskaia istoriia narodov Severa*. I.S. Gurvich (ed.), 43–77. Moscow: Nauka.

— 1975b. *Etnicheskie protsessy u narodov Nizhnego Amura i Sakhalina* [Ethnic Processes Among the Peoples of the Low Amur and Sakhalin]. Moscow: Nauka.

— 1991. Shaman: Lichnost', funktsii, mirovozzrenie (narody Nizhnego Amura) [The Shaman: Personality, Functions and Worldview (Peoples of the Lower Amur River]. Moscow: Nauka.

— 1994. K voprosu ob "izbranichestve v religii" [On the Question About "Divine Election in Religion" (Answer to Reviewers)]. *Etnograficheskoe obozrenie* 3: 174–175.

Smoliak, A.V., and A.A. Sirina A.A. 2002. Obzor "Lev Shternberg: The Social Organization of the Gilyak" [Review of "Lev Shternberg: The Social Organization of the Gilyak"]. *Etnograficheskoe Obozrenie* 4: 168–170.

Sobolev, V.S. (ed.), Anfert'eva A.N. (comp.) 1995. *Gebraistika i istoriia evreiskoi kul'tury v Rossii: tematicheskii ukazatel dokumentov po fondam Sankt-Peterburgskogo Arkhiva Rossiiskoi akademii nauk*. [Hebraic Studies and History of the Jewish Culture in Russia]. St. Petersburg. Ierusalim, 5785. Issue 2.

Staniukovich, T.V. 1971. Iz istorii etnograficheskogo obrazovaniia (Leningradskii geograficheskii institut i geograficheskii fakultet LGU) [From the History of Ethnography Education (The Leningrad Institute and Geographic Faculty LGU)]. *Ocherki Istorii Russkoi Etnografii, Fol'kloristiki i Antropologii* 5, 121–138, Moscow: Akademiia nauk SSSR.

— 1986. Lev Iakovlevich Shternberg i Muzei antropologii i etnografii [Lev Iakovlevich Shternberg and the Museum of Anthropology and Ethnography]. *Sovetskaia Etnografiia* 5: 81–91.

Taksami, Ch.M. 1961. Issledovatel', drug i uchitel nivkhov [Researcher, Friend and Teacher of the Nivkh]. In *Issledovateli Sakhalina i Kuril'skikh ostrovov*. I.A. Cenchenko (comp.), 108–131. Iuzhno-Sakhalinsk: Sakhalinskoe knizhnoe izdatel'stvo.

— 1975. *Osnovniye problemy etnografii i istorii nivkhov*. [Main Issues of Nivkh Ethnography and History]. Leningrad: Nauka.

— 2000 (ed.). *285 let Peterburgskoi Kunstkamere: Materialy itogovoi nauchnoi konferentsii MAE RAN, posviashchennoi 285-letiu Kunstkamery* [285 Years to the Petersburg Kunstkamera: Materials of the Concluding Scientific Conference at the MAE RAN, Devoted to the 285th Anniversary of the Kunstkamera]. St. Petersburg: Nauka, Peterburgskoe otdelenie.

Tarasova, A.I. 1979. Pis'ma L.Ia. Shternberga k V.K. Arsen'evu. [Letters of L.Ia. Shternberg to V.K. Arsen'ev]. In *Strany i Narody Vostoka. Pamiati V.K. Arsen'eva* 20: 57–80. Moskva: Nauka.

— 1985. Vladimir Klavdievich Arsen'ev. Moscow: Nauka.

Teriukov, A.I. 1993. Kollektsii A.V. Zhuravskogo v MAE [A.V. Zhuravskii's Collections at the MAE]. *Kunstkamera: Etnograficheskie Tetradi* 2-3: 254–265. St. Petersburg.

Tokarev, S.A. 1949. K postanovke problem etnogeneza [On the Question of Ethnogenesis]. *Sovetskaia Etnografiia* 3: 12–36.

Tsintsius, V.I. (ed.) 1975–77. *Sravnitel'nyi slovar' tunguso-manchurskikh iazykov.* [Comparative Dictionary of the Manchu-Tungusic Languages], vol. 1, 2. Leningrad: Nauka.

Tumarkin, D.D. (comp.) 1999. *Repressirovannye etnografy* [Repressed ethnographers], vol. 1, 1st edition. Moscow: Vostochnaia literatura.

Vakhtin, N. 2001. Franz Boas and the Shaping of the Jesup Expedition Siberian Research, 1895–1900. In *Gateways: Exploring the Legacy of the Jesup North Pacific Expedition, 1897-1902.* I. Krupnik and W.W. Fitzhugh (eds.), 71–89. Washington, D.C.: Arctic Studies Center, National Museum of Natural History, Smithsonian Institution.

Vigasin, A.A. 2003. Aleksandr i Liudmila Mervart: u istokov otechestvennogo tseilonovedeniia i dravidologii [Aleksandr and Liudmila Mervart: At the Beginning of Domestic Ceylon and Dravide Studies]. *Repressirovannye etnografy,* 2nd edition. D.D. Tumarkin (comp.), 375–398. Moscow: Vostochnaia literatura.

Vinnikov I.N. 1928. Leo Shternberg. *Anthropos* 23: 135–140.

— 1930 L.Ia. Shternberg kak issledovatel' pervichnikhh sotsial'nykh form [L.Ia. Shternberg as Researcher of Primordial Social Forms]. *Pamiati L.Ia. Shternberga 1861-1927.* S.F. Ol'denburg and A.N. Samoilovich (eds.), 51–84. Leningrad: Akademiia nauk SSSR.

Vologdina, V.N. 1994. Iz istorii Kunstkamery: museinye rabotniki v gody voiny i blokady [From the History of the Kunstkamera: Museum's Workers in the Years of War and Blockade]. *Kunstkamera: Etnograficheskie Tetradi* 4: 161–184. St. Petersburg.

Zhmoida, A.I. 1999. V muzee antropologii i etnografii v kontse 30-ykh godov [In the Museum of Anthropology and Ethnography at the End of the 1930s]. *Kur'er Petrovskoi Kunstkamery* 8–9. St. Petersburg.

Zolotarev, A.M. 1933. Novye dannye o gruppovom brake. [New Data About Group Marriage]. *Sovetskaia Etnografiia* 3-4: 197–204.

— 1934. Amurskie orochi [The Orochi of the Amur River]. *Sovetskii Sever* 6: 80–85.

— 1937. The Bear Festival of the Olcha. *American Anthropologist* 1: 37–43.
— 1939. *Rodovoi stroi i religiia ul'chei.* [Clan System and Religion of the Ulch]. Khabarovsk: Dal'giz.
— 1964. *Rodovoi stroi i pervobytnaia mifologiia* [Clan System and Primitive Mythology]. Moscow: Nauka.

8 WAS LEV SHTERNBERG
JUST ANOTHER CLASSICAL EVOLUTIONIST?

Sergei Kan

The majority of scholars, both Russian and Western, have long regarded Lev Iakovlevich Shternberg (1861–1927) as a leading representative of the classic evolutionist school who, like the rest of them, was only interested in studying the present-day culture of the non-Western peoples or the past culture of the Western ones.[1] Given the fact that most of Shternberg's published works on social organization and religion were heavily influenced by Lewis H. Morgan and E.B. Tylor (whom his friend and colleague Waldemar Bogoras [Vladimir Bogoraz] called the heroes of Shternberg's youth), such viewpoint is quite natural. In my view, however, a more careful reading not only of his scholarly publications but also his academic manuscripts, lectures, letters and other archival materials as well a careful analysis of his complex and rather contradictory scholarly views in the context of world ethnology demonstrates that in his worldview (*Weltanschauung*) classical evolutionism coexisted with ideas that resembled those of Durkheim, Mauss, Boas and even Radcliffe-Brown.

It seems particularly important to include Shternberg's numerous articles and essays published in various Russian periodicals of both liberal and more left-wing socialist leaning between the mid-1890s and the early 1920s. Some of these writings appeared in publications aimed at a Russian audience; others addressed the Russian-speaking Jewish *intelligentsia*, which Shternberg himself belonged to.

In addition one should take into consideration the fact that between the 1890s and the 1920s, Shternberg's scholarly views underwent some modifications. Lev Iakovlevich corresponded and interacted with quite a few foreign colleagues, many of them prominent scholars, and carefully monitored new developments in ethnology and such related disciplines as linguistics, psychology, etc. While never abandoning his evolutionism, Shternberg was open to modifying it to a significant extent, both in response to some major new developments in Western anthropology and especially in the wake of the dramatic economic, social and ideological upheavals and changes caused by the First World War, the Russian Revolutions, and the Civil War. The aim of this brief essay is to present several key examples of Shternberg's theoretical views that either contradicted or went far beyond what has usually been described as his "classical" evolutionism.[2]

---

1   See Gagen-Torn (1975); Grant (1999); Roon and Sirina (2004, see also *this volume*).
2   Much of the data and some fo the arguments presented in this paper can be found in my earlier publications. See Kan (2009a; 2009b; 2012a; 2012b; 2016).

The Nivkh Clan as Seen by Shternberg the *Narodnik*

Beginning with his very first scholarly publication "The Gilyak of Sakhalin," Shternberg demonstrated his special interest in *both* the evolution of social organization (and especially of kinship and the marriage system) as well as the role of certain social institutions in the everyday as well as the religious life of this indigenous people of the Far East. So far most anthropologists have focused on the first but not the second aspect of his scholarly agenda, which, in my view, is just as significant.

Shternberg first describes the Gilyak (Nivkh) clan (*rod*) (*khal*) as an institution that regulates marriage, the laws and customs related to blood revenge, the structures and principles of conducting the bear festival, as well the basic social identification of each person, and then offers a virtual hymn to that positive influence, which in his opinion, the primitive (*pervobytnyi*) clan had and continues to have on the character (or what later anthropologists would call "ethnic" or "national psychology" of the Nivkh person. In his own words,

> The fact that each Gilyak must belong to large clan left a major imprint on his entire spiritual tone (*sklad*), his personality, customs and mental development. This habit of discussing everything collectively, this necessity to take the interests of one's kin into consideration, this custom of collective responsibility in matters of blood revenge, these communal festivals and sacrifices, this brotherly union of numerous fathers, brothers and children, and, finally, this necessity and custom to dwell in large yurts along with dozens of people just like oneself – a necessity, which makes every Gilyak to live while always being seen by others – all of this must have contributed to the development a personality that is sociable, inclined to conversation, serious and sensitive as far as issues of honor as concerned (1893:17–18).

In his positive characterization of the Nivkh people's personality, the Russian ethnographer also mentions their hospitality, their system of primitive equality and other "good qualities of primitive tribes" (*dobrodeteliakh pervobytnykh plemen*), which in his view had still survived into the 1890s among the Nivkh of both Sakhalin and the lower Amur, despite a negative influence of the Russians and the Manchu who had been exploiting them. Shternberg's admiration for the "traditional" Nivkh clan as well as his concluding comments on the future of Nivkh society clearly reflect both his evolutionist as well as his Russian Populist (*narodnicheskii*) ideology, "The fate of their society is undoubtedly doomed. Within one or two generations, the mainland [Amur] Gilyak will become completely Russified and along with the benefits of [higher—S.K.] culture he will acquire all of its bad habits" (ibid.:19).

Whereas his reconstruction of the evolution of the Nivkh system of marriage was clearly a product of the work of Shternberg an *evolutionist theorizer*, this description of the clan's key role in Nivkh life was undertaken by a *field ethnographer* and is more reminiscent of the work of Durkheim, Mauss, Radcliffe-Brown and Malinowski than that of Morgan and Tylor. Thus one could definitely argue that already in this early works on social organization of the peoples of the Russian Far East, classical evolutionist coexisted somehow with a (kind of) structural-functionalist. Moreover, Shternberg's enthusiastic description of the major role played by the clan in the social and spiritual life of the Nivkh as well as in the development of their distinct ethnic character and identity (or may be even what Geertz called "ethos") is clearly reminiscent of Durkheim's concept of "mechanical solidarity." This should not come as a surprise: after all both of them (as well as Marcel Mauss) were late 19th–early 20th century socialists who saw in the so-called "primitive" societies some very important forms of social relations and institutions, which in their view, had disappeared from the modern capitalist/industrial ones.[3]

Shternberg and Boas

Considering Boas's rejection of Shternberg's evolutionist theorizing, it seems difficult to argue that their anthropological ideas had much in common. Thus, in his memorializing of Shternberg at the 1930 International Congress of Americanist in Berlin "the father of American anthropology" called him the "Russian Bastian" and evaluated very highly his "fundamental studies of the ethnology of the Amur peoples" as well as his work at the MAE. However, he also characterized his friend and colleague as "one of the brightest modern-day defenders of the Morgan's and the entire evolutionist theory" (Boas 1934:XL–XVI). In conclusion Boas made it clear that while he viewed Shternberg's ethnographic work very highly, he was not impressed with his evolutionist theorizing. In his words, "No matter what our attitude towards these [evolutionist] theories might be, the important ethnographic data he had collected must be taken into very serious consideration" (ibid.).

Nonetheless, aside from this major disagreement, the two scholars had quite a bit in common. For example, just like Boas, Shternberg were convinced that an ethnographer could not understand "the true life of a people" he was studying and especially "its psychological aspects" without a solid knowledge of its language (Bogoras 1928:5). It is this conviction that explains why, despite his special interest in "primitive" social organization, the Russian ethnologist had collected such a large body of linguistic and folklore materials on the Nivkh. Thus, despite the fact that Boas had entered ethnology from the hard sciences and Shternberg from the social ones, both eventually arrived at the same conclusion about the centrality of language in culture and the need for the ethnographer to master it and collect a variety of texts in it.[4]

---

3   See, for example, Gane (2014), Fournier (2006).

4   I might add that while the Western canon of the history of anthropology usually credits Malinowski with the "discovery" fieldwork as the #1 method for collecting ethnographic

There are also similarities in these two scholars' views on what constitutes a single *culture*. Thus Boas saw culture as a historical phenomenon or as a total of all of the patterns of and for behavior that a member of a society acquired in the process of growing up and acquiring that culture. And here is how Shternberg defined the meaning of "culture" in his lecture course "The Introduction to Ethnography" delivered at the Leningrad State University in 1926–1927: "Culture is a group of people, whose unity rests on their common historical experience, which in turn creates a combination of such powerful memories and emotions that they unite millions of people into a single psychological and historical body" (SPF ARAN/F. 282, op. 1, d. 21, l. 26). Such historical/psychological and idealistic understanding of culture seems much more akin to Boas's than that of Morgan or even Tylor, let alone Marx and Engels.

Fig. 1 Shternberg, Boas, and Bogoras at the 21st International Congress of Americanists, 1924, in the Hague. Franz Boas Papers (Mss.B.B61), # U5-1-34. American Philosophical Society.

data, one could definitely argue that the Russian political exiles, like Shternberg, Bogoras and Jochelson, "discovered" it as well and did so a couple of decades earlier. Eventually Shternberg and Bogoras began referring to it as the "stationary method" (*statsionarnyi metod*) of research and made it a key part of their students' education (Kan 2009:101–111; Arziutov and Kan 2017: 39–50).

Judaism as the Highest Stage of the Evolution of Religion

Over the years Shternberg developed a theory that Judaism's most important contribution to the world's "cultural capital" was the "discovery of monotheism". He articulated it in his articles published in the 1910s in *Novyi Voskhod* and *Evreiskaia Nedelia*, the main Russian language Jewish newspapers, as well as in a lecture course entitled "Evolution of Religion" offered on a regular basis at the Ethnography Division of the Geography Institute and the Ethnography Division of the Geography Faculty of the Leningrad University throughout most of the 1920s. These ideas were most clearly articulated in his presentation "Aspects of Jewish Ethnic Psychology" delivered at the Jewish Historic and Ethnographic Society (JHES) in the early 1920s and then published in its journal *Evreiskaia Starina* in 1924 (Shternberg 1924a).

In his lectures on the evolution of religion, Lev Iakovlevich outlined a more or less traditional scheme of the evolution of religious ideas from primitive animatism to complex polytheism (Shternberg 1936:519). Like his predecessors from the classical evolutionist school, Shternberg argued that monotheism was the next stage in the evolution of world religion. However, in his own scheme, monotheism was divided into two types: a more primitive one (called "animistic"), typical for such peoples as the ancient Egyptians, and the "ethical" one, which, in his view, had been created, by the "Semitic peoples" (ibid.). While in the former type, the deity still retained some anthropomorphic features, in the latter one, it lost them and became a "special ethical being" (ibid.). In the concluding lecture of the course, Shternberg did not focus specifically on Judaism. However, even his brief comments on the subject made it perfectly clear that he favored this ethical monotheism over the other one. Thus he insisted that the former included a strong emphasis on social justice, e.g., in contrast to the more primitive one, the former could not reconcile itself with the existence of socioeconomic inequality typical for the Ancient Near East and openly advocated a struggle for "the kingdom of God" on Earth rather than in Heaven.

One can imagine Shternberg being reluctant to openly extoll Judaism in front of an audience of Soviet students; however in 1924, he could still do so openly among his colleagues and friends—members of the JHES. So let us return to the presentation on the subject of the Jewish national psychology he gave to that audience. He began by drawing its attention to a particular fact, which was supposed to completely confuse an evolutionist ethnologist. As he put it, why was it that, if each type of sociopolitical system usually had a corresponding religious one, the pure monotheism did not develop among such advanced peoples as the Babylonians, the Egyptians, or the Persians, who "created enormous empires with their despotic monarch, supreme deities, and highly elaborate astral cults [...] while, on the contrary, it did develop among a small people, which had barely advanced from the stage of a tribal organization and which did not know such monarchs or such astral cults" (Shternberg 1924a:19).

According to him, the solution to such a paradox had to be searched for in that unique Jewish monotheism, which "*stood alone in world history* [italics—S.K.] and could not fit into the common evolutionary boundaries" [*ramki*] (ibid.: 21). His own interpretation of the origin of such monotheism was to attribute it to the type of phenomena that developed thanks to a kind of "leap" [*skachok*] and represented "individual discoveries of geniuses" (ibid.). Shternberg did allow for a possibility of such monotheism having been discovered in a different sociocultural environment; however, in his words, "in order for it to become the shared by an entire ethnic group it is necessary for that group to possess certain inherited psychological attributes facilitating an understanding and acceptance of such purely intellectual concept" (ibid.). Thus he attributed a major evolutionary development in the realm of religion not to economic or social factors but psychological ones.[5]

It is interesting that in the rest of his presentation and article Shternberg focused specifically on what he called the "intellectual-rationalist character of Jewish monotheism", while also arguing that its ritual dimension represented a later and externally introduced phenomenon (ibid.). An intellectual, who from his childhood days, had absorbed both the traditional Jewish religious learning as well as the secular European late 19th century education and high culture, Lev Iakovlevich favorite aspect of Judaism was precisely its humanistic-philosophical and cultural-historical aspects rather than the mystical and rituals ones. Thus while appealing to the assimilated Jewish intelligentsia of Russia in his 1907–1916 newspaper articles to "return to its people," he also instructed it that while it was important to observe such holy days as Passover and Chanukah, it was not necessary to follow every letter of the ancient religious law. Instead such observance represented a wonderful opportunity to acquaint one's children with the heroic history of the Jewish people (Kan 2009a:218–223).

Not surprising, this old *narodnik* was particularly fond of the Biblical prophets who preached universal social justice and combined rationalism with what he referred to as "social emotionalism" (a quality he himself possessed) (ibid.:36). Shternberg viewed the prophets as the precursors of Socialists, while in light of his hypothesis, the Jewish national psychology explained high political engagement of the Jews and the presence of so many Jews in the internationalist socialist movement (Shternberg 1924a:37).

Without going into a detailed discussion of Shternberg's hypothesis of the development of Jewish national psychology and Jewish ethical monotheism, which undoubtedly contains a good deal of errors, I would like to point out that it does represent a good example of how this Jewish patriot's views influenced his social evolutionism. At the very least these views obviously made him modify such key postulate of classical evolutionism as the idea that all of world's people had to pass inevitable through the same stages of evolution, including in the realm of spiritual culture.

---

5   This view is also reminiscent of some of Boas's ideas on the relationship between psychology and culture.

The Dramatic Upheavals Caused by World War I and the Russian Revolutions

The most serious challenge to Shternberg's evolutionist theorizing was posed by the radical economic and sociopolitical upheavals that took place in much of Europe and especially in his own country between 1914 and the early 1920s, i.e., the beginning of World War I and the end of the Russian Civil War. Although as a former Narodnik-turned-Socialist-Revolutionary (SR) he welcomed the February Revolution, Lev Iakovlevich opposed the Bolshevik coup and for a few months contributed to a newspaper run by the right wing of the SR party. In 1918 he abandoned politics in order to concentrate on museum work (Kan 2009a:237–258). While he chose to remain in Soviet Russia and cooperate with the new regime, he never fully embraced it, remaining loyal to the democratic socialist ideology of his youth (Kan 2009a:267–302, 2012b). From Shternberg's correspondence we know that between from the mid-1910s through the early 1920s he was deeply troubled not only by the drastic loss of lives but also such catastrophic disruptions of normal daily life as lack of food, fuel, transportation, and other basic necessity. As an intellectual and a scholar he was equally troubled by the breakdown of communication between scholars across international borders and the total interruption of the flow of scholarly literature and correspondence between them.

These new developments in the world he was living in forced the Russian ethnologist to turn his ethnographer's gaze to the present, and not just the past, and to rethink some of the postulates of his evolutionist theorizing. Although the only evidence of these new developments in Shternberg's thinking is an unfinished or only partially preserved typescript of a lecture, it is nonetheless a very important document for understanding his overall scholarly worldview.

Entitled "Anthropological Suggestions and Perspectives during the Revolutionary Years in Russia" this paper must have been written at the end of the Civil War and prepared for some public presentation.[6] The paper opens with an observation that Russia of that recent era "represents an enormously interesting phenomenon for an anthropologist interested in the general issues of culture" because it allows him to observe culture in its "dynamic" rather than just its "static" state (Shternberg 2009b:271). It is especially rare, according to Shternberg, for a social scientist to be able to observe how a person who shares our own culture acts creatively under such circumstances, when normal conditions of life are disturbed, regular cultural resources disappear, and one can no longer rely on familiar scientific ideas and technical habits, and instead one has to adapt to conditions, under which people occupying lower levels of cultural development normally live (ibid.:271–272). As Shternberg points out, during the period

---

6   I discovered this manuscript in the Shternberg files in the St. Petersburg Branch of the Archive of the Russian Academy of Sciences, while conducting research on his biography (PFA RAN. F. 282. op. 1. d. 81. l. 1–9). My English translation of the full text of this manuscript and commentary appear in the journal *Ab Imperio* (Kan 2009b).

under discussion, industrial production in Russian cities came almost entirely to a standstill. In order to survive Russian urban population simply returned to the long abandoned forms of production. As for the peasantry, it had an easier time adjusting to this chaos. In the countryside the old customs had not yet been forgotten. In the absence of matches, for example, the peasants returned to the old practice of preserving the fire under the ashes the way their ancestors did. When commercially made fabrics disappeared, the country folk found in their attics the old looms and turned to some old women who still remembered how to use them. Domestic cloth making began to flourish all over Russia and was still competing with the factory-based one at the time he wrote the paper. When cattle herds began to shrink and leather footwear began to disappear, hand woven *lapti* began to be made and worn not only in the country but the city as well. This demand for new materials affected the choice of crops raised: many peasants began growing hemp and linen instead of other kinds. With the decline of commercial vodka and tobacco coming from the city, an increasing number of peasants turned to growing their own tobacco and brewing their own vodka.

Having examined the peasants' adjustment to industrial crisis, Shternberg turned to the urbanites to argue that they had had a much more difficult time surviving. Many of them simply fled to the countryside. Even the *intelligentsia* tried to learn to be farmers. Those who remained in the cities survived by relying on a few inventions of their own such as, for example, the miniature iron stove (*bourzhuika*). However, by and large, in Shternberg's opinion, the civilized urban dweller returned to a primitive (*pervobytnyi*) condition. As he put it, "When the accumulated material resources are lost, a thousand-year-old culture immediately lowers a civilized person to the level of a primitive (*pervobytnyi*) one. And this is true not only in the sphere of the struggle for survival but in the moral one as well" (ibid.:275). For Shternberg this represented clear evidence that the so-called "primitive" peoples, including the present-day inhabitants of the outlying regions of the USSR were not at all inferior to the more "civilized" (*kul'turnye*) peoples of the European part of the country and in some respects, even superior to them.[7]

This short unpublished article suggests two things about Shternberg's evolving views on the development of human society and culture. Firstly, as a progressive thinker he clearly could not accept the classic evolutionists' notion that the evolution of technology, economy, social institutions and ideology was also inevitably accompanied by the evolution (i.e., progress) in the sphere of morality and intelligence. Secondly, as a witness to an incredible setback in the lives of millions of his contemporaries he could no longer share the optimistic belief in the inevitability of progress and unilineal sociocultural evolution he himself used to share with the previous generation of evolutionists.

---

7   Thus he pointed out that the indigenous peoples of Siberia had a much easier time adjusting to the scarcity of commercially made objects than the Russian city folk (Shternberg 2009b:275–276).

Not surprisingly in his 1920s lectures, while discussing evolution, Lev Iakovlevich did mention such factors as diffusion, borrowing, and other phenomena that played only a very minor role in his evolutionist theorizing some twenty to thirty years earlier.

Shternberg's Program for the Study of the Present-Day Culture of Soviet Jews

As someone who had received a traditional religious Jewish education, Shternberg was well acquainted with the Hebrew Bible and throughout his academic career often drew on it as a source of examples for his discussion of the evolution of social organization and religion. Several of his publications addressed this subject directly.[8] This type of scholarly interest was typical for evolutionist anthropologists, beginning with E.B. Tylor. That same interest in the "old ways" and "traditional customs" of the inhabitants of the small *shtetls* of the Pale of Settlement was behind his involvement in helping prepare a detailed research program for the famous An-sky's Jewish Ethnographic Expedition of 1912–1914 (Kan 2009a:216–218; Deutsch 2011, 2016).

However, not until after the monumental upheaval in the life of the Jews of the Russian Empire as a result of World War I, the Revolution and the Civil War, which Shternberg referred to as a "catastrophe," did he develop a strong interest in ethnographic research on their present-day social life and culture. Two sources illustrating this change in the ethnographer's thinking exist: an article entitled "Issues in Jewish Ethnography" based on a talk given at the Jewish Historical and Ethnographic Society and published posthumously (Shternberg 1928) and an unpublished "Instruction for the Study of the Jewish Population from an Ethnographic and Economic Point of View." The latter is based on the notes taken by students who attended Shternberg's lectures given at the Leningrad Institute of Jewish History and Literature in 1923-1924.[9]

Echoing the argument presented in his unpublished paper discussed above, Shternberg argued that precisely because "such colossal" changes had been taking place in all aspects of Jewish life in Russia since 1917, "the present moment in the life of the Jewish people is a uniquely interesting one for an ethnographer" (1928:14). To make sure his audience understood why an ethnologist would want to study contemporary life of a relatively 'advanced' ethnic group, he explained,

"Ethnography is no longer understood as only a study of the curious phenomena from the life of primitive peoples. Most importantly ethnography is a

---

8   See Shternberg's article on the "preservation of names in Jewish levirate" (1924b) or his well known essay "Divine Election in Primitive Religion" (1925).

9   This document was discovered in the Rossiiskii Gosudarstvennyi Arkhiv Sankt-Peterburga (RGASPb) by Deborah Yalen who kindly shared it with me.

sociological discipline, which studies both the static and the dynamic aspects of a people's life. It studies both the manifestations of the traditional culture and the processes of the creation of a new one such as the present-day social and economic relations" (ibid.:12).

Once again, Lev Iakovlevich saw this type of ethnographic research as a golden opportunity to study the reactions of individual people to change as well as the psychological significance major changes had for an individual. As he put it, "A whole set of psychological shifts have been taking place, which say something about not only human psychology in general but the unique national [Jewish] psychology" (ibid.:15).

As far as the actual aspects of the present-day Jewish life that Shternberg instructed the future ethnographers among his students to concentrate on those ranged from economic activities to the status of women, and from education to social and religious life. He encouraged them to pay particular attention to such new developments as the Jewish collective farms (*kolkhozy*), Jewish sections of the Communist Party and the Young Communist League (*Komsomol*), the impact of the new secular schools and on the traditional religious ones, and so forth. He did not tell them to avoid such sensitive topics as the persistence of anti-Semitism among the Gentile neighbors of the Jews.[10]

Fig. 2 Shternberg, before his departure to the 21st International Congress of Americanists in the Hague, 1924. SPbF RAN Archive. F282/O1/D194/ L22. Copy from the author's personal collection.

---

10   Some of the less sensitive and controversial topics of of ethnographic research mentioned by Shternberg in his lecture were actually put into practice by the students of Waldemar Bogoras, who conducted fieldwork in 1924 in two small shtetls, a Jewish agricultural colony, and the town of Gomel with its large Jewish population. The results fo their research appeared in a collected entitled *Evreiskoe Mestechko v Revoliutsii* (The Jewish Shtetl During the Revolutionary Years) (see Yalen 2007).

Conclusion

Examples drawn from Lev Shternberg's published and unpublished writing as well as lectures clearly support my argument that the prevailing view of him as a typical late 19th – early 20th century evolutionist is not entirely accurate, especially if one considers the changes that occurred in his views in the wake of the dramatic transformations in all of the spheres of Russian (and the broader European) life following World War I, the February Revolution, the Bolshevik Coup, and the Civil War.

Fig. 3 From left to right around the table: Waldemar Bogoras, P.P. Semyenov-Tyan-Shanskiy, wife of A.P. Pinkevich, A.P. Pinkevich, L.B. Panek, O.I. Kolenkina, Sarra Ratner-Shternberg, A.A. Kolenkin, Lev Shternberg, L. Vittenburg, at the Second Soviet Kraevedcheskii (Local Regional Studies) Congress in Batumi (Georgian SSSR), 1925. SPbF RAN Archive. F282/O1/D194/L16.

References

Boas, Franz 1934. Lev Shternberg. In *Proceedings of the Twenty-fourth International Congress of Americanists:* 40–41. Hamburg.

Deutsch, Nathaniel 2011. *The Jewish Dark Continent: Life and Death in the Russian Pale of Settlement.* Cambridge, MA: Harvard University Press.

— 2016. Thrice Born; or Between Two Worlds: Reflexivity and Performance in AN-sky's Jewish Ethnographic Expedition and Beyond. In *Going to the People: Jewish Ethnographic Impulse.* J.Veidlinger (ed.), 27–44. Bloomington: Indiana University Press.

Fournier, Marcel 2006. *Marcel Mauss: A Biography.* Jane Marie Todd, trans. Princeton: Princeton University Press.

Gagen-Torn, Nina I. 1975. *Lev Iakovlevich Shternberg.* Leningrad: Vostochnaia Literatura.

Gane, Michael (ed.) 2014. *The Radical Sociology of Durkheim and Mauss.* London/New York: Routledge.

Grant, Bruce 1999. Foreword. In *The Social Organization of the Gilyak by Lev Shternberg. Anthropological Papers of the American Museum of Natural History* 82: xxiii–lvi.

Kan, Sergei 2009a. *Lev Shternberg: Anthropologist, Russian Socialist, Jewish Activist.* Lincoln: University of Nebraska Press.

— 2009b. An Evolutionist Ethnologist Confronts Post-Revolutionary Russia: Lev Shternberg's "Anthropological Suggestions and Perspectives during the Revolutionary Years in Russia." *Ab Imperio* 1:259–269.

— 2012a. Nauchnye vzgliady L.Ia. Shternberga v kontekste mirovoi etnologii and ego sobstvennoi ideologii narodnika i evreiskogo patriota [Lev Shternberg's Scholarly Views in the Context of World Ethnology and His Own Ideology of Populism and Jewish Patriotism]. In *Lev Shternberg – Grazhdanin, Uchenyi, Pedagog.* E.A. Rezvan (ed.), 179–190. St. Petersburg: MAE RAN.

— 2012b. Grazhdanskoe muzhestvo uchenogo: L.Ia. Shternberg posle Oktiabria 1917 g. [A Scholar's Civic Courage: Lev Shternberg after October 1917]. In *Lev Shternberg – Grazhdanin, Uchionyi, Pedagog.* E.A. Rezvan (ed.), 305–315. St. Petersburg: MAE RAN.

— 2016. "To Study Our past, Make Sense of Our Present and Develop Our National Consciousness": Lev Shternberg's Comprehensive Program for Jewish Ethnography in the USSR. In *Going to the People: Jewish Ethnographic Impulse.* J. Veidlinger (ed.), 64–84. Bloomington: Indiana University Press.

Roon, Tat'iana P. and Anna A. Sirina 2004. Lev Iakovlevich Shternberg: u istokov Sovetskoi Etnografii [Lev Ia. Shternberg: The Beginning of Soviet Ethnography]. In *Vydaiushchiesia otechestvennye etnologi i antropologi XX veka.* V. Tishkov and D. Tumarkin (eds.), 49–94. Moscow: Nauka.

Shternberg, Lev Ia. 1893. Sakhalinskie giliaki [The Gilyak of Sakhalin]. *Etnografi-cheskoe Obozrenie* 2: 1–46.

— 1924a. Problema evreiskoi natsional'noi psikhologii [Issues in Jewish National Psychology]. *Evreiskaia Starina* 11: 5–44.

— 1924b. Rol' sokhraneniia imion v evreiskom levirate [The Role of the Preservation of Names in the Jewish Levirate] *Evreiskaia Starina* 11:177–179.

— 1925. Divine Election in Primitive Religion. *Proceedings of the Twenty-first International Congress of Americanists:* 472–512. Göteborg.

— 1928. Problema evreiskoi etnografii [Issues in Jewish Ethnography]. *Evreiskaia Starina* 12: 11–16.

— 1936. *Pervobytnaia religiia v svete etnografii* [Primitive Religion in Light of Ethnography]. Leningrad: Institut Narodov Severa.

— 2009. Anthropological Suggestions and Perspectives during the Revolutionary Years in Russia. *Ab Imperio* 1: 271–276.

Yalen, Debra 2007. Documenting the "New Red *Kasrilovke*": Shtetl Ethnography as Revolutionary Narrative. *East European Jewish Affairs* 37(3): 353–375.

NOTES ON THE CONTRIBUTORS

Tatiana Argounova-Low is senior lecturer at the Department of Anthropology, University of Aberdeen. She works predominantly in Sakha (Yakutia) and Evenkiia. Her research interests include the history and ethnography of the Sakha people, and recently include aspects of their mobility, movement and transport. In her recent AHRC-funded project she focused on the craft of carving, the ancient skill of working with mammoth tusk, and the revitalization of traditional Sakha celebrations.

Michael Dürr is an anthropological linguist specializing in Mesoamerica and the North Pacific Rim. He works as a librarian in Berlin and also teaches anthropology and Mayan languages at the Free University of Berlin. His publications include studies on Franz Boas's text collections for the languages Sm'algyax and Kwak'wala of the northwest coast. He also co-authored an introduction to descriptive linguistics (in German) and participates in the language preservation and publishing activities of the Kulturstiftung Sibirien. Currently he is focusing on an edition of 16th to 18th century dictionaries and grammars in K'iche' and Mixtec. http://www.lai.fu-berlin.de/homepages/duerr/index.html

Sergei Kan is a professor of Anthropology and Native American Studies at Dartmouth College. He is also affiliated with the Davis Center for Russian and Eurasian Studies at Harvard University. He is the author of numerous articles and several edited volumes and monographs on the history and culture of the Tlingit people of Alaska and the history of Russian and American anthropology, including symbolic immortality: Tlingit Potlatch of the Nineteenth Century (1989), Memory Eternal: Tlingit Culture and Russian Orthodox Christianity Through Two Centuries (1999), Lev Shternberg: Anthropologist, Russian Socialist, Jewish Activist (2009), and Sharing Our Knowledge: the Tlingit and Their Coastal Neighbors (2015). Currently he is working on several major projects: a biography of Alexander Goldenweiser (1880-1940), an ethnohistorical study of the Creole community of southeastern Alaska (1867–1967), and an annotated volume of Franz Boas's correspondence with his Russian/Soviet colleagues.

Erich Kasten studied social and cultural anthropology and taught at the Free University of Berlin. He has conducted extensive field research in the Canadian Pacific Northwest and in Kamchatka and has curated international museum exhibitions. As the first coordinator of the Siberian research group at the Max Planck Institute for Social Anthropology in Halle, he studied transformations in Post-Soviet Siberia. In ensuing projects for UNESCO and the National Science Foundation, he documented and analyzed indigenous knowledge. Since 2010 he has been the director of the Foundation for Siberian Cultures in Fürstenberg/Havel (Germany). More recently he has also applied himself to developing web archives and Internet interfaces with the pur-

pose of enhancing access and sustaining endangered cultural heritage. http://www.
kulturstiftung-sibirien.de/kasten_E.html

Igor Krupnik received his Ph.D. in Anthropology/Cultural Ecology at what was then
the Institute of Ethnography in Moscow, Russia (1977) and has been active in Arctic
socio-cultural and heritage research since the 1970s. He currently works as Curator of
Arctic and Northern Ethnology collections at the National Museum of Natural History of the Smithsonian Institution in Washington D.C. He has conducted fieldwork
in local communities in the Russian Arctic and in Alaska, especially in the Northern Bering Sea-Bering Strait region. From 1992 to 2002 he co-chaired (with William
Fitzhugh) the international "Jesup-2" program dedicated to the centennial of the
Jesup North Pacific Expedition, 1897–1902.

Elena Liarskaya is an anthropologist working at the European University at Saint
Petersburg (Russia). She conducted long-term anthropological fieldwork in the Russian Arctic (predominantly on Yamal) with indigenous people and recent arrivals,
reindeer herders and city dwellers. Among her research interests are various aspects
and cultural consequences of the interaction between native and non-native people,
the anthropology of education, gender in the Arctic, migration and connectivity, and
the history of Russian anthropology.

Thomas R. Miller (https://berkeleycollege.academia.edu/ThomasMiller) is an anthro-
pologist focusing on sound, shamans, media and museology. He holds a Ph.D. from
Columbia University and worked as senior scientific assistant in the Division of
Anthropology at the American Museum of Natural History. He was a guest curator of
the museum's Franz Boas centenary exhibition "Drawing Shadows to Stone: Photographing North Pacific Peoples (1897–1902)" and created the intermedia installation
"Schamanenreise" for Schamanen Sibiriens, curated by Erich Kasten at the Linden
State Museum of Ethnology in Stuttgart, Germany. He has been a visiting professor
in museum studies at the University of Iceland, and is currently focusing on radio
and environmental sound art in the circumpolar north. He is a founding member of
the UArctic thematic research network CAFÉ: Circumpolar Archives, Folklore and
Ethnography, established by the University of the Arctic in 2018. He lives and teaches
in New York City.

Tatiana P. Roon is an ethnologist specializing in traditional ethnic culture and the
economy of the indigenous people of the Russian Far East. She completed her Ph.D. at
the Museum of Anthropology and Ethnography in St. Petersburg (Russian Academy of
Science) in 1997. She worked as a senior researcher at the Sakhalin Regional Museum
in Yuzhno-Sakhalinsk, and from 2003 until 2015 as the director of this museum. For
many years she has been active in the study and preservation of the indigenous peo-

ple's vanishing cultural heritage on Sakhalin Island. She gathered museum collections and published on them. She also participated in the long-time museum's project on the research history of the region that was devoted to Bronislav Pilsudski, Leo Shternberg and Erukhim Kreinovich, and published on its outcomes. Her current research focuses on questions of ethnic history with regard to the indigenous peoples of the Amur and Sakhalin regions.

Anna A. Sirina received her Ph.D. in 2012 in Ethnology and Anthropology at the Institute of Ethnology and Anthropology of the Russian Academy of Sciences in Moscow, where she currently works as a leading research fellow. Since 1981 she has been conducting field work in Siberia and the Russian Far East. She has published extensively on the history of anthropology and on different aspects of the cultures of old-Russian settlers and indigenous peoples in Siberia, in particular Evenk and Even identity, nature use and world view. She is co-editor (with V. Davydov) of the first Russian translation (2017) of S.M. Shirokogoroff's book *Social Organization of the Northern Tungus* (1929).

Matthias Winterschladen is a historian of Eastern Europe from the University of Bonn (Rheinische Friedrich-Wilhelms-Universität) who is specializing in the history of culture contact and civilization policy towards the indigenous peoples of the North Pacific Rim at the turn of 19th and in the first half of the 20th century, especially by the United States of America and the young Soviet state. At Bonn University he worked as an assistant lecturer and is now finishing his Ph.D. His main publication close to the topic of this anthology dealt with the Jesup North Pacific Expedition in northeastern Siberia and the special role of Franz Boas's Russian colleagues W. Jochelson, W. Bogoras and L. Shternberg in the entanglement and reciprocal influences in science and politics between North America and Europe (especially Russia). Besides this he has done some research into the beginnings of modern soccer and old orthodox entrepreneurship in late imperial Russia.

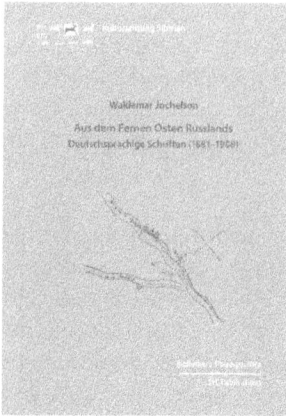

Waldemar Jochelson

Aus dem Fernen Osten Russlands
Deutschsprachige Schriften (1881–1908)

Herausgegeben von Erich Kasten
2017, Fürstenberg: Kulturstiftung Sibirien
159 pp., 16 x 22,5 cm
Euro 28; Hardcover
ISBN: 978-3-942883-91-7

Bibliotheca Sibiro-Pacifica
http://www.siberian-studies.org/publications/bisp.html

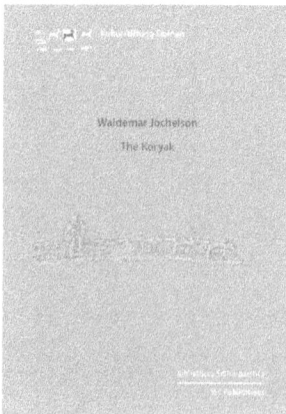

Waldemar Jochelson

The Yakut

Edited by Erich Kasten and Michael Dürr
2018, Fürstenberg: Kulturstiftung Sibirien
253 pp., 26 color photos, 16 x 22,5 cm
Euro 38; Hardcover
ISBN: 978-3-942883-92-4

Bibliotheca Sibiro-Pacifica
http://www.siberian-studies.org/publications/bisp.html

Waldemar Jochelson

The Koryak
Part I. – Religion and Myths
Part II. – Material Culture and Social Organization
Edited by Erich Kasten and Michael Dürr

2016, Fürstenberg/Havel: Kulturstiftung Sibirien
884 pp., 1 Farbabbildung, 16 x 22,5 cm
Euro 68; Hardcover
ISBN: 978-3-942883-87-0

Bibliotheca Sibiro-Pacifica
http://www.siberian-studies.org/publications/bisp.html

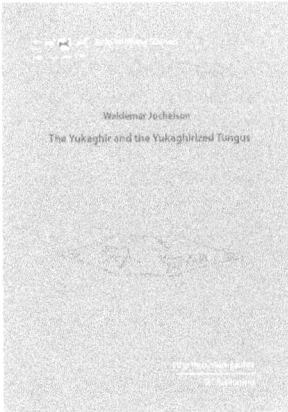

Waldemar Jochelson

The Yukaghir and the Yukaghirized Tungus
Edited by Erich Kasten and Michael Dürr

2018, Fürstenberg/Havel: Kulturstiftung Sibirien
564 pp., 16 x 22,5 cm
Euro 58; Hardcover
ISBN: 978-3-942883-90-0

Bibliotheca Sibiro-Pacifica
http://www.siberian-studies.org/publications/bisp.html

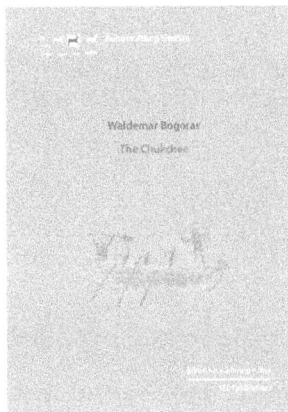

Waldemar Bogoras

Chukchee Mythology
Edited by Michael Dürr and Erich Kasten

2016, Fürstenberg/Havel: Kulturstiftung Sibirien
204 pp., 16 x 22,5 cm
Euro 34; Hardcover
ISBN: 978-3-942883-89-4

Bibliotheca Sibiro-Pacifica
http://www.siberian-studies.org/publications/bisp.html

Waldemar Bogoras

The Chukchee
Part I-III: Material Culture, Religion,
Social Organization
Edited by Michael Dürr and Erich Kasten

2017, Fürstenberg: Kulturstiftung Sibirien
860 pp., 16 x 22,5 cm
Euro 68; Hardcover
ISBN: 978-3-942883-88-7

Bibliotheca Sibiro-Pacifica
http://www.siberian-studies.org/publications/bisp.html

Alexandra Lavrillier and Semen Gabyshev

An Arctic Indigenous Knowledge System
of Landscape, Climate, and Human Interactions:
Evenki Reindeer Herders and Hunters

2017, Fürstenberg/Havel: Kulturstiftung Sibirien
467 pp., ca. 300 color photos, 15,5 x 22 cm
Euro 68; paperback
ISBN: 978-3-942883-31-3

Studies in Social and Cultural Anthropology
http://www.siberian-studies.org/publications/studies_E.html

Matthias Winterschladen, Diana Ordubadi, and
Dittmar Dahlmann (eds.)

Auf den Spuren der modernen Sozial- und
Kulturanthropologie: Die Jesup North Pacific
Expedition (1897-1902) im Nordosten Sibiriens

2016, Fürstenberg/Havel: Kulturstiftung Sibirien
400 pp., 15,5 x 22 cm
Euro 38; paperback
ISBN: 978-3-942883-26-9

Exhibitions and Symposia
http://www.siberian-studies.org/publications/exsym_E.html

Kasten, Erich (Hg.)

Reisen an den Rand des Russischen Reiches:
Die wissenschaftliche Erschließung der nordpazifischen Küstengebiete im 18. und 19. Jahrhundert

2013, Fürstenberg/Havel: Kulturstiftung Sibirien
320 pp., 9 color photos, 15,5 x 22 cm
Euro 32; paperback
ISBN: 978-3-942883-16-0

Exhibitions & Symposia
http://www.siberian-studies.org/publications/exsym_E.html

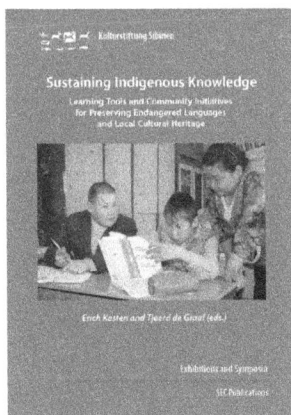

Kasten, Erich and Tjeerd de Graaf (eds.)

Sustaining Indigenous Knowledge: Learning Tools and Community Initiatives for Preserving Endangered Languages and Local Cultural Heritage.

2013, Fürstenberg/Havel: Kulturstiftung Sibirien
284 pp., 22 color photos,15,5 x 22 cm
Euro 26; paperback
ISBN: 978-3-942883-12-2

Exhibitions and Symposia
http://www.siberian-studies.org/publications/exsym_E.html

Cecilia Odé (ed.)

Илья Курилов: Моя жизнь, песны
Il'ia Kurilov: My Life, Songs (Yukaghir)

2016, Fürstenberg/Havel: Kulturstiftung Sibirien
56 pp., 13 color photos,15,5 x 22 cm
Euro 18; paperback
ISBN: 978-3-942883-28-3

Languages and Cultures of the Russian Far East
http://www.siberian-studies.org/publications/lc_E.html

Erich Kasten (ed.)

Духовная культура коряков-нымыланов, с. Лесная, Камчатка
Worldviews and Ritual practice, Coastal Koryaks (Nymylans), Lesnaya, Kamchatka

2017, Fürstenberg/Havel: Kulturstiftung Sibirien
ca. 163 pp.,15,5 x 22 cm
Euro 18; paperback
ISBN: 978-3-942883-32-0

Languages and Cultures of the Russian Far East
http://www.siberian-studies.org/publications/lc_E.html

www.ingramcontent.com/pod-product-compliance
Lightning Source LLC
Chambersburg PA
CBHW031413270326
41929CB00010BA/1441